Current English Grammar and Usage

CURRENT ENGLISH GRAMMAR AND USAGE

S.M. GUPTA
Emeritus Professor of English
Sobhasaria Group of Institutions
Sikar, Rajasthan

PHI Learning Private Limited
Delhi-110092
2013

₹350.00

CURRENT ENGLISH GRAMMAR AND USAGE
S.M. Gupta

ISBN-978-81-203-4743-4

Published by Asoke K. Ghosh, PHI Learning Private Limited, Rimjhim House, 111, Patparganj Industrial Estate, Delhi-110092 and Printed by Mudrak, 30-A, Patjparganj, Delhi-110091.

Contents

Preface

The book 'Current English Grammar and Usage' is a distillation of my forty-six years of experience as a teacher of English Language and Literature in academic and professional colleges in India and abroad. This experience was further enriched by my fourteen years of teaching communication techniques in engineering colleges of Rajasthan.

The question arises, when there are hundreds of books on grammar in English, why is there a need to write yet another book on grammar? The answer to this question is that while teaching students of all streams (science, arts, commerce, engineering, law and medicine), I realized that most of the grammar books do not go beyond Wren and Martin's traditional grammar. They even religiously include topics such as transformation and synthesis of sentences. The students find these grammar books very boring. Hence, a new grammar book is required that looks at the discipline of grammar from a new perspective. This book breaks a new ground in the sense that it incorporates the latest insights from linguistic research (from structural to transformational linguistics) in the conceptualization and presentation of the material. The material has been developed in innumerable class-room interactions and interaction with colleagues all over India whom I taught Modern English grammar at UGC seminars and refresher courses. The book presents the matter in such a way that the students will find it quite exciting, challenging as also interesting.

Unlike traditional grammar's meaning-based definitions of parts of speech, the book points out the morpho-syntactic features of word classes which makes the learning experience quite rewarding. It has been observed that the category of tense is best taught through its linking with the adverbials. In equipping students with developing proficiency in sentence structure, the approach of Syntactic Structures (1957) by the famous linguist Naom Chomsky of MIT has been followed. It is believed that his insights into phrase structure and transformational grammar are valid even today from the pedagogical point of view.

In reading comprehension and précis sections, passages have been taken from newspapers and current magazines related to biography, philosophy, religion, science, economics, technology and sacred texts. The purpose is to acquaint the readers with different kinds of experience on the one hand and vocabularies and sentence construction, on the other. In letter writing section, authentic letters received from different countries such as the USA, the UK, Australia, Canada, Egypt and Saudi Arabia have been quoted to sensitise the readers with different styles of letter-writing. The distinguishing feature of the book is that lots of examples have been given for every activity. A number of exercises with answers have also been provided. Theory has been kept to the minimum.

I am sure the book will go a long way in improving the language proficiency and communication skills of the students of all streams at the tertiary level. The book will prove quite useful for budding engineers, MBA students, business professionals, arts and commerce students and students preparing for various competitive examinations.

I will be very grateful for any suggestions and comments to improve the quality of the book conceptually and linguistically.

S.M. GUPTA

Acknowledgements

I express my heartfelt thanks to all the writers and publishers whose books I have consulted while writing this book. In addition, I am also grateful to *The Times of India*, *The Hindustan Times*, and *The Hindu*, *Outlook* and numerous other magazines and dailies.

I owe a lot of ideas on grammar to my Indian teachers such as Prof. N. Krishnaswamy, the late Dr. S.K. Verma and Prof. Yadurajan of CIE (now EFLU), Prof. Pit Corder, Prof. Henry Widdowson and Prof. John Lyons of Edinburgh University, Prof. Greg Lee of the University of Hawaii, and Prof. Braj B. Kachru and Prof. Yamuna Kachru of the University of Illinois, the USA. I am grateful to each of them.

Finally, I would like to thank my family members, Mrs. Vimla Gupta, Asha Gupta, Madhu Gupta, Kalpana Gupta, Alpana Gupta, Dr. Ashok Gupta, Susheel Singhal, Hanish, Utsav, Honey and Archie for their encouragement in writing the book.

My grateful thanks are due to PHI Learning, New Delhi for their careful and speedy processing of the book.

S.M. GUPTA

1

Word Classes

"Grammar is a piano I play by ear. All I know about grammar is its power."

—Joan Didion

Introduction

Traditional grammarians have used the term 'parts of speech'; structural linguists call them word classes. We have preferred the term 'word classes' because it is not confusing like the traditional term. In this unit, we define what word classes are and discuss all the eight word classes in great detail. In our discussion, we take into consideration the view of both traditional and structural linguists to enrich our discussion. The objective of the lesson is to enable the readers to identify major and minor word classes in English quite competently and to use them in their speech and writing flawlessly.

Word Classes Defined

Words are divided into different grammatical categories according to the function they perform in an utterance or a sentence. Study the following extract:

Sex	**money**	**power**	**promises**	
noun	noun	noun	noun	
But	**Chantal**	**decided**	**to pretend:**	
conjunction	noun	verb	to-infinitive	
That	**she**	**was**	**expecting**	**some**
conjunction	pronoun	auxiliary verb	progressive participle	determiner
amazing	**revelation;**			
adjective	noun			
men	**take**	**the**	**oddest**	**satisfaction**
noun	verb	determiner	adjective	noun

in	**feeling**	**superior**		
preposition	gerund	adjective		
without	**knowing**	**that**	**most of**	
preposition	gerund	conjunction	pre-determiner	
the	**time**	**they**	**are**	**being**
determiner	noun	pronoun	helping verb	progressive participle
utterly	**predictable**			
adverb	adjective			

(*Source:* The Devil & Miss Prim, 13)

As we know, a language has a hierarchical structure. This extract consists of sentences; the sentences consist of many phrases; and the phrases contain a number of words. These words perform different grammatical functions and depending upon those functions, each has been labelled as **noun, pronoun, preposition, conjunction, adjective**, **adverb**, **verb**, etc. and these grammatical categories are called word classes.

There are eight word classes in English: nouns, verbs, adjectives, adverbs, pronouns, prepositions, conjunctions and interjections.

1. A **noun** is a word used as the name of a person, place, thing or an idea.
   Examples: Delhi, Bangalore, book, beauty, honesty.
2. An **adjective** is a word that describes an attribute of a noun.
   Examples: interesting, amazing, lovely, yellow.
3. A word that expresses an action, state or process is called a **verb**.
   Examples: go, weep, dance, read, write, paint, give, seem, look.
4. An **adverb** is a word that modifies a verb, an adjective or another adverb in a sentence.
   Examples: very, extremely, fast, slowly, quite, rather.
5. A **pronoun** is a sub-class of nouns. It can replace a noun or a noun phrase in a sentence; it can replace a sentence also.
   Examples: I, we, you, he, she, it, they, nobody.
6. **Prepositions** are used before nouns or pronouns and they show relation of nouns/pronouns with another word class.
   Examples: on, in, at, by, above, according to, from, with, concerning
7. **Conjunctions** are words used to express a connection between words, phrases and clauses.
   Examples: but, or, yet, and, that, although, because, since.
8. **Interjections** are words that express sudden feelings and emotions.
   Examples: ah, eh, oh, hum, ouch, ugh, phew.

Further, word classes have been classified into two categories: major word classes and minor word classes (Figure 1.1).

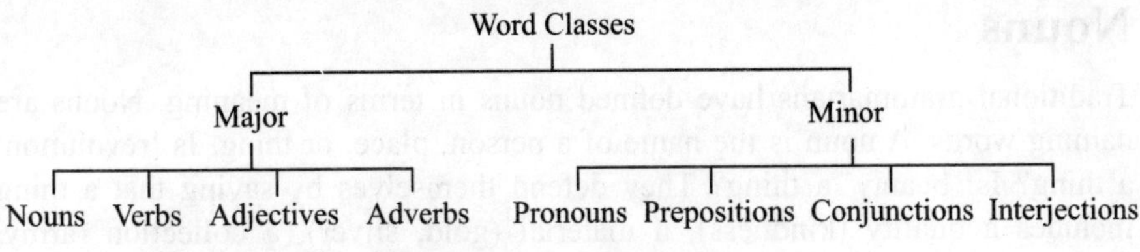

FIGURE 1.1 Word classes.

The major word classes are also called **open class words** or **form classes**. They are called 'open' in the sense that new words can be added to this class. Further, we cannot make a list of these classes and can say that there are no more nouns in English because new nouns are being added every day.

Minor classes or function words, on the other hand, form a close class or set in that their number is limited. We can make an inventory of pronouns, prepositions, conjunctions and interjections. The list cannot be easily extended by the addition of new function words.

One interesting thing about these word classes is that one word form can belong to more than one word class. This makes English a highly productive language.

The word 'up' belongs to the following word classes:

(i) Adverb: The girl climbed *up* to a high branch of the tree.
(ii) Adjective: It is early in the morning and Harish is not *up* yet.
(iii) Verb: The government has decided to *up* the price of gas by fifty rupees.
(iv) Preposition: She climbed *up* the ladder.
(v) Noun: She hit the ball on the *up*.

EXERCISE 1.1

Identify word classes of the bold words in the following sentences:

Example: He ran **down** the budget.
Down: adverb

1. He has been living in Sikar **since** his birth.
2. He has been living in Sikar **since** he was born.
3. She **hates** him too much.
4. Why do you look at me with **hate** in your eyes?
5. There is no **table** of contents at the front of this book.
6. He tabled the resolution for consideration in the Parliament.
7. She disappeared **round** the corner.
8. I have to do my daily round of cooking and washing.
9. Medha Patkar broke her **fast** with a glass of orange juice.
10. She ran very **fast** to catch the bus.

Nouns

Traditional grammarians have defined nouns in terms of meaning. Nouns are naming words. A noun is the name of a person, place, or thing. Is 'revolution' a thing? Is 'beauty' a thing? They defend themselves by saying that a thing includes a quality (kindness), a material (gold, silver), a collection (army, crowd), a state (childhood, youth) and an action (laughter, theft, movement). In such a case, the definition becomes uneconomical and imprecise.

Therefore, it would be better to discuss the morphological and syntactic properties of nouns. But before that, a word about types of nouns is in order.

Types of Nouns

There are several ways of classifying nouns. The broad classification of nouns is in terms of **concrete** and **abstract nouns** (Figure 1.2).

Concrete nouns are those nouns that we can perceive through five physical senses: touch, sight, taste, hearing, and smell. Shyam, tea, silver, fan, chair, etc. are concrete nouns. Abstract nouns are just the opposite. They cannot be perceived through five physical senses or have no existence. They are the nouns of qualities, states, processes, ideas, etc. Joy, honesty, beauty, poetry, happiness, evaporation, socialism, etc. are abstract nouns.

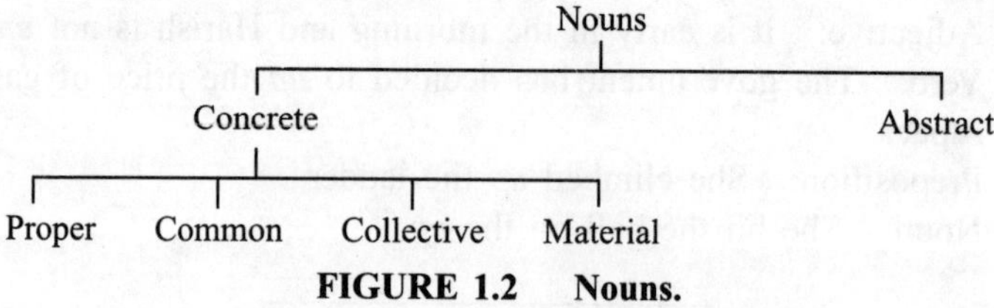

FIGURE 1.2 Nouns.

Nouns that name specific persons or places are termed **proper nouns**: David, Ram, Alice, Bangalore and many more.

Some proper nouns contain more than one word:

South Wales	Ram Kumar
Pacific Ocean	White House
Queen Elizabeth	

Names of months, days and important festivals are also proper nouns.

Examples: March, Monday, October, Christmas, Easter, Thanksgiving.

Proper nouns refer to unique persons or places; they do not have plurals. They may have plurals only when a proper noun is specifically referred to.

(i) There are three **Rams** in this class.
(ii) We met three **Dipawalis** ago.

No determiners occur before proper nouns except when they are used as common nouns:

He is **a Shakespeare** of the college. (The meaning is that he is as great a dramatist as Shakespeare was.)

Proper nouns begin with a capital letter.

The opposite of a proper noun is a common noun. It refers to a person, place or thing in a general sense. Examples of common nouns are: **girl**, **boy**, **pen**, **pencil**, **fan**, **table**, **chair**.

A collective noun refers to a group of things, animals or persons. Though the members of the group are countable, we think of the group as one unit.

Examples: flock, jury, committee, class, crowd, mob, herd, army, family, nation, parliament, fleet.

Material nouns refer to materials or substances out of which other things are made.

Examples: milk, water, gold, tea, wood, air, smoke, silver.

However, this classification of nouns is not satisfactory. There are several reasons for this. Firstly, all these definitions are meaning based and meaning is a slippery term. Secondly, there are many nouns that do not 'fit into the above pigeon-holes'. What about *cricket*, *God*? Are they concrete or abstract?

A better classification would be the one that has syntactic consequences. The classification of nouns in terms of countable versus uncountable is syntactically significant because it governs the use of determiners (Figure 1.3).

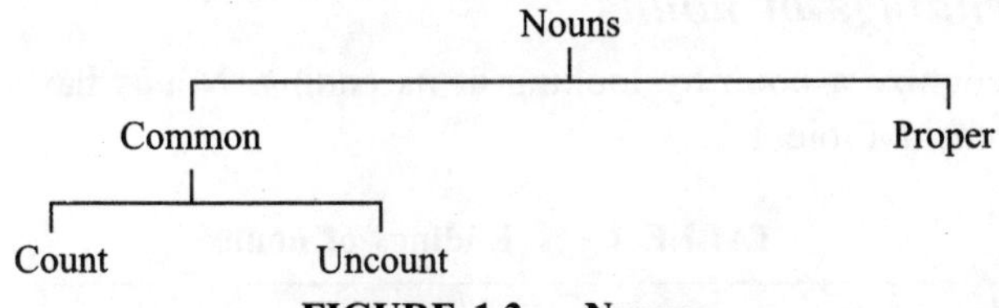

FIGURE 1.3 Nouns.

Countable nouns are those nouns that can be counted. For example, one apple, two apples, three apples; one pen, two pens, three pens. Count nouns have plural forms.

Uncount nouns cannot be counted. They refer to indivisible wholes. They are mass nouns. Collective nouns are also uncountable and so are abstract, and material nouns.

The interesting thing about countable and uncountable nouns is that they can be recategorized as uncountable and countable respectively.

(i) I prefer tea to coffee (uncountable).
(ii) Give me three teas, please (countable).
(iii) Ram is a man (countable).
(iv) Man is mortal (uncountable).

EXERCISE 1.2

Identify nouns given in bold as common, collective, abstract and proper in the following sentences and phrases:

1. A social **worker.**
2. An environmental **activist**.
3. He has tremendous **expertise** in **marketing**.
4. He likes **reading, writing**, **thinking** about the **state** of the **world**.
5. She likes classical **music**.
6. **Lata Mangeskar** is the most acknowledged **singer** in **India**.
7. She is good at **art** and **craft**, **drawing**, and **photography**.
8. She has a **crowd phobia**.
9. **The jury** gave the **verdict** in his **favour.**
10. **Gold** is more expensive than **silver**.

More about Nouns

Meaning based definition of a noun is not satisfactory. Therefore, it would be better if we could consider the morphological and syntactic characteristics of nouns.

Typical endings of nouns

You can recognize a noun by looking at its ending. Nouns have some of the endings given in Table 1.1.

TABLE 1.1 Endings of nouns

S.No.	*Ending of nouns*	*Examples*
1.	-er, -or	inspector, director, teacher, learner, preacher, dealer
2.	-ism	baptism, communism, socialism, idealism
3.	-ist	artist, fatalist, guitarist, humanist
4.	-ment	development, improvement, engagement, arrangement, agreement, attachment, enjoyment
5.	-ation -tion	examination, recognition, attention, annihilation, assumption, vacation, expectation
6.	-ness	happiness, tardiness, highness
7.	-hood	boyhood, childhood, womanhood
8.	-ee	payee, employee, examinee
9.	-ance	attendance, maintenance, assistance, sustenance, importance, variance, assurance
10.	-al	dismissal, approval, burial, nuptial, refusal

The list can be multiplied.

Other morphological features of nouns

Most nouns (countable nouns) show the **number contrast**. They have singular and plural forms (Table 1.2). The following patterns are available.

The regular plural of nouns is formed by the addition of –s or –es.

Examples: car=cars, pen=pens, cat=cats, dog=dogs, house=houses, box=boxes, bush=bushes, church=churches, judge=judges

TABLE 1.2 Singular and plural nouns

Singular	*Plural*
Mass nouns: advice, applause, cash, evidence, food, furniture, garbage, hospitality, money, music, knowledge, waste, butter, wood, rock, iron, glass, oil, water, milk, smoke, air	Proper nouns: the West Indies The Wilsons, the Netherlands
News, classics, mathematics, linguistics, physics, statistics, billiards, darts, ninepins	sunglasses, people, police, trousers, police, pants
Proper nouns: the Ganges, Athens, Mars, Naples, Wales, the USA, the UN	Tools: scissors, binoculars, pincers, pliers, tongs, scales
Names of diseases: measles, mumps, rickets, AIDS	Other nouns that are used as plurals only: arms, ashes, funds, oats, odds, outskirts, premises, quarters, headquarters, spirits, stairs, steps, surroundings, thanks

In compound nouns the plural –s is added to the last part (Table 1.3)

TABLE 1.3 Compound nouns

Singular	*Plural*
assistant district attorney	assistant district attorneys
breakdown	breakdowns
onlooker	onlookers
grown-up	grown-ups
stand-by	stand-bys
check-up	check-ups

In some compound nouns, where the head noun comes first, –s is added to the first part.

Examples: editors-in-chief, mothers-in-law, runners-up, passers-by, etc.

In some compounds, the first and the last part both are pluralized.

Examples: women doctors, women writers, men students, etc.

TABLE 1.4 Irregular plurals

S.No.	*Singular*	*Plural*	*Explanation*
1.	calf	calves	nouns ending
	knife	knives	in **f** change to **v**
	life	lives	exceptions:
	wife	wives	beliefs, chiefs, cliffs,
	wolf	wolves	proofs, roofs, safes
	leaf	leaves	
2.	month	months	notice the sound
	mouth	mouths	(*θ*) in singular changes to
	oath	oaths	(ð), in plural in speech
	truth	truths	
	wreath	wreaths	

In plural formation of some nouns, there is a change in the vowel.

foot	feet	tooth	teeth
goose	geese	man	men
mouse	mice	woman	women

There is zero plural in the following words.

singular	*plural*
sheep	sheep
deer	deer
salmon	salmon
grouse	grouse
pike	pike
trout	trout
carp	carp
moose	moose

Note some nouns have both regular and unchanged forms, e.g. antelope(s), fish(es), flounder(s), herring(s).

- Note further that *dozen* and *foot* have no plural forms except when they are followed by post modifiers.

  (i) He won a dozen lotteries.
  (or He won dozens of lotteries.)

  (ii) He is 5 foot 1 inch. (Also possible to say, He is five feet 1 inch.)

When plural expressions are used as pre-modifiers, their singular forms are used.

Examples: A four-day week, an eight cylinder engine, a five-month old baby.

Notice *series* and *species* can be used either as singular or plural.

Examples: One series of lectures
Two series of lectures

Words borrowed from foreign languages either keep their foreign plural or in some cases can have English as well as foreign plurals (Table 1.5).

TABLE 1.5 Plurals of foreign words

Singular	*Plural*
stimulus	stimuli
bonus/ corpus/ circus	bonuses /corpuses/circuses
cactus	cactuses/cacti
focus	focuses / foci
radius	radiuses/radii
terminus	terminuses/termini
syllabus	syllabuses/syllabi
alumnus	alumni
bacillus	bacilli
alumna	alumnae
alga	algae
larva	larvae
formula	formulas/formulae (their use is register based)
antenna	antennas/antennae
album/museum/forum/stadium/ultimatum	albums/museums/forums/stadiums/ ultimatums
memorandum/symposium	memorandums/memoranda/symposiums/ symposia
datum/medium	data/media (data and media can be used as singular or plural subject)
index	indices/indexes
apex	apexes/apices
appendix	appendixes/appendices
matrix	matrixes/matrices
basis	bases
metropolis	metropolises
analysis/axis/crisis	analyses/axes/crises
diagnosis/ellipsis/hypothesis	diagnoses/ellipses/hypotheses
oasis/parenthesis/synopsis/thesis	oases/parentheses/synopses/theses
criterion/phenomenon	criteria/phenomena
automaton	automatons/automata
corpus/schema	corpora/corpuses/schemata

Gender Distinctions

English gender is limited only to certain pronouns. Nouns, adjectives and articles have no gender distinction. The choice between *he* and *she* mostly depends on whether the person is male or female though there are some exceptions. Notice sex is a semantic concept whereas gender is a formal concept.

Sex (semantic)	*Gender* (formal)
male	masculine
female	feminine
neutral or sexless	neuter

Notice further that there is no one-to-one relationship between sex-based and gander-based classification. Consider the following sentences:

(i) I saw **a huge bison** in the zoo. **It** was sitting on the ground. (bison = male sex but neuter gender)

(ii) **The ship** is at the harbour. **She** leaves at 8.00 am. (ship: neutral sex but feminine gender)

(iii) Hey, why is **the child** crying? **It** is hungry. (child could be male or female but neuter gender)

There is a movement against the use of gender biased language. Most of the writers/speakers use non-sexist language these days. Look at the following sentences:

Each student is responsible for revising *his/her/their/one's* papers.

There is a tendency to use *their* as a non-sexist pronoun in the above cases. This is called the singular use of *they*. Below we give alternatives for sexist-language (Table 1.6):

TABLE 1.6 Sexist and non-sexist language

Sexist language	*Non-sexist language*
Mankind	Humanity/people/human beings
Man's achievement	Human achievements
Man-made	Synthetic/manufactured/machine made
The common man	The average person/ordinary people
Man the stock room	Staff the stock room
Eight man hours	Eight stuff hours
Chairman	Chairperson/presiding officer/head coordinator
Businessman	Business executive
Fireman	Firefighter
Steward/stewardess	Flight attendant
Mailman	Mail carrier
Policeman/police woman	Police officer
Congressman	Congressional representative

Case

Like Latin or Sanskrit, there is no case system in English. Only personal pronouns are marked for three cases: nominative (I, we, he, she, etc.), objective (me, us, him, her, etc.), and genitive (my/mine, our/ours, his, her/hers, etc.). Nouns are marked only for genitive case.

We shall talk about genitive (marked by apostrophes + s) of singular nouns and singular names; of regular and irregular plural nouns; of construction; genitive of nouns phrases and head nouns and double genitive. Consider the following examples:

(i) A boy's books
(ii) A girl's dress
(iii) The cook's salary
} Genitive of singular nouns

(i) Boys' books
(ii) Girls' dresses
(iii) The two cooks' salaries.
} Genitive of regular plural nouns

Notice the apostrophe is placed after the plural marker without **s**.

Consider the following genitive of irregular plural nouns:

The child's toy	the children's toy
The man's umbrella	the men's umbrella
Keats' poetry	Keats's poetry.

The alternative of genitive is *of constructions*.

What's the building's name (genitive)?

What's the name of the building (of construction)? But notice that genitive and of construction are not always replaceable. There are some differences in their use (Table 1.7)

TABLE 1.7 Genitives and of constructions

Genitives	*Of constructions*
• Used with nouns denoting people: Ram's car *the car of Ram	• Used with nouns denoting things The legs of a table *a table's leg
• With human, animal and human group nouns The boy's departure The flemingo's beak The government's policy	• With mass and abstract nouns The discovery of penicillin. The progress of science. The discovery of Newton (some body discovered Newton)
• Used for subject-verb relationship Newton's discovery (Newton discovered something)	• Is preferred when the modifying NP is long: The departure of the 4.30 flight for London
• Time and place nouns are frequently used in the genitive Today's menu Three week's holiday The town's oldest pub The town's best ice cream	

So far, we have looked at genitive as a case of nouns. It can also be considered as an ending belonging to a NP. In that case, the whole genitive noun phrase functions as a determiner to the head of the NP.

The Indian government's	**recent**	**accession**
determiner	adj.	N

(i) Hemingway's best novel.
(ii) A famous women's college in Hyderabad.
(iii) The chairman of the Finance committee's pertinent remarks.
(iv) He gave two months' notice.
(v) An hour and a half's discussion.
(vi) My house is better than Ram's (i.e. Ram's house).
(vii) I went to the dentist's clinic.
(viii) He is a friend of my sister's (double genitive).
(ix) She is Sita's sister.
(x) She is a sister of Sita's (has more than one sister).

Syntactic Features of Nouns

Nouns can be preceded by determiners:

All	**his**	**favourite**	**colours.**
Pre-det	det.	adj.	N

Nouns can be followed by post-modifiers.

(i)	**The book**	**which is red.**
	NP	post-modifier
(ii)	**A girl**	**staring at me.**
	NP	non-finite clause
(iii)	**A reason**	**to control oneself.**
	NP	to infinitive clause
(iv)	**A boy**	**in blue jeans.**
	NP	PP

The examples can be multiplied. Notice in the preceding discussions we have tried to point out some morphological and syntactic features of nouns rather than meaning based approach of traditional grammars.

EXERCISE 1.3

After each question, an instruction has been given. Follow the instruction and answer the question accordingly.

1. Give the plurals of the following nouns:
   pike, mouse, foot, antelope, dozen, leaf, wreath, father-in-law, woman,

doctor, stand-by, house, analysis, alumna, index, basis, axis, oasis, criterion, automaton, schema.

2. Change the following sexist words into non-sexist words:
   Chairman, man-made, policeman, fireman, businessman, congressman.
3. In the following expressions, either genitive or of construction has wrongly been used. Correct them by using genitive or of construction appropriately.
   The dress of the girl, the door's knob, the salary of the teacher, insulin's discovery, a notice of two months, the clinic of the dentist.

Pronouns

Pronouns are words that can substitute nouns or noun phrases.

(i) **John** is a teacher. **He** is quite knowledgeable. ('he' replaces a noun, John)
(ii) **A very beautiful girl** walked into the room. **She** was in blue jeans. ('she' replaces the NP 'a very beautiful girl').

As pronouns replace NPs, they cannot be preceded by determiners like NPs.

What are the morpho-syntactic features of pronouns?

Pronouns agree with the NPs they substitute in *number* and *gender*.

(i) **Lata** is studying linguistics in the USA. **She** is coming to India next month. (**she** agrees in *number* and *gender* with **Lata**.)
(ii) **These boys** are very naughty. T**hey** always play **their** musical instruments very loudly. ('**their**' agrees with 'they' in number; **these boys** (plural) agrees with **they** (third person plural).

Number and gender concord in pronouns is visible in case marking of personal possessive and reflexive pronouns. Since some pronouns refer to people, they are called **personal pronouns**. They are marked for case.

Consider the following examples:

	Subjective case	*Objective case*	*Possessive case*
1st person	I, we	me, us	mine, ours
2nd person	you	you	yours
3rd person	he, she, it, they	him, her, it, them	his, hers, its, theirs

There are several types of pronouns that are presented in Table 1.8.

TABLE 1.8 Pronouns

Pronoun type	*Members of the sub class*	*Examples*
Interrogative	who, what, why, where, when, whether	What is your name?
Possessive	mine, ours, yours, his, hers, its, theirs	This big house is mine.
Reflexive	myself, yourself, himself, herself, itself, oneself, ourselves, yourselves, themselves	She killed herself yesterday.
Reciprocal	each other, one another	They love each other.
Relative	that, which, who, whom, whose, where, when	The book that you bought yesterday has been prescribed for BEI.
Demonstrative	this, that, these, those	This is a grand house.
Indefinite	anything, anybody, something, somebody, someone, nothing, nobody, none, no one	There is somebody at the door.

Uses of Pronouns

Personal pronouns can be divided as 1st, 2nd, and 3rd person singular and plural.

The first person singular (I, me, my, mine) refers to *the speaker*. The first person plural (we, us, our, ourselves) refers to *a group of people including the speaker.* The second person (you, your, yourself, yourselves) refers to the *hearer* (singular) and the second person plural refers to a *group of people including the hearer* but excluding the speaker.

The use of *we* is very interesting. It sometimes includes the hearer (inclusive 'we') and sometimes excludes the hearer (exclusive 'we'),

(i) Let's go to the party, shall we? (inclusive 'we')
(ii) We've enjoyed talking to you. (exclusive 'we')

Third person pronouns refer to the persons (or in some cases things) other than the speaker and the hearer. Their uses can be summarized below.

(i) He (him, his, etc.) refers to a male person or animal.
(ii) She (her, etc.) refers to a female person or animal.
(iii) It (its, etc.) refers to an inanimate thing or animal.
(iv) They (them, etc.) refers to either animate or inanimate. For family pets, instead of it, he/she may be used:

Fido keeps awake all night and does **his** duty of watching the house very faithfully.

We generally use *it* for animals and babies, whose sex is not known.

(i) He has **a ferocious dog**. **It** barks at a stranger systematically.
(ii) She has **a beautiful baby**. But **it** cries a lot.

It is also used for mass nouns and singular abstract nouns.

(i) The prices of **gold** have recently gone up. **It** is selling ₹ 10,000 per ten gram.
(ii) **Success** is slippery. **It** cannot be attained easily.

Notice *she* is used for inanimate objects like *ships* and *countries*.

(i) **The ship** has arrived in the harbour. **She** will sail tomorrow for Singapore.
(ii) I love **India**. **She** is the most diverse country in the world.

When a human noun whose sex is not known is replaced by a pronoun, the usual tendency is to replace it by *he*. But now under the influence of feminists, it is better to use *they* or *their*.

(i) **A patriot** is one who sacrifices **their** (instead of **his** or **her**) life for the country.

This is known as the singular use of they/their.

If all the persons (1st, 2nd and 3rd) are used in the same sentence, the formula of **2 3 1** (i.e. 2nd person + 3rd person + 1st person) is used:

(i) **You, Sita and I** will go to see a movie tomorrow.

It is also used for time weather, distance, cleft sentences, to infinitive clauses and to introduce subject clauses.

(i) It is 5 O' clock.
(ii) It is very cold in here.
(iii) It is 10 km from here.
(iv) It was Jamuna who helped me.
(v) It is not easy to succeed.
(vi) It seems that he will arrive today.

Third person pronouns (they, them, etc.) replace not only plural noun phrases but also coordinated singular noun phrases.

Ram and Shyam both are teachers. **They** are very popular teachers.

Sometimes first and second person pronouns are coordinated and if this happens, the agreement is with the first person.

You and I are very close friends and hence **we** should plan a trip together to the USA.

If second person is there, use that the first person, the agreement is with the second person pronoun.

You and Ram can go home now. **You** must come back tomorrow at 8.00 am.

One, **you**, and **they** are used for people in general. One is used for people in general including you and me.

(i) One never knows what may happen.
(ii) You never know what may happen.

'They' is also used for 'people' but excluding *you and me.*

(i) **They** say India is going to win the match in the West Indies. (People say…)

Reflexive pronouns (myself, ourselves, yourself, yourselves, himself, herself, themselves) have two uses. They are used as objects, complements and prepositional complements.

(i) **He** cut **himself**.
(ii) **He** certainly has a high opinion **of himself**.

After **as**, **like**, **but for**, and **except for**, reflexive pronouns are used as alternatives to the objective forms of personal pronouns.

(i) As for **me/myself**, I won't leave any stone unturned to get the criminal arrested.

Reflexive pronouns are also used to reinforce the meaning. This is called the **emphatic** use of reflexive pronouns:

(i) **I myself** have done this.

The alternative way of saying the same thing is:

(i) He cooks **his own** dinner = He himself cooks his dinner.

Interrogative pronouns are *who*, *what*, *which*, *when*, *where*, etc. Notice except *what*, other words are used as relative pronouns also. The uses of these pronouns can be summarized as given in Table 1.9.

TABLE 1.9 Interrogative pronouns

	Personal	*Non-personal*
Subjective case	who, what, which	what, which
Objective case	who, whom (formal), which	what, which
Genitive case	whose	
Interrogative + prep.	who, what (formal) + prep.	what, which + preposition
Preposition + Interrogative	preposition + whom (formal)	preposition + what, which (formal)

Based on *A Communicative Grammar of English* by Geofftery Leech and Svartvik.

As said earlier, pronouns are referring words. They can refer backward or forward to persons or non-persons. They are governed by case, number and gender. The reference can be *definite* or *indefinite*. Look at Figure 1.4.

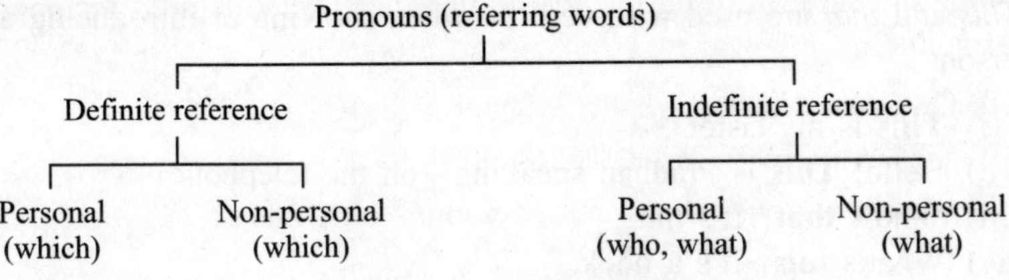

FIGURE 1.4 Pronouns.

(i) **Which** do you like more: Rita or Geeta?
(ii) **Which** did you study: Linguistics or ELT?
(iii) **Who** broke the window?
(iv) **What** teachers do you like best?
(v) **What** do you want?
(vi) **What** towns do we go through on the way? (The speaker does not know the area)
(vii) **Which** towns do we go through on the way? (The speaker knows the area)

Notice that *what* has a number of uses.

(i) **What's** your name?
(ii) **What's** the time?
(iii) **What's** the date?
(iv) **What's** he studying?
(v) **What's** he like? (asks about appearance and character)
(vi) **What** does he look like? (asks about appearance)
(vii) **What's** the weather like? (asks about characteristic quality)
(viii) **What's** your father? (asks about profession)
(ix) **Who** is your husband? (asks about identity)
(x) **Which** is her husband? (asks about choice from a group)

Notice that *who* and *whom* are used only for persons whereas *whose* can be used for both persons and non persons. With prepositions only *whom* is used and *whose* is used only in formal English.

(i) **Who** brought you here?
(ii) **Who** do you want to see?
(iii) **Whom** do you want to see? (formal)
(iv) **Who** did you give the book to?
(v) To **whom** did you give the book? (formal)
(vi) **Whose** is this house?
(vii) **Whose** is this child?

Demonstrative pronouns are *this*, *these*, *that* and *those*. *This* and *that* refer to things ideas, etc. which are understood, stated, etc.

(i) Who told you **this**?
(ii) Come at 5. **That** seems early enough.

This and *that* are used with verb *be* when showing or introducing a thing or person.

(i) **This** is my sister.
(ii) Hello! **This** is Pradhan speaking. (on the telephone)
(iii) Who's **that**? It's me.
(iv) What's **this**? It's a book.

This and *that* can also be used for a previously mentioned noun phrase or clause:

(i) He plays football every evening. **This** he has been doing for the last several years.
(ii) He is playing the guitar. He does **that** every morning.

Each other and *one another* are called **reciprocal pronouns** because they express a mutual relationship. Notice that they form a unit. Generally, *each other* is used for two persons and *one another* for more than two persons. But it is not a fixed rule.

(i) John and Marry kissed **each other**.
(ii) They live in **one another's** houses.
(iii) We should all love **one another**.

Who, *whom*, *that*, *which*, and *whose* are **relative pronouns** because they relate or refer to the noun phrases occurring before them. These noun phrases are called **antecedents** and these govern the use of relative pronouns. Relative pronouns can function as a subject, an object of or a complement to a preposition. Further, *who* is used for persons in the subjective case, *whom*, too, for persons in the objective case and after a preposition. *Which* is used for things; *that* can be used for both persons and non persons and so is the case with *whose*. Consider the following sentences:

(i) *This is the boy* **who** *is wearing a red shirt*. (relative pronoun as subject)
(ii) *This is the book* **that/which** *I bought yesterday*. (relative pronouns as object of the verb to buy)
(iii) *This is the boy to* **whom** *I gave a good thrasing yesterday.* (relative pronoun as complement to a preposition)
(iv) *The house* **the roof of which/whose** *roof collapsed yesterday belongs to Ram.*
(v) *The boy* **whose** *father is a magistrate is a student of this college.* (relative pronoun in genitive case referring to the boy)

Pronouns such as *all*, *each*, *every*, *both*, *none*, *nobody*, *anybody*, *everybody*, *no one*, *somebody*, *someone*, *something*, *anything*, *nothing*, etc. are indefinite pronouns.

(i) **All** enjoyed the quality ice cream.
(ii) I bought **all** of them.
(iii) **Each** of the students was awarded at the function.
(iv) **Everybody** has arrived, haven't they?
(v) **Anybody** can succeed if they try.
(vi) I continued studying in the library when **everyone** else had gone home.
(vii) All the books are free: you can take **any** (of them) you like.
(viii) She asked for money and I gave her **some**.
(ix) **Some** say only fools make money and I don't believe it.
(x) You **both** can join the party.
(xi) We expected 10 guests at the party but **none** came.
(xii) **Somebody** called you last night but didn't tell his name.

EXERCISE 1.4

Supply the appropriate pronouns in the blanks.

Example: She fought the case against the wishes of .... father-in-law.

Answer: her.

1. What's .... ? It's a toy.
2. .... is your brother among the people sitting there?
3. .... of these paintings were done by you?
4. .... do you think of my work?
5. .... was the weather like in London?
6. I've got coffee and tea .... would you prefer?
7. If .... comes to see me, tell them that I am busy.
8. While you are typing, I'll get on with .... else.
9. I don't think there is .... wrong with her eyes.
10. Can you get some tea when you go shopping. There isn't .... left.
11. It's nice to know that you .... have passed the English exam.
12. The boy .... parents came to meet you yesterday is studying in BEI.
13. It seems that they have packed .... baggage and are ready to move.
14. .... knows who fired at Mr. Pramod Mahajan.
15. .... of the criminals has/have been arrested yet.
16. My sister was wearing a bullet proof jacket and so .... didn't get injured.
17. When she was shifting the heavy luggage, she hurt ....
18. I know Ram and Shyam well. .... are both brothers.
19. You and I should get together over a cup of tea and exchange .... ideas.

20. Cheating never pays. .... always brings bad luck.
21. Come and meet .... in my office. I am there till 5.30 pm.
22. They love .... so much that .... are thinking of marriage.

Verbs

Verbs are words that denote a state, a process or an action.

(i) She is **happy**. (state)
(ii) The rice is **cooking**. (process)
(iii) He is **cooking** the rice. (action)

There is another way of looking at verbs. We can say that verbs may refer to *an event* or *a state*. Now what is an event? An event is "a happening thought of as a single occurrence with a definite beginning and end, e.g. *become*, *get*, *come*, *leave*, *hit*" (Leech and Svartvik:65).

A state, on the other hand, refers to "a state of affairs which contains over a period of time and does not need to have a well-defined beginning and end, e.g. *be*, *remain*, *contain*, *know*". (*ibid*:65)

Notice our process and action correspond to an event in the present discussion and, therefore, there is not much of a difference in these two interpretations.

What are the *morpho-syntactic* features of verbs? Below we discuss some of these features.

Certain endings are characteristics of the base forms of the verbs (Table 1.10).

TABLE 1.10 Endings of verbs

Ending	*Base form*
-ate	remonstrate, adjudicate, demonstrate, abdicate, saturate, dictate, corrugate
-ify	signify, magnify, horrify, beautify, electrify, justify, exemplify
-ise/-ize	hypnotize, mesmerize, canonize, monopolize, apologize, characterize, sympathise

A verb has past and present forms. –s inflection added to the verb indicates present tense and –ed inflection added to the verb shows past tense.

There is agreement between the subject and the verb with the third person in the present tense, but there is no concord in the past tense.

(i) She **goes** to Jaipur every day.
(ii) They **go** to Jaipur every day.
(iii) She **went** to Jaipur yesterday.
(iv) They **went** to Jaipur yesterday.

A verb has a *to-infinitive* form when it follows to: *to go*, *to read*. Without *to*, the verb is called the base form. A verb also has present participle and past participle forms. When *–ing* is added to the base form of a verb (*go* + *ing* = *going*), it is called **present participle** and when *–ed* is added to the base form (*walk* + *ed* = *walked*), it is called **past participle** form. All these different morphological forms of a verb are presented in Table 1.11.

TABLE 1.11 Verb forms

Base form of a verb	*Present tense form*	*Past tense form*	*-ing form*	*-ed form*	*To-infinitive form*
read	reads	read	reading	read	to read
walk	walks	walked	walking	walked	to walk
play	plays	played	playing	played	to play
sing	sings	sang	singing	sang	to sing

There is another way of looking at the verb forms. Verbs may be *finite* or *non-finite*. The element of the verb or auxiliary verb that carries *tense* is called **finite** and a verb without the finite element is called **non-finite**. There is usually person and number concord between the subject and the finite verb.

Consider the following sentences:

(i) Ram **plays** tennis every day.
finite

(ii) Ram **played** the guitar.
finite

(iii) He **wants** **to eat** a mango.
finite non-finite

(iv) He **wanted** **to eat** a mango.
finite non-finite

(v) **Studying** in the morning **can be** a nuisance.
non-finite finite.

(vi) **Being tired** she **went** to bed early.
non-finite finite.

In fact, in progressive and perfective aspects, the first part of the verb phrase is finite and the second part is non-finite, but then we can say that they function in finite verb phrases.

(i) She **is** **working** very hard.
(present participle)
finite non-finite
finite verb phrase

(ii) I **have** completed the work.
(past participle)
finite non-finite
finite verb phrase

(iii) I **can** **do** it.
finite (base form)
non-finite
finite verb phrase

(iv) I **could** **do** it.
finite non-finite
finite verb phrase

Another morphological feature of a verb is that it is marked for *tense* and *aspect*. Tense refers to the absolute location of an event or action in time, either the present or the past. It is marked by an inflection of the verb. (Internet Grammar)

There are only two tenses in English because there is no inflection on the verb for future tense. There is no one to one correspondence between tense and time. Look at the following sentences:

(i) He **is leaving** tomorrow. (future time)
present tense
(ii) He **leaves** tomorrow. (future time)
simple present
(iii) He **will be** at home now. (present time)
(future tense according to traditional grammar)
(iv) I **have done** my homework. (past time)
present tense
(v) If I were the Prime Minister of India, I would remove poverty. (past tense referring to hypothetical state in the present time)
(vi) He **might take** the exam sometime next year. (future time)
past tense
(vii) He **walked** to the college yesterday. (past time)
past tense

Notice that the past tense may refer to present time, past time and future time.

The future tense can be expressed by modal auxiliaries (*will*, *shall*, etc. and semi-auxiliaries (*going to*, *about to*, etc.)

(i) The train is about to leave (immediate future).
(ii) He is going to buy a car next month.

According to Internet Grammar, *aspect* refers to how an event or action is to be viewed with respect to time rather than to its actual location in time. Whereas aspect includes *tense*, tense can occur without aspect (play football, played football). There are two aspects in English: *progressive* and *perfective*. The progressive aspect denotes that the action or event is in progress at the moment of speaking, while the perfective aspect shows that the action or event is completed. The progressive aspect is expressed through *be+ing*, whereas the perfective aspect is expressed through *have + en*. Many more forms of verbs can be generated by combining modals, perfective, progressive and passive:

(i) The house **must have been being built.**

(ii) It **is raining** now.
progressive aspect

(iii) He **has been living** in Sikar for the last two years.
perfective + progressive aspect

(iv) I **have done** my homework.
perfective aspect

(v) The patient **had died** before the doctor arrived.
past perfective

(vi) He **was watching** TV when I reached home.
past progressive

Syntactic Features of Verbs

Now we discuss some of the syntactic features of verbs.

Verbs can be preceded by *auxiliary* or *helping verbs*. They are called **helping verbs** because they help the main or lexical verb in specifying the action of the verb.

She **is** **writing** a letter.
helping verb main verb

Here, the helping verb *is* denotes that the action of writing is still in progress.

Auxiliaries can be divided into three categories as show in Figure 1.5.

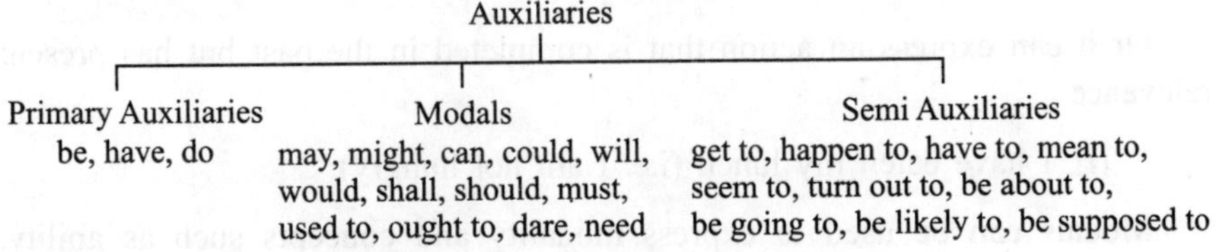

FIGURE 1.5 Types of auxiliaries.

Be has the eight forms as shown in Figure 1.6.

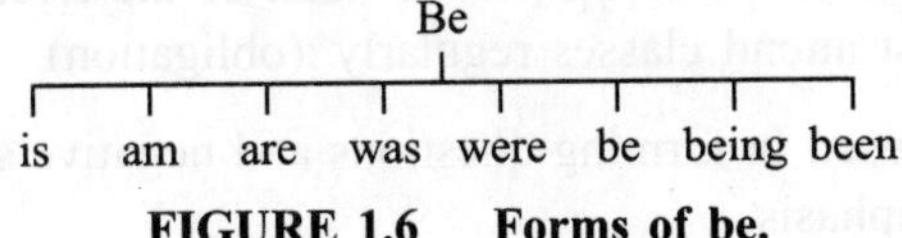

FIGURE 1.6 Forms of be.

Have has three forms as shown in Figure 1.7.

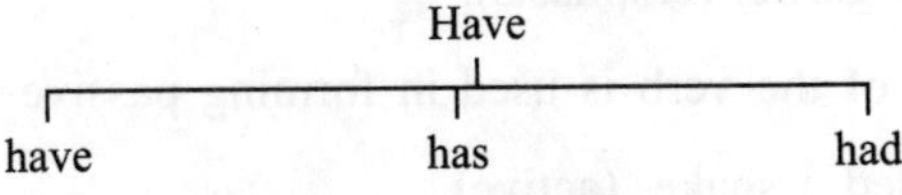

FIGURE 1.7 Forms of have.

Do has three forms as shown in Figure 1.8.

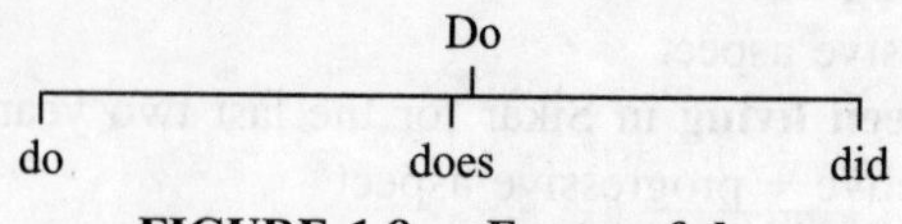

FIGURE 1.8 Forms of do.

Look at the following examples:

(i) She **is** reading a book.
(ii) I **have** earned my M.A. from Edinburgh University.
(iii) **Did** you see a ghost last night?
(iv) You **can** get first division if you work hard.
(v) You **ought to** respect your parents.
(vi) He **seems to** be very lucky.
(vii) I **tend to** disagree with you.
(viii) He is **likely to** win the race.
(ix) I **happened to** miss the train.

From semantic-syntactic point of view, *auxiliaries* have the following properties.

They are used in forming aspect, i.e. either progressive or perfective. It can express an action in progress.

(i) She is watching television.

Or it can express an action that is completed in the past but has present relevance.

(i) I have eaten my lunch (i.e. I am not hungry).

Modals can be used to express modality and concepts such as ability, obligation, prediction, intention, dedication, duty, advice, etc.

(i) She can speak French. (ability)
(ii) She would sit for hours on the bank of the river. (past habit)
(iii) You must attend classes regularly. (obligation)

Dummy *Do* is used in forming questions and negative sentences. It is also used to express emphasis.

(i) Do you like tea or coffee? (question)
(ii) I don't like onions. (negative sentence)
(iii) I do like garlic. (emphasis).

Be + 3rd form of the verb is used in forming passive sentences:

(i) John killed a snake. (active)
(ii) A snake was killed by John. (passive)

Apart from *do*, *does* and *did*, other 21 auxiliaries are also used in forming negative sentences.

(i) He can't attend the party tomorrow.
(ii) She hasn't applied for the job.
(iii) She isn't working hard for the exam.
(iv) She need not work hard.

In forming all types of questions (**yes-no, wh-**, etc.), the operator is inverted, i.e. it is put before the subject.

(i) John is a doctor. Is John a doctor?
(ii) What is John?

All the 24 auxiliary verbs (*is*, *am*, *are*, *was*, *were*, *do*, *does*, *did*, *have*, *has*, *had*, *can*, *could*, *will*, *would*, *shall*, *should*, *must*, *may*, *might*, *ought to*, *need*, *used to*, and *dare*) are used in forming question and negative sentences.

Further**,** *an auxiliary* may occur stranded where the main verb has been left out. Consider the following sentences:

(i) I never play tennis but my brother **does.**
(ii) She can never sing a song but her sister **can.**

The form of the verb shows whether the subject is the doer of the action of a verb or is the affected one. The former is called **active voice** and the latter **passive voice**. In a change from active to passive voice, it is not only the verb that undergoes a change (be + third form of the verb and where *be* has eight forms: *is*, *am*, *are*, *was*, *were*, *be*, *being*, and *been*) but what comes before the verb, i.e. subject and what follows the verb, i.e. object also undergo a change. **Object** becomes **subject** and **subject** becomes **by + object** and the verb becomes **be + third form** (of the verb). Consider the following sentences:

(i) John broke the window. (active)
(ii) The window was broken by John. (passive).
(iii) He was killed in an accident. (agentless passive)
(iv) English is spoken all over the world. (agentless passive)

Another syntactic feature of the verbs is the kind of **complement** it takes. Verbs can be categorized into different patterns on the basis of the sentence elements (**object, complement, adverbial**, etc.) it takes after it. English is an SVO (subject-verb-object) language unlike Hindi, which is an SOV (subject-object-verb) language, and Tagaloq, which is a VSO (verb-subject-object) language. On the basis of these sentence elements, verbs can be divided into six basic verb patterns given below.

(i)	**She**	**is**	**a nurse.**
	S	verb (be)	subject complement.
(ii)	**She**	**is reading**	**a book.**
	S	verb (transitive)	object

(iii)	**She**	**wants**	**you**	**to go.**
	S	V	O	V
(iv)	**She**	**sent**	**him**	**flowers.**
	S	V	IO (indirect object)	DO (direct object)
(v)	**She**	**painted**	**the room**	**yellow.**
	S	V	O	object complement
(vi)	**The stone**		**moved.**	
	S		V	

Having discussed the syntactic features of the verbs, we shall now describe the types of verbs that are available in the English language.

Types of Verbs

On the basis of their meaning and syntactic properties (the kinds of complements/objects following the verbs), verbs can be classified into different categories.

Linking verbs are followed by subject complements. These are realized by noun phrases or adjectives:

(i) She is a doctor.
(ii) She is very intelligent.

Verb **be** (is, am, are, was, were) falls in this category.

Current linking verbs indicate a state. The verbs that fall into this category are *appear*, *feel*, *look*, *remain*, *seem*, *lie* (*awake*), *stay* (*alive*), *table*, *sound*, *prove*, etc.

(i) You sound very convincing.

Resulting linking verbs are *become*, *fall* (sick), *get* (angry), *grow* (suspicious/old, etc.), *turn* (nasty), etc.

Notice some of these linking verbs can be followed by *–ing*, *-ed*, adjectives and adverbials in addition to noun phrases and adjectives. In some verbs *to be*, construction intervenes between the verb and the complement.

(i) After seeing the papers, he looked rather **confused**.
(ii) His performance of the concert was very **interesting**.
(iii) She appears to be very intelligent.
(iv) She would be in London for a few weeks.

Transitive verbs are followed by objects. These verbs can be simple transitive or phrasal prepositional verbs, followed by a single object. These verbs are too numerous to be listed here. Some of these verbs are *finish*, *hear*, *believe*, *telephone*, *cause*, *blow up* (a phrasal verb), *call on* (prepositional verb), *come across*, *bump into*, *do away with*, etc.

(i) She would telephone me today at 5.00 p.m.
(ii) Ravi called on me at 4.00 p.m. yesterday.

These single transitive verbs may be followed by *to* – infinitive clause, which acts as an object.

(i) I want **to see you** tomorrow.

Verbs such as *decide, expect, discuss, long, promise, can't afford, ask, dislike, forget, hate, help, hope, learn, love, need, offer, prefer, refuse, remember, try,* etc. are followed by a base infinitive clause.

Another category of *single transitive* verbs is followed by *–ing clauses.*

(i) Why have you stopped **talking to me**?

Some of the other verbs that fall into this category are *avoid, enjoy, dislike, admit* (can't) *bear, confirm, deny, finish, forget, hate, help, keep, like, love,* (not) *mind, prefer, remember* (can't) *stand,* etc.

The next category of *single transitive verbs* is followed by *that- clause*: I **admit** that I made mistakes in the past.

Other verbs in this category are *agree, discover, think, announce, bet, claim, complain, cater, declare, deny, explain, guarantee, insist, mention, object, predict, promise, reply, say, state, anger, warn, write, believe, hope, say, suppose, order, request, suggest, command, ask, decide, demand, prosper, recommend, require, urge,* etc.

Single transitive verbs may be followed by *wh-clauses* (beginning with *how, why, where, who, whether* (or if), etc.)

(i) I wonder **whether** he will pass or not.

Some of the other verbs in this category are *ask, care, decide, depend, doubt, explain, forget, hear, mind, prove, realize, remember, see, tell, think, know, notice, say, forget, learn, see,* etc.

Intransitive verbs are those that are not followed by any object or complement. They may be followed by adverbial. Some verbs may be used both as transitive and intransitive.

(i) The stone moved. (intransitive)
(ii) He moved the stone. (transitive)

It is difficult to list all the intransitive verbs here. Some of the intransitive verbs are: *go, laugh, weep, jump, come, return, reach, give up, come in, lead, sleep, run, stand, lie, sit, fall, happen, matter, swim, wait,* etc.

Then there are *transitive verbs* that are followed by an object and an object complement.

(i) He found her attractive.
(ii) They appointed him monitor of the class.

Some of the verbs in this category are *find, consider, appoint, leave, imagine, make, name, suppose, think, vote, declare, find, judge, keep, learn, make, wash, believe, feel,* etc.

There are a number of verbs in English that are called *ditransitive*, i.e. they take two objects after them. One of them is generally an indirect object and the other one is a direct object.

(i) She sent **him** a bouquet.
(ii) Bring **me a glass of water**.

Some of the other verbs in this category are *give*, *teach*, *write*, *offer*, *bring*, *hand*, *lend*, *owe*, *promise*, *read*, *send*, *show*, *buy*, *get*, *find*, *make*, *order*, *save*, *spare*, *ask*, etc.

With intransitive verbs, we sometimes find that these verbs are followed by an indirect object + **that or wh-** *clause*.

(i) I told *him* **that I would go to Jaipur tomorrow.**
(ii) I asked **him why he behaved like that**.

Verbs that fall into this category are *advise*, *assume*, *bet*, *convince*, *inform*, *persuade*, *promise*, *remind*, *show*, *teach*, *warn*, *write*, *ask*, *tell*, *teach*, etc.

The next category of verbs includes verbs like *hear*, *help*, *let and make* that are followed by an object and a bare infinitive.

(i) I **heard** him sing.
(ii) I **let** him go.
(iii) I **make** him wash the clothes.
(iv) Will you **help** me pack my suitcases?

Other verbs such as *advise*, *allow*, *ask*, *want*, *behave*, *force*, *order*, *permit*, *teach*, *tell*, *urge*, etc. require an object plus *to-infinitive construction.*

(i) I am not **allowed** to see a movie.
(ii) She **advised** me to do exercise for half an hour every day.

There is another way of dividing the verbs on semantic grounds. Verbs can be categorised as *activity* or *state verbs*. This distinction becomes crucial because it has syntactic implication. *Activity verbs* can be used with progressive aspect, but *state verbs* cannot.

(i) I **am writing** a letter to my brother. (activity verb)
(ii) I **am not understanding** what you are saying. (state verb cannot be used with progressive aspect)

Process verbs such as *change*, *grow*, *widen*, and *improve*, and momentary verbs such as *knock*, *jump*, *have*, and *kick* can be used with progressive aspect.

But verbs of *perception* (feel, hear, see, smell, taste, etc.), *verbs of feeling* (believe, adore, desire, detest, dislike, doubt, forget, hate, hope, imagine, know, like, love, mean, prefer, remark, suppose, understand, want, wish, etc. , *verbs of relationship* (be, belong to, concern, consist, contain, cost, depend on, deserve, equal, fit, have, invite, matter, owe, own, possess, remain, require, resemble, etc.) are not used in the progressive aspect.

(i) I am having a headache.

EXERCISE 1.5

For each sentence below, two alternatives have been given, and one of them is correct. Choose the correct alternative.

Example: I don't understand

(i) that he is late.
(ii) why he is late.

Here, why he is late is correct.

1. Can you find out
   (i) whether she has joined the service or not?
   (ii) that she has joined the service or not?
2. She taught me
   (i) how to play cricket.
   (ii) that I should work hard.
3. I would not figure out
   (i) who he was.
   (ii) that he was.
4. He has discovered
   (i) how effectively he can learn to communicate.
   (ii) that effectively he can learn to communicate.
5. He warned me
   (i) that I should be careful of the new office assistant.
   (ii) which I should be careful of.
6. Did you hear the donkey
   (i) braying all night?
   (ii) to have brayed all night?
7. Did he advise you
   (i) to take exercise every day?
   (ii) taking exercise every day?
8. I remember
   (i) seeing him sitting in the chair.
   (ii) to see him sitting in the chair.
9. He admitted
   (i) to be in college around noon.
   (ii) being in college around noon.
10. Have you noticed
    (i) how he prepares tea?
    (ii) that he prepares the tea?

EXERCISE 1.6

Identify the finite and non-finite elements in the following sentences.

Example: He **wants** **to go** today.
finite non-finite

1. His wife disapproved of his drinking liquor.
2. He stopped to smoke a cigarette.
3. I saw the tiger leaping towards me.
4. Being tired, the teacher slept in the class.
5. I'd advise you to study 8 hours a day if you want to pass the RPET.
6. I am starting to learn French.
7. The student admitted having copied in the examination.
8. The consumer threatened the shopkeeper to report his cheating him to the police.
9. She agreed to pay the fine.
10. I'll help you (to) arrange the flowers if you like.

Adjectives

Adjectives are words that describe the attributes of nouns:

hot	**weather**	
Adj.	N	
A	**red**	**car**
	Adj.	N
A	**yellow**	**dress**
	Adj.	N

What are the morphological and syntactic characteristics of adjectives? Below, we discuss some of the *morphological characteristics* of adjectives. Adjectives have some of the following typical endings (Table 1.12).

TABLE 1.12 Endings of adjectives

Ending	*Examples*
-ous	joyous, fabulous, nebulous, vacuous, stupendous, notorious, ceremonious, adventurous
-less	breathless, senseless, faithless, limitless, merciless
-ic	characteristic, rustic, terrific, angelic, climatic, dramatic
-able -ible	venerable, advisable, corrigible, negligible
-al	accidental, classical, autumnal, inimical, facial, natural
-ive	authoritative, protective, stative, expensive
-ful	faithful, harmful, fanciful, peaceful

But a number of adjectives do not conform to the above endings. They are given below:

timid	accurate
patient	abundant
transparent	broad
	large
ignorant	big
	small
inferior	calm
superior	cruel
innocent	false
brilliant	free
happy	human
humble	merry
mortal	necessary
novel	obedient
perfect	poor
proud	pure
real	rival
vain	true
vacant	vital
weak	wide
wise	young
busy	brief
cheap	deep
gay	grand
hot	long

They are too many to list.

Adjectives take different forms on a scale of comparison. They are marked for comparative and superlative degrees.

Absolute	**Comparative**	**Superlative**
weak	weaker	weakest
hot	hotter	hottest
bright	brighter	brightest
young	younger	youngest
able	abler	ablest
happy	happier	happiest

There are some irregular forms to be seen such as:

good	better	best
bad	worse	worst
far	farther	farthest
little	less	least

Longer adjectives take *more* and *most* before them on the scale of comparison.

brilliant	more brilliant	most brilliant
beautiful	more beautiful	most beautiful
wonderful	more wonderful	most wonderful

Syntactic features of adjectives provide the tests for words to qualify as adjectives. Some of the syntactic features are given below

Some adjectives take adverbs such as *extremely*, *very*, *less*, *fairly*, *immensely*, *reasonably*, etc. before them.

(i) An extremely beautiful girl
(ii) A very poor farmer
(iii) An immensely important leader
(iv) A fairly rich foreigner
(v) A less violent person

Notice that the use of the above adverbs before the adjectives indicates that a thing or person has more or less of a particular quality. That means the adjectives are *gradable*. Gradable adjectives are *effective*, *difficult*, *hard*, *angry*, *disappointed*, *sorry*, *entertaining*, *enjoyable*, *successful*, etc.

The opposite of gradable adjectives is *ungradable adjectives*. Ungradable adjectives already have the highest position on the scale of comparison and hence they do not need the above modifying adverbs. Some of the ungradable adjectives are given below.

main	amazed	invaluable
principal	awful	terrible
sheer	dreadful	wonderful
unique	huge	useless
major	impossible	meaningless
certain	true	devastated
absurd	clear	exhausted
terrified	necessary	unbearable
essential	sure	unrecognizable

Some of the ungradable adjectives can be modified by *absolutely*, *completely*, *entirely*, *really*, *totally*, *simply* and *utterly*.

For example:

(i) utterly devastated (ii) simply valueless
(iii) totally absurd (iv) completely terrified
(v) absolutely essential

The second syntactic feature of adjectives is that most adjectives can occur before the nouns they modify or after the linking verbs. This is called *attributive* and *predicative* uses of adjectives.

Attributive use	Predicative use
the **red** car	The car is **red**.
the **young** man	The man is **young**.
the **happy** woman	The woman is **happy**.

After linking verbs such as *appear*, *become*, *feel*, *get* and *seem*, an adjective is used which is called the predicative use of the adjective.

(i) She seemed to be happy. (ii) He looked very cool.
(iii) He got angry for no reason. (iv) I feel very hot.

Notice that there are some adjectives that seldom have attributive use: most of them start with *a* = *afraid*, *alight*, *alike*, *alive*, *alone*, *ashamed*, *asleep*, *awake*, *aware*, (content, fine, glad, ill, when they describe health or feeling), *well*, *unwell*, *sure*, *unsure*, *sorry*, *poorly*, and *upset*.

Notice further that the synonymous of *ill*, i.e. *sick* can be used attributively (*a sick child*); *ill* can occur before a noun if preceded by an adverb.

(i) a terminally ill person

There is a mechanism in language that if a particular part of speech does not have one type of use, then it invents a related word that can be used in that particular use. Thus, there is a gap filling strategy available. This applies to *a*-type adjectives where language users have evolved related adjectives that can be used attributively.

alive = living
afraid = frightened
alike = similar
asleep = sleeping
alone = lonely
ashamed = shy

Further, there are classifying adjectives such as *atomic*, *cubic*, *digital*, *medical*, *phonetic*, *chief*, *entire*, *initial*, *main*, *only*, *whole*, *eventual*, *occasional*, *northern*, *maximum*, *minimum*, *underlying* and emphasizing adjectives such as *absolute*, *complete*, *mere* and *utter* are not used predicatively.

(i) The main accused did not turn up in the court.
(ii) The accused who is main did not turn up in the court.

In institutionalized expressions, adjectives are used after nouns.

(i) The Governor General
(ii) Akbar the great
(iii) The Princess royal

Adjectives are used after pronouns.

(i) Something useful
(ii) Everyone present
(iii) Those responsible

Some adjectives ending with *–ible* and *–able* come after the nouns when these nouns follow words such as *first, last, next* and *superlative adjectives* or when a propositional phrase follows the adjective.

(i) Only suggestion suitable
(ii) An offer available to club members only
(iii) The shortest route possible
(iv) The best hotel available

There are certain adjectives that can come before or after nouns. Their meaning changes accordingly. These adjectives are *concerned, involved, opposite, present*, and *responsible*.

(i) My present address (my address now)
(ii) All the students present (who were there)
(iii) All the teachers concerned (involved)
(iv) All the concerned teachers (worried)

Types of Adjectives

There are two types of adjectives mainly *central* and *peripheral*. The adjectives that satisfy the criteria of gradability, comparisons, attribution, predication are *central* and the rest are *peripheral*.

Adjectives can be classified into different types based on their meaning and syntactic behaviour.

Inherent vs non-inherent adjectives

In order to understand the difference between inherent and non-inherent adjectives, look at the derivation of two sets of noun phrases containing adjectives (Table 1.13).

TABLE 1.13 Derivation of noun phrases

Inherent adjectives	*Non-inherent adjectives*
• A small car = A car which is small	• A small businessman = A businessman whose business is small
• An old man = A man who is old	• An old friend = An old person who has been a friend for a long time.
• A heavy burden = A burden which is heavy	• A heavy smoker = A smoker who smokes heavily (too much)
• A dancing girl = A girl who dances	• A walking stick = A stick for walking

Notice that in the two columns, the adjectives are different. In the first column, the adjective *small* in *a small car* refers to the inherent qualities of the car, i.e. its small size. Therefore, it is an inherent adjective.

In the second column, the word *small* in the phrase *a small businessman* does not modify the businessman but business which is small, i.e. it indirectly or less directly refers to the attributes of the part of the noun. It is a non-inherent adjective. The same thing applies to other adjectives given in Table 1.13.

Stative vs dynamic adjectives

Adjectives are classified as *stative* vs *dynamic* on the basis of their meaning. The term *stative* refers to the permanent state or condition of the adjective whereas the term *dynamic* shows that the quantity is under the control of the possessor. Table 1.14 gives examples of *stative* and *dynamic* adjectives.

TABLE 1.14 Stative and dynamic adjectives

Stative adjectives	*Dynamic adjectives*
small	brave
big	patient
red	cool
yellow	foolish
tall	friendly
short	rude
soft	suspicious
hard	hard working

This distinction is important because it has syntactic implications. Notice that with stative adjectives, imperatives and progressive aspect are not possible whereas these syntactic operations are permissible with dynamic objectives.

(i) Be tall.
(ii) He is being small.
(iii) Be smart.
(iv) He is being rude.

Nominal adjectives

As the name suggests, these adjectives have some of the characteristics of nouns and some of adjectives. These adjectives denote a class by describing one of the qualities of that class:

(i) *the French* (all people belonging to France)
(ii) *the old* (all are old)
(iii) *the brave French*
(iv) *the very old*
(v) *the poor*
(vi) *the English* (refers to the English people – nationality)
(vii) *the Germans*
(viii) *the Russians*
(ix) *the Americans*

Denominal adjectives

When adjectives are derived from nouns, they are called **denominal adjectives**.

(i) *a linguistic problem* (a problem based on linguistics)
(ii) *a steely determination* (determination as hard as steel)
(iii) *a woollen garment* (a garment made of wool)
(iv) *French wine* (wine that comes from France)

Notice further that even a noun can be used to modify another noun though it does not have the characteristic of an adjective. For example:

(i) a family car
(ii) the Sikar public
(iii) the college student

Participle adjectives

They are called *participle adjectives* because they have the same endings (*-ing*, *-ed*) as those of participles. Look at the following examples (Table 1.15):

TABLE 1.15 Participle adjectives

-ed form	self-centered, renowned, talented, alarmed, amazed, bored, excited, frightened, pleased, surprised, tired, worried, delighted
-ing form	alarming, amazing, boring, exciting, frightening, pleasing, surprising, tiring, worrying, welcoming

Notice a few important things about these adjectives.

They can be modified by adverbs.

(i) very alarming
(ii) most alarmed

Some of them are derivable from verbs.

Frightening = frighten
Pleased = please

Others are not.

self-centered = self centre
talented = talent
renowned = renown

If a participle adjective has both *–ing* form and *–ed* form, then the *–ing* form describes something and *–ed* form describes someone.

(i) The movie was frightening.
(ii) The frightened children shouted for help.

Sometimes it becomes difficult to separate the verbal and adjectival use of participles. In these cases, you should apply the *very* test. If the *very test* applies, then it is adjectival, otherwise it is verbal.

(i) I was disappointed to hear the news. (adjectival, because we can say *very disappointed*)
(ii) I was disappointed by the news. (verbal, because we cannot say *very disappointed*)

Ordering of Adjectives

Sometimes, we use a number of adjectives in a row. What should be the order? Should the size precede the colour?

According to Hewings (1999:166), the preferred order (though not fixed) is: *opinion + size/physical quality/shape/age + colour + participle adjectives + origin + material + type + purpose + noun*

In other words, gradable adjectives (describing opinion, size, quality, shape, age) precede ungradable adjectives (participle adjectives and adjectives describing origin, material, type and purpose). Look at the following examples.

(i) a new wooden box (= age + material + noun).
(ii) a soft white toy (= quality + colour + noun).
(iii) an exciting Japanese story (= opinion + origin + noun).
(iv) a round biscuit container (= shape + purpose + noun).
(v) a big broken table (= size + participle + adjective + noun).
(vi) a useful digital alarm clock (= opinion + type + purpose + noun).

According to Internet Grammar of English, "the more adjectival a word is, the farther it will be from the noun; the less adjectival (the more nominal) it is the nearer to the noun it will be."

Internet Grammar of English lists the five sequences for the ordering of adjectives.

1.	central	+ denominal	+ nouns		
	heavy	wooden	tables		
	complex	biological	problems		
2.	central	+ colour	+ nouns		
	big	red	cars		
	small	white	rabbits		
3.	colour	+ denominal	+ nouns		
	green	Japanese	toys		
	white	Indian	rabbits		
4.	central	+ participle	+ denominal	+ nouns	
	heavy	carved	wooden	tables	
	small	dancing	Indian	rabbits	
5.	non-gradable	+ central	+ colour	+ denominal	+ nouns
	certain	expensive	green	Japanese	toys

What happens if the adjectives of the same type occur?

rich, young people (use either a *comma* or *and* between two adjectives). Here, the choice depends upon premodification. If one of them is premodified by *very*, then it comes in the beginning.

A very rich and young man

A rich and very young man (not acceptable)

EXERCISE 1.7

Adjectives have been put in bold letters in the following sentences. Identify gradable and non-gradable adjectives.

1. This house needs **major** repairs.
2. The actress from Japan was given only a **minor** role in the film.
3. I'm **certain** that she stole the watch.
4. He won the gold medal by **sheer** luck.
5. The Ganges is one of the **principal** rivers in India.
6. My **main** meal is in the morning.
7. I want to live a very **comfortable** life.
8. His contribution to the college has been **invaluable.**
9. He is an utterly **useless** person.
10. He is an **angry, young** man who wants to bring about a social revolution in the country.
11. She is a really **marvellous** woman.
12. This is an extremely **complicated** problem that needs **careful** handling.
13. You look **absurd** in this dress.
14. This is the most **important** day in my life.
15. Can I see you tomorrow? Sorry! I am very **busy** tomorrow.
16. I cannot come to meet you in this **awful** weather.
17. When I saw my result in the newspaper, I was **disappointed.**
18. I was utterly **devastated** by the news.
19. He is a very **popular** teacher among the students.
20. He is a very **famous** doctor in this part of Rajasthan.

EXERCISE 1.8

Put the adjectives in brackets in the following sentences in the most appropriate order.

1. Ram has a .... (big, American, red) car.
2. She is wearing .... (black, soft, woolen) clothes.
3. She has .... (curly, long) hair.
4. He is an .... (enthusiastic, young) teacher.
5. He is a .... (very boring, ignorant, depressing) fool.

6. Life is .... (very happy, exciting, interesting).
7. He came and saw that two .... (oblong, wooden) tables were laid in the central courtyard.
8. This room has been painted in a mixture of .... (yellow, white).
9. He hit me with a .... (long, wooden) stick.
10. Nobody could escape from his ever .... (watchful, probing) eye.
11. Amitabh Bachchan is a .... (famous, rich, renowned) actor.

Adverbs

Adverbs are words that are used to modify a verb, an adjective or another adverb.

(i) Rama ran **fast**.
adverb
(modifies verb, ran)

(ii) Rama ran **very** **fast**.
adverb adverb
(modifies another adverb, fast)

(iii) Rama is **extremely** beautiful.
adverb
(modifies adjective, beautiful)

What are the morphological and syntactic characteristics of adverbs?

Morphological Characteristics of Adverbs

Most adverbs are formed by the addition of *–ly* to adjectives.

Adjectives	*Adverbs*
slow	slowly
quick	quickly
hard	hardly
soft	softly
gradual	gradually

These adverbs are called *–ly* adverbs.

Notice that all adverbs do not end in *–ly*. Adverbs like *always*, *never*, *seldom*, *quite*, *rather*, *still*, *yesterday*, *twice a week*, *often*, *very*, *too*, *even*, *only*, *alone*, etc. do not end in *–ly*. Further, there are some adjectives such as *deadly*, *friendly*, *kindly*, *manly*, *silly*, *timely*, *lively*, *cowardly*, *daily*, *lovely*, *elderly*, etc. that end in *–ly*.

Adverbs also have comparative and superlative forms like adjectives.

Absolute	**Comparative**	**Superlative**
hard	harder	hardest
recently	more recently	most recently
far	farther	farthest
frequently	more frequently	most frequently
bravely	more bravely	most bravely
fast	faster	fastest
well	better	best
badly	worse	worst
little	less	least
much	more	most
soon	sooner	soonest
late	later	latest

Syntactic features of adverbs

Like adjectives, adverbs are also gradable. They can be modified by *very* or *extremely*.

softly	very softly
suddenly	very suddenly
slowly	extremely slowly

Notice that *very* and *extremely* are degree adverbs because they specify the degree to which an adjective or adverb applies. Other degree adverbs are *almost*, *entirely*, *highly*, *quite*, *slightly*, *totally*, *utterly*, *completely*, *fairly*, *rather*, *too*, *very* (*much*).

Very means to a high degree, *too* means 'more than is wanted or needed', and *quite* means to a particular degree' and with ungradable adjectives means *completely*.

(i) The weather is very cold these days.
(ii) The weather is too cold to stay outdoors.
(iii) I am quite satisfied with the request. (= fairly)
(iv) I am quite certain that he will come tomorrow. (= completely)

Notice that *enough* comes after the adverb/adjective.

You won't pass the test if you don't work hard enough.

It will be in order to understand the difference between *quite* and *rather*. Take for example:

He is quite popular.

It means less than very popular but more than a little.

Rather is used with negative words and negative ideas.

How was the exam?

Rather difficult, I suppose.

If *rather* is used with positive words, then it means *unusually* or *surprisingly*.

The apples are rather nice. (unusually nice, nicer than expected)

Adverbs vs Adjectives

As said above, adverbs and adjectives have several things in common. For example, the concepts of *gradability* and *comparison* apply to both. The characteristics of + attributes and predications of adjective do not apply to adverbs. The following words are used as both adjectives and adverbs:

early, *far*, *fast*, *hard*, *late*, *better*, *best*, *daily*, *weekly*, *monthly*, *well*, *kindly*, *back*, *direct*, *enough*, *ill*, *left*, *right*, *still*, *most*, *pretty*, *deep*, *low*, *high*, *little*, *long*, *straight*, *short*, *near*, *wronged*, *amazed*, etc.

Notice further that some adverbs have two forms.

I will be there as **quickly** as possible.

Other adverbs of this type are *loud*, *loudly*, *cheap*, *cheaply*, *clean*, *cleanly*, *clear*, *clearly*, *fine*, *finely*, *slow*, *slowly*, *thin*, *thinly*.

In formal style, the form ending *–ly* is preferred.

Then, adverbs without *–ly* and with *–ly* have different meanings.

(i) I arrived late for the play.
(ii) I haven't seen her **lately** (recently).

This meaning difference is summarized in Table 1.16:

TABLE 1.16 Meaning difference in adverbs

direct = without stopping	directly = very soon = straight
hard	hardly = rarely
high	highly = praise somebody for something
short	shortly = soon
wide = completely	widely = many places

Types of Adverbs

There are different types of adverbs based on meaning. Degree adverbs (*very*, *extremely*, *rather*, *quite*) have already been discussed. Now we discuss other types of adverbs.

1. Circumstantial adverbs: Adverbs describing the circumstance of an event or action are called circumstantial adverbs. They are of four sub types as shown in Figure 1.9.

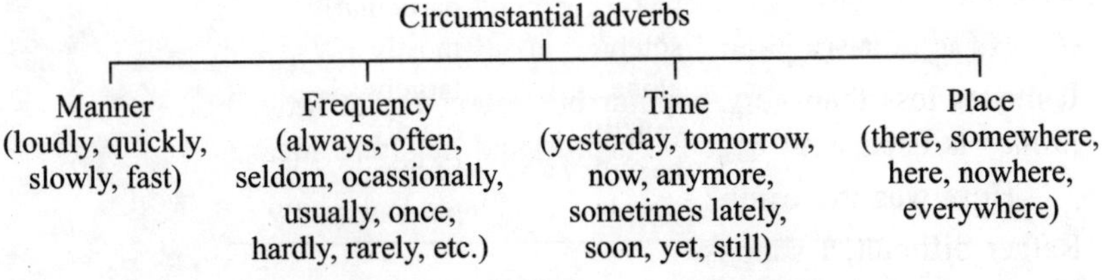

FIGURE 1.9 Circumstantial adverb

(i) He ran **quickly** to catch the bus.
(ii) He **occasionally** attends the club to play bridge.
(iii) I haven't seen him **anywhere**.
(iv) Come **soon**, I'll miss you.

2. Wh- adverbs Another sub-class of adverbs begins with *wh- words* such as *when, where, why, where, whereby, wherein, whereupon,* and *how*. Consider the following sentences.

(i) **When** are you going to Hyderabad?
(ii) **Why** did you do this?
(iii) **How** did you do this?
(iv) **Where** did you park the car?

3. Sentence adverbs Sentence adverbs modify the whole sentence.

(i) Frankly speaking, he beat her very badly during the interval.
(ii) Unfortunately, he failed in the examination.

Sentence adverbs often convey speakers' comments on the content of what they are saying.

Strangely enough, he has behaved quite contrary to his nature.

Some of the sentence adverbs are given below.

yet, naturally, frankly, to be frank, to put it frankly, if I may be frank, certainly, hopefully, of course, to be sure, surely, unfortunately, actually, admittedly, definitely, in fact, indeed, luckily, officially, possibly, preferably, superficially, surprisingly, technically, theoretically, etc.

They are too many to be listed here.

Some sentence adverbs are used to link one sentence with the preceding one. These sentence adverbs are *however, accordingly, consequently, therefore, yet,* etc.

The college didn't pay me the house rent. However, I didn't sue them.

4. Additives, exclusives and particulizers First of all, we give a list of three types of adverbs, based on Internet English Grammar, in Table 1.17.

Table 1.17 Types of adverbs

Additives	*Exclusives*	*Particulizers*
too	just	particularly
also	solely	mostly
	alone	largely
	exactly	mainly
	heavily	primarily
	simply	predominantly

Let us now look at the meaning and use of these adverbs.

Additives, as the name suggests, *add* two or more constructions/ideas, together emphasizing that they are equal in meaning or status.

(i) American students are very hard-working and research-oriented. Indian students **too** are no less researchers and hard workers.

(ii) Mohan, after doing B.Tech. from IIT Kanpur, got a package of ₹ 10,0000 from Infosys. **Also** his brother got a pay package of 9 lac from Satyam.

Exclusive adverbs, as the name suggests, focus attention on the following idea to the exclusion of all other possibilities:

The meeting was called **just** to vote on the budget. (There was no other purpose of the meeting except voting on the budget.)

Particulizers also focus attention on the following matter but do not exclude other possibilities.

Ramgarh Shekhawati is particularly famous for frescoes on havelis.

When certain adverbs are placed in the beginning of a sentence, there is an inversion of the operator.

(i) Never before **have** I seen such a beautiful temple.

(ii) Hardly **had** he reached the college **when** the principal called him.

(iii) No sooner **had** he started taking breakfast **than** he discovered a fly in the milk.

(iv) Only in India **can** you buy cottons like that!

EXERCISE 1.9

Identify in each sentence whether the bold word has been used as an adjective or adverb.

1. He is a very **fast** runner.
2. She ran as **fast** as she could.
3. He went **straight** to meet the principal.
4. She has **straight** not curly hair.
5. Can you direct me to the railway station? Go straight two blocks and then turn **right**.
6. After 5 minutes she asked me whether she was going in the **right** direction.
7. I hope for an **early** reply to my letter.
8. He arrived rather **early** for the meeting.
9. It's a very **cold** day today. I am shivering.
10. When she asked him to marry her, he refused her **cold**.
11. Our income falls **short** of our expenses.
12. Coloured TVs are in **short** supply.
13. The sum is **wrong**, but I don't know where it went **wrong**.
14. He is working very **hard** to get very good marks in the examination.

15. But he found some **hard** questions in the paper which he could not answer.
16. The train arrived 10 minutes **late.**
17. The train was 10 minutes **late**.
18. Which is the most **direct** route to Delhi?
19. The next train doesn't go **direct** to Delhi; it goes to Aligarh.
20. How are you? **Pretty** good.
21. She made a **pretty** fortune by selling her jewellery.
22. She is the most **kindly** person I have ever met.
23. Would you **kindly** shut the door?
24. Keep **still** while I pull out your tooth.
25. It's **still** unfair that I have not been given a pay raise.

Prepositions

Prepositions are words that come before noun phrases and they show the relationship between one **noun** and **another**. In the definition, we said noun phrases because after the preposition, a determiner or an adjective may intervene.

(i)	**Under**	**the**	**table**	
	Prep	Det	N	
(ii)	**Under**	**the**	**round**	**table**
	Prep	Det	Adj	N

We start the discussion of prepositions by listing them and by pointing out their types. The uses of prepositions will be dealt with in a separate chapter.

Types of Prepositions

There are three types of prepositions in English as shown in Figure 1.10.

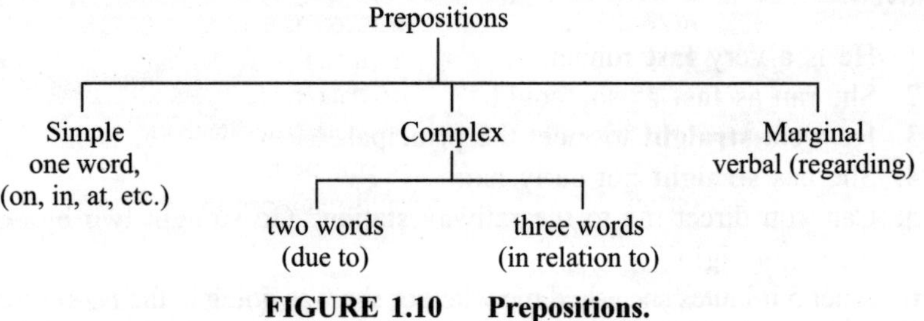

FIGURE 1.10 Prepositions.

Simple prepositions

Most common prepositions in English are one word prepositions called **simple prepositions**. They are listed below.

about	between	on	up
above	by	onto	with
across	down	over	without

after	for	past	along
from	since	around	in
till	at	through	before
into	to	below	of
under	beside	off	until

If a preposition does not come before the NP and is moved to the end or beginning position, it is called a stranded preposition.

(i) Which pen did you write **with**?
(ii) With which pen did you write?

Complex prepositions

Complex prepositions consist of two words or three words. If they are made up of two words, then the second word is the preposition. If they contain three words, then the pattern is:

preposition + noun + preposition
in relation to

A list of complex prepositions is given in Table 1.18.

Table 1.18 Complex prepositions

Two word prepositions	*Three word prepositions*
according to	in relation to
along with	by means of
apart from	in comparison with
because of	on top of
contrary to	in front of
due to	
except for	in addition to
instead of	with respect to
prior to	in aid of
	on behalf of
regardless of	in accordance with
as for	in line with
out of	with reference to
away from	
except for	
up to	
etc.	etc.

Examples:

(i) **according to** the supervisor
(ii) **contrary to** my expectations

(iii) **due to** sickness
(iv) **with reference to** your application
(v) **in line with** previous decision
(vi) **in accordance with** your directions

Marginal prepositions

Marginal prepositions are derived from other parts of speech. Some of them are derived from verbs (see Figure 1.11).

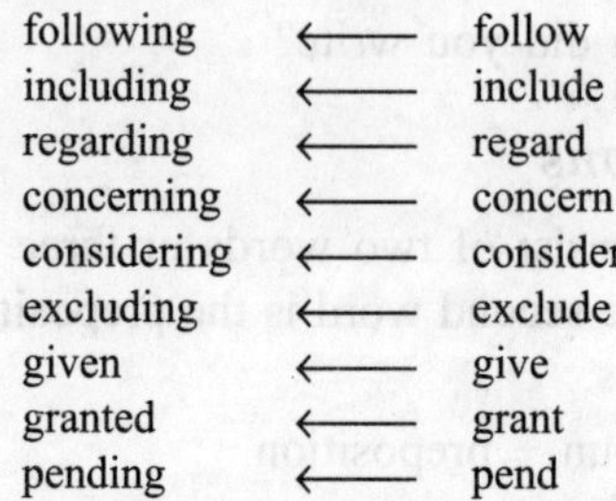

FIGURE 1.11 Derivation of marginal prepositions.

Worth and *minus* are non-verbal marginal prepositions.
Examples:

(i) I am writing to you regarding the electricity and water problem facing the village.
(ii) Concerning his performance, I would like to say that he is doing wonderfully well.
(iii) The decision will be held in abeyance pending the court decision.
(iv) His time is worth a million dollars.
(v) Twenty five minus ten is fifteen.

Conjunctions

Conjunctions are words that link or connect two words or phrases of the same word class. Sometimes, longer units such as two simple sentences having some semantic connection can also be connected.

For example:

(i) Ram and Sita
(ii) the boy and the girl
(iii) hot and humid
(iv) poor but honest
(v) hot or cold
(vi) tea or coffee
(vii) Ram plays tennis and Shyam plays badminton.

But you cannot say:

Ram plays tennis and Armstrong landed on the moon. (Do not make any semantic connection, hence it is ruled out.)

There are two types of conjunctions as shown in Figure 1.12.

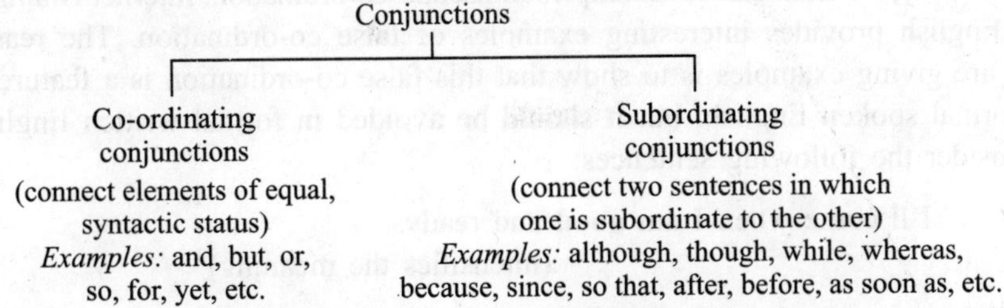

FIGURE 1.12 Conjunctions.

Notice that the sentences joined by co-ordinators (*and*, *but*, *or*, etc.) are called **conjoins** and the co-ordinator occurs in between them. The order of conjoins can be reversed without affecting the meaning.

Shyam went to Delhi	and
conjoins	co-ordinator
Gopal went to Calcutta.	
conjoins	

The order can be reversed without affecting the meaning.

Gopal went to Calcutta	and
conjoins	co-ordinator
Shyam went to Delhi	
conjoins	

In this regard, subordinating sentences are different. First, it is not necessary for the subordinator to come between the main clauses and the subordinate clauses. Secondly, if we reverse the order, the meaning is affected.

(i) I cannot come to college **because** I am ill.
subordinator

(ii) Because I am ill, I cannot come to college. (Notice *because* can come in the beginning.)

If the order is reversed:

(i) If you are tired, rest for a while.

(ii) Rest for a while, if you are tired.

(iii) I am ill because I cannot come to college. (This sentence makes no sense.)

The reason is that the relationship between the main clause and the subordinate clause is that of **syntactic dependency**, whereas there is no such relationship between co-ordinate clauses. It is a kind of equal relationship.

A detailed discussion of the process of co-ordination and subordination will be given in the chapter on compound and complex sentences.

Finally, we shall discuss examples of pseudo-co-ordination. Internet Grammar of English provides interesting examples of false co-ordination. The reason we are giving examples is to show that this false co-ordination is a feature of informal spoken English, but it should be avoided in formal written English. Consider the following sentences:

I'll come when I am **good** and ready.
(intensifies the meaning)

This sentence can be derived from:

I'll come when I am good and when I am ready, but that is not the meaning. The meaning is,
I'll come when I'm completely ready.

So here *good* and *ready* are examples of false or pseudo-coordination. Another example is:

Please try and come early.

It can be derived from:

(Please try) and (Please come early).

The meaning is:

Please try to come early.

This is informal English. *But* and *and* are used as false coordination.

Interjections

Interjections are words that express a number of emotions. They are used in spoken English or in novels or in plays. Common English interjections are reproduced below.

Oh (surprise)
Oh, what a big achievement!
Ah (satisfaction, recognition, etc.)
Ah, that's the job I was looking for.
Aha (great satisfaction, recognition)
Aha, I've found my lost book.
Wow (great surprise)
Wow, what a jackpot you have hit.

Yippee (excitement, delight)

Yippee, I've found the toy.

Ouch (sudden pain or disgust)

Ouch, my foot hurts!

Ow (pain)

Ow, that wound!

Ugh (disgust)

Ugh, what a noise!

Ooh (pleasure, pain)

Ooh, this pudding's tasty.

Shit (exasperation)

Shit, I dropped my pen again.

Yuck (disgust)

Oh, yuck, I hate pudding.

Eh (surprise, doubt, agreement)

Let's have another drink, eh.

Hum (uncertainly)

Hum, I may go tomorrow.

Phew (glad that worrying experience is over)

Phew, we have done it.

Tsk (disapproval)

Tsk, tsk, you shouldn't do it.

Uh-huh (yes)

Can I smoke in here? Uh- huh

Uh-uh (no)

Is Paul here yet? Uh-uh

Huh (shows that you have not heard or understood a question)

John, are you listening to me? 'Huh?'

EXERCISE 1.10

Identify prepositions in the following excerpts. Also, point out type of preposition each one is (i.e. simple or complex).

1. Seventeen-year-old Cory was working on his car and was covered with grease. "That boy is going to leave his mark on the world some day," said his father proudly.
   "The question is," Cory's mother remarked, "Will I be able to get it off?" (Elaihe Redway, from the Reader's Digest.)
2. Once someone wrote to Sir Winston Churchill, suggesting that he should avoid using prepositions at the end of his sentences. Churchill wrote back: "This is the kind of arrant nonsense up with which I will not put."
3. I started playing cricket when I was about 11. With hard work I managed to get into my class team. I played four matches and then was removed

as I was out for a duck in all four matches. I managed to get into the team again. I played two matches in which I didn't score. Then, in my third match, I could hardly believe I scored a half century and I was the highest scorer. Since then, I always played well and I was never removed from the class team. I even played for the school.

4. According to senior tax officials, if the amounts roughly matched the date provided by the third parties through annual information returns, the need for any further scouting and investigation would not arise.
5. This is in response to your advertisement for the post of lecturers in English published in the Times of India of June 14, 2006.
6. Following riots in Delhi, the curfew was imposed for 18 hours in the walled city area.

EXERCISE 1.11

Choose the correct alternative.

1. One of his books has been acclaimed internationally. (so that, as a result), he thinks he is a great writer.
2. Your argnment is powerful, (however, though) I beg to differ.
3. (Even so/Even though) I know that I would fail, I took the test.
4. He has worked in this college for 5 years. (even though/nevertheless) the principal does not give him the recognition he deserves.
5. I first listened to Bajpai's speech in 1963. (after/after that), I didn't miss any of his speeches.
6. We have worked together in the same college for years (yet/however) we hardly exchanged a word.
7. We were all enjoying the concert, (meanwhile/while) Shyam sat gloomily looking at the ceiling.
8. They first had coffee at a restaurant and (afterwards/since) they went for sight seeing.
9. (However/Yet) hard he tried, he couldn't clear the paper of Management Information System.
10. (Meanwhile/While) I was waiting for the city bus, my eyes fell on a very poor boy sitting on the pavement and asking for alms.

Conclusion

In this chapter, an attempt was made to define and illustrate word classes. Two types of word classes, major and minor were discussed. Under major word classes was included the discussion of nouns, verbs, adjectives, and adverbs. The discussion of minor word classes included pronouns, auxiliaries, conjunctions, prepositions and interjections.

The traditional way of discussing parts of speech in terms of meaning was replaced by the morphological and syntactic properties of these word classes. It is hoped the readers would benefit from the presentation of parts of speech in this chapter.

Key to Exercise 1.1

1. preposition
2. conjunction
3. verb
4. noun
5. noun
6. verb
7. preposition
8. noun
9. noun
10. adverb

Key to Exercise 1.2

1. common
2. common
3. abstract, abstract
4. abstract, abstract, abstract, abstract, abstract
5. abstract
6. proper noun
7. abstract, abstract, abstract, abstract
8. collective, abstract
9. collective, abstract, abstract
10. material, material

Key to Exercise 1.3

1. pike, mice, foot (in measurement) feet (parts of the body), antelope(s), dozen (if followed by of construction, dozens of … possible), leaves, wreaths, fathers-in-law, women doctors, stand-bys, houses, analyses, alumnae, indices, bases, axes, oases, criteria, automata, schemata
2. chairman/chair, synthetic, police officer, firefighter, business executive, congressional representative
3. The girl's dress, the knob of the door, the teacher's salary, the discovery of insulin, two month's notice, the dentist's clinic.

Key to Exercise 1.4

1. this
2. which
3. which
4. what
5. what
6. which
7. anybody
8. something
9. anything
10. much
11. all
12. whose
13. their
14. everyone/everybody
15. none
16. she
17. herself
18. they
19. our
20. it
21. me
22. each other, they

Key to Exercise 1.5

1. whether she has joined the service or not.
2. how to play cricket.
3. who he was.
4. how effectively he can learn to communicate.
5. that I should be careful of the new office assistant.
6. braying all night.
7. to take exercise every day.
8. seeing him sitting in the chair.
9. being in college around noon.
10. how he prepares tea.

Key to Exercise 1.6

1. Finite: disapproved.
2. Finite: stopped, non-finite: to smoke
3. Finite: saw, non-finite: leaping
4. Non-finite: being tired, finite: slept
5. Finite: would advise, non-finite: to study, finite: want, non-finite: to pass
6. Finite: am starting, non-finite: to learn
7. Finite: admitted, non-finite having copied
8. Finite: threatened, non-finite: to report
9. Finite: agreed, non-finite: to pay
10. Finite: will help, non-finite: (to) arrange

Key to Exercise 1.7

1. ungradable
2. ungradable
3. ungradable
4. ungradable
5. ungradable
6. ungradable
7. gradable
8. ungradable
9. ungradable
10. gradable, gradable
11. ungradable
12. gradable, gradable
13. ungradable
14. gradable
15. gradable
16. ungradable
17. gradable
18. ungradable
19. gradable
20. gradable

Key to Exercise 1.8

1. big, red, American
2. soft, black, woolen
3. long and curly
4. enthusiastic and young
5. very boring, ignorant and depressing

6. very happy, exciting and interesting
7. oblong, wooden
8. yellow and white
9. long, wooden
10. watchful and probing
11. famous, rich and renowned

Key to Exercise 1.9

1. adjective
2. adverb
3. adverb
4. adjective
5. adverb
6. adjective
7. adjective
8. adverb
9. adjective
10. adverb
11. adverb
12. adjective
13. adjective, adverb
14. adverb
15. adjective
16. adverb
17. adjective
18. adjective
19. adverb
20. adverb
21. adjective
22. adjective
23. adverb
24. adjective
25. adverb

Key to Exercise 1.10

1. with, on (simple)
2. to, at, of, up, with (simple).
3. about, with, into, in, for, in, after, into, in, from, for (all simple prepositions)
4. according to (complex), by, through, for (simple).
5. in response to (complex), for, of, in, of (all simple)
6. following (marginal), in, for, in (simple)

Key to Exercise 1.11

1. as a result
2. though
3. even though
4. nevertheless
5. after that
6. yet
7. while
8. afterwards
9. however
10. while

2

Phrases

Introduction

A language has a hierarchical structure. To discover the hierarchical structure of a language, we can adopt the top-down or bottom-up approach. A sentence is made up of clauses; a clause is made up of phrases; a phrase is made up of words; and a word is made up of morphemes. Take for example:

John killed a tiger.

This sentence consists of one clause (*John killed a tiger*); three phrases (*John* (NP)), *killed* (VP) and *a tiger* (NP); and four words (*John*, *killed*, *a*, *tiger*) and five morphemes (*John*, *kill*, *-ed*, *a*, *tiger*).

In this chapter, we shall describe different types of phrases such as:

(i) Noun phrases (NPs)
(ii) Verb phrases (VPs)
(iii) Adjective phrases (APs)
(iv) Prepositional phrases (PPs)

We will also discuss their constituents. It is hoped, after reading this chapter, the reader will be able to understand different kinds of phrases, their constituents and will be able to use them properly.

What is a Phrase?

A phrase consists of a group of words that constitute a single unit and that unit participates in a syntactic operation as such.

For example, the following sentence

The lazy boy	**did not read**	**the yellow book on the table.**
NP	VP	NP

consists of three phrases at one level of analysis, *the yellow book on the table* is a single phrase because it participates in passivization as a single unit:

The yellow book on the table was not read by the lazy boy.

Consider the following sentence:

I don't know **what you are saying**.
NP

In the above sentence, *what you are saying* is an NP which consists of a noun clause (what you are saying). It is an NP because it can be replaced by *it*, which is a pronoun and we know that a pronoun is a kind of noun. There are three characteristics of an NP:

(i) Can be replaced by a pronoun.
(ii) Participates in a syntactic operation such as passivization.

A single word dogs in the sentence '*Dogs* are faithful animals' is a noun phrase at one level of analysis because it can be expanded to form longer strings, e.g. *German dogs* are faithful animals.

Consider the following extract in which the phrases of different kinds have been made bold.

The first stage	**is**	**the production stage.**	**The human**
NP	VP	NP	NP
mind	**can be**	**extremely productive**	**for a short period.**
	VP	Adj. Phrase	Prepositional Phrase
The speaker	**should dig**	**into his memory bank**	
NP	VP	Prepositional Phrase	

intensively	**and**	**should extract**	**quickly**	**from it**
Adv. Phrase (adverb)	conjunction	VP	Adv. Phrase	PP
the range of ideas	**he has on his subject.**			
NP	NP (reduced relative clause).			

(*Source: The Skills of Communication*, Bill Scott, p. 10.)

Notice in the above extract, even some of the single words have been labelled as phrases. A language can be analyzed at several levels, i.e. at the level of clause, at the level of phrase, and at the level of word.

Noun Phrases

A noun phrase is called so because its head or main part is a noun. The head can be preceded by determiners or modifiers and these strings are called **pre-head strings**. The head can be followed by post-modifiers and these strings are called **post-head strings**. In the structure of an NP, *head* is the obligatory element whereas pre-modifiers and post-modifiers are optional. Look at the following NPs:

All **those** good **places** **I want to visit.**
predet det adj. head noun reduced relative clause
Pre-head strings Post-head strings

Tall **students** **on the playground.**
adj. head noun prepositional phrase
Pre-head strings Post-head strings

Notice that *pronouns* and *numerals* can also function as heads of NPs. Pronouns do not have pre-head strings; they may be followed by post-head strings.

(i) **He** visits his hometown twice a month.
head

(ii) Teachers don't like **those** **who arrive late in class.**
head post-head string

(iii) **Three** **of my students** have failed in the exam.
head post-head strings.

(iv) He was **the** **first** **to go.**
det head post-head string
pre-head string

Functions of NPs

A noun phrase can perform several functions. Look at the following sentences:

(i) **Sita** is a black beauty.
subject

(ii) This is **my sister, Sita.**
complement

(iii) Ram saw **Sita.**
object

(iv) Ram sent **Sita** **flowers.**
indirect object direct object

(v) Ram cannot live **without Sita**.
object of the preposition without

Constituents of NP

An NP has several constituents. It may consist of a *noun* or a *pronoun* or a wh-word:

(i) **Ram** is very intelligent.
NP
N

(ii) **He** was expelled from Ayodhya.
NP
pronoun

(iii) **Who** caused his expulsion?
NP
wh-pronoun

(iv) **This** saddened every citizen of Ayodhya.
NP
pronoun

A noun phrase may consist of a determiner plus a noun. A determiner comprises an article (*a* or *an* or *the*); a possessive adjective (*his*, *her*, *its*, *my*, *our*, *their*, and *your*); a demonstrative adjective (*this*, *these*, *that*, *those*); a wh-word (*what*, *which*, *whatever*, *whichever*, etc.) and a quantifier (*some*, *any*, *many*, *much*, *little*, *a little*, *few*, *a few*, *one*, *two*, *three*, *first*, *second*, *third*, etc.). Consider the following examples:

(i)	**a** art.	**book** N		
(ii)	**his** det.	**book** N		
(iii)	**this** det.	**book** N		
(iv)	**your** det.	**name** N		
(v)	**which** wh-word	**boy** N		
(vi)	**the** art.	**second** ordinal	**building** from here N	
(vii)	**many** quant	**girls** N		
(viii)	**her** det.	**first** ord.	**ten** cardinal	**lovers** N

A noun phrase can be preceded by an adjective phrase. An adjective phrase may consist of an *intensifier* and an adjective.

A	**very**	**interesting**	**book**
art.	int.	adj.	N
	adj. phrase		

Some nouns are also used before nouns and they modify the following nouns. These modifying nouns are called **classifiers**.

Commerce	**building**	
N	N	
A	**buy-now and pay-later**	**scheme.**
art.	classifier	N

All	**these**	**forget-me-not**	**gifts**
pre-det	det	classifier	N

On the basis of the above discussion of the constituents, we are now in a position to give the longest expansion of an NP:

All	**these**	**first**	**five**	**very**	**intelligent**
pre-det.	det.	ord	cardinal	int.	adj.
Alwar	**students.**				
classifier	N				

An NP may contain all the constituents or some of the constituents or none of the constituents. The use of one or more constituents depends upon what the speaker wants to say. The more the number of constituents, the more difficult it would be to process the NP under consideration.

Other examples of NPs are the following:

(i)	**a**	**very**	**interesting**	**anecdote**
	art	int.	adj.	N
(ii)	**friend's**	**daughter's**	**husband**	
	genitive	genitive	N	
(iii)	**some of**	**the**	**boring**	**lecturers**
	pre-det	det.	adj.	N
(iv)	**many**	**very**	**promising**	**students**
	quan	int.	adj.	N
(v)	**half of**	**my**	**textbooks**	
	pre-det.	det.	N	
(vi)	**both**	**the**	**top-ranking**	**students**
	pre-det.	det.	adj.	N
(vii)	**those**	**bad**	**boys**	**from Delhi**
	det.	adj.	N	PP
	pre-head string		head	post-head string
(viii)	**those**	**unforgettable**	**moments**	**in life**
	det.	adj.	N	PP
	pre-head string		head	post-head string
(ix)	**several**	**irrefutable**	**arguments**	**against reservation**
	quant	adj.	N	PP
	pre-head string		head	post-head string
(x)	**indefinite**		**strike**	**by medicos**
	adj.		N	PP
	pre-head string		head	post-head string

NPs may also contain two types of clauses. They may be relative clauses or complement clauses.

(i) **I** **know** **the student** **who stood first in the university.**
NP VP NP NP
pronoun V relative clause

(ii) **That Armstrong landed on the moon is not known**
NP VP
to everybody.
PP

EXERCISE 2.1

Identify NPs in the following paragraph. Ignore other phrases.

Excellent examples of the distinction between formal and informal were to be seen on British television during the time of the Folklands crisis. The professional spokesman from the Ministry of Defense adopted an attitude and a tone massively more formal than his counterparts in Argentina. He was seen to be the dispassionate expert, not the impassioned partisan.

Verb Phrases

Verb phrases are called so because their heads are verbs. Like noun phrases, they are preceded by *pre-* and *post-*head strings. Pre-head strings that may occur before verbs are negatives (*not* or *never*) and adverbial phrases such as *knowingly* or *slowly*. They may be followed by complements in that part of the VP which is required to complete the meaning of *head*. A verb is followed by a direct object if it is a transitive verb (*He kicked the ball*); or by an indirect object if it is an intransitive verb (*He gave him biscuits*). If the verb is a linking verb (*He is a doctor*), then it is followed by subjective complement. As the post-strings occur after a head, verbs are of many types. It is better to use the general term *complement*, which will encompass direct object, indirect object and subjective complement. Below some examples of verb phrases are given.

(i)	[He NP	[VP **never** pre-head string	**tells** head	**a lie**.]] post-head string complement
(ii)	[I NP	[VP **cannot** pre-head string	**say** head	**who stole the purse.**]] post-head string complement
(iii)	[She NP	[VP **brought** head	**him** post-head string complement	**flowers.**]] complement
(iv)	[He NP	[VP	**is** head	**a doctor.**]] post-head string complement

(v) [Gaurav Goyal [VP **has** **become** **an IAS officer.**]]
NP pre-head string head post-head string
complement

A verb phrase consists of an auxiliary verb and a main verb. An auxiliary or helping verb helps the main verb in specifying the action thereof. Auxiliaries include primary auxiliaries (*do, have, be*); tenses (*present* and *past*); modals (*may, might, can, could, shall, should, will, would,* and *must*); progressive aspect (*be* + *ing*); perfective aspect (*have* + *en*); and passive form (*be* + *past participle*).

There are two types of verbs: lexical verbs and phrasal verbs. Lexical verbs are *go, turn, break,* etc. and phrasal verbs are *go in for, go off, turn down, break down,* etc.

There are two types of verb phrases: finite and non-finite. **A finite verb phrase** carries tense and a non-finite verb is without tense. Non-finite phrases include *infinitival, gerundial* and *participial forms:*

(i) **To err** **is** human.
non-finite finite
infinitival

(ii) Kartikeyan **made** a mistake.
finite

(iii) **Being** **tired**, she **went** to bed early.
non-finite non-finite finite
present participle past participle

(iv) **Flying** planes **is** dangerous.
non-finite finite
present participle

(v) He **wants** **to eat** a mango.
finite non-finite
infinitival

(vi) He **wanted** **to eat** a mango.
finite non-finite
infinitival

Notice that the non-finite takes over the tense of the finite. The paraphrase of Example (v) above will be:

He wants it. He eats a mango.

The paraphrase of Example (vi) above would be

He wanted it. He ate a mango.

EXERCISE 2.2

Identify finite and non-finite verb phrases in the following sentences:

1. Being rich, he had no respect for the poor.
2. The sun having risen, we started for the village.
3. Entering the room, he discovered that all his valuables had gone.
4. He came, he saw and he conquered.
5. To work is to worship.
6. The aim of his life is to earn as much money as possible.
7. He is doing engineering so that he can go to the United States of America.
8. He is going to the States to do his M.S.
9. He earned his doctorate at the University of Hawaii.
10. The Hawaiin girls like to dance hula.

EXERCISE 2.3

Identify auxiliary and main verbs in the following sentences.

Example: you must be joking.
Auxiliaries: must, be + ing
Main verb: joke

1. A house must have been being built by him.
2. He cannot live without her.
3. He has been living in Sikar for the last two years.
4. Mary had a little lamb.
5. He will pass the examination.
6. He must be reading a book.
7. They had been playing football for two hours when I reached the playground.
8. A burglary must have been committed for sure.
9. A book has been being written by her for the last two years.
10. Coffee was being drunk by him when I entered the room.

Operator in the Verb Phrase

In addition to tense and aspect, auxiliaries also play an important part in some other constructions. The first auxiliary of the verb phrase functions as an operator in the following constructions:

(i) The auxiliary verb functions as an operator in yes-no questions.

Will you **marry** me?
operator main verb

(ii) In the formation of negative sentences, the auxiliary verb functions as an operator.

Sorry, I **can't** marry you.
operator

(iii) 'Do' is used as an operator to create *emphasis*.

He **does** study for ten hours every day.
operator

(iv) In imperative sentences, *do* is used as an operator.

Do come and see me.
operator

(v) In responses, an operator can stand alone.

Have you ever met her?

Yes, I **have**.
operator.

EXERCISE 2.4

Identify whether the bold words are an operator or not. Choose yes or no.

1. He **does** the cooking and she **does** the washing.
   ◯ Yes ◯ No
2. I **haven't** seen her for ages.
   ◯ Yes ◯ No
3. You **can't** go home now.
   ◯ Yes ◯ No
4. **Will** you appear at the exam or not?
   ◯ Yes ◯ No
5. She **plays** the piano well.
   ◯ Yes ◯ No

Adjective Phrases or Adjectival Phrases

Adjectival phrases are called so because their *heads* are adjectives. They may be preceded by pre-head string and be followed by post-head string. Consider the following sentences:

(i) Shyam is [AP intelligent].

(ii) The teacher is [AP **very** **late**].
pre-head string

(iii) She is [AP **extremely** **beautiful.**]
pre-head string head

(iv) I am [AP **delighted** **to meet you.**]
head post-head string

(v) She is [AP **ready** **to leave.**]
head post-head string

(vi) She is [AP **afraid** **of dogs.**]
head post-head string

(vii) He is [AP **very** **fond** **of dates.**]
pre-head string head post-head string.

Notice adverbs *very* and *extremely* are generally used as pre-head strings in adjective phrases.

Some adjectives must be followed by post-head strings without which their meaning would be incomplete. Among these adjectives are *afraid of, fond of, conscious of, uncertain of, independent of, convinced of,* etc.

Adjectives can have different kinds of complements.

(i) Adjectives followed by PPs:
He feels [AP **sorry** **for her.**]
head PP
post-head string

Other adjectives following this pattern are *interested in, convinced of, conscious of, uncertain of, based on, depended on.*

(ii) Adjectives followed by *that clauses:*
Her parents are [AP **pleased** **that she is doing so well.**]
head that clause
Post-head string

Other adjectives following this pattern are *sure, confident, glad, surprised, amazed, certain, proud, sad, alarmed, annoyed, astonished, disappointed.* (*annoyed at, certain of, pleased with are also possible.*)

(iii) Adjectives followed by *to + infinitive*:
I am [AP **happy** **to note]** that she has qualified for the IAS.
head to infinitive
post-head string

Other adjectives that fall in this pattern are *wrong, hard, delighted, quick, clear, cruel, good, kind, naughty, nice, rude, silly, splendid, stupid, easy, impossible, able, bound, ready, unable, prompt, slow, furious,* etc.

(iv) Adjectives are also used with introductory *it* as *subject.*
It is [AP **strange** that **she has failed in the exam.**]
head that clause
post-head string

Other adjectives that occur in the above pattern are *certain, curious, disconcerting, embarrassing, evident, extraordinary, fitting, fortunate, frightening, important, irritating, likely, odd, obvious, possible, probable, sad, shocking, surprising, true,* etc.

EXERCISE 2.5

Rewrite the following constructions by using *it constructions*.

Example: you are kind to say these encouraging words.
It is kind of you to say these encouraging words.

1. You are wrong to accuse me of stealing.
2. Virtuous people are hard to find these days.
3. She was delighted to go on a journey to London.
4. Many students of Computer Science and Engineering were eager to learn C++.
5. Journey to Great Britain is very easy to arrange.

Prepositional Phrases

Prepositional phrases are the phrases whose *heads* are prepositions. They are followed by *post-head string* which can be called **complements** of the prepositions. They are rarely preceded by *pre-head string*, though there are a few exceptions. Consider the following sentences:

(i) He went	[	**through**	**the forest.**]
	PP	head	post-head string complement

(ii) He went	[	**across**	**the field.**]
	PP	head	post-head string complement

(iii) He woke me up	[	**early**	**in**	**the morning.**]
	PP	pre-head string	head	post-head string complement

(iv) He jumped	[	**over**	**the fence.**]
	PP	head	post-head string complement

We said earlier that pre-head strings are rarely found. Here are some exceptions.

(v) The arrow went	[	**straight**	**through**	**his heart.**]
	PP	pre-head string	head	post-head string complement

(vi) He jumped	[	**right**	**over**	**the fence.**]
	PP	pre-head string	head	post-head string complement

(vii) I went to meet him	[	**just**	**after**	**midnight.**]
	PP	pre-head string	head	post-head string complement

As we said earlier, prepositions are followed by complements. These complements could be different kinds of constructions.

(i) **Preposition + an NP**

I met her **in** **the canteen.**

prep. NP

(ii) **Preposition + a wh- clause**

She belongs **to** **what she calls a God forsaken place in the world.**

prep wh- clause

(iii) **Preposition + an –ing clause**

He got first division **by studying ten hours per day for the exam.**

prep -ing clause

(iv) **Preposition + an adverb**

It will take you two hours **from** **here.**

prep adverb

Notice, however, that a preposition is *not followed by a that clause and a to – infinitive construction.* If we use one of these constructions, the preposition is dropped or an NP *the fact* is introduced after the preposition.

Look at the following sentences:

(i) I was shocked at the news.
(ii) I was shocked that he met with a terrible accident. (**at** is dropped.)
(iii) I was shocked to hear the news of the accident. (**at** is dropped.)
(iv) I was shocked at what had happened. (the preposition **at** is retained before a wh-clause.)
(v) I reckon that he is conscious of his fortune.
(vi) I reckon that he is conscious that he is rich.
(vii) I reckon that he is conscious of the fact that he is rich.

Notice further that a prepositional phrase has several grammatical functions. These functions are illustrated below.

(i) **A PP functioning as an adverbial.**

I'll see you **in the morning.**

adverbial of time

(ii) **A PP as a complement to an adjective.**

She is terribly **bad at mathematics.**

adj p complement

(iii) **A PP as a subject**

After breakfast is the best time for work.

subject

(iv) **A PP as a complement to a verb**

You will have to **pay** a great deal **for this.**

verb complement

(v) **A PP as a modifier to an NP**

I have bought **this house** **in the city** for progress and prosperity.

NP modifier

Adverb Phrases

Adverb phrases are called so because their *heads* are *adverbs*. Adverb heads are preceded by *very*, *quite*, *rather* as *pre-head string*. They are rarely followed by post-head string. Consider the following sentences:

(i) She read her poems **very** **slowly** and **softly.**
pre-head string head head

(ii) He jumped **quite** **quickly** into the river.
pre-head string head

(iii) **Unluckily** **for him** his fiancée failed in the exam.
head post-head string

There are different kinds of adverbial phrases such as time, manner, degree, etc. Below are given some examples.

(i) Can we meet **very late** in the afternoon?
adv ph. of time

(ii) I do my work **very honestly.**
adv ph. of manner

(iii) I **very much** appreciate your contribution.
adv. ph of degree

Other adverbial phrases are *entirely*, *fully*, *hardly*, *nearly*, *rather*, *simply*, *definitely*, *thoroughly*, *scarcely*, etc.

Onion Like Structure of Language

Language has a structure like an onion. There are layers within layers. One can find phrases within phrases; clauses within phrases and clauses within clauses. This is what is called the recursive property of human language and this makes language highly productive. Below we shall give some examples of this property of human language.

(i) [NP a [adj. ph very small] car].

In the above phrase, an AP occurs within an NP. It is an example of a phrase occurring within another phrase.

(ii) [clause I think [clause that I will go to London next week]].
NP
This is an example of a clause within a phrase.

(iii) [clause I will ring you again [adv. clause before I leave]].
This is an example of a clause occurring within another clause.

(iv) [[NP The boy][clause who is wearing a red shirt] is my brother].

In the above example, a clause (who is wearing a red shirt) has been embedded within an NP. It is an example of a clause within a phrase.

EXERCISE 2.6

In each of the sentences below, a phrase has been bracketed. Find the type of that bracketed phrase.

Example: He is not [in the office].

o NP
o PP
o AP
o VP
o Adv P

Answer : o PP

1. [A white boy] is chasing [the black girl].

o NP
o PP
o AP
o VP
o Adv P

2. A [very beautiful] girl walked into my office.

o NP
o PP
o AP
o VP
o Adv P

3. He took his exams [very carefully].

o NP
o PP
o AP
o VP
o Adv P

4. When I reached there, the house [was being built].

o NP
o PP
o AP
o VP
o Adv P

5. Karuna was suffering [from fever] when her mother reached her house.

o NP
o PP
o AP
o VP
o Adv P

6. He came, he saw and he [conquered].

o NP
o PP
o AP
o VP
o Adv P

7. She [never comes] late to classes.

o NP
o PP
o AP
o VP
o Adv P

8. He has won [many battles].

o NP
o PP
o AP
o VP
o Adv P

9. She finds it difficult to live [without him].

o NP
o PP
o AP
o VP
o Adv P

10. She has been appointed as [a senior lecturer].

o NP
o PP
o AP
o VP
o Adv P

Key to Exercise 2.1

NP: excellent examples of the distinction between formal and informal
NP: British television
NP: the time of the Folklands crisis
NP: the professional spokesman
NP: the Ministry of Defense
NP: an attitude
NP: tone
NP: his counterparts in Argentina
NP: he

NP: the dispassionate expert
NP: the impassioned partisan

Key to Exercise 2.2

1. finite: had
   non-finite: being
2. finite : started
   non-finite: having
3. finite: discovered, had gone
   non-finite: entering
4. finite: came, saw, conquered
5. finite: is
   non-finite: to work, to worship
6. finite: is
   non-finite: to earn
7. finite: is doing, can go
8. finite: is going
   non-finite: to do
9. finite: earned
10. finite: like
    non-finite: to dance

Key to Exercise 2.3

1. auxiliaries: must, have+ en, be+ing, be+en
   main verb: build
2. auxiliary: can
   main verb: live
3. auxiliaries: have+en, be+ing
   main verb: live
4. auxiliary: -ed (past tense)
   main verb: have
5. auxiliaries : will, have+en,
   main verb: pass
6. auxiliaries: must, be+ing
   main verb: read
7. auxiliaries: past tense, have +en, be+ing, -ed(past tense)
   main verbs: play, reach
8. auxiliaries : must, have+en, be+en
   main verb: commit
9. auxiliaries: have+en , be+ing, be+en
   main verb: write
10. auxiliaries: be(past tense)-ing , be+en
    main verb: drink

Key to Exercise 2.4

1. no
2. yes
3. yes
4. yes
5. no

Key to Exercise 2.5

1. It's wrong of you to accuse me of stealing.
2. It's hard to find virtuous people these days.
3. It's made her delighted to go on a journey to London.
4. It's made many students of Computer Science and Engineering eager to learn C++.
5. It's very easy to arrange a journey to Great Britain.

Key to Exercise 2.6

1. NP, NP
2. AP
3. Adv. P
4. VP
5. PP
6. VP
7. VP
8. NP
9. PP
10. NP

3

The Sentence Different Types

Introduction

Look at the following sentences:

1. She is a black beauty.
2. She is from the States.
3. She plays tennis well.
4. Her name is Serena Williams.

The above four sentences are called **declaratives**. They generally make statements; they state facts, describe things or narrate events. They are also called **assertives**. Those declaratives that make positive statements are called **affirmative declaratives** and those that make negative statements with the help of (*no*, *not*, *never*, *etc.*) are called **negative declaratives**. Declaratives can also occur as questions if uttered with a rising intonation.

(i) You are leaving ↗ tomorrow?

(ii) You have passed ↗ the test?

There are 24 helping verbs that are used in the formation of negatives and questions (see Table 3.1).

TABLE 3.1 List of auxiliary verbs

do	have	is	will	would	ought to
does	has	am	can	could	used to
did	had	are	shall	should	need
		was	may	might	dare
		were	must		

Table 3.2 illustrates how negatives and questions are formed with the help of helping verbs. In colloquial English, the contracted form (will + not → won't) is used.

TABLE 3.2 Formation of negatives and interrogatives

Positive	*Negative*	*Interrogative*
do, did, does	do not, did not, does not; don't, didn't, doesn't	do I does he did he
ought to, used to, dare, need	ought not to, used not to, dare not, need not; oughtn't to, usedn't to, daren't, needn't	ought he to, dare he to, used he to, did he use to, need he

Look at Tables 3.3 and 3.4 that give the short forms of auxiliary verbs in the positive and negative sentences.

TABLE 3.3 Short forms of auxiliaries

'm = am	I'm						
's = is or has		He's	She's	It's			
're = are					You're	We're	They're
've = have	I've				You've	We've	They've
'll = will	I'll	He'll	She'll		You'll	We'll	They'll
'd = had, would	I'd	He'd	She'd		You'd	We'd	They'd

TABLE 3.4 Negative short forms

isn't (= is not)	haven't (=have not)	shan't (=shall not)
aren't (= are not)	hasn't (=has not)	shouldn't (=should not)
wasn't (= was not)	hadn't (=had not)	mightn't (=might not)
weren't (= were not)	can't (=cannot)	mustn't (=must not)
don't (=do not)	couldn't (=could not)	needn't (=need not)
doesn't (=does not)	won't (=will not)	daren't (=dare not)
didn't (=did not)	wouldn't (=would not)	

EXERCISE 3.1

Say that the following statements are not true. That is, turn them into negatives. Also, use the contracted **n't form.**

Example:

(i) He is a doctor.
(ii) He is not a doctor.
(iii) He isn't a doctor.

1. The BE I classes have started from today.
2. The timetable has been put up on the notice board.
3. The students have noted the timetable.
4. Most of them located their classes.

5. Some of them have failed to find the class.
6. They went to the principal to complain about it.
7. The principal called the HODs meeting.
8. The HOD reframed the timetable.
9. Helpers were made available to the students to locate the rooms.
10. Classes are running smoothly.

Questions

Questions are sentences that **ask for information**. There are mainly two types of questions: *yes-no* questions and *wh-questions*.

A question which expects a yes or no in answer is called a yes-no question.

Are you a doctor?
Yes, I am.
No, I ain't/aren't/am not.

A yes-no question is formed by moving *the operator* before the subject:

She is a black beauty.
→Is she a black beauty?
She can play the guitar.
→Can she play the guitar?
She has been living in Sikar for the last 20 years.
→Has she been living in Sikar for the last 20 years?
She does dance well.
→Does she dance well?
She sang well at the party.
→Did she sing well at the party?

Notice *operator* is one of the 24 auxiliary verbs and it is an *operator* that is moved to the front of the sentence to make a *yes-no* question.

In the case of sentences where there is no overt operator, a dummy *do* or *does* or *did* is assumed to be there before the main verb and that is shifted to the front.

Wh- questions begin with *wh-words* such as *what*, *where*, *why*, *how*, etc. and can be answered in a word or a phrase or in a complete sentence:

(i) Who broke the window?
Ganesh.

(ii) Where are you going?
To the college.

(iii) Which is your favourite teacher?
I don't like any of them.

Wh-questions are formed by putting the *wh-word* at the beginning and then the operator is moved in front of the subject.

He will be going **to Jaipur tomorrow.**

where when

Where he will be going tomorrow?

Where he will be going to tomorrow?

Where will he be going to tomorrow?

When he will be going to Jaipur?

When will he be going to Jaipur?

The above sentences show that a word or phrase about which we want to ask a question is *replaced* by a suitable *wh-word.* Then it is *moved* to the front. Thirdly, *the operator is moved* in front of the subject. Table 3.5 shows the common *wh-words* and what information they convey.

TABLE 3.5 Common wh-words

Wh-word	*Concept they convey*
where	place
how	manner
when	time
who	doer
whom	object or sufferer or affected
why	reason
which	choice to be made form a known set
how far	distance
how long	duration
how much	quantity
how many	number
how often	frequency
what	choice to be made from an unknown number or amount

When the *wh-* element is subject, *no operator* or *no do-construction* is used.

(i) Who is there?

(ii) Who met you in the college?

(iii) Which guests are attending the party?

Notice yes-no questions are *limited* whereas wh-questions are *unlimited* in that out of two answers (*yes or no*), one is possible in the case of yes-no questions and a number of answers are possible in the case of wh-questions.

Another type of limited question is *alternative questions* where the answer is one or out of two or more *alternatives*

Would you like tea or coffee?

Coffee, please.

Shall we go by train or by air?
By air.

Tag questions are added at the end of a statement to ask for 'confirmation of the truth of the statement' (Leech et al. 127). If the statement is positive, the expected answer is 'yes'; if the statement is negative, the expected answer is 'no'.

Tag questions are formed by adding an operator plus a pronoun. If the statement is positive, the tag is negative and if the statement is negative, the tag is positive. Consider the following sentences:

She is a doctor, isn't she?
She is not a doctor, is she?

Besides, there are miscellaneous questions that we discuss below briefly:

(i) It is possible to have *more than one question word* in a question:
Who's going where?
Shyam is going to Kolkata.
Where and when did you buy it?
I bought it (the laptop) in Delhi yesterday.

(ii) By adding *please* or *could you tell me*, a question can be made more polite.
What is your father, please?
Could you tell me whether you would lend me the money?

(iii) There are also *echo questions*. They involve a kind of response. The speaker is asked to repeat some information in these questions.
I didn't like going there.
Did you say you didn't like going there?

(iv) A *rhetorical question* is a forceful statement. There are two types of rhetorical questions: positive and negative.
A positive rhetorical question is a strong negative statements and a negative rhetorical question is a strong positive statement.
Who knows him? (Nobody knows him.)
Who doesn't know Rajeev Gandhi? (Everybody knows Rajeev Gandhi.)

EXERCISE 3.2

Turn the following sentences into *wh-questions* and *yes-no questions*. The bold word has to be replaced by a *wh-word*.

He went **to Jaipur** yesterday.
Did he go to Jaipur yesterday?
Where did he go yesterday?

1. Sunita Gogoi has come to this college **from Assam.**
2. She has taken admission in **BEI.**
3. She has chosen **computer science and engineering.**

4. She finds this college **very exciting.**
5. She likes **Mr. Ramesh Sharma,** the computer teacher very much.
6. She doesn't like **the Rajasthani food** being served in the hostel.
7. She misses **her family** very much.
8. She has decided **to phone them every night**.
9. Her mother cannot forget **her** at all.
10. She will go back to Assam **during Dipawali Break.**

EXERCISE 3.3

Respond to the following miscellaneous questions.

Example: Where are you going to?
Response: To Jaipur.

1. Do you like novel or poetry?
2. He is a teacher, isn't he?
3. He isn't a teacher, is he?
4. Who killed whom?
5. What and when did you buy it?
6. Could you please tell me what discipline I should go in for?
7. Did you say you didn't do it?
8. Who doesn't know Jawahar Lal Nehru?
9. Who cares for him?
10. Would like to have pastry or chocolate?

Imperatives

Sentences that express commands or requests are called **imperatives**. The commands can be positive or negative. Consider the following sentences:

(i) Come here. (positive command)
(ii) Don't go there. (negative command)
(iii) Don't eat it, please. (negative request)
(iv) Eat it, please. (positive request)

Notice an imperative sentence starts with a verb and a negative command starts with *do* auxiliary.

There are two types of commands: 2nd person commands and 1st and 3rd person commands.

(i) Open the door, will you? (second person command)
(ii) Do let me know when you can come here. (second person command)

Notice the subject is not generally expressed in commands. However, sometimes we find the subject *you*.

(i) You keep the volume down. (rather impolite)
(ii) Let me teach you how to do it. (1st person command)
(iii) Let us go to the party. (1st person command)
(iv) Now somebody shut the window. (3rd person, informal command)

Exclamations

These clauses express the speaker's feelings or attitudes. They start with a predeterminer *what*, followed by an NP or with *how*, followed by an adjective or adverb.

(i) What a beautiful woman!
(ii) How well you dance!
(iii) What a grand building it is!
(iv) What great poetry you write!
(v) What a boy!
(vi) How stupid!
(vii) Good! Excellent!
(viii) Well done!
(ix) Bravo!
(x) Oh! My God!

Fragments

Look at the following conversation:

What are you doing this Sunday?
Nothing much.
What about going for a picnic?
Good idea!

The bold responses are called **fragments**. Fragments do not have their own subjects and predicates. They are words or phrases doing the function of full sentences. It is possible to convert them into full sentences.

I am doing nothing much.
It's a good idea.

EXERCISE 3.4

Complete the following dialogue by filling in with the appropriate type of sentences:

A: Hello! I am Gopal.
B: Hai! I am Ganesh.
A: Nice to meet you.

B: .... is mine.
A: Where are you from?
B: I am ....
A: What is Assam famous for?
B: ....
A: Is it a folk dance?
B: Yes ....
A: Would you like to see a performance.
B: Sure ....
A: Then come tomorrow at four.
B: ....
A: In the college. The college is organizing a freshmen's party.
B: O.K. ....
A: I've to go now. Bye. See you tomorrow at four.
B: Sure ....

Key to Exercise 3.1

1. (a) The BE I classes have not started from today.
   (b) The BE I classes haven't started from today.
2. (a) The timetable has not been put up on the notice board.
   (b) The timetable hasn't been put up on the notice board.
3. (a) The students have not noted the timetable.
   (b) The students haven't noted the timetable.
4. (a) Most of them have not located their classes.
   (b) Most of them haven't located their classes.
5. (a) Some of them have not failed to find their classes.
   (b) Some of them haven't failed to find their classes.
6. (a) They did not go to the principal to complain about it.
   (b) They didn't go to the principal to complain about it.
7. (a) The principal did not call the HODs meeting.
   (b) The principal didn't call the HODs meeting.
8. (a) The HODs did not reframe the timetable.
   (b) The HODs didn't reframe the timetable.
9. (a) Helpers were not made available to the students to locate the rooms.
   (b) Helpers weren't made available to the students to locate the rooms.
10. (a) Classes are not running smoothly.
    (b) Classes aren't running smoothly.

Key to Exercise 3.2

1. (a) Has Sunita Gogoi come to this college from Assam?
   (b) Where has Sunita Gogoi come from?

2. (a) Has she taken admission in BEI?
   (b) In which class has she taken admission?
3. (a) Has she chosen computer science and engineering?
   (b) Which discipline has she chosen?
4. (a) Does she find the college very exciting?
   (b) What is the college like?
5. (a) Does she like Mr. Ramesh Sharma, the computer teacher very much?
   (b) Who does she like very much?
6. (a) Does she not like the Rajasthani food being served in the hostel?
   (b) What does she not like?
7. (a) Does she miss her family?
   (b) What does she miss very much?
8. (a) Has she decided to phone them every night?
   (b) What has she decided?
9. (a) Can her mother forget her?
   (b) Whom can her mother not forget at all?
10. (a) Will she go back to Assam during Dipawali Break?
    (b) When will she go back to Assam?

Key to Exercise 3.3

1. Poetry
2. Yes, he is.
3. No, he isn't.
4. Ram killed Ravan.
5. I bought a DVD yesterday.
6. Science, I suppose.
7. I didn't do it.
8. Yes, you are right. Everybody knows Jawahar Lal Nehru.
9. Yes, you are right. Nobody cares for him.
10. Chocolate.

Key to Exercise 3.4

B: the pleasure
B: from Assam
B: Bihu
B: it is
B: I would.
B: where?
B: I'd be there.
B: Bye

4

Sentence Patterns

Sentence Pattern Defined

'Sentence pattern' refers to the way the elements in a sentence are organized or arranged. The elements of a sentence can be described in terms of functional labels such as subject, verb, object, complement or adverbial or in terms of categorical labels such as noun phrase, verb phrase, adjectival phrase or adverbial phrase. The classification of sentence patterns depends upon the nature of verbs, that is, whether a verb is of be-type, become-type, have-type, intransitive or transitive. Look at the following sentence:

S V C
John is a very good teacher.

(S = Subject, V = Verb, C = Complement, O = Object and A = Adverbial.)

The pattern of the above sentence is:

S + V + C

Innumerable sentences can be framed on the above pattern. For example:

	S	V	C
(i)	**She**	**is**	**a nurse.**
(ii)	**She**	**is**	**a black beauty.**
(iii)	**She**	**is**	**in the room.**

Before we discuss the basic sentence patterns from which other sentences are derived, we shall discuss the following sentence elements:

(a) subject (b) verb
(c) object (d) complement
(e) adverbial

Elements Defined

English is an SVO language whereas Hindi is an SOV language. That is, the subject comes in the beginning in a normal sentence.

Defining the subject as an actor is misleading because in sentence (i), it functions as an actor but in sentences (ii–iv), it is a sufferer.

(i) **John** killed a tiger.
actor
(ii) **The man** received a blow.
sufferer
(iii) **I have** stomach ache.
sufferer
(iv) **He** suffered a defeat.
sufferer

Some grammarians define the subject as the topic of a sentence. But the notion of the topic does not always work. Take, for example, the sentence given below where the topic and the subject are different.

This house,	**I**	don't live in.
topic	subject	

The subject has certain syntactic characteristics and it is better to describe the subject in terms of these. The following characteristics are noticeable.

Inversion: In question formation, the operator is placed before the subject.

(i) There is a book on the table.
(ii) There are some books on the table.

Their yes-no question counterparts would be:

(i) Is there a book on the table?
(ii) Are there some books on the table?

Now the question arises what the subjects are in (i) and (ii). From inversion point of view, 'there' is the subject but from 'concord' point of view, 'a book'. Some grammarians, therefore, make a distinction between 'inversion' and 'concord' subjects. Sentences (i) and (ii) above justify this distinction. Some scholars call 'there' an **introductory subject**.

A distinction is made between grammatical and logical subject. A grammatical subject is that which conforms to the principles and processes of sentence construction.

Look at the following sentences:

(i) **Sita** was reading a book.
grammatical subject
\+
logical subject

(ii) **A book**	was being read	**by Sita**.
Gammatical subject		logical subject

If we accept this division, then we can say that a grammatical subject can be divided into 'inversion' and 'concord' subject.

TABLE 4.1 Features of a subject

Functional label	*Examples*	*Description*
(i) Subject	1. *She* is a nurse. 2. *There* is *a book* on the table. 3. *There* are *two books* on the table. 4. Come here. 5. Fish *I* like. 6. *I* like bananas, but *bananas* don't like me.	(i) Subject comes in the beginning of a normal sentence. *Fish* in sentence (5) is an object. It is not a normal sentence. The normal sentence would be: I like fish. (ii) There is an agreement between subject and verb. From this point of view, *a book* is subject in sentence (2) and *two books* is subject in sentence (3). *There* in both the sentences is *introductory subject*. This happens whenever an indefinite NP is made subject in English. (iii) *Subject* becomes *by* + *object* and *object* becomes *subject* in passive constructions. For example, the passive of (6) would be: S V by + object Bananas are liked by me.

Verb

A verb refers to a state, process or action. Look at the following Table 4.2.

TABLE 4.2 Types of verbs

Verb	*Examples*	*Description*
Linking: be (is, am, are was, were), become, have, seem, resemble, appear, look, etc. Intransitive: weep, laugh, go, fly, run, etc. Transitive: read eat, drink, play, write, give, send, etc.	(i) Ram *is* good. (ii) The rice is cooking. (iii) He is running. (iv) Ram became a manager of the bank. (v) He has a big car. (vi) The room measures 30 × 30 square feet. (vii) Birds fly in the sky. (viii) He is eating a banana. (ix) She gave me flowers.	Sentence (i) refers to a state, (ii) to a process and (iii) to an action. Sentence (i) refers to be-type verb, (iv) to *become-type*, (v) to have type, (vii) to intransitive and (viii) to transitive verbs. Transitive verbs have objects whereas Intransitive verbs have no objects.

Object

Object refers to things or persons that are affected by the action denoted by the verb. Only transitive verbs have objects. There are different kinds of objects. Reciprocal object (each other/one another), reflexive object (himself/herself), etc. are not passivizable.

Look at the following table (Table 4.3).

TABLE 4.3 Types of object

Object	*Examples*	*Description*
There are two types of objects. direct object and indirect object Direct object is affected whereas indirect object is the recipient or beneficiary of the action of the verb.	(i) He is eating a banana (ii) They sent her flowers (iii) They explained the matter to him (iv) He reported the matter to the police	Only transitive verbs have objects. An object becomes subject in passive constructions. Sentence (i) becomes: *A banana* is being eaten by him. Send, give, bring, buy, tell, etc. are double object verbs. In sentences (iii) and (iv) the object *matter* is followed by complements (*to him* and *to the police*)

Complement

The term 'complement' refers to NPs or adjectival phrases without which the sentence is not complete. Look at the following table (Table 4.4).

TABLE 4.4 Types of complements

Complement	*Examples*	*Description*
Subjective complement refers to subject S C **She** is **a teacher** Objective complement refers to object. They appointed **him leader** O C	(i) She is a black beauty (ii) Two and two make four (iii) They have a book (iv) This room measures 30 × 30 square feet (v) He became a king (vi) He became happy (vii) They elected him monitor (viii) She put the book on the table (ix) The car lay in the garage	There is a three-way distinction in complement: subject complement, object complement and complement After linking verbs, we get subject complements (see sentences (i)–(vi)). Verbs like put and lie are verbs of incomplete predication and require complement (see sentences (viii) and (ix)). Verbs like elect, select,

(*Contd.*)

TABLE 4.4 Types of complements (*Contd.*)

Complement	*Examples*	*Description*
	(x) He didn't behave himself at the party (xi) This soup tastes good (xii) She prides herself on her appearance	nominate, name, call, make, paint, appoint, etc. take object complements (see sentence (vii)). Verbs like resemble, suit, cost, fit, taste, pride, and behave take complements Other verbs are: have, smell, feel, stay, alive, appear, look, get angry, grow old, turn traitor, etc. (see sentences (x)–(xii))

Adverbials

Adverbials refer to words or prepositional phrases, or clauses, denoting time, place, manner, frequency, condition, result, or purpose. Adverbials are optional elements of a sentence. Therefore, they are also called **adjuncts**. Look at the following table (Table 4.5).

TABLE 4.5 Features of adverbials

Adverbials	*Examples*	*Description*
	S V A (i) He went **to Jaipur** A **yesterday.** S V (ii) **He is playing** O A **football now.** A (iii) **In America,** S V **broad ties have gone** C **out of fashion** S V (iv) **They appointed** O C **him secretary** A **yesterday.** S V C (v) **He is waiting for you**	Optional prepositional phrases are adverbials. *In America* in sentence (iii) and *for you* in sentence (v) are examples. Adverbials are optional elements in a sentence. They provide a time or place framework. Prepositional phrases which are obligatory after certain types of verbs are complements. For example, out of fashion in sentence (iii)

Basic Sentence Patterns

After having discussed the sentence elements, let us now list basic sentence patterns. These patterns are called **basic** or **fundamental** because other sentences can be derived from them.

There are 10 sentence patterns and they are reproduced below.

TABLE 4.6 List of basic sentence patterns

Subject	*Verb be (be: is, am, are, was, were)*	*Complement (SC, formally, realized as NP Adj. P or PP)*
The lawyer	is	very clever
The teacher	is	in the room
The new nurse	is	quite disgusting

The second type of verb is *become* (Table 4.7). It shows change in the state whereas *be* shows a state. We can use an adjective (phrase) or a noun (phrase) after these verbs.

TABLE 4.7 Basic sentence patterns

Subject	*Verb become*	*Complement (realized as Adj. (phrase)) Noun (phrase)*
The king	became	very angry
He	has become	a minister

The third type of verbs is *seem*, *look* and *appear* (Table 4.8). These verbs are also called **linking verbs** and they can be followed by an adjective (phrase) or a noun (phrase). Linking verbs are followed by complements.

TABLE 4.8 Basic sentence patterns

Subject	*Verb seem*	*Complement (realized as Adj. (phrase)) Noun (phrase), PP*
He	seems	(to be) happy
She	appears	(to be) a flirt
He	looked	extraordinarily brilliant
It	looks	like rain

The fourth type of verb is *have-type* (Table 4.9). This verb has complements or noun (phrase) after it. This verb is not used in progressive tense.

TABLE 4.9 Basic sentence patterns

Subject	*Verb have*	*Complement (realized as NP)*
The lawyer	has bought	a big house
The inspector	has	a brand new Toyota

The next sentence pattern consists of an intransitive verb, followed optionally by an adverbial (Table 4.10). The intransitive verb is one which does not have an object. The intransitive verbs include *weep*, *laugh*, *sleep*, *jump*, *dance*, *go*, *walk*, *run*, etc.

TABLE 4.10 Basic sentence patterns with intransitive and transitive verbs

Subject	*Verb*	*(Adverb phrase or PP)*	*Description*
(i) Birds	fly	in the sky	PP functions as an adverbial
(ii) ……	come	here	Here is an adverb of place in sentence (ii)
(iii) The stone	moved	…	
(iv) He	is eating	…..	Some verbs can be used both transitively and intransitively He *moved* the stone. (transitive) The stone moved. (intransitive) He *walked* the horse. (transitive) He *is walking* towards me. (intransitive) *Eat* is a transitive verb, but it allows object deletion. See sentence (iv)

Transitive verbs are those that are followed by objects. The test for a transitive verb is that it can have a passive construction. There are two types of transitive verbs: single and double transitive. Single transitive verbs have only one object whereas double transitive verbs have two objects (Table 4.11). Two objects are direct object and indirect object

TABLE 4.11 Basic sentences with IO and DO

Subject	*Verb*	*Object*
Ram	gave	**him a book** IO DO
He	is eating	**an orange** O
He	reported	**the matter to the police** O C
The teacher	explained	**the lesson to the students** O C

The double transitive verbs can be expressed in two ways:

She sent him flowers.

She sent flowers to/for him.

Transitive verbs with one object are *finish*, *learn*, *believe*, *telephone*, *equal*, *blow up*, *call on*, etc.

Verbs with double objects are *bring*, *hand*, *lend*, *offer*, *owe*, *promise*, *show*, *teach*, *show*, *write*, *buy*, *sell*, *ask*, etc.

There are other transitive verbs such as *appoint*, *select*, *nominate*, *call*, *make*, *and name* which are followed by object and objective complement (Table 4.12). Objective complements refer to objects.

TABLE 4.12 Basic sentence patterns

Subject	*Verb*	*Object*	*Objective complement (realized as NP or Adj. Phrase)*
They	appointed	him	monitor of the class
They	painted	the door	red
They	called	her	a fool
The priest	named	the ship	Queen Elizabeth

Other verbs in this pattern are *find*, *consider*, *imagine*, *suppose*, *think*, *vote*, *declare*, *find*, *judge*, *keep*, *leave*, *wash*, etc.

Then there are transitive verbs which are followed by an object and complement (Table 4.13). These verbs are *put* and *lay*.

TABLE 4.13 Basic sentence patterns

Subject	*Verb*	*Object*	*Complement (realized as PP)*
He	laid	the car	in the garage
He	put	the book	on the table

Thus, there are ten basic sentence patterns. All the sentences in English can be analyzed in terms of these sentences. Even complex and compound sentences can be analyzed so.

Look at the following analysis.

S V O
(i) **Every body knows that Armstrong landed on the moon.**

S V A Con S V A
(ii) **Ram went to America and Sita went to London.**

S V C
(iii) **There seems to be every hope that he will come.**

S V O AP
(iv) **I saw him going.**

Some Untypical Sentence Patterns

There are some sentences that do not conform to the sentence patterns described above. These are discussed in the following sections.

Extraposition

In this type of pattern, the subject is postponed till the end of the sentence. Consider the following sentences:

(i) **The reservation policy** is the most important problem facing the
subject
country today.

(ii) **Two income-tax officers** were inside the house.
subject

(iii) **Thunderbolt beer** is in the first place.
subject

In the three sentences above, the subject can be extraposed and when it is done, the sentences would be like given below.

(i) The most important problem facing the country today is **the reservation policy.**
subject-extraposed

(ii) Inside the house are **two income-tax officers.**
subject-extraposed

(iii) In the first place is **thunderbolt beer.**
subject-extraposed

The extraposition or postponement of subject is done for achieving end-focus and end-weight.

Another situation when the subject is extra-posed is the introduction of the sentence with the anticipatory *it*. Consider the following.

(i) **That he failed in the examination** is known to everybody.
(ii) To make reservation two months in advance is a nice idea.

The above two sentences can begin with the anticipatory it.

(i) It is known to everybody **that he failed in the examination.**
(ii) It is a nice idea **to make reservation two months in advance.**

Notice certain verbs obligatorily take extra-posed subjects after them.

(i) It seems that he will come again.
*That he will come again seems (not possible).

(ii) It turned that he sold the army secrets to the enemy.
*That he sold the army secrets to the enemy turned out (not possible).

Notice further that even *direct object* can also be extraposed:

(i) She made **it** very clear **that her husband would control the next union election.** Object–extraposed.

The un-extra-posed sentence used cannot be correct.

She made that her husband would control the next union election it very clear (not possible).

Cleft Sentences

A simple sentence can be divided into two separate sentences, each having its own verb. Consider the following sentences:

Sobhasaria Engineering College bought several original softwares for its electronics laboratory last year.

The above sentence can be divided into the following two sentences:

(It was Sobhasaria Engineering College) (that bought several original softwares for its electronics laboratory last year)
is called a cleft sentence.

The above sentence can be divided into several cleft sentences depending upon what element the writer or the speaker wants to emphasize. In the above sentence, it is *Sobhasaria Engineering College*, which is brought into focus. Other elements such as *several original softwares* and *for its laboratory* and *last year* can also be focused.

(i) It was several original softwares that Sobhasaria Engineering College bought for its electronics laboratory.
(ii) It was for its electronics laboratory that Sobhasaria Engineering College bought several original softwares.
(iii) It was last year that Sobhasaria Engineering College bought several original softwares for its electronics laboratory.

Notice the second part of the sentence is similar to a restrictive relative clause and this fact is corroborated by the use of relative pronouns such as *which* and *that*.

There are two types of cleft sentences: **it-type cleft sentence** and **wh-type cleft sentence.** Suppose we want to emphasize several original softwares. We can use either it-type cleft sentence or wh-type cleft sentence as given below:

(i) It was several original softwares that Sobhasaria Engineering College bought for its electronics laboratory last year.
(ii) What Sobhasaria Engineering College bought for its electronics laboratory last year was several original softwares.

EXERCISE 4.1

Analyze the following sentences in terms of sentence elements (SVOCA).

Example: He killed a snake with a stick. (S: He; V: killed; O: a snake; A: with a stick)

1. Birds fly in the sky.
2. There is a book on the table.
3. It is raining very hard.
4. Fish I like very much.
5. The assumption is that he will pass.
6. That he has come to Alwar is the assumption.
7. The boy who is wearing a red shirt is my brother.
8. They are cooking rice.
9. John killed a tiger.
10. John painted the door green.
11. I gave him a book.
12. She sent him flowers.
13. They reported the matter to the police.
14. She told me a story.
15. She bought sweets for her.
16. He killed himself.
17. He laughed a merry laugh.
18. He dreamt a horrible dream.
19. They hate each other.
20. They like one another.
21. They distributed the sweets among themselves.
22. She is a doctor.
23. They elected him chairman.
24. Last evening, he came to my house.
25. I often go to college.
26. If you work hard, you will pass.
27. I cannot come to college because I am ill.
28. He did it beautifully.
29. George Orwell was born in India in 1903.
30. Much of his writing is a record of his experiences.
31. He became a policeman in 1922.
32. In 1944, he wrote 'Animal farm'.
33. The sheep are silly.
34. The pigs teach them a rhyme.
35. Meera sang a song.
36. He looked an actor.
37. She looked smart.
38. He bought her a saree.

39. They named her Hema.
40. He called her a taxi.
41. I shall need at least two weeks to finish the job.
42. There was a large crowd.
43. The secretary showed me into the reception room.
44. They put the books on the table.
45. They nominated her secretary.
46. Both your fairness and impartiality have been appreciated.
47. We considered him a genius.
48. You must see him off.
49. You have grown up.
50. They are growing tomatoes in their garden.
51. On July 7, DDT was sprayed on the Marsh from a helicopter.
52. I smell something burning.
53. This soap smells good.
54. The grammarian shot himself.
55. I had my breakfast at 8:30 yesterday.
56. The girl giggled.
57. The boy is sleeping in the room.
58. The silly old man laughed noisily.
59. Every one knows that big bully.
60. The students looked up the word in the dictionary.
61. My father bought me a guitar on Monday.
62. It will make me very sad.
63. He became a thief.
64. The silk feels soft.
65. She got the first prize.
66. The boy ran down.
67. He ran down the budget.
68. Why did he marry her with such unseemly haste?
69. Sometimes we feel fed up with the whole world.
70. Only afterwards did I come to know of the truth.
71. She cooked her husband a delicious meal.
72. She gave her teacher a stern look.
73. They found her a charming wife.
74. I have found him a dull partner.
75. I am tasting the soup.

EXERCISE 4.2

Make five sentences of each of the following patterns:

1. S + V + C
2. S + V + O + OC
3. S + V_{seem} + C
4. S + $V_{transitive}$ + IO + DO

5. $S + V_{transitive} + O + A$
6. S + V + O + C
7. S + V + A
8. $S + V_{have} + C$
9. $S + V_{become} + C$
10. $S + V_{intransitive} + C$

Key to Exercise 4.1

1. S + V + A
2. Introductory Subject + V + Real Subject + A
3. S + V + A
4. O + S + V + A
5. S + V + O (that – clause)
6. S + V + C
7. S + V + C
8. S + V + O
9. S + V + O
10. S + V + O + OC
11. S + V + IO + DO
12. S + V + IO + DO
13. S + V + O + A
14. S + V + IO + DO
15. S + V + O + A
16. S + V + RO (Reflexive object)
17. S + V + CO (Cognate object)
18. S + V + CO
19. S + V + RO (Reciprocal object)
20. S + V + RO (Reciprocal object)
21. S + V + O + A
22. S + V + C
23. S + V + O + OC
24. A + S + V + A
25. S + A + C + A
26. A + S + V
27. S + V + A + A
28. S + V + A
29. S + V + A + A
30. S + V + C
31. S + V + C + A
32. A + S + V + O
33. S + V + C
34. S + V + IO + DO
35. S + V + O
36. S + V + C
37. S + V + C

38. S + V + IO + DO
39. S + V + O + OC
40. S + V + IO + DO
    or
    S + V + O + OC
41. S + V + A + O + A
42. Introductory Subject + V + Real Subject
43. S + V + O + A
44. S + V + O + OC
45. S + V + O + OC
46. S + V
47. S + V + O + OC
48. S + V + O + Particle
49. S + V
50. S + V + O + A
51. A + S + V + A + A
52. S + V + O + OC
53. S + V + C
54. S + V + O
55. S + V + O + A + A
56. S + V
57. S + V + A
58. S + V + A
59. S + V + O
60. S + V + O + A
61. S + V + IO + DO + A
62. S + V + O + OC
63. S + V + C
64. S + V + C
65. S + V + O
66. S + V
67. S + V + O
68. A + V + S + V + O + A
69. A + S + V + C + A
70. A + A + V + S + V + O
71. S + V + IO + DO
72. S + V + IO + DO
73. S + V + IO + DO
74. S + V + O + OC
75. S + V + O

Key to Exercise 4.2

Free exercise

5

Compound and Complex Sentences

(Including Infinitival, Gerundial and Participial Constructions)

Introduction

In the previous chapter, we discussed the basic sentence patterns. We stated that basic sentence patterns are affirmative (not negative or interrogative); active (not passive) or imperative; carrying only one verb (notice we say *finite* verb because we want to rule out any infinitival constructions in basic patterns) and they are not further reducible. They are called **basic** because other sentences are derivable from them.

The classification of basic sentence patterns depends on the type of verbs and the nuclear and non-nuclear elements (subject, object, complement, adverbial) that go with them. To refresh the memory of readers and to establish a link between basic sentences and what follows in this chapter, we give basic sentence patterns below once again.

1. Subject + Verb_{be} + Subjective complement

(i)	Ram	is	a teacher.
(ii)	He	is	very intelligent.
(iii)	He	is	here.

2. Subject + $\text{Verb}_{\text{become}}$ + Complement

(i)	Ram	became	monitor of the class.
(ii)	It	grew	dark.
(iii)	He	turned	traitor.

3. Subject + $\text{Verb}_{\text{seem}}$ + Complement

   (i) He seems (to be) happy.
   (ii) It looks like rain.
   (iii) He appears calm.

4. Subject + $\text{Verb}_{\text{have}}$ + Complement

   (i) He owns a big house.
   (ii) They have a big car.

5. Subject + $\text{Verb}_{\text{intransitive}}$ + (Adverbial)

   (i) Birds fly ....
   (ii) Birds fly in the sky.
   (iii) She is laughing ....

6. Subject + $\text{Verb}_{\text{transitive}}$ + Object

   (i) They killed a snake.
   (ii) He is eating his dinner.

7. Subject + $\text{Verb}_{\text{transitive}}$ + IO + DO

   (i) I gave him a book.
   (ii) He sent her flowers.

8. Subject + $\text{Verb}_{\text{transitive}}$ + O + OC

   (i) They appointed him chairman.
   (ii) They elected him leader of the group.

9. Subject + $\text{Verb}_{\text{transitive}}$ + O + C

   (i) They reported the matter to the police.
   (ii) The teacher explained the lesson to the student.
   (iii) They put the car in the garage.

10. Subject + $\text{Verb}_{\text{intransitive}}$ + C

    She lay in bed.

These ten sentences illustrate the basic sentence patterns in English. All the sentences of the English language are derivable from these patterns. That is to say, if a student learns what type of verb he is using, he will be able to use the correct participants and circumstances. Above, we discussed three types of verbs, which can be diagrammatically represented as shown in Figure 5.1.

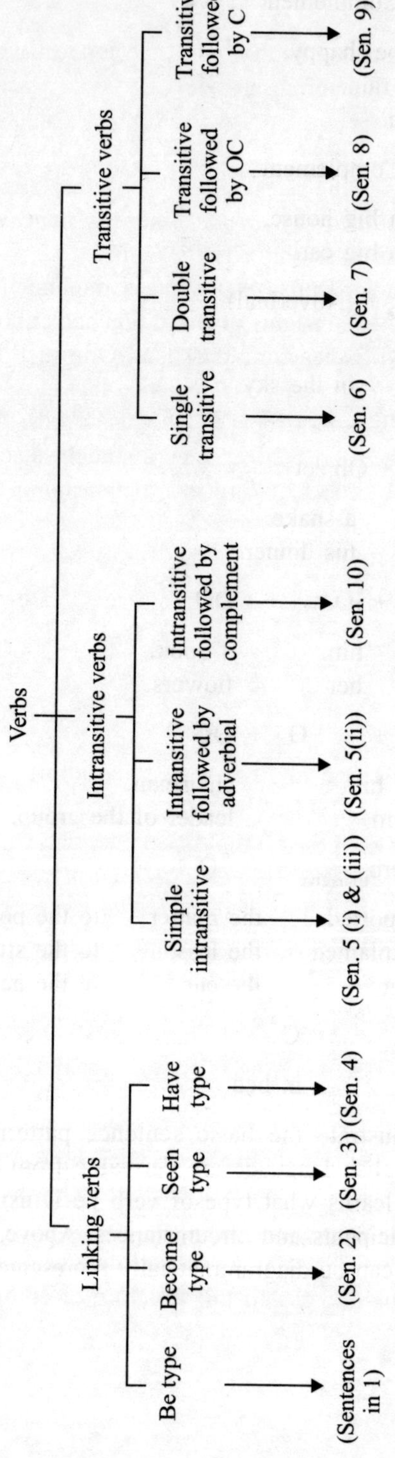

(***Note:*** Linking verbs are followed by complements, transitive verbs by objects and intransitive verbs carry no objects.)

FIGURE 5.1 Types of verb.

Complex Sentences

In class, sometimes a question is asked: what is the longest word in English? Usually the students come out with an answer.

Antidisetablishmentarianism

Quite mind-boggling, isn't it?

But no student can answer the question: What is the longest sentence in English? Because it is difficult to say. *In fact*, there is none. A sentence can be as long as the Mississippi or as short as *Birds fly.*

Chomsky, a famous linguist from MIT, wrote a monumental book called *Syntactic Structures* in 1957. The insights given in this book about the structure of English are still very valid for teaching purposes. One such insight is that a simple sentence carries only *one verb*. If a sentence has more than one verb, it will have more than one simple sentence. In other words, there will be as many simple sentences as there are verbs. Once a student discovers the basic simple sentences, he will be able to figure out the meaning of the complex sentence and he will also be able to figure out the series of transformational operations that yield the sentence under consideration. Let us start with an example:

(i) Jack **built** a house.
a

(ii) This **is** the house that Jack **built.**
a b

(iii) This **is** the cat that **lived** in the house that Jack **built.**
a b c

(iv) This **is** the cat that **chased** the rat that **lived** in the house that Jack **built.**
a b c d

(v) This **is** the dog that **killed** the cat that **chased** the rat that **lived** in the
a b c d
house that Jack **built.**
e

(We can go on making sentences as long as we want by a process of embedding. It is the psychological constraints of memory that force us to keep sentences within a reasonable length so that we can process them easily.)

Notice sentence (i) is simple, but sentence (ii) onwards are complex sentences because they contain more than one verb. Below (in Table 5.1) we give simple sentences for each of them and show in the case of one sentence how, through a series of transformational operations, we get the sentence under discussion. This will help us understand the structure of complex sentences.

TABLE 5.1 Complex sentences

Complex sentence	*Simple sentences contained therein*
This **is** the house that Jack **built.**	Two verbs, so two simple sentences: (i) This is the house. (ii) Jack built the house. *Transformational operations:* The house in (ii) is shifted to the front of (ii) and then the co-referentiality of *the house* in (i) and the house in (ii) gives us *that* (relativizer) which is substituted for the fronted *the house* in (ii) and we get a complex sentence.
This **is** the cat that **lived** in the house that Jack **built.**	Three verbs, so three simple sentences: (i) This is the cat. (ii) The cat lived in the house. (iii) Jack built the house. Fronting of the house in (iii). Two operations of replacement of *that* because of co-referentiality and the resultant sentence is as given.
This **is** the cat that **chased** the rat that **lived** in the house that Jack **built.**	Four verbs, four simple sentences: (i) This is the cat. (ii) The cat chased the rat. (iii) The rat lived in the house. (iv) Jack built the house. *Transformational operations:* In (iv), there is fronting of the *house.* The co-referential noun phrases (*the cat, the rat, the house* are replaced by *that* in each case and what we get is the resultant sentence.
This **is** the dog that **killed** the cat that **chased** the rat that **lived** in the house that Jack **built.**	Five verbs, so five simple sentences: (i) This is the dog. (ii) The dog killed the cat. (iii) The cat chased the rat. (iv) The rat lived in the house. (v) Jack built the house. *Transformational operations:* Fronting of *the house* in (v). Replacement of the second occurrence of each co-referntial NP by *that* resulting in sentence as given.

The diagrammatic representation of transformational operations in case of the following sentence is given below:

This **is** the dog that **killed** the cat that **chased** the rat that **lived** in the house that Jack **built.**

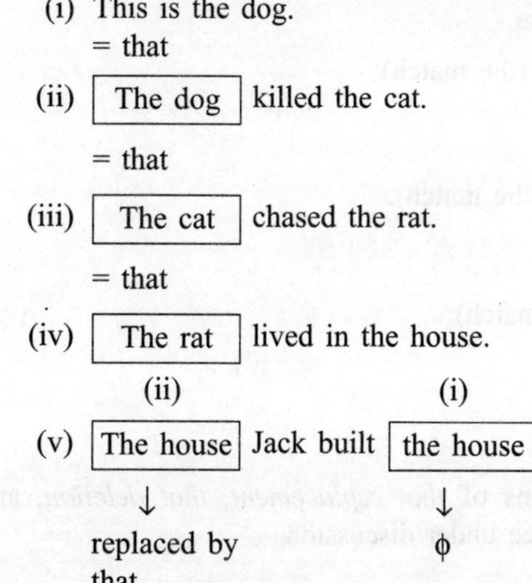

Participial Constructions

Notice in the heading of this chapter, we have included gerundial, infinitival and participial constructions under complex sentences. This is quite reasonable given the position that there are as many simple sentences as there are verbs. This postulation holds true for the above constructions.

The bus **coming** now **is** ours.

↓

(participial construction)

There are two verbs in the above sentence, and so two simple sentences.

(i) The bus is ours.
(ii) **The bus** is coming
that replacement
that is coming.
deletion
coming

These two operations (*that* replacement and *that be* deletion) give us the participial construction.

Infinitival Constructions

Notice the following infinitival relative clause:

United **were** the first team to **win.**

These are two verbs in the above sentence so two simple sentences.

(i) United were the first team.
(ii) United won (the match).

(i) United were the first team.

(ii) United past tense win (the match).

⇓ that

that past tense win (the match).

⇓ deletion

φ past tense win (the match).

⇓ to

to win (φ)

The transformational operations of *that replacement*, *that deletion*, and *to-replacement* give us the sentence under discussion.

Gerundial Constructions

Gerund means a verbal noun. This is formed by adding *–ing* to the verb. A gerund functions as a noun. Examples:

(i) I **like driving** fast. (gerund)

(ii) **Swimming is** a good exercise. (gerund)

In (i), there are two verbs, so there are two simple sentences:

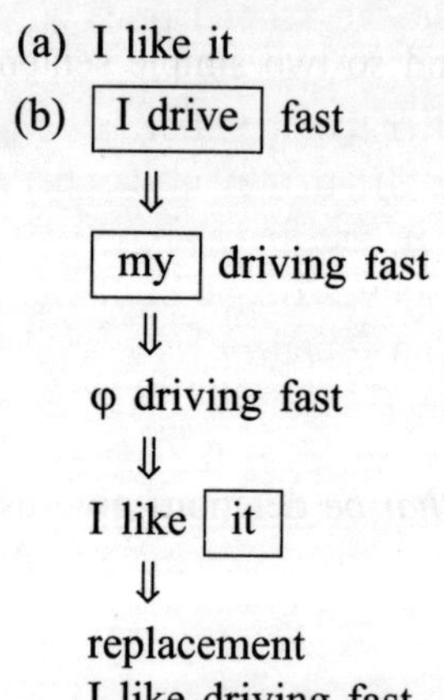

Notice *I drive* is replacement by genitive + gerund; then there is *genitive deletion* and lastly *it* is replaced by the gerund, which gives us sentence (i).

On the basis of the above discussion, it is reasonable to include gerundial, participial and infinitival constructions under the rubric of complex sentences because they also involve the formula of more than one verb and a series of transformational operations. This proposition has neurological backing because this is how we understand and process these constructions.

EXERCISE 5.1

Below are given some relative clauses. Give simple sentences for each of them:

Example: The boy who is wearing a red shirt is my brother.
Simple sentences

(i) The boy is my brother.
(ii) The boy is wearing a red shirt.

1. The man who lives next to us has five children.
2. The building for sale was the house which had an RCC roof and was by the stream.
3. We have a neighbour who plays the guitar.
4. She showed us the beds she had brought back from Badrinath.
5. That's the young man I met at Sita's party.
6. He is an actor whom most of people think is at the peak of his career.
7. The danger of driving is something which worries me each time I travel.
8. The park which I usually go running in is across the road.
9. We received on offer of ₹ 800000 for the house, which we accepted.
10. Ram, who is 60 years old, is a well-known linguist.
11. Professor Sharma, whom I have held in high esteem, is to visit the college next week.
12. Nancy, whose parents are both bankers, won the second prize in the competition.
13. The bandages will be taken off a few days after the operation, at which point we will be able to judge how effective the treatment has been.
14. Whoever wins will go on to play in Athens in the final.
15. We stood on the bridge connecting the two halves of the building.
16. The weapon used in the murder has now been found.
17. The girls being chosen for the team are under 15.
18. The people being asked to take retirement are all over the age of 70.
19. Glancing over the shoulder, he could see the dog chasing him.
20. Having completed the book, he had a holiday.

Complex Sentences

Complex sentences involve a main clause and one or more subordinate clauses; the subordinate clauses are joined to the main clause by means of a subordinate conjunction such as that, why, what, where, whether, if, etc. *A subordinate clause is part of the main clause in the same way as a phrase is a part of the sentence.*

For example:

S V O

He confessed his crime.

S V O

He confessed that he had committed the crime.

There are three types of subordinate clauses:

- Noun clauses
- Adjective clauses
- Adverb clauses

The classification of these clauses depends upon the function they play in the main clause.

Noun Clauses in Different Positions

A noun or noun phrase can function as a subject, an object, a complement or object to a preposition or in apposition to another noun or noun phrase. A noun clause also performs the same function in a complex sentence. Let us look at some examples (Table 5.2).

TABLE 5.2 Noun clauses

Function	*Example*
Subject	• *That Armstrong landed on the moon* is known to everybody • *What he is doing these days* is not known to anybody. • *Why he did this* is a secret.
Object	• Ram knows *that he will pass in first division.* • He thinks *that he will be able to pull through the difficult time.* • I noticed *that he was fast asleep.*
Complement	• The assumption is *that he is a thief.* • The idea is *that we shall catch him red handed.* • My view is *that we should start the counselling sessions.*
Object to preposition	• Your job will depend *on how hard you work.* • We had a discussion *about when we should hold the party.* • He gave books *to whosoever came to the meeting.*
In apposition to a noun or pronoun	• The fact *that he did not do his duty sincerely* cost him his job. (in apposition to the noun *fact*) • It is widely known *that he is the trouble maker.* (in apposition to the impersonal pronoun *it*) • It is obvious *that he has committed the crime.*
After an adjective	• I was ashamed *that I had failed in the examination.* • I am afraid *that we haven't* any money. • We were worried *that it did not rain for days together.*

(Contd.)

TABLE 5.2 **Noun clauses** (*Contd.*)

Function	*Example*
	• Some adjectives used in this pattern are : afraid, amused, annoyed, anxious, aware, certain, confident, conscious, pleased, sorry, surprised, convinced, delighted, determined, eager, glad, happy, horrified, impatient, proved, sure, willing
As DO and IO with double transitive verbs	• I gave *whatever I had in my pocked* to the beggar. • I gave the books *whosoever came to the meeting.* (The italicized noun clause functions as DO and IO respectively).

Below we give a list of verbs after which noun clauses are generally used (Table 5.3).

TABLE 5.3 List of verbs

accept	discover	notice	see
add	doubt	object	show
advise	dream	observe	state
agree	estimate	order	suggest
announce	expect	point out	suppose
answer	explain	predict	suspect
anticipate	fear	prefer	swear
argue	feel	presume	teach
arrange	find	pretend	think
ask	forecast	promise	threaten
assume	forget	propose	understand
beg	guarantee	protest	undertake
believe	guess	prove	urge
check	hear	realize	warm
claim	hope	recognize	wish
command	imagine	recommend	worry
complain	imply	regret	write
confirm	indicate	remark	
consider	insist	remember	
decide	know	reply	
declare	learn	report	
demand	mean	request	
demonstrate	mention	reveal	
	mind	say	

Subordinating Conjunctions

That is a subordinate conjunction which is frequently used to connect a subordinate clause to the main clause. Question words such as **what, which, why** and **where** are also used as subordinate conjunctions when the questions are transformed into statements. *Yes–no questions*, when subordinated to the main clause, begin with *if* or *whether* subordinate conjunction. Consider the following sentences:

(i) I want to know (When will you come?) **when you will come.**

(ii) I want to know (Are you married?) **whether you are married.**

(iii) I can't imagine (How can you behave like this?) **how you can behave like this.**

(iv) (What do you say?) **What you say** is non-sense.

Similarity between Noun Clauses and Non-finite Constructions

Finite verb forms are marked for a tense. The verb forms that are not marked for *tense* and *derive* their time reference form the finite verbs are called **non-finite verb forms**. Infinitives and *–ing* forms are called **non-finite forms**:

(i) I want (finite) to go (non-finite) home.

(ii) I wanted (finite) to go (non-finite) home.

(iii) I saw them going (non-finite) home.

(iv) I saw him cross (non-finite) the road.

Finite verb forms are used to create compactness in the description.

There are similarities between noun clauses and *to-infinitive* forms in their occurrences.

TABLE 5.4 Functions of to-infinitive

Function of to-infinitive	*Examples*
after adjectives	• He is ready *to go.* • I am sorry to *be late.* • She is excited to go to *London.* • I will be delighted to meet you.

(*Contd.*)

TABLE 5.4 Functions of to-infinitive (*Contd.*)

Function of to-infinitive	*Examples*
	Other adjectives that occur in this pattern are good, kind, nice, helpful, silly, stupid, wrong, etc. Alternative way of stating the above sentence could be: It's *nice* of you to come.
after verbs	• He has decided to go to the school. • She agreed to help me. • I want to eat a mango. There are some verbs that are followed by an *object* and *to-infinitive.* I have invited *him to come* to the party. Here are some verbs followed by to-infinitive: agree, arrange, attempt, can afford, choose, dare, decide, expect, fail, forget, hate, hope, intend, learn, like, manage, need, offer, plan, promise, refuse, seem, try, used, want, wish. Some verbs are followed by an object + to-infinitive. Ask, advise, command, expect, help, force, persuade, tell, want warn.
after certain verbs, occurrence of bare infinitive	After *let, make, hear, see* and modal verbs except (used and ought), bare infinitives are used: • They made him *give up* smoking. • They let him *go.* • We heard him *cry.* • We saw him *cross* the road.
as subject, complement and object	• **To err** is human subject • **To see** is to **believe** subject complement • She hopes **to pass the examination** DO ***Note:*** Some uses of to infinitive will be discussed with adverb clauses.

The above discussion shows that to-infinitive behaves like noun clauses in some of its uses. Therefore, it is quite appropriate to discuss it along with noun clauses.

Verbal Nouns or Gerunds

A gerund or verbal noun is formed by the addition of *–ing* to the verbs. It has the same function as that of a noun or a noun phrase (Table 5.5).

Table 5.5 Functions of gerund

Function	*Examples*
Subject	*Swimming* is a good exercise. *Reading book* is a good habit.
DO	I like *eating bananas.* I like *swimming.*
Object of preposition	I am fond *of swimming.* They are ignorant *of trespassing.*
Subject complement	*Seeing* is *believing.* S SC
OC	She stands in knee deep water and splashes about and she calls it swimming
Noun in apposition	Radha likes one exercise—*jogging.*

Note: Most common verbs and other fixed expressions followed by a gerund are *avoid, begin, can't help, dislike, enjoy, finish, go on, imagine, keep, mind, practise, risk, suggest, worth, it's no fun, it's no good, it's worth, it's no use.*

EXERCISE 5.2

Below are given complex sentences (including infinitival and gerundial constructions). Mark as bold the complex sentences and indicate their function in the sentences in terms of subject, object, complement, object of preposition, noun in apposition.

Example: I know **that she will buy a property in Alwar.**

Ans: The complex sentence has been put in bold letters. It functions as an object.

1. I heard him open the door.
2. She hopes to go to the States.
3. Do you know how to defeat him?
4. I am pleased to meet you.
5. The box is too heavy to move.
6. I have arranged to meet him at the airport.
7. He avoids meeting me.
8. I can't help going there.
9. Do you mind opening the window?
10. After working all morning, I want to attend a meeting.
11. I don't like your driving the car carelessly.
12. I expected that he would arrive in time.
13. Ram wouldn't say where he was going.
14. We regret that you don't like our detergent.
15. No one believes that he will win the election.

16. I suppose you aren't used to this kind of behaviour.
17. The assumption is that he will be a force to reckon with.
18. The news that the plane had crashed came as a terrible shock.
19. The fact that he bought a plot of land in Jaipur surprised everybody.
20. There is a rumour that he manipulated the result of his son.
21. I am delighted that you have enjoyed your stay here.
22. I wasn't sure when the guests would arrive.
23. He wanted to know whether I would join him in his trip to Dehradun.
24. That he reached New York safely is known to the members of his family.
25. Why he has come here is not known to me.

EXERCISE 5.3

Rewrite the following sentences by using one main clause and one or more (as the case may be) noun clauses.

Example: I admire his expertise in computers.
Ans: I admire the fact that he is expert at computers.

1. I am sure of giving you satisfaction.
2. I am delighted to hear of your success.
3. He is generally believed to have died of poison.
4. No one can tell the time of his arrival.
5. We must hope for better days.
6. His departure will depend upon his grant of leave.
7. He wanted to know the nature of his offence.
8. The burial place of Moses was never known to the Jews.
9. He was reported to have lost a lot of money.
10. We know the name of the writer of that book.
11. His death at so early an age is sad.
12. Tell me the date and place of your birth.
13. We need not disbelieve his word.
14. I cannot prove my innocence.
15. They were surprised to hear him confess.
16. I promise to meet you tomorrow.
17. He denied telling a lie.
18. They did not believe his declaration of his innocence.
19. Everyone believed him to be guilty.
20. The principal insisted on the students arriving on time for classes.
21. Your decision to work hard is laudable.
22. Your ignorance of not knowing the rule cannot absolve you from punishment.
23. His not apologizing for his rudeness made everyone angry.

24. His mistake of not wishing the seniors was unpardonable.
25. The reason for sending me to a boarding school was never revealed to me.

Adjective Clauses

Adjective clause is also called **relative clause**. As the name suggests, the function of an adjective clause is to *define* or identify or classify the noun phrase after which it occurs.

(i) The boy **who is wearing a red shirt** is my brother.
adjective clause

The relative clause 'who is wearing a red shirt' refers to a particular boy and selects him out of a number of boys, only that boy is my brother.

(ii) What is the name of the player who was injured?
identifying which player

(iii) A player who is injured has to leave field. (Classifying, what kind of player)

Notice in sentence (i), *who* (a relative pronoun) functions as a conjunction. The other relative pronouns that are used in adjective clauses are *that*, *which*, *whom*, *whose*, *of which*. Below we discuss their uses along with examples.

TABLE 5.6 Different relative pronouns

Relative pronoun	*To what it refers*	*Function*	*Examples*
who	persons	subject	(i) The students *who* study in this college are quite disciplined. (ii) The boy *who* has come from Chennai will take admission in this college.
whom	persons	object	(i) The students **whom** I teach English are quite attentive in classes. (ii) The girls *whom* she teaches pay more attention to dancing than to engineering subjects. (iii) The boy *whom* he is talking to is my brother. (iv) The boy to *whom* he is talking is my brother. ***Notice:*** *whom* is formal.
which	things	subject object	(i) The bananas *which* you have bought (object) from the Mumbai market are all rotten.

(*Contd.*)

TABLE 5.6 Different relative pronouns (*Contd.*)

Relative pronoun	*To what it refers*	*Function*	*Examples*
			(ii) The books *which* are lying on the table belong to my brother. subject
that	persons and things	subject and object	(i) The boy *that* is studying in class X is my brother's brother-in-law. person/subject (ii) The book *that* is lying on the table is mine. subject/thing (iii) The book *that* I bought yesterday has been written by a well-known writer. object/thing (iv) The boy *that* Sita married is quite intelligent. object/person (v) The boy *that* (person + object of preposition) he was talking to is my brother. (vi) The boy *to that* he was talking is my brother. (not possible). *Note:* Notice that 'that' relative pronoun can be used for both, things and persons and for subject and object functions. However, there are certain restrictions on its use. It is preferred when we use *that* as subject after *something* and *anything;* words such as *all*, *little*, *much* and superlatives. We use *that* or *zero* pronoun as object after these: (i) These walls are *all that* remain of the city. (ii) She is one of the kindest people (that I know). (iii) Is there anything (that) I can do to help? (from AEG by Martin Hewings, p. 140).
who, whom, which, that and	which and that, who, whom that to persons	object of to things, preposition	(i) The man *who* we talked *to* has come from the States. (ii) The girl *that* we talked *to* has come from the States. (iii) The girl φ we talked to has come from the States.

(*Contd.*)

TABLE 5.6 Different relative pronouns (*Contd.*)

Relative pronoun	*To what it refers*	*Function*	*Examples*
	to things and persons		(iv) The black nurse *whom* we talked *to* belongs to the States. (v) The white man to whom we talked comes from New York. (vi) The music *which* we listened *to* last night was *jazz.* (vii) The music *that* we listened *to* last night was pop. (viii) The music φ we listened to last night was classical. (ix) The music *to which* we listened last night was Hindi pop. *Note: Zero* relative pronoun is used when the relative pronouns (*that*, *which*, *who*, *whom*) are object to verb or object to preposition. Notice sentences (iii) and (viii) above.
whose	persons	possessive	(i) The person *whose* courage I admire fought bravely with the hooligans in the street last night. (ii) The people *whose* houses were damaged by the storm complained to the mayor. ***Note:*** Sometimes, *whose* can also be used with things: (iii) I wouldn't fly with an airline *whose* record is so poor. (This use is restricted only to towns, countries and organizations.)
of which	things	possessive	(i) The house the roof *of which* was damaged last night belongs to my brother.
where, when whereby why	place, time, means and reason	adverbial	(i) This is the place *where* I was born. (ii) He was looking forward to the time *when* he would be called for the interview. (iii) The government has to introduce a system *whereby* (by which) poor students can get free education. (iv) I didn't know the reason *why* he did not come for the evidence. *Note:* In formal English we can use preposition + which for the italicized relative adverbs in (iii).

(*Contd.*)

TABLE 5.6 Different relative pronouns (*Contd.*)

Relative pronoun	*To what it refers*	*Function*	*Examples*
who, what whatever, whoever, whichever,	the people that, the thing that, anything, any person or group, one thing or person from a limited number of things or people	nominal	(i) Can you tell me *who* has been invited? (ii) Ram didn't know *what* to do next. (iii) I'm sure I'll enjoy eating *whatever* you have. (iv) *Whoever* wins in the national games will go in to play at Athens in the final. (v) *Whichever* one of you broke the window will have to pay for it.

Two Types of Relative Clauses

There are two types of relative clauses in English:

1. My sister who *lives* in Chennai is a lecturer (defining).
2. My wife, who lives in Chennai, is a lecturer (non-defining).

Sentence (1) is an *identifying defining relative* clause and specifies my that sister who lives in Chennai, i.e. I have more than one sister and here I am talking about the sister who lives in Chennai, not the one who lives in Bangalore.

Sentence (2) is called **non-defining relative clause** because here *wife* does not need any identification and the relative clause gives *additional* information about my wife. In writing, a non-defining relative clause is written between commas.

Another feature of a non-defining clause is that *that* and *zero* relative pronouns are not used in these clauses. However, *who*, *whom*, *which*, *whose*, and *preposition* + *which* can be used in non-defining clauses.

Yet another feature of non-defining clauses is that antecedents such as *wife*, *father*, *mother*, a proper name of a person or a place, will be followed by non-defining relative clauses because these antecedents are self-identifying. A few more examples will not be out of place.

(i) The Taj Mahal, *which was built by Shahjahan*, is one of the seven wonders in the world.
(ii) Ram's hobby is internet surfing *on which* he spends a *lot of money.*
(iii) Ram dropped a box of chocolate, *all of which broke.*
(iv) Ram, whose father is an MP from Bhopal, is visiting the States next month.

(v) The Indian Hockey team lost to Pakistan by 1 goal to 2 last night, *which is very disappointing.* (Here, *which* refers to the whole main clause. In this use, *that* or *zero* relative pronoun cannot be used.)

After words such as *all, both, each, many, most, neither, none, part, same,* a number (one, two, three, first, second, half, third, etc.) and superlatives (the best, the biggest, etc.), we can use a *non-defining relative clause* beginning with *of which* or *of whom.*

(i) The bank was held up by a group of men, *four of whom* were armed.
(ii) The P.M. has made many visits to China, the *most recent of which,* began today.

Further, at the beginning of a non-defining relative clause, we can use expressions like at *which point/time, by which point/time, during which time, in which case:*

(i) It might rain this week, *in which case* we won't go to Jaipur.
(ii) The next RPET exam will be in May next year, *by which time* Ram will be 16.

Participle Clauses are Reduced Relative Clauses

Participles are those *–ing* forms which have the function of an adjective or an adverb.

Look at the following sentences:

(i) I saw a man **crossing the street.**
participle (adverbial function)
(ii) The boy **sitting in the corner** is my friend.
Participle (adjectival)
(iii) I like **your living in the country**.
gerund (nominal)

There are two types of participles (Figure 5.2)

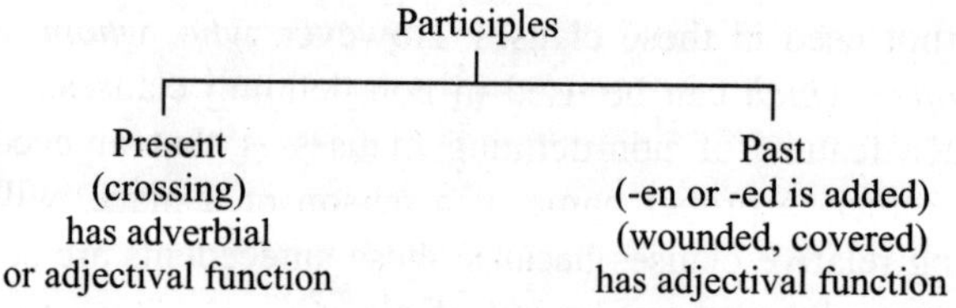

FIGURE 5.2 Participles.

Some examples of past participle are given below.

(i) The boy **covered** with blood came here (adjectival, who was covered with blood).

(ii) The window is **broken.**
adjectival

(iii) The book **published** last week is meant for children.
adjectival

(iv) The boys **being chosen** for the team are under 15.

Notice the bold words in sentences (i), (iii) and (iv) are reduced relative clauses, which is clear by their paraphrases:

(i)' The boy who was covered with blood came here.
(iii)' The book which was published last week is meant for children.
(iv)' The boys who are being chosen for the team are under 15 (passive construction).

A present participle sometimes can also be put before the antecedent.

a ringing telephone (a telephone which is ringing)
a dancing girl (a girl who is dancing)

EXERCISE 5.4

Join the sentences below by turning the second sentence into a relative clause.

Example: *The book is* very interesting.
You lent me *the book.*

Ans.: The book (that) you lent me is very interesting.

1. The pen is missing. I wrote a letter with the pen.
2. The boy has topped the senior secondary examination. The boy belongs to Indore.
3. The boy appeared at the RPET Examination 2004. His result has come out today.
4. The boy has secured the second rank in the examination. His parents live in Delhi.
5. A friend of mine helped me. He is a lecturer.
6. Mohan has sold his old motorbike. He was given it by his father-in-law.
7. The car is for sale. It is Maruti 800, 2000 model.
8. A lecturer had to retire because of ill health. We know him.
9. My brother came to see us. He is in the navy.
10. It is one of the most interesting books. I have read it this year.
11. The park is across the road. I usually go running in it.
12. I bought the present in New York. I gave him it for Diwali.
13. The film is about the lives of seven men. Amitabh Bachchan plays all the men.
14. He has two elder sisters. Neither of his sisters went to school.
15. Several of his friends came to the railway station to welcome him back. Some of them had travelled long distance.

16. I hadn't seen Radha for nearly five years. I had got married and had one child during that period.
17. The film was made in Rajasthan. Its deserts are the largest in India.
18. This is the place. I was born here.
19. Do you know the date? We have to submit the first assignment on that date.
20. I did not know of it. I should do it next.
21. I have managed to get all the cassettes. You have asked for those cassettes.
22. The college is closing down. She is principal of that college.
23. We are grateful to Ram. We had travelled home in his car.
24. That boy backed out of his promise to take admission at our college. This is very disappointing.
25. Sita was able to switch between Hindi, Gujarati, and English. She spoke all the three languages fluently.
26. The dragonfly is an insect. We know very little of it.

Adverbial Clauses

An adverbial clause is a subordinate clause which functions as an adverb and is a part of the sentence in the same way as an adverbial phrase is.

(i) We could pay **later.**
adverb

(ii) We could play **after the meals.**
adverbial phrase

(iii) We could play **after we've eaten.**
adverbial clause

There are three characteristics of an adverbial clause.

1. Like an adverb, an adverbial clause can modify a verb or a predicate.

   (i) I saw him **as he was crossing the street** (modifies the verb *saw*).
   (ii) She spent her entire holiday in Lucknow **as she had never been there before**. (modifies the predicate *spent her entire holiday in Lucknow*)

2. Like an adverb, an adverbial clause can occur in a sentence initially, medially or finally.

   (i) **While he was in England**, he learnt to speak English as an Englishman. (initial position)
   (ii) He learned, **while he was in England**, to speak English as an Englishman. (medially)
   (iii) He learned to speak English as an Englishman, **while he was in England**. (in final position)

The usual position for an adverbial clause is initial or final.

3. Adverbial clauses like adverbs express concepts of (i) time, (ii) place, (iii) reason, (iv) result, (v) concession, (vi) condition, (vii) purpose, and (viii) manner.

   Accordingly, there are *eight types* of adverbial clauses.

Adverbial Clauses of Time

Adverbial clauses of time are introduced by the following subordinate conjunctions (Table 5.7). They answer the questions starting with *when*, *since*, and *how long*.

TABLE 5.7 Adverbial clauses of time

Subordinate conjunction	*Example*
while	*While he was* sleeping, a fire broke out.
when	He came *when she was sleeping.*
before	The patient had died *before the doctor arrived.*
after	We reached the station *after the train had come.*
since	He has lived in Delhi *since he was a child.*
till	We will wait *till he comes back.*
until	Vijay was a little known student *until he topped the college.*
as	I met him *as he was going to college.*
as long as	You can keep the book *as long as you want.*
as soon as	I ran out of the room *as soon as I saw a snake.*
once	*Once you see him*, you can't help falling in love with him.

Adverbial Clauses of Place

Where or wherever introduces adverbial clauses of place.

(i) Leave the books **where you found them**.
(ii) The boy followed the girl **wherever she went**.

EXERCISE 5.5

Complete the following sentences by suitable conjunctions of time or place.

Example: I'll wait for you ......
I'll wait for you *till you come back.*

1. I waited for her .... but she didn't come.
2. You are not going home ....
3. I rushed out of the house ....
4. Once you visit Nainital ....

5. She injured her knee ....
6. I'll trace you out ....
7. Put the pressure cooker back ....
8. Two months have passed ....
9. When the procession passed through the street ....
10. While she was writing letters, ...

Adverbial Clauses of Reason

Adverb clause of reason gives the reason for the happening in the main clause. *As*, *since*, *now that*, *because*, *seeing that* introduce these clauses (Table 5.8).

TABLE 5.8 Adverbial clauses of reason

Subordinate conjunction	*Example*
as	*As it was raining hard*, we decided not to go out.
since	*Since he was not well*, he did not attend classes.
now that	*Now that he has won a jackpot*, he does not have to work for living.
seeing that	There is no point in recruiting him *seeing that his knowledge of the subject is very poor*.
because	I am sure to win this scholarship *because* my performance at the test was excellent.

Notice adverbial clause of reason can start with *as*, *since* and *now that*, but a clause beginning with *because* seldom comes at the beginning of a sentence.

Adverbial Clause of Result

There is a close relationship between *reason* and *result.* There cannot be a result without a reason.

reason ↔ result

Compare the following

Subordinate clause (reason) Since he is ill	Main clause (result) he cannot attend classes.
Main clause (reason) He is so ill	Subordinate clause that he cannot attend classes (result).

Now study the following table (Table 5.9).

TABLE 5.9 Adverbial clauses of result

Subordinate conjunction	*Example*	*Alternative way of stating result*
So that (i) so + adj + that	He is so *ill that* he cannot attend classes.	On account of his illness/ owing to his illness/ because of his illness, he did not attend the classes. (Prepositional phrase + abstract noun) or He is too ill to attend classes. (too + adjective + infinitive phrase).
(ii) So + adverb + that	He behaved *so badly that* he was turned out of the class.	*In view of* (on account of, owing to) the *fact* that he did not attend classes. (Prepositional phrase followed by *the fact that*) or *Being ill*, he did not attend classes. (participle phrase) He behaved *too badly* to be turned out of the class.
Such....that (i) such + countable noun + that	It was *such* a hot day *that we dropped the idea of eating out.*	
(ii) such + uncountable noun + that	She had *such* good luck *that she won a jackpot.*	
so that	He worked hard so that he passed in *first division.*	

EXERCISE 5.6

Change the bold phrase into adverbial clause of result.

Example: **Owing to poverty**, he could not continue his studies.
Ans.: He was so poor **that he could not continue his studies**.

1. **Owing to caste considerations**, people did not elect the able candidates.
2. **On account of their ability to win the election**, about hundred criminals have been allowed to contest the election.
3. **Owing to drought in the eastern part of Maharashtra**, there is scarcity of drinking water.
4. He is too selfish **to help anybody**.
5. **Being tired**, he went to bed immediately.

6. **On account of his being ill**, he did not attend the seminar.
7. **Because of his poor performance at the district level**, he could not be selected for the national games.
8. **Because of the government's bad economic policies**, the poor have become poorer.
9. Sita is **too week to participate in the competition**.
10. **Owing to his bad nature**, nobody likes him.

EXERCISE 5.7

In the following sentences, the subordinate clauses are adverbial clauses of reason. Convert the following sentences in such a way that the main clause states the reason and the subordinate clause becomes a clause of result.

Example: Since he is ill, he cannot attend college.
Ans.: He is so ill that he cannot attend college.

1. Since he is lucky, he will win a lottery ticket.
2. As he is good at English, he will get this job.
3. Since you can't answer the question, we'd better ask someone else.
4. As she has no money, she cannot buy a car.
5. As she is not feeling comfortable in this house, she will shift the house.
6. As Maya is gaining weight every day, she is having problems in walking.
7. Since she speaks English with a strange accent, nobody can understand her.
8. He has no friends because he is a selfish person.
9. Seeing that Ram is a cheat, Mohan gave up his company.
10. Now that he has invented this wonderful machine, he will soon be very rich.

Adverb Clause of Concession

Concession implies a *contrast* or *opposition* in idea. This contrast may be *partial* or *total.*

(i) *Although he worked hard*, he did not pass the examination. (He worked hard and therefore should have passed *but* he did not.)
(ii) *Although I admire his guts*, but I don't like him. (partial contrast)
(iii) *While I was working*, you were sleeping. (total contrast)

In Table 5.10, we discuss adverb clause of concession with examples. Also, we discuss the alternative ways of expressing concession or contrast.

TABLE 5.10 Adverb clause of concession/contrast

Subordinate conjunction	*Example*	*Alternative way of expressing adverb clause of concession*
although (formal)	*Although he is a hard worker,* he is not successful.	*In spite of/despite his hard work*, he is not successful in life. (a prepositional phrase followed by a noun or a gerund) or *Though/although a hard worker*, he is not successful in life. (elliptical concessive clause)
though (less formal)	*Though I admire her for her beauty*, I hate her for her character.	
even though (strong form)	*Even though I did not like to take admission at college*, I did so to please my mother.	
while	*While I am attending classes*, he is abstaining from them.	
whereas	Male students love sports *whereas female students love studies*.	
however + adverb	*However hard you try*, you cannot satisfy him.	
however + adjective	*However rich he may be*, he is quite a miser.	
no matter + wh-word (what, who, where, how)	*No matter what you say*, he won't believe you. or *No matter how bad things are*, we should not lose heart. or The police will catch the thief *no matter where he hides*. or I am going to arrest you, *no matter* who you are.	

Adverb Clauses of Condition

Conditional clauses express different kinds of conditions. The condition may be *likely*, *less likely* or *impossible*. For these three types, we use the following constructions.

(i) If I go to Agra, I shall see the Taj. (likely, i.e. I may go to Agra or I may not. If I go, I shall see the Taj.)
(ii) If I were the Prime Minister of India, I would introduce several new proposals for removing poverty. (My becoming PM is quite hypothetical.)
(iii) If I went to Agra, I would see the Taj. (My going to Agra is less likely or doubtful.)
(iv) If I had gone to Agra, I would have seen the Taj. (It is impossible. It did not happen.)

As we have already discussed in great detail all these three types of conditions in a separate chapter, here we shall refer to only those points that we have not mentioned there (see Table 5.11).

TABLE 5.11 Adverb clauses of condition

Subordinating conjunctions	*Examples*	*Alternative way of expressing conditions*
If	*If you go past the post office*, post this letter for me.	*If possible*, post this letter for me. (elliptical clause)
Unless (if not)	*Unless you work hard*, you won't pass the test.	By working hard, you will pass the test. (preposition followed by a gerund) or Without hard work, you won't pass the test. (preposition followed by a noun) To pass the test/for you to pass the test, you must work hard.
in case	Ring up 100, *in case there is a theft.*	*In case of theft*, ring up 100.
as long as (refers to necessary condition)	*As long as you attend classes*, you will pass.	
so long as (necessary condition)	*So long as you do your work sincerely*, you will not lose your job.	
provided (necessary condition)	He will help you *provided that you don't pressure him.*	
only if (necessary condition)	Textile industries will do well in this area *only if there is abundant harvest of cotton.*	

Notice for unfulfilled condition: If I had worked hard, I *would/should/might/could* have passed the examination. The alternative way of expressing the same is with *but for + noun* construction. Look at the following sentence:

But for your help, it would not have been possible for me to arrange this function.

Adverb Clause of Purpose

Adverb clauses of purpose refer to clauses showing intention or plan (see Table 5.12). They are different from clauses of reason or result.

(i) They moved to the town from the village **so that they could give good education to their son (purpose)**.
(ii) **Since they wanted to give good education to their son**, they moved from the village to the town (clause of reason).

In case of (i), we can ask a question: what was the purpose of their moving to the town? In case of (ii), the question will start with 'why', i.e. why did they move to the town?

TABLE 5.12 Clauses of purpose

Subordinate conjunction	*Example*
so that	They took a taxi to the bus station *so that they might be in time for the bus*.
in order that	They took a taxi to the airport *in order that they might be in time for the flight*.
lest	They took a taxi to the railway station *lest they might miss the train*.

Notice this *so that* is different form the result *so that*.

(i) He ran fast **so that** he could catch the bus (purpose).
(ii) He worked hard **so that** he passed the examination (result).

The first sentence can be replaced by *in order that;* further modals such as *may*, *might*, *can*, *could*, *shall*, *should*, *will*, *would* occur in the subordinate clause.

The second sentence cannot be replaced by *in order that*. It can be paraphrased as he *worked hard, as a result of which he passed.*

The *alternative way of* expressing purpose is with infinitival phrase *in order to* or *so as to*.

The above can be alternatively expressed as:

1. He ran fast **in order** to catch the bus.
2. He ran fast **so as to** catch the bus.

Adverb Clause of Manner

Adverb clause of manner is used when two persons are *compared* in their manner of *being* or *doing*. Table 5.13 shows adverb clauses of manner.

TABLE 5.13 Adverb clauses of manner

Subordinate conjunction	*Example*
as	My teacher treats me *as* (he treats) *his own daughter*. He is as strict as *he was*.
as if/as though	He acts *as if he owns this place*. He looks *as though he is the father of the girl*.
like	Are you going to watch TV *like you did yesterday*.
the way, in a way, in the way (refers to someone's manner of behaving or doing)	She behaved with me *in a way I was not used to*. I am not allowed to live *the way I like*. I have the right to live *in the way I like*.

EXERCISE 5.8

Fill in the blanks with suitable conjunctions of concession, purpose, manner and condition.

Example: (*Although*) he is rich, he is honest.

1. Ram stayed at work .... he could complete the pending work.
2. Seminar is being held .... students can be guided to choose the best courses.
3. Ram gave up his job .... he could take care of his mother.
4. She hid the chocolate .... children could not find it.
5. The train was .... slow. I was almost two hours late.
6. It all happened .... quickly .... I never got a good look at his face.
7. It was .... unusual .... it seemed almost a joke.
8. I gave Ram my address .... he could contact me.
9. Rama has bought a video camera. .... he can film his daughter's marriage.
10. We have planted the rose bush in the middle of the garden .... it is always in a sun.
11. We had turned down the television .... we could hear the door bell.
12. He is going to have a period of training .... he will be ready to take over the job.
13. .... Ram failed the examination, he helped Rama to pass.
14. She bought a car .... she was still too young to learn to drive.
15. .... the night air was hot, they slept soundly.

16. .... it was extraordinary, Thiruanantpuram had less rain than Hyderabad.
17. .... I enjoyed the holiday, I was glad to be at home.
18. .... she doesn't speak French, I think she should still visit Paris.
19. This shirt is still dirty .... I have washed it twice.
20. They drank from the stream .... they knew it was polluted.
21. If we had travelled together, we .... saved money.
22. If you .... of spiders, don't go into the garden.
23. Where .... you .... if you could live anywhere in the world?
24. She'll be furious if she .... the truth.
25. You .... the answer if you read the book.
26. You .... to take a taxi if you want to leave now.
27. If you had taken that job in English, you .... to speak English.
28. If you .... excuse me, I have to make a telephone call.
29. If you .... leave your name and telephone number, I .... you back as soon as I can.
30. If you .... stay here until I return, I'd appreciate it.
31. It looks .... it is going to rain.
32. He looks .... he has been in a pigsty.
33. It looks .... the baby is suffering from cough and cold.
34. The food will be served just in time for the party .... it may be served hot.
35. The bank robbers went into hiding and grew beards .... they are not caught by the police.

Compound Sentences

Compound sentences are the sentences in which two or more *main clauses* (= clauses of equal rank) are conjoined by means of coordinating conjunctions (*and*, *but*, *or*, *so*). The sentences also show how one clause is *related* (*i.e.* relationship of addition or contrast of choice) to the other. Look at the following table for details (Table 5.14)

TABLE 5.14 Coordinate clauses

Conjunction	*Example*	*Meaning of coordinating conjunction*
and	He was born in Delhi *and* (he was) *educated in Madras.*	addition
	To live in a village is cheap *and* it provides a healthy atmosphere.	similarity
but	He is rich *but* honest.	contrast
yet	She worked hard, *yet* she failed.	concession

(*Contd.*)

TABLE 5.14 Coordinate clauses (*Contd.*)

Conjunction	*Example*	*Meaning of coordinating conjunction*
so	I did not buy the textbooks, *so* I borrowed from my classmate.	cause
for	Father asked daughter to meet him after dinner, *for* he had something important to tell her.	effect
or	You had better hurry up *or* you will be late for the exam.	negative condition
	Would you like to drink tea *or* coffee?	choice

More about Coordination

Two negative clauses can be joined by *and:*

(i) I haven't gone to my village for the last four years, **and** I don't intend to go this year also.

Use *or* instead of *and* if both the negative clauses have the same subject and the same auxiliaries:

(i) He does not speak English **or** French.
(ii) I don't drink **or** chew tobacco as a matter of policy.

Negative clauses can alternatively be linked by using *and, neither, and nor* or *nor.* In such a case, an auxiliary verb (*be* or *do*) is placed before the subject:

(i) I don't like sweets, **nor** do the rest of my family.
(ii) He was not happy with the arrangements made in the party **and neither** were others.
(iii) He is not rich, **nor** is he poor.

The conjunction *and*, if it comes after an imperative sentence followed by a clause which contains a future tense verb, expresses a *condition.*

Pay me ₹ 200 **and** you'll have no trouble. (= if you pay me ₹ 200, you will face no trouble.)

Leave now **and** you will be at the station in time.

Sometimes, a coordinate conjunction is followed by another coordinate conjunction.

(i) She was rich **and yet** not happy.
(ii) The college was closed **and so** I could not collect my certificates back from the clerk.

Conjunctive Adverbs

Conjunctive adverbs are adverbs that function as conjunctions. Study the following table (Table 5.15):

TABLE 5.15 Conjunctive adverbs

Conjunctive adverbs	*Example*	*Meaning*
moreover	Tamil Nadu has a number of engineering colleges, sufficient for the population here; *moreover* several new colleges are being added to the existing ones.	addition
furthermore	Urban children spend a lot of time in watching television; *furthermore* they are losing interest in outdoor sports.	addition
however	He did not work hard for the examination; *however* his result was in no doubt.	contrast
nevertheless	I doubt whether he will grant me leave; *nevertheless* I am going to request him for it.	contrast
consequently/ therefore	He wasted his time in gossiping with his friends; *consequently* he failed in the relationship. I have to go to Delhi; *therefore*, I request you to grant me leave.	cause and effect
otherwise	He sleeps too much; *otherwise* he is all right.	a condition or qualification

Coordinate clauses can also be expressed with the help of a semicolon (;):

He was sick; he did not attend classes.

To form coordinate clauses, sometimes a conjunctive adverb is used with coordinate conjunction.

(i) It will take me a lot of time to tell the full story **and besides** it is not necessary.
(ii) The building is not without flaws **but still** it is a fabulous attempt by a young architect.
(iii) I have seen her behave like that before, and **therefore**, there was no shock.

Correlative Conjunctions

Correlative conjunctions are conjunctions that go together (Table 5.16). They are *both ... and, neither... nor, either ... or, not only ... but also*, (sometimes) *not only ... but as well. Correlative conjunctions are stronger form of coordinate conjunctions.*

TABLE 5.16 **Correlative conjunctions**

Coordinate conjunction	*Correlative*
The collector is an able administrator *and* a fine man.	The collector is *both* an able administrator *and* a fine man. or The collector is *not only* an able administrator *but* a fine man as well.
The director or the principal will preside over the function.	*Either* the director *or* the principal will preside over the function.
Ram doesn't speak English nor does Sita.	*Neither* Ram *nor* Sita speaks English.

Conclusion

In this long chapter, we have discussed the principles and processes of embedding and coordination. We started with the phrase structure rules by stating that the complex and compound sentences are part of a basic sentence the same way a phrase is. These structures are embedded either in the NP (in the case of noun clauses) or beside NP in the case of relative clauses. Adverbial clauses occur as daughters of adverbial phrases.

Unlike traditional grammars, we have assumed that infinitival, gerundial and participial constructions also have the same kind of abstract embedding and then through a series of transformations, we get the surface constructions. Though we know that this earlier view of transformational generative grammar was later on revised, done away with, but still we have retained it because we find it pedagogically rewarding and viable.

EXERCISE 5.9

Below are given pairs of sentences. Make a coordinate clause by combining each pair. Use only correlative conjunctions.

Example: He is intelligent. He is handsome.
Ans.: He is *both* intelligent *and* handsome.

1. The road was closed. I couldn't go right or left.
2. A deaf-mute is someone. He can't hear or speak.
3. The post office was not open. The bank was not open.
4. He is rich. He is honest.
5. He has gone to Jaipur. He has gone to Delhi.
6. Ganesh does not speak Tamil. Suresh does not speak Telgu.
7. Ram is outspoken. Ram is hard-working.
8. Ram will go to London on holidays. Ram will go to Paris on holidays.
9. Krishna is a good dancer. Krishna is a good singer.
10. Suresh is not clever. Suresh is not pragmatic.

EXERCISE 5.10

Fill in the blanks with suitable coordinating conjunctions.

Example: Ram has passed in RPET-2004 *but* Sita has not been able to qualify.

1. Krishna had no food. .... he also had to pay the rent.
2. Neil Armstrong was an American astronaut .... his landing on the moon was stage managed. That is the rumour.
3. Sita is right handed .... Geeta is left handed.
4. It has not rained for months .... the ground is very dry.
5. There was a widespread earthquake .... only 7 people died.
6. I have left my bag either on the bus .... at the office.
7. He was not only a boxer .... he .... lectured at Rajasthan University.
8. The family have no money .... they enjoy themselves.
9. I'm too busy to travel all that way .... there is the expense.
10. I know travelling is safe .... you won't find me on an airplane.

EXERCISE 5.11

Fill in the blanks with conjunctive adverbs such as *however*, *nevertheless*, *moreover*, *furthermore*, *consequently*, *therefore*, *and otherwise*.

1. What you said was true but (it was) .... unkind.
2. The rent is too high and .... it isn't conveniently located.
3. The school is quite small and .... it is quite far from our house.
4. He did not work hard for the exam .... he failed in the exam.
5. Work had for the exam .... you will fail.
6. He had a bad cold .... he did not go to work.
7. India has done badly once again in the Olympics. .... we have had success in the archery by wining a gold medal.
8. The principal is unwilling to admit that he can make mistakes. .... he is totally incapable.
9. Maybe what you say is correct. .... I cannot agree with you.

List of Verbs Followed by Complement Clauses

Below we give a list of *verbs* (Table 5.17) which take *that clause* as object, or which are followed by *to-infinitive construction* or *object + to-infinitive construction* or *gerund* or *to-infinitive construction*. If a student has mastered 2500 words from General Service List, as suggested by Michael West, and about 1000 words from the field in which he is specializing plus the knowledge of complement clauses that occur after these verbs, he will be able to speak or write English with complete mastery. Many educated people make this mistake when they say *I want that you should go* which is not acceptable. You should say *I want you to go.*

Classification of some of the verbs commonly used in terms of their capacity to take *that-clauses*, *infinitives*, or *gerunds*.

TABLE 5.17 List of verbs taking different complements

+that clause as object	*+ to-infinitive*	*+ object + to-infinitive*	*+gerund*	*+gerund or to-infinitive*
accept	ache	advise	abhor	attempt
acknowledge	afford	allow	admire	begin
admit	agree	appoint	admit	can't bear
advertise	aim	ask	advocate	cease
advocate	appear	assist	anticipate	continue
affirm	arrange	bear	appreciate	dread
agree	aspire	beg	avoid	fear
allege	attempt	beseech	await	forget
announce	beg	bribe	bear	hate
answer	bother	bring	burst out	hesitate
appreciate	care	cause	can't help	intend
ascertain	chance	caution	can't resist	leave
ask	choose	challenge	can't stand	like
assert	claim	choose	cherish	love
assume	commence	charge	commence	mean
believe	condescend	coax	complete	neglect
certify	consent	coerce	consider	omit
charge	contrive	command	continue	plan
claim	dare	commission	contemplate	prefer
comment	decide	condemn	criticize	propose
complain	decline	compel	curse	regret
conceive	deserve	convince	defend	remember
confess	determine	dare	defer	start
confide	endeavor	challenge	delay	try
conjecture	expect	defy	deny	deserve
content	fail	desire	deplore	merit
contest	happen	detail	deprecate	need
decide	hasten	direct	detest	want
declare	hope	dislike	discredit	
decree	learn	drink	discuss	
deduce	look	empower	dislike	
demand	long	enable	encourage	
demonstrate	lust	encourage	endorse	

(*Contd.*)

TABLE 5.17 List of verbs taking different complements (*Contd.*)

+that clause as object	*+ to-infinitive*	*+ object + to-infinitive*	*+gerund*	*+gerund or to-infinitive*
deny	manage	enjoin	endure	
deplore	mean	entice	enjoy	
desire	need	entitle	escape	
discern	often	entreat	eschew	
disclose	persist	exhort	evaluate	
discover	plead	expect	examine	
dislike	plot	forbid	excuse	
divulge	pray	force	fancy	
doubt	prepare	get	finish	
dream	presume	(= cause)	forgive	
emphasize	pretend	hate	give up	
estimate	proceed	help	glorify	
expect	profit	impel	go on	
explain	promise	implore	grudge	
rumour			guard against	
say			harp on	
see			indulge in	
(=understand)			inquire into	
sense			insist upon	
show			intrude upon	
specify			jeer at	
state			joke about	
stipulate			know about	
submit			laugh at	
suggest			long for	
suppose			muse on	
suspect			participate in	
swear			persist in	
teach			plan on	
testify			pore over	
theorize			protest against	
think			provide against	
tolerate			puzzle over	
understand			react against	
verify			rebel against	
warn			rebel against	
(somebody)			reflect on	
			rejoice at	
write			rely upon	
appear			scoff at	

(*Contd.*)

TABLE 5.17 List of verbs taking different complements (*Contd.*)

+that clause as object	*+ to-infinitive*	*+ object + to-infinitive*	*+gerund*	*+gerund or to-infinitive*
come to pass			slum over	
happen			sneer at	
matter			subsist on	
seem			succeed in	
turn out			talk of	
advise			think about	
apprize			weak at	
assure			wince at	
convince			wonder about	
inform				
notify				
persuade				
reassure				
remind			**write about.**	
tell			Object +	
			preposition	
warn			**+ gerund.**	
			absolve + **o** + of	
			accuse + **o** + of	
			bully + **o** + into	
			cajole + **o** + into	
			caution + **o** + about	
			coax + **o** + into	
			coerce + **o** + into	
			convict + **o** + of	
			cure + **o** + of	
			deter + **o** + from	
			discourage + **o** + from	
			dissuade + **o** + from	
			entice + **o** + into	
			exclude + **o** + from	
			fool + **o** + into	
			force + **o** + into	
			goad + **o** + into	

(*Contd.*)

TABLE 5.17 List of verbs taking different complements (*Contd.*)

+that clause as object	*+ to-infinitive*	*+ object + to-infinitive*	*+gerund*	*+gerund or to-infinitive*
			lecture + (to) **o** + about	
			pester + **o** + into	
			prevent + **o** + from	
			provoke + **o** + into	
			remind + **o** + of	
			save + **o** + from	
			scare + **o** + into	
			suspect + **o** + of	
			trick + **o** + into	
			+ Reflexive + gerund	
			imagine	
fancy	reckon	incite	imagine	
fear	refuse	induce	justify	
feel	resolve	inspire	keep	
(= understand)	seek	instruct	keep on	
	seem	intend	leave off	
figure	strive	invite	mean	
find	struggle	lead	mention	
force	succeed	(=cause)	mind	
forget	swear	leave	miss	
gamble	thirst	like	neglect	
gather	threaten	love	necessitate	
guarantee	turnout	mean	notice	
guess	venture	motivate	overlook	
hate	volunteer	pardon		
hear	wait	oblige	postpone	
(= be told)	want	order	practice	
hint	wish	permit	praise	
hope	yearn	persuade	preach	
ignore		prefer	preclude	
imagine		prepare	prevent	
imply		press	publicize	
indicate		(=urge)	put off	
infer		prompt	question	
inform (some		promise	quit (=stop)	
body)		provoke	recollect	

(*Contd.*)

TABLE 5.17 List of verbs taking different complements (*Contd.*)

+that clause as object	*+ to-infinitive*	*+ object + to-infinitive*	*+gerund*	*+gerund or to-infinitive*
insist		remind	recommend	
insinuate		request	reconsider	
intimate		schedule	relish	
know		stimulate	renounce	
learn		teach	report	
like		tell	repudiate	
love		tempt	resent	
maintain		train	resist	
mean		trouble	ridicule	
mention		trust	risk	
mind		urge	sanction	
(=take care)		want	shirk	
mutter		warn	spend	
note		**wish**	stand	
notice		object +	stop	
object		present	suggest	
observe		**participle**	survive	
order		behold	tolerate	
overlook		catch	try (= make)	
own		detect	an experiment	
perceive		discern	with)	
point out		feel	understand	
pray		find	value	
preach		hear	veto	
predict		imagine	vindicate	
prefer		keep	welcome	
prescribe		leave	**withhold**	
presume		listen to	approve of	
profess		notice	arrange for	
promise		observe	bank on	
pronounce		overhear	beware of	
prophesy		pass	blush at	
prove		see	brag about	
postulate		set	check on	
realize		watch	comment upon	
reason		witness		
reckon			conceive of	
recall			consent to	
reckon			consent to	

(*Contd.*)

TABLE 5.17 List of verbs taking different complements (*Contd.*)

+that clause as object	*+ to-infinitive*	*+ object + to-infinitive*	*+gerund*	*+gerund or to-infinitive*
recognize			concentrate on	
recollect			cope with	
recommend			correspond	
regret			count on	
reiterate			decide on	
rejoice			delight in	
remark			depend on	
remember			disapprove of	
remind (some-body)			dispense with	
			elaborate on	
report			engage in	
request			escape from	
require			gamble on	
represent			gloat over	
reveal			gloss over	

Source: Modern English Grammar by Professor N. Krishnaswamy.

Key to Exercise 5.1

1. (i) The man has five children.
   (ii) He lives next to us.
2. (i) The building for sale was the house.
   (ii) The house had an RCC roof.
   (iii) The house was by the stream.
3. (i) We have a neighbour.
   (ii) He plays the guitar.
4. (i) She showed us the beads.
   (ii) She had brought back the beads from Badrinath.
5. (i) That's the young man.
   (ii) I met the young man at Sita's party.
6. (i) He is an actor.
   (ii) Most people think of him.
   (iii) He is at the peak of his career.
7. (i) Someone drives in danger (Someone's driving in danger—The danger of driving).
   (ii) The danger of driving is something.
   (iii) It worries me each time.
   (iv) I travel each time.

8. (i) The park is across the road.
   (ii) I usually go in the park.
   (iii) I usually run in the park.
9. (i) We received an offer of ₹ 800000 for the house.
   (ii) We accepted the offer.
10. (i) Ram is a well-known linguist.
    (ii) He is 60 years old.
11. (i) Professor Sharma is for something.
    (ii) Professor Sharma visits the college next week.
    (= For him to visit the college next week.)
    (iii) I have held him in high esteem.
12. (i) Nancy won the second prize in the competition.
    (ii) Her parents are both bankers.
13. (i) Someone will take the bandages off a few days after the operation.
    (ii) At which point we will be able for it.
    (iii) We judge it.
    (iv) The treatment has been effective to some degree.
14. (i) Someone wins it.
    (ii) Someone will go on for something.
    (iii) Someone plays in Athens in the final.
15. (i) We stood on the bridge.
    (ii) The bridge connects the two halves of the building.
16. (i) Someone has now found the weapon.
    (ii) Someone used the weapon.
17. (i) The girls are under 15.
    (ii) Someone is choosing the girls for the team.
18. (i) The people are all over the age of 70.
    (ii) Someone asked people it.
    (iii) People take retirement.
19. (i) He glanced over the shoulder.
    (ii) He could see the dog.
    (iii) The dog chased him.
20. (i) He had completed the book.
    (ii) He had a holiday.

Key to Exercise 5.2

1. **open the door**, adverbial.
2. **to go to the States**; object.
3. **how to defeat him**; object.
4. **to meet you**; adverbial.
5. **to move**; adverbial
6. **to meet him at the airport**; object.
7. **meeting me**; object.
8. **going there**; object.
9. **opening the window;** object.
10. **after working all morning**; adverbial, **to attend a meeting**; adverbial.
11. **your driving the car carelessly**; object.

12. **that he would arrive in time**; object.
13. **where he was going**; object.
14. **that you don't like our detergent**; object.
15. **that he will win the election**; object.
16. **you aren't used to this kind of behaviour**; object.
17. **that he will be a force to reckon with**; complement.
18. **that the plane had crashed**; noun in apposition.
19. **that he bought a plot of land in Jaipur**; noun in apposition
20. **that he manipulated the result of his son**; noun in apposition.
21. **that you enjoyed your stay here**; adverbial
22. **when the guests would arrive**; adverbial.
23. **whether I would join him in his trip to Dehradun**; object.
24. **that he reached New York safely**; subject.
25. **Why he has come here**; subject.

Key to Exercise 5.3

1. I am sure that I shall give you satisfaction.
2. I am delighted that you have succeeded.
3. It is generally believed that he died of poison.
4. No one can tell the time when he arrived.
5. We must hope that better days will come.
6. That he will leave depends upon his grant of leave.
7. He wanted to know what offence he had committed.
8. It was never known to the Jews where Moses was buried.
9. It is reported that he lost a lot of money.
10. We know who has written that book.
11. The fact that he died at so early an age is sad.
12. Tell me when and where you were born.
13. We need not disbelieve what he says.
14. I cannot prove that I am innocent.
15. They were surprised to hear that he had confessed.
16. I promise that I shall meet you tomorrow.
17. He denied that he had told a lie.
18. They did not believe his declaration that he was innocent.
19. Everyone believed that he was guilty.
20. The principal insisted that the students should arrive on time for classes.
21. It is laudable that you have decided to work hard.
22. The fact that you did not know the rule cannot absolve you from punishment.
23. The fact that he did not apologize for his rudeness made everyone angry.
24. The mistake that he did not wish his seniors was unpardonable.
25. It was never revealed to me why I was sent to a boarding school.

Key to Exercise 5.4

1. The pen which I wrote a letter with is missing.
2. The boy who belongs to Indore has topped the senior secondary examination.
3. The boy, whose result has come out today, appeared at the RPET Examination 2004.
4. The boy, whose parents live in Delhi, has secured the second rank in the examination.
5. A friend of mine who is a lecturer helped me.
6. Mohan, who was given an old motorbike by his father-in-law, has sold it.
7. The car which is Maruti 800, 2000 model is for sale.
8. A lecturer whom we know had to retire because of ill health.
9. My brother who is in the navy came to see us.
10. It's one of the most interesting books that I have read this year.
11. The park in which I usually go running is across the road.
12. I bought the present which I gave him for Diwali in New York.
13. The film is about the lives of seven men all of whom are played by Amitabh Bachchan.
14. He has two elder sisters neither of whom went to school.
15. Several of his friends, some of whom had travelled long distance, came to the railway station to welcome him back.
16. I hadn't seen Radha for nearly five years, during which period I had got married and had one child.
17. The film was made in Rajasthan, the deserts of which are the largest in India.
18. This is the place where I was born.
19. Do you know when we have to submit the first assignment?
20. I did not know what to do next.
21. I have managed to get all the cassettes that you have asked for.
22. The college of which she is principal is closing down.
23. We are grateful to Ram, in whose car we had travelled home.
24. That boy backed out of his promise to take admission at our college, which was disappointing.
25. Sita was able to switch between Hindi, Gujarati, and English, all of which she spoke fluently.
26. Dragonfly is an insect which we know very little of.

Key to Exercise 5.5

1. until 6 O' clock.
2. until you've finished the report.
3. as soon as I heard an explosive noise.
4. you can never stop visiting it again and again.

5. as she was playing.
6. wherever you go.
7. where I picked it from.
8. since I wrote you a letter.
9. everybody came out to watch.
10. I was watching TV.

Key to Exercise 5.6

1. People were so caste conscious that they did not elect the able candidates.
2. About hundred criminals are so able to win the election that they have been allowed to contest the election.
3. The eastern part of Maharashtra is so drought-stricken that there is scarcity of drinking water.
4. He is so selfish that he cannot help anybody.
5. He was so tired that he went to bed immediately.
6. He was so ill that he did not attend the seminar.
7. He performed so badly at the district level that he could not be selected for the national games.
8. The government's economic policies are so bad that the poor have become poorer.
9. Sita is so weak that she cannot participate in the competition.
10. He has such a bad nature that nobody likes him.

Key to Exercise 5.7

1. He is so lucky that he will win a lottery ticket.
2. He is good at English that he will get this job.
3. He is so ignorant that we'd better ask someone else.
4. She is so poor that she cannot buy a car.
5. She is so uncomfortable in this house that she will shift the house.
6. Maya is so heavy that she has problems in walking.
7. She has such a strange accent that nobody can understand her English.
8. He is so selfish that he does not have friends.
9. Ram is such a cheat that Mohan gave up his company.
10. He is so good at inventing machine that he will soon be very rich.

Key to Exercise 5.8

1. in order that/so that
2. in order that/so that
3. so that
4. so that
5. so slow that
6. so quickly that
7. so unusual that
8. so that
9. so that
10. so that
11. so that
12. so that

13. although
14. although/though
15. though
16. though
17. though
18. even though
19. even if
20. even though
21. would have
22. are scared
23. would choose
24. finds out
25. would know
26. will have
27. would have learnt
28. would
29. would, will call
30. would stay
31. as though
32. as though
33. as though
34. so that
35. so that

Key to Exercise 5.9

1. As the road was closed, I couldn't go either left or right.
2. A deaf-mute is someone who can neither hear nor speak.
3. Neither the post office nor the bank was open.
4. He is both rich and honest.
5. He has gone either to Jaipur or to Delhi.
6. Ganesh speaks neither Tamil nor Telgu.
7. Ram is not only outspoken but also hard-working.
8. Ram will go either to London or to Paris on holidays.
9. Krishna is not only a good dancer but a good singer as well.
10. Suresh is neither clever nor pragmatic.

Key to Exercise 5.10

1. and
2. and
3. but
4. so
5. but/however/ nevertheless
6. or
7. but, also
8. yet
9. and then
10. still

Key to Exercise 5.11

1. nevertheless
2. moreover
3. furthermore
4. and therefore
5. otherwise
6. therefore
7. however
8. moreover
9. however

6

Conditional Sentences

Introduction

There are three types of conditional sentences in English

(i) If the bus reaches by 10 am, I will be able to reach the MREC by 11 am. (open condition)

(ii) If the bus did not break down, it would reach Jaipur by 10 am. (improbable condition)

(iii) (a) If I had started a day earlier, I would have already been in Jaipur. (unfulfilled condition, with past consequence)

(b) If the diamond merchant had not given me lift, I wouldn't be here. (unfulfilled condition with present consequence)

Below we discuss all the three types of conditional clauses.

Open Condition

Study the following sentences:

(i) If you **work** hard, you will pass the exam.

(ii) If Ram **goes** to Agra, he **will see** the Taj.

(iii) If Radha **marries** Krishna, she **will be** happy.

(iv) If I am **called** for the interview, I **will be selected**.

Notice the following points about the sentences:

If I work hard, I will pass the exam.

Conditional clause   result clause.

The clause beginning with *if* is called the **conditional clause** and the main clause is called the **result clause**.

In the *if* clause, we use simple present tense and in the result clause, we use *will* + *first form* of the verb.

In this respect, this type of clause is different from Hindi conditional sentences. In Hindi, in both the clauses, we use simple future tense.

Therefore, a word of caution is required for Hindi speakers using English. They should avoid using will + first form of the verb in the conditional clause.

Though the most common form to be used in this pattern is simple present + will /shall + first form of the verb, other tenses are also possible as illustrated by the following sentences.

(i) If you go past the post office, please post this letter for me. (Simple present +imperative)
(ii) If your car is not working, you can use mine. (present continuous + can + first form of the verb)
(iii) If you heat water at 100°C, it starts boiling. (simple present + simple present)
(iv) If you leave now, you may reach by 10 am. (simple present + may + first form of the verb)
(v) I shall be grateful if you will do me a favour. (shall + first form + will + first form; shows polite request)

The *if* clause states a condition and if this condition is satisfied, the result will follow.

The time denoted by this type of conditional sentence is generally future.

Improbable/Rejected Condition

This condition is also called **doubtful** or **hypothetical condition**. Look at the following sentences:

(i) **If you worked hard, you would pass the exam.**
Conditional clause result clause.
(ii) If a ghost **came into** your room, what **would** you do?
(iii) If I **had** wings, I **would** fly.
(iv) If I **were** the Prime Minister of India, I **would make** revolutionary changes in the field of IT.

Note the following points about this condition.

1. This condition is called improbable or doubtful condition. Look at the sentence (i) above. The teacher is doubtful about the student's working hard and hence he is also doubtful about his passing the exam. In (ii), it is improbable that a ghost would come into the room. Sentence (iii) states a hypothetical condition, which is unlikely to be fulfilled.
2. The tense used in the conditional clause is simple past and the tense used in the result clause is would + first form of the verb. Other configurations are also possible with *might*, *could*, etc.

(i) If you started earlier, you **might reach** in time. (You will perhaps reach in time.)
(ii) If you **worked hard**, you **could pass** the exam. (You will perhaps pass the exam.)

The time denoted by this conditional type of sentence is *future*.

Please note this type of conditional sentences are not available in Hindi. Therefore, Hindi speakers using English make a lot of mistakes.

Unfulfilled Condition

Look at the following sentences:

(i) If you had worked hard, you would have/could have passed the exam. (You did not work hard. You did not pass the exam.)
(ii) If he had helped her, she could have gotten the job. (He did not help her. She did not get the job.)
(iii) If I had known it before, I would have applied for the job. (I did not know it before. I did not apply for the job.)
(iv) If they had played well, they could have won the match. (They did not play well. They did not win the match.)

Note the following features about this condition:

1. This condition is called unfulfilled condition because the condition was not satisfied and hence the result did not follow. For example Sentence (i) above shows that he did not work hard and hence he did not pass.
2. In this type of sentences, we use had + third form of the verb in the conditional clause and would/could/might + have + third form of the verb in the result clause.

   Sometimes, we see a variation in the form:

   (i) If you had not given me a ride, I wouldn't be here. (present consequence of a past action)
   (ii) If you had not given me a ride, I wouldn't have reached the college in time. (past consequence of a past action)

3. This type of conditional sentence shows *past time*.
4. This type of conditional sentence has a negative meaning and can be paraphrased by 'not'.

If you had worked hard, you would have passed the exam.
(You did *not* work hard. You did *not* pass the exam.)

Tips for Solving the Questions

In the tests, generally a completion type exercise is given:

If you go ....

The student should first figure out the tense to be used and later he can complete the remaining part in such a way that the sentence does not sound non-sensical. For example, in the above sentence, *go* (simple present) is given, to complete this sentence will + first form of the verb is required.

If you go .... will see.

After completing this part, a student can insert other elements.

If you go to Agra, you will see the Taj.

EXERCISE 6.1

Put the verbs in the brackets in the following sentences into the correct form.

1. If you (not work) hard now, you (be) sorry afterwards.
2. If you (earn) 2 lac rupees, you (be able) to buy a car.
3. If you (have) a car, you (be able) to reach office in time.
4. I don't work hard. If I (work) hard, I (pass) the exam.
5. I don't like him. If I (like him), I (stay) with him in the same room.
6. I don't write letters to him. If I (write) letters to him, I (know) where he is.
7. If you (boil) water, it (start) evaporating at 100°C.
8. If your scooter (go) out of order, (use) my car.
9. I don't have a car. If I (have) a car, I (go) to office by car.
10. You seem to be poor. If you (be) rich, you (send) your kids to a good public school.
11. You seem to be weak. If you (be) strong, you (not cry) with pain like this.
12. I am not a rich man's daughter. If I (be) rich, I (distribute) all my wealth among the poor.
13. If I (have) the money, I would have bought a car.
14. If she had money, she (buy) gold ornaments.
15. I don't like wearing gold jewellery. If I (like) it, I (buy) it.
16. I have not seen a ghost till today. If I (see) a ghost now, I (scream) at the top of my voice for help.
17. This plant does not flower in winter. If it (flower) in winter, it (be) a pleasant spectacle.
18. He did not work hard. That is why he failed in the exam.
    If he (work) hard, he (not fail) in the exam.
19. He did not know how to drive. That is why he did not use a car. If he (know) how to drive, he (use) a car.

20. He did not know how to flatter the management. That is why he lost his job.
    If he (know) how to flatter the management, he (not lose) his job.
21. I don't like driving fast. If I (drive) fast, I (meet) with an accident.
22. I don't like his tactics. If I (like) his tactics, I (follow) his example.
23. He did not like wearing a dhoti. That is why he was wearing a pair of trousers. If he (not like) wearing a dhoti, he (wear) a pair of trousers.
24. I don't know how to interact with people. If I (know) they (come) to my room too.
25. He did not teach in the class. That is why his result was poor.
    If he (teach) in the class, his result (not be) so poor.
26. He was no longer popular. That is why his popularity graph declined.
    If he (be) popular, his popularity graph (not decline).

EXERCISE 6.2

Complete the following sentences:

1. If you go to Kolkata ....
2. If you go to college by bus ....
3. If a ghost came into my room ....
4. If I had enough money ....
5. ....the result would be good.
6. .... what would happen?
7. ....the plants would be fresh and green.
8. If you had attended the interview ....
9. ....he would have been selected.
10. If you go out of the room ....
11. If you happen to meet him ....
12. If he had posted the letter in time ....
13. If you served humanity…………..
14. If you worshipped two hours every day ....
15. Look me up ....
16. If you were an MP, ...
17. If you win a lottery ....
18. If he had been brought up well ....
19. If you see a butterfly ....
20. If it is raining now, ...

EXERCISE 6.3

Complete the following sentences:

1. If x-rays had not been discovered ....
2. If you believe in ghosts ....

3. If they offered him US $ 1.5 lac ....
4. I shall never permit you to attend a Refresher Course if ....
5. If you think it is absolutely necessary ....
6. If he had not fallen in the pig sty ....
7. Oil floats if ....
8. If I met your friend in the street ....
9. If he wastes his time ....
10. If I had the sort of son people have these days ....
11. .... I'll consent as well.
12. If May had not gone to Italy. ....
13. If I won a lottery ....
14. If it rains tomorrow,
15. What will you do if ....
16. If many people board the boat ....
17. If a metro had been built in Chennai ....
18. Unless you are more careful ....
19. Would it affect your pension if ....
20. If I had known there was ginger in it ....
21. Hurry or else ....
22. Dial 007 if ....
23. He will not answer unless ....
24. If it had not been a hot day ....
25. If the driver had a nap ....
26. If you put salt in water ....
27. If he didn't smoke so much ....
28. If I pass this exam ....
29. The milk wouldn't have turned sour if ....
30. Should you lose your way ....
31. .... I would have been seriously injured.
32. ....you might succeed.
33. What would you do if ....
34. If he did not return ....
35. Remind him to phone me if ....
36. If you had gone to bed earlier ....
37. Unless he switches off the radio ....
38. The flight is generally postponed ....
39. They generally play football if ....
40. People earn a lot of money if they ....
41. He could buy a new car if they ....
42. If I were the Prime Minister, I ....
43. If the car hadn't broken down, we ....
44. If the policeman hadn't shown me the way, I ....
45. He could have never won his case if his lawyer ....
46. If I worked hard ....

47. If a ghost came into the room. ....
48. .... I would have seen the Taj.
49. .... you should have passed the exam.
50. If I were rich ....
51. If you do not walk carefully ....
52. If you were to buy a car ....
53. Were they to arrive tomorrow ....
54. Had I known he would pass ....
55. Should you go past the college ....

Key to Exercise 6.1

1. do not work, will be
2. earn, will be able
3. have, will be able
4. worked, would pass
5. liked, would stay
6. wrote, would know
7. boil, starts
8. has gone, use
9. had, would go
10. were, would send
11. were, would not cry
12. were, would distribute
13. had had
14. would have bought
15. liked, would buy
16. saw, would scream
17. flowered, would be
18. had worked, would not have failed
19. had known, would have used
20. had known, would not have lost
21. drove, would meet
22. liked, would follow
23. had not liked, would have worn
24. knew, would come
25. had taught, would not have been
26. had been, would not have declined.

Key to Exercise 6.2

Note: Other alternatives are possible.

1. bring a pair of goggles for me
2. take a bus pass

3. I would chant “Hanuman Chalisa”
4. I would buy a car
5. If I taught well
6. If you kicked the dust
7. If he watered the plants
8. you would have been selected
9. If they had called him for the interview
10. switch off the lights
11. don’t forget to tell him that I still cherish him
12. he would have received it in time
13. God would reward you
14. all your sins would be over
15. if you happen to come this side next time
16. what would you do?
17. what would you do with the money
18. he would have behaved nicely
19. don’t catch it
20. don’t go out

Key to Exercise 6.3

1. Many people would have died of deadly diseases
2. you will be called anachronistic
3. he would buy a decent house in Mumbai
4. you don’t finish your courses in time
5. you should do it
6. he would not have broken his bones
7. you pour it on water
8. I would recognize him
9. he will regret it
10. I would have disinherited him
11. If you agree. ....
12. John would not have fallen in love with Catherine
13. I would buy a car
14. I won’t be able to go to Kolkata
15. you win a lottery
16. the boat will capsize
17. the traffic situation would have been much better
18. you will harm yourself
19. you accepted this job
20. I would not have drunk it
21. you will miss the train
22. you are in trouble
23. you goad him

24. I would not have felt tired
25. he would meet with an accident
26. dissolves
27. he wouldn't be sick
28. I will go abroad
29. you had put it in the fridge
30. you must give me a call
31. If you had not saved me
32. If you worked hard
33. you won a lottery
34. in time, I would be worried
35. he is in trouble
36. you would have woken up on time
37. I will not be able to concentrate
38. if visibility is low
39. the weather is fine
40. are hard working
41. had money
42. would introduce free education up to secondary schools
43. wouldn't have been late
44. would not have reached here
45. hadn't helped him
46. I would pass the exam
47. I would scream loudly
48. If I had gone to Agra
49. If you had really worked hard
50. I would distribute my wealth among the poor
51. you will fall
52. which brand would you buy?
53. we should be unprepared
54. I would not have snubbed him
55. give this message to the street vendor there

7

Indirect Speech

I ent have no gun, I ent have no knife, but mugging de queen's English is the story of my life, I don't need no axe to split up you syntax, I don't need no hammer to mash up you grammar.

—From Firdous Azim

Introduction

Reporting event is a very important activity and is needed in everyday life. If somebody steals your car, you would like to report the theft to the police. If you are Secretary of the College Union, you will have to record the minutes of the union meeting. There are a number of other occasions when you would like to report your experiences and the events of that place. In this chapter, we shall tell you how to report statements, questions, commands and requests.

Distinctions between Direct and Indirect Speech

If we reproduce the exact words of a particular person at a particular time and place, this would be an instance of direct speech. Conversely, if we paraphrase or state in our own words the speech of a person, in that adding nothing on our own, this would be an example of indirect speech. The conversion from direct speech into indirect speech involves changes in person, tense and adverbials of time and place and time of reporting. Consider the following sentences and study the changes that take place from direct to indirect speech (Table 7.1).

Reporting of Statements and Exclamations

Note the following points about the changes:

1. The reporting verb *say* changes to *tell*, *advise*, *recommend*, *believe*, *feel*, *know*, *admit*, *agree*, *announce*, *argue*, *assume*, *claim*, *complain*, *confess*, *decide*, *declare*, *deny*, *disagree*, *exclaim*, *inform*, *mention*,

TABLE 7.1 Changes from direct into indirect speech

Direct speech	*Indirect speech*	*Change from direct to indirect speech*
Mohan said to Sohan, "I'll get a house constructed next year."	Mohan *told* Sohan *that* he'd get a house constructed the following year.	There is a change in the reporting verb, *say* becomes *tell*. There is a change in the pronoun. *I* has become *he*. There is a change in the tense. If the reporting verb is in the past tense, *will* changes to *would*. There is a change in the time adverbial, *next year* becomes the *following year*. The connecting word used is *that*.
He said to me, "you should see the doctor."	He *advised me* to see the doctor.	The reporting verb *say* changes to *advise*. The pronoun *you* changes to *me*. The reported speech is the paraphrase of the direct of speech.

promise, *remember*, *report*, *remind*, *state*, *suggest*, etc. depending on the kind of speech act involved in the reported speech. Look at some more examples:

(i) Mohan said to me, "I need Karunakaran."
Mohan **told** me that he needed Karunakaran.

(ii) The boy said, "I have copied in the exam."
The boy **confessed** that he had copied in the exam.

(iii) The accused said, "I deny the charge."
The accused **denied** the charge.

(iv) My dad said to me, "I'll get you a camera."
My dad **promised** that he would get me a camera.

(v) He said, "I am rich."
He **claimed** that he is rich.

2. The connecting word used in *statements* is *that*. The reporting of an exclamatory sentence is just like reporting a statement with an added feeling of joy, surprise, sorrow, etc. This added feeling is expressed by the reporting verbs such as *exclaim with joy*, *exclaim with sorrow*, *realize*, *notice*, *see*, *remember*, *understand*, etc. The connecting word used is *that* or *how/what*. Look at the following sentences:

(i) She said, "What a bore he is."
She **realized what** a bore he was.
She **realized that** he was a great bore.

(ii) The maid servant said, "How hot it is."
The maid servant **noticed how** hot it was.
The maid servant **noticed that** it was very hot.

(iii) He said, "Alas! his father is dead."
He **exclaimed with sorrow that** his father was dead.

(iv) He said, "Hurrah! We have won the match."
He **exclaimed with joy that** they had won the match.

3. *Change in pronoun:* The changes in pronoun depend upon the reporter and the person he is reporting to. Look at the following sentences:

(i) Mohan said to Lata, "I can speak English very well."
Imagine that Mohan is the reporter and he is reporting this to some other person than Lata. This is how he will report.
I told Lata that **I could** speak English very well.
Now imagine that Lata is the reporter and she is reporting Mohan's statement to Mohan himself. The report will be:
You told me that **you** could speak English very well.
Now suppose that Lata is the reporter and she is reporting Mohan's statement to someone else. She will report like this:
Mohan told me that **he** could speak English very well.
The rule of the thumb is:

- Change the first person according to the subject of the reporting verb.
- Change the second person according to the object of the reporting verb.
- The third person does not change.

4. *Tense changes in reported speech:* When we report a statement or an exclamatory sentence, one other change that we have to make is in the tense form. If the reporting verb is in the past tense in the direct speech, it changes to the corresponding past tense in the reported speech. Consider the following examples:

(i) Kalpana said, "I **will study** Physics at MREC next year."
Kalpana *said* that she would study Physics at MREC the following year.

(ii) Kalpana **said**, "I **am taking** the interview next week.
past tense present continuous
Kalpana **said** that she **was taking** the interview the following week.
past tense past continuous

The rules for the modification in the indirect speech are given in Table 7.2.

TABLE 7.2 Modification of tense

Tense in the direct speech	*Tense in the reported speech*
Simple present (write)	Simple past (wrote)
Present continuous (is writing)	Past continuous (was writing)
Present perfect (has/have written)	Past perfect (had written)
Present perfect continuous (has/have been writing)	Past perfect continuous (had been writing)
Simple past (wrote)	Past perfect (had written)
Past continuous (was writing)	Past perfect continuous (had been writing)
Can, shall, will, may, must	Could, should, would, might, must/had to

5. *Adverbial and other changes in the reported speech:* If the time reference is different in indirect speech from the time reference of the utterance, the reporter has to make adjustment in the adverbials. Consider the following sentences:

   (i) She said, "I'll see you **tomorrow**." (July 1)
   She said that she would see me **tomorrow**.
   (if reported on July 1)
   She said that she would see me **the next day**.
   (if reported on July 3 or later)

   Further, adverbial of place and demonstratives also change.

   (ii) She said, "I'll see you **here**."
   She said that she would see me **here**.
   (if reported at the same place)
   She said that she'd see me **there**.
   (if reported at a different place)

   The change in the demonstratives depends upon the situation. Look at the following sentences:

   (iii) She said, "**This** is my house."
   She said that **this** is his house.
   (if reported near the house)
   She said that **that** is his house.
   (if reported away from the house)

Table 7.3 illustrates the changes.

TABLE 7.3 Changes in adverbials

today	that day
yesterday	the previous day
tomorrow	the next day
next week	the following week
now	then
ago	before
here	there
this	that
these	those
come	go

EXERCISE 7.1

Change the following into indirect speech:

1. Ram said to Mohan, "I will visit the Hanging Gardens in Mumbai."
2. Ram said to Mohan, "He will go to the Zoological Park."
3. Ram said to Mohan, "When in Mumbai, he stayed at the Taj Mahal Hotel for two days."
4. Ram said to Mohan, "When in Mumbai he spent five hours on the Juhu Beach."
5. Ram said to Mohan, "I will visit the Red Fort in Delhi on 15 August."
6. Ram said to Mohan, "I cannot live without you."
7. Ram said to Mohan, "I'm glad I came to Delhi University."
8. Ram said to Mohan, "I find all the professors quite learned here."
9. Ram said to Mohan, "There are a number of good labs here."
10. Ram said to Mohan, "I find myself very busy here."
11. Ram said to Mohan, "The students here are from all over India."
12. Ram said to Mohan, "You will get a job here after completing the Ph.D."
13. Ram said to Mohan, "I will take five years in completing my Ph.D."
14. Ram said to Mohan, "I am having problems with my studies."
15. Ram said to Mohan, "He will pass the exam in first division."
16. The captain said to the team, "Alas! We have lost the match."
17. The teacher said to the students, "Two and two make four."
18. The teacher said to the students, "The sun sets in the west."
19. Ram said to Mohan, "I can't lend you ₹ 2000."
20. Ram said to Mohan, "You are always late in the class."

EXERCISE 7.2

Assuming that the reporting verb is in the past tense, supply the correct form of the expression in column II for the expression given in column I.

	I	II
1.	simple present	
2.	present continuous	
3.	simple past	
4.	present perfect	
5.	past continuous	
6.	shall	
7.	can	
8.	will	
9.	may	
10.	must	
11.	today	
12.	yesterday	

Reporting of Questions and Imperatives

Look at Table 7.4.

TABLE 7.4 Reporting of questions and imperatives

Questions	*Reporting of the questions*
What is your name?	Ram *asked* Mohan *what his name was.*
Where are you from?	Ram *asked* Mohan *where he was from.*
Why did you come here?	Ram *asked* Mohan *why he had come here.*
Are you married?	Ram *asked* Mohan *if/whether he was married.*

The rules are as follows:

1. The reporting verb used is *ask*, *enquire of*, and *demand*.
2. The connecting word used in wh-questions is the question word itself and in yes-no questions, it is *if* or *whether*.
3. The word order of the question formation is undone. The word order becomes like that of a statement.
4. The question mark is replaced by a full stop.
5. The changes in *pronoun*, *tense*, *adverbials* are like the changes in statements.

Reporting of Orders and Requests

Look at Table 7.5.

TABLE 7.5 Reporting of orders and requests

Commands/requests	*Reporting of commands/requests*
'Get out of here,' he said.	He *told me* to get out of there.
'Have another cup of coffee,' said Radha.	Radha *asked me* to have *another cup of coffee.*
'Please shut the door,' he said.	He *requested me to shut* the door.
'Don't make a noise,' the teacher said.	The teacher *told the class not* to make a noise. or The teacher *forbade* the class to make a noise.

The rules are as follows:

1. Orders are reported with *tell* + *object* + to infinitive.
2. Requests are reported with *request* + *object* + to infinitive.
3. The connecting word used is *to-infinitive.*
4. The changes in pronouns and adverbials are the same as in statements.
5. Advice is reported with *advise* + object + to infinitive.

EXERCISE 7.3

Sita's mother is suffering from hyper-tension and diabetes. She goes to a doctor for consultation. The doctor advises her to do and not to do certain things. Here is a list of those things. Report what the doctor told Sita's mother. Begin with 'The doctor advised her to … or the doctor advised her not to …

1. Take the prescribed medicine every day.
2. Don't eat salt.
3. Don't eat sugar, potatoes and rice.
4. Don't eat bananas, *cheeku* and grapes.
5. Go for a walk both in the morning and in the evening.
6. Don't overeat.
7. Take your meals four times a day.
8. Reduce the quantity of food intake.
9. Eat a lot of salads.
10. Stop worrying.
11. Take regular exercise.
12. Do meditation and *pranayam.*
13. Do *yoga* for half an hour every day.

14. Reduce your weight.
15. Get lipid profile done.
16. Get the blood sugar test done.
17. Try to be happy.
18. Develop positive thinking.
19. Be hopeful and optimistic.
20. Banish negative thoughts from your mind.

EXERCISE 7.4

Integrated exercise on indirect speech.
Change the following sentences into indirect speech:

1. He said, "I am trying to write a book on civilization."
2. She said, "We should now have foremothers instead of forefathers."
3. The teacher said, "A convex mirror produces a virtual and erect image."
4. The others said, "Please, have patience."
5. She said, "Why do you think Mr. Trent has stolen your picture?"
6. John said, "Is there anything I can do for you, Joan?"
7. The Prince said, "Tell her I don't want any milk."
8. The teacher said, "Pi is the ratio of the circumference of a circle to its diameter."
9. Lucy said, "I don't think that they are at all civilized."
10. He said, "This is all I have."
11. The speaker said, "Two wrongs do not make a right."
12. Father said, "Why are you under your bed instead of on it."
13. He said, "Are they just going to repeat what they said today?"
14. He said, "Solar eclipse occurs when the moon comes between the sun and the earth.
15. Peter said, " Your mother will be terribly worried, Aurthur."
16. Paul said, "Why aren't you taking your exams, Bill?"
17. Tom said, "Let's put the tape recorder under the table and record the conversation."
18. I said, "It is ridiculous to take three suitcases for a weekend."
19. "What did you miss most when you were in London?" Sheela asked Meeta.
20. He said, "Columbus discovered America and Vasco da-Gama discovered India."
21. James said, "Are you interested in sound and light show?"
22. She said, "Sweep up that broken glass."
23. He said, " My wife has gone out."
24. "Are you free tomorrow," she said to me.
25. "All the noble gases are inert," said the teacher.
26. He said, "Why did they suspend Bill?"

27. "Who has been using my typewriter?" said my mother.
28. "Let us put your tape recorder under the table," said Tom, "and make a recording."
29. "I have made a terrible mistake!" said Ram.
30. "Would you mind getting out of the car?" said the driver, "I have to change a wheel."
31. "I'm going out now, but I will be in by nine," he said.
32. "Don't put sticky things in your pockets," said his mother.
33. He said, "Will there be a general strike of the coal miners from tomorrow?"
34. "Please buy a few books on teaching English as a foreign language," he said to her.
35. She said, "They were playing tennis when I saw them."
36. She said, "We were thinking to sell this house but now we have decided not to."
37. The manager said, "Which person are your referring to?"
38. She said to me, "Is that girl in the corner your wife?"
39. He said, "Can you meet me tomorrow?"
40. She said, "I will never forgive him for his outrageous behaviour."
41. The servant said to the master, "Please don't take me to the police station."
42. Raju said, "I tried to contact you yesterday but I could not succeed, Ramesh."
43. Ram said, "I will marry an army officer if I am given a choice."
44. He said, "I worked in a factory for two years and my employers considered me to be very efficient."
45. The teacher said, "Do your work with dedication."
46. She said, "I am proud of you, my son."
47. The Principal said to the Manager, "The growing indiscipline in the college is a matter of great concern."
48. The management said to the undisciplined students, "Mend your ways or leave college."
49. The erring students said to the Management, "We shall never repeat the mistake."
50. The Management said to the Principal, "Let us wait and watch."
51. One student said to the other, "Do you think that they will honour their promise."
52. "Don't use bent coins in a stop machine," I warned him.
53. "What is your father?" he asked.
54. I said to him, "Shall we meet at the theatre?"
55. Ram said to Mohan, "I don't know what Shyam is doing."
56. "Ugh!" She exclaimed and turned the programme off.

(*Hint to the students:* You will notice that in the tests generally each type of indirect speech is asked, i.e. there are two statements, two questions and one imperative sentence. Sometimes there is an exclamation or a *let-type* sentence.)

For doing let-type sentences, pay attention to the following rules:

1. Use *suggest* or *propose* as a reporting verb.
2. Use *that* as a connective.
3. Use should + first form after the subject in the that clause. For example, sentence (28) is done for you:

Tom suggested to Bill that they should put the tape recorder under the table and make a recording.

Key to Exercise 7.1

1. Ram told Mohan that he would visit the Hanging Gardens in Mumbai.
2. Ram told Mohan that he would go to the Zoological Park.
3. Ram told Mohan that when in Mumbai, he had stayed at the Taj Mahal Hotel for two days.
4. Ram told Mohan that when in Mumbai, he had spent five hours on the Juhu Beach.
5. Ram told Mohan that he would visit the Red Fort in Delhi on 15 August.
6. Ram told Mohan that he could not live without him.
7. Ram told Mohan that he was glad he had come to Delhi University.
8. Ram told Mohan that he found all the professors quite learned there.
9. Ram told Mohan that there were a number of good labs there.
10. Ram told Mohan that he found himself very busy there.
11. Ram told Mohan that the students were there from all over India.
12. Ram told Mohan that he would get a job there after completing the Ph.D.
13. Ram told Mohan that he would take five years in completing his Ph.D.
14. Ram told Mohan that he was having problems with his studies.
15. Ram told Mohan that he would pass the exam in first division.
16. The captain exclaimed with sorrow and told the team that they had lost the match.
17. The teacher told the students that two and two make four.
18. The teacher told the students that the sun sets in the west.
19. Ram told Mohan that he could not lend him ₹ 2000.
20. Ram told Mohan that he is always late in the class.

Key to Exercise 7.2

1. simple past
2. past continuous
3. past perfect
4. past perfect
5. past perfect continuous
6. should
7. could
8. would
9. might
10. must
11. that day
12. the previous day

Key to Exercise 7.3

1. The doctor advised her to take the prescribed medicine every day.
2. The doctor advised her not to eat salt.
3. The doctor advised her not to eat sugar, potatoes and rice.
4. The doctor told her not to eat bananas, *cheeku* and grapes.
5. The doctor asked her to go for a walk both in the morning and in the evening.
6. The doctor forbade her to overeat.
7. The doctor advised her to take her meals four times a day.
8. The doctor told her to reduce the quantity of food intake.
9. The doctor asked her to eat a lot of salads.
10. The doctor asked her to stop worrying.
11. The doctor asked her to take regular exercise.
12. The doctor advised her to do meditation and *pranayam*.
13. The doctor told her to do *yoga* for half an hour every day
14. The doctor advised her to reduce her weight.
15. The doctor asked her to get lipid profile done.
16. The doctor asked her to get the blood sugar test done.
17. The doctor asked her to try to be happy.
18. The doctor told her to develop positive thinking.
19. The doctor asked her to be hopeful and optimistic.
20. The doctor told her to banish negative thoughts from her mind.

Key to Exercise 7.4

1. He said that he was trying to write a book on civilization.
2. She said that they/we should now/have foremothers instead of forefathers.
3. The teacher told us that a convex mirror produces a virtual and erect image.
4. The others requested us to have patience.
5. She asked me why I thought Mr. Trent had stolen my picture.
6. John asked Joan if there anything he could do for her.
7. The Prince told me to tell her that he didn't want any milk.
8. The teacher told the class that Pi is the ratio of the circumference of a circle to its diameter.

9. Lucy said that she didn't think that they were at all civilized.
10. He said that that was all he had.
11. The speaker said that two wrongs do not make a right.
12. Father asked Mohan why he was under his bed instead of being on it.
13. He asked me whether they were just going to repeat what they had said that day.
14. He said that the solar eclipse occurs when the moon comes between the sun and the earth.
15. Peter told Aurther that his mother would be terribly worried.
16. Paul asked Bill why he was not taking his exams.
17. Tom suggested to Aurther that they should put the tape recorder under the table and record the conversation.
18. I said that it was ridiculous to take three suitcases for a weekend.
19. Sheela asked Meeta what she had missed when she had been in London.
20. He said that Columbus discovered America and Vasco da-Gama discovered India.
21. James asked Joan if he was interested in sound and light show.
22. She told him to sweep up that broken glass.
23. He said that his wife had gone out.
24. She asked me if I was free the next day.
25. The teacher said that all the noble gases are inert.
26. He asked me why they had suspended Bill.
27. My mother asked me who had been using my typewriter.
28. Tom suggested to me that they should put his tape recorder under the table and make a recording.
29. Ram said that he had made a terrible mistake.
30. The driver asked me whether I would mind getting out of the car as he had to change a wheel.
31. He said that he was going out now, but he would be back by nine.
32. His mother asked him not to put sticky things in his pockets.
33. He asked me whether there would be general strike of the coal-miners from the next day.
34. He requested her to buy a few books on teaching English as a foreign language.
35. She said that they had been playing tennis when she had seen them.
36. She said that they had been thinking of selling that house but then they had decided not to.
37. The manager asked me which person I was referring to.
38. She asked me if that girl in the corner was my wife.
39. He asked me if I could meet him the next day.
40. She said that she would never forgive him for his outrageous behaviour.
41. The servant requested the master not to take him to the police station.
42. Raju told Ramesh that he had tried to contact him the previous day but he could not succeed.

43. Ram said that he would marry an army officer if he was given a choice.
44. He said that he had worked in a factory for two years and his employers had considered him to be very efficient.
45. The teacher advised the students to do their work with dedication.
46. She told her son that she was proud of him.
47. The Principal told the Manager that the growing indiscipline in the college was a matter of great concern.
48. The management asked the undisciplined students to mend their ways or leave college.
49. The erring students promised to the Management that they would never repeat the mistake.
50. The Management suggested to the Principal that they should wait and watch.
51. One student asked the other whether he thought that they would honour their promise.
52. I warned him not to use bent coins in a stop machine.
53. He asked me what my father was.
54. I asked him if they should meet at the theatre.
55. Ram told Mohan that he did not know what Shyam was doing.
56. She had expressed her disgust and turned the programme off.

8

The Uses of Articles

Introduction

Articles belong to the class of determiners; other determiners being possessives, demonstratives and quantifiers. The use of articles depends upon the kind of nouns they precede. There are two kinds of nouns in English—countable and uncountable. Countable nouns refer to objects, people, ideas that can be counted. Countable nouns have plurals whereas uncountable nouns refer to unindividuated mass, material and quality. Mostly abstract and material nouns are uncountable. Below is given a short list of countable and uncountable nouns (Table 8.1).

TABLE 8.1 Countable and uncountable nouns

Countable nouns	*Uncountable nouns*
boy, girl, table, chair, fan, bucket, pen, pencil, cup, teacher, doctor, architect, engineer, book, leaflet, clerk, window, gate, door, blackboard, spoon, kettle, pan, etc.	accommodation, advice, applause, assistance, baggage, camping, cash, chaos, chess, clothing, conduct, courage, cutlery, dancing, dirt, employment, equipment, evidence, fun, furniture, harm, health, music, news, etc.

Relationship between the Types of Nouns and Articles

There are three articles in English: *a*, *an* and *the*. Some grammarians consider *some* and *zero* also as articles.

a is used before singular, countable, and unidentified nouns, beginning with consonant sounds whereas **an** is used before singular, countable and unidentified nouns beginning with vowel sounds (Table 8.2).

TABLE 8.2 Examples of the use of indefinite article

a	*an*
a university	an orange
a European	an Italian
a one parent family	an umbrella
a NATO general	an hour
a FIFA official	an honest child
a pen	an heir
a pencil	an MP
a dog	an FBI agent
a cat	an IOU
a chair	an elephant
a book	an inkpot
	an ass
a is pronounced as /ə/	an is pronounced as /ən/

Uncountable nouns refer to unindividuated mass. They are preceded by *zero*, *some* or *the* but not *a* or *an* unless the noun under discussion is re-categorized as a countable noun. Similarly, a countable noun is also re-categorized as uncountable. That is to say, there are countable and uncountable uses of nouns. Let us consider the following examples (Table 8.3).

TABLE 8.3 Countable and uncountable uses of nouns

Uncountable use	*Countable use*
I prefer tea to coffee.	Give me three *teas* please. (cups of tea)
There's *cheese* in the fridge.	There are dozens of *cheeses* (= kind of cheese) to choose from.
She has brown *hair*.	There's a *hair* in my soup. (= example of a concrete thing)
The statue was made of *stone*.	I had *a stone* in my shoe. (a particular instance)

There is a very interesting example of a countable noun being used as uncountable.

There is *egg* on your chin (refers to the substance of the egg).

Then there are nouns that can be used as both countable and uncountable nouns.

(i) She lives in **luxury.**
(u)

(ii) A refrigerator is **a luxury.**
(c)

(iii) **Man** (mankind) is mortal.
(u)

(iv) Ram is a **man.**
(c)

Uses of the Indefinite Articles

A and *an* are called **indefinite articles** because they precede the nouns whose reference is not known to the listener, whereas *the* is a definite article because the noun referred to is known both to the speaker and to the listener. Below are given some important uses of the indefinite articles.

Classifying and Describing Function of *a* and *an*

A class-membership or type token relationship is created with the use of *a* or *an*. Look at the following examples:

(i) She is **a nurse**.
(ii) Ram is **a doctor**.
(iii) That's **a blackbird**.
(iv) That's **a pen**.

Here in sentence (i), *a nurse* refers to a member of the class of nurses; sentence (ii) refers to a member of the class of doctors, and so on and so forth.

A and *an* are also used to describe a noun pharse:

(i) Mumbai is **a beautiful city**.
(ii) English is **an international language**.

Here sentences (i) and (ii) state what type of something is.

Other Uses of *a* and *an*

Here are some other uses of the indefinite articles.

1. *a*(*n*) is a shortened form of *one*. In some of its uses, it still retains the meaning of *one* though *one* is considered to be more emphatic:

   (i) He was in India for a (one) year.
   (ii) Wait here for a (one) minute.
   (iii) She scored a (one) hundred and eighty points.

2. Here only *one* is used, not *a*(*n*):

   (i) Do you want **one** apple or two?
   (ii) Are you staying just **one** night?
   (iii) Close **one** eye, and then **the other**.
   (iv) **One** day, **one** evening, **one** summer, etc.

3. Only *a*(*n*) is used, not *one:*

   (i) I really need **a** cup of tea (anyone of a particular type of thing).
   (ii) Three times **a** year.
   (iii) half **an** hour
   (iv) **a** quarter of **an hour**

(v) **a day** or so
(vi) **a** week or two
(vii) 50 rupees **a** liter
(viii) **a few, a little**
(ix) **a huge number of, a lot of**
(x) **a** colleague of mine
(xi) **a** friend of Ram's

4. *a*(*n*) is used for non-specific things. Here, it has the meaning of *any:*
   (i) I need **a stamp** for this letter.
   (ii) I want **a pen.**

5. *a*(*n*) is also used for specific but indefinite (i.e. not mentioned before) objects:
   (i) There is **a stamp** in the drawer.
   (ii) I want to marry **an American**.
   (iii) I saw **a Korean.**

6. *a*(*n*) is also used for making generalization:
   (i) **A stamp** often tells a story.
   (ii) **A corkscrew** is a gadget for getting corks out of bottles. (Notice to define something, we use *a*/*an* rather than *the.*)
   (iii) **An oar** is a thing you row a boat with.

7. For referring to a particular instance of something, we use *a* or *an:*
   (i) She plays tennis well but she will never be **a** Martina Navratilova. (has the particular excellent qualities of the famous tennis star.)
   (ii) There is **a Dr. Gupta** on the phone. (I haven't heard of him before.)
   (iii) There is **a cold wind** blowing from the north.
   (iv) She dreamt of **a future** (a particular instance) where she could spend more time for painting.

Uses of the Definite Article

The is used before nouns that are singular or plural or uncountable and *they* have been identified in some way. There are different ways of identifying a noun.

1. Anaphoric (backward) reference: If a noun is mentioned the second time, *the* is used before it because it can be identified by both the speaker and the listener.
   (i) I saw a **tiger**. **The tiger** was ferocious.
   (ii) The police questioned **a man** about the incident. **The man** was arrested when he arrived at the airport.

(iii) We hired **a car** to go to Delhi. **The car** broke on the way.
(iv) She's got two children: **a boy** and **a girl**. **The boy** is fourteen and **the girl** is eight.
(v) Sita took **a cake** and **an apple pie** to the party but only **the apple pie** was eaten.
(vi) There was a serious fire in **a block of flats** in Jaipur last night. **The building** was totally destroyed.
(vii) We had a good time on holiday. **The hotel** was comfortable and **the beach** was only 10 minutes away.

2. Cataphoric (forward) reference: *The* is used before those nouns that are specified or identified by a following phrase or clause.

(i) Ours is **the house on the corner.**
(ii) **The book yellow with age.**
(iii) **The boy who came her yesterday** is my brother.
(iv) We came to **the edge of a lake.**
(v) **The roof of a house** was blown off in the storm.
(vi) **The water of this well** is tasty.
(vii) He is reading **the plays of Shakespeare.**

3. Homophoric (situational) reference: A situation makes a noun unique and requires the use of *the* before the noun. Situations can be of three types as shown in Figure 8.1.

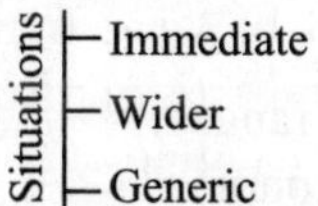

FIGURE 8.1 Situations.

Immediate situation: It refers to the situation which is within the experiential range of the interlocutors. Notice the following sentences:

(i) Close **the window**. (The listener knows which *window* the speaker is referring to. Maybe, there is only one window in the room.)
(ii) Clean **the blackboard**. (There is only one blackboard in the classroom.)
(iii) Pass **the sugar**, please.
(iv) **The bus is coming**. (It's the bus we are waiting for.)
(v) **The Japanese** student had to go home. (The Japanese student we have previously talked about.)

(vi) What do you think of **the table**. (The table we are looking at.)
(vii) What's in **the curry**? (The curry in my plate)

Wider situation: Such situations include all the situations which are away from the immediate situations of the interlocutors and which are the part of their general knowledge. Examples:

- the English Channel
- the Prime Minister (there is only one)
- the President
- the sun
- the moon
- the tallest building (with superlative degree)
- the French (people)
- the poor/rich (people)
- the Russians (nationalities)
- the Times of India
- the North Pole
- the late Stephen King
- the artist William Turner
- the wonderful actor Harrison Ford, the Robinsons (the Robinson family)

Note: With winter, summer, spring, autumn and new year, we can use either *the* or *zero* article.

- the morning
- the evening
- in the afternoon
(but compare *at night*, *at midday*, *at midnight*).

The following place names attract *the* before them:

- the Atlantic (seas)
- the Himalayas (mountain ranges)
- the West Indies (island groups)
- the Rhine (rivers)
- the Sahara (deserts)
- the Grand Hotel (most hotels)
- the Odeon: the playhouse (most cinemas and theatres)
- the British Museum (museums)

We usually use no article with: continents, countries, states, departments, etc. (Africa, Brazil, Texas)

- Oxford (towns)
- New Street (streets)
- Lake Michigan (lakes)

but:

- the People's Republic of China
- the United Kingdom
- the United States
- the Netherlands
- the Hague

also:

- Oxford University (without *the*), British Zoo, Delhi City Council.

Generic situation: Where a noun refers to the whole class, there are three ways of expressing it:

(i) **Camels** can close their noses.
(ii) **A camel** can close its nose.
(iii) **The camel** can close its nose.
(iv) **Life** is complicated (zero article).

Notice in all these sentences, the bold noun phrase refers to the whole class or genus of camels

For making generalizations, the most preferred way is to use plural nouns in case of countable nouns and zero article in case of uncountable nouns. Notice:

(i) Railway platforms are horrible places.
(ii) Time waits for no one.
(iii) People expect good behaviour.

Other examples with *the* are:

(i) Nobody has an idea who invented **the wheel**.
(ii) Can you play **the guitar**?

We use *the* before the musical instruments such as *the piano*, *the word processor*, etc. Note nouns related to games and sports are uncountable; so they carry *zero* articles in the generic sense:

He plays tennis/chess.

Notice further that *the* is used in a general sense for *some institutions*, means of transport and communication and with some jobs:

(i) There has been a revival of **the cinema**.
(ii) I go to work on **the bus**.
(iii) Your cheque is **in the post**.
(iv) Ram will go to **the dentist** tomorrow.

Other nouns that take *the* in this way are the countryside, the establishment, the doctor, the media, the newspaper, the police, the press, the sea-side, the working class, etc.

But *television* and *radio* as an institution do not take any article.

He is watching TV.

While talking about parts of the body, use of *the* is preferred.

(i) He hit her **in the stomach**.
(ii) Can you look me **in the eye**.
(iii) She was shot **in the leg**.
(iv) He's broad across **the shoulders**.

For measuring expressions beginning with *by*, we use *the*.

(i) by the kilo or by the dozen
(ii) by the liter
(iii) by the hour
(iv) by the month

Uses of Zero Article and Some

Zero article and *some* are used with uncountable nouns. *Some* is used in affirmative sentences and questions with plural and uncountable nouns when we talk about *limited* but indefinite or unknown numbers or quantities of things:

(i) **Some furniture** arrived for me this morning.
(ii) There is **some good news** for you.

Some is also used for particular but unspecified people or things:

(i) **Some** students never get bored in the classroom.
(ii) I enjoy **some** classic music.

Some is used before a number denoting *approximately*.

There were **some** 20,000 people in the stadium (= approximately 20,000).

Here *some* is pronounced as /s∧m/.

Some can also be used with a singular noun if we want to emphasize that we do not really remember which person or thing we are talking about.

I was asked a really difficult question by **some student** in class four.

Below we discuss the uses of zero article.

1. Zero article used for making *generalizations* with uncountable and plural nouns:

(i) She always likes to get **good news**. (= good news in general)
(ii) **Furniture** is expensive these days. (furniture in general)
(iii) **Students** like having long holidays. (= all students)
(iv) I enjoy **classical music**. (classical music in general)
(v) **Sugar** is bad for teeth. (sweet in general).

2. Zero article is used for institutions such as *hospital*, *university*, *prison*, *school*, *college*, or *church* when they are used for the intended purpose, i.e. medical treatment in hospital, studying in college or university, and so on. We also talk about *bed* in the same way. When these nouns are used for particular places or buildings, they are preceded by articles. Notice the following expressions:

   to school, at school, in school (US)
   from school
   to/in/from college (US) — I met her at college.
   to/at/from college (BE) — cf. I'll meet you at the college (= building)
   to church
   in bed
   in hospital
   at work
   at sea
   from town
   from home
   leave home
   by day
   by night
   by bus/car/plane/train/boat
   on foot
   by radio/phone/letter/mail

3. Double expressions are often used with zero article.

   with knife and fork
   on land and sea
   day after day
   with hat and coat
   arm in arm
   bread and butter
   ice cream and cake
   husband and wife
   from top to bottom
   inch by inch
   man and woman were created equal.

4. Zero article is preferred after *kind of*, *sort of*, *type of* and similar expressions.

   What **kind of** (a) person is she? Have you **got a cheaper** sort of tape recorder? They have developed a **new variety** of sheep.

5. Zero article is used with the names of days, months, seasons, illnesses unless they refer to particular instances.
   (i) See you next **Monday**.
   (ii) See you in **April**.
   (iii) Rome is lovely in **spring**.
   (iv) He is suffering form **measles/appendicitis/toothache** (but *a cold*, *a headache* are acceptable.)
   (v) By midnight, midday, noon

6. Zero article is generally used for meals.

   What shall we have for **dinner**?
   When do you have **breakfast**.
   He doesn't have **lunch**.

7. Zero article is used before the names of particular persons:

   President Kalam
   The name of Gandhi.

8. We use zero article in abbreviated styles:

Newspaper headlines, Headings	Man Killed in Hotel
	Introduction
	Chapter 3
	Section A
Picture captions	Father and Child
Notices, poster, etc.	Super Opera, Ashoka Hotel
Instructions	Open packet at other end
Numbering and labeling	Control to car 30, can you hear me?
Turn to page 230.	

Conclusion

In this chapter, we discussed the uses of *a*, *an*, *the*, *zero* and *some*. We gave their rules in detail. What we said in the chapter was that *a* or *an* has predominantly a classifying function whereas *the* has an identifying function. This identification takes place through various reference devices of anaphoricity, cataphoricity and homophoricity. We also discussed the use of *some* with uncountable and countable plural nouns where they refer to the limited quantity of a thing. Zero article seems to have a number of interesting uses. We shall be doing an exercise before we go to the next chapter.

EXERCISE 8.1

Insert articles in the blanks if necessary.

1. .... horse is a faithful animal.
2. .... dogs are faithful animals.
3. .... dog is more faithful than .... cat.
4. .... radio has changed our way of life.
5. .... radios have changed our way of life.
6. .... student should attend classes.
7. .... students should attend classes.
8. I bought .... new radio.
9. I bought .... cat last week and .... cat died after a few days.
10. I' ll be there for .... hour or two.
11. Ram paid .... hundred rupees for his pen.
12. Ram goes to his village twice .... week.
13. You look sick. You ought to see .... doctor.
14. Mr. Sharma is .... principal of .... college.
15. He turned .... traitor.
16. I have got .... cold and .... toothache.
17. He is not .... Shakespeare.
18. There is .... Dr. Menon to see you.
19. Goa is .... paradise for all hippies.
20. Money can buy .... life of ease.
21. .... knowledge of Hindi is essential for all of us.
22. I sold it at .... profit.
23. He was in .... great hurry.
24. She is .... most beautiful woman.
25. He is as stupid as .... ass.
26. I have never met so sensible .... person as he.
27. How brilliant .... idea!
28. Mr. Sharma is .... Marxist first .... historian second.
29. He is .... fool enough to believe everything they say.
30. .... fool that he was, no one could convince him.
31. This house is made of .... stone.
32. He entered .... store.
33. .... fire is .... great destroyer.
34. We lit .... fire.
35. .... man is the highest form of creation.
36. Please open .... door.
37. .... dog entered my bedroom .... dog saw .... cat .... cat was sitting on .... table.
38. .... boy who is sitting near .... gate is my brother.

39. .... rich should not hate .... poor.
40. He is .... best athlete in .... college.
41. He came on .... Monday.
    .... following day he went to .... movie.
42. .... majority of .... students in this class passed .... examinations.
43. He is .... cleverer of .... two.
44. .... sooner you finish it, ... better it is.
45. He played .... lover.
46. What is .... matter?
47. There is .... American in my class.
48. .... British are very conservative.
49. He is studying .... English language.
50. He is .... Kalidas of our time.
51. .... milk is good for health.
52. I don't think .... father has come home yet.
53. He goes to .... college every day at 10 O' clock.

EXERCISE 8.2

Rewrite the following passages by inserting articles where necessary.

Gramophone

It is device for recording and reproducing sound and music. It has disc on which sound record is cut in form of special groove. It is mounted on rotating spindle for reproduction of recorded sound. Reproducer consists of sensitive diaphragm and needle, which is attached to moving tabular arm. Steel needle runs in wavy groove corresponding to original sound vibrations. These movements are communicated to diaphragm, which in turn produces original sound. These days, however, diaphragm is being replaced by electromagnetic system of reproduction with valve implication.

EXERCISE 8.3

Leonardo da Vinci's last supper is masterpiece of monumental composition. Group is located in rather tight space; mighty figures crowd around table; if they were to stand up there would not be enough for them. This illustrates for first time one of principles of classic composition: super proportions of figures in relation to space. Correct perspective of setting is still maintained; apparent continuation of refractory required clearly comprehensible and unambiguous space construction. This is achieved by use of apparently simple but expert demarcations of coffered ceiling, tapestry – hung walls and background windows. Within this space than there actually is. This space creating force which pervades their movements is one of secret causes of monumental effect of picture. We shall see how far Leanardo himself developed this principle of "Super dimensions" in his subsequent compositions, the St. Anne and Battle of Anghiari. Through Leonardo, it became from then on, formal principle of classic High Renaissance style; Raphael makes use of it; as well as Michelangelo, who in his Sistine ceiling develops conscious imprisonment of colossal forms in tight space ad extremism. (from Ludwig H. *Heydenreich: Leanardo da Vinci*).

Key to Exercise 8.1

1. a or the	2. φ	3. a, a
4. the	5. φ	6. a
7. φ	8. a	9. a, the
10. an	11. a	12. a
13. a	14. φ	15. φ
16. a, φ	17. a	18. a
19. a	20. a	21. a
22. a	23. a	24. a
25. an	26. a	27. an
28. φ φ	29. a	30. φ
31. φ	32. a	33. φ, a
34. a	35. φ	36. the
37. a, the, a, the, a	38. the, the	39. the, the
40. the, the	41. φ, the, a	42. the, the, the
43. the, the	44. the, the	45. the
46. the	47. an	48. the
49. the	50. the	51. φ
52. φ	53. φ	

Key to Exercise 8.2

It is *a* device for recording and reproducing sound and music. It has *a* disc on which sound record is cut in *the* form of *a* special groove. It is mounted on *a* rotating spindle for *the* reproduction of recorded sound. *The r*eproducer consists of *a* sensitive diaphragm and *a* needle, which is attached to *a* moving tabular arm. *The s*teel needle runs in *the* wavy groove corresponding to *the* original sound vibrations. These movements are communicated to *the* diaphragm which in turn produces original sound. These days, however, diaphragm is being replaced by electromagnetic system of reproduction with valve implication.

Key to Exercise 8.3

Leonardo da Vinci's last supper is *a* masterpiece of monumental composition. *The* group is located in *a* rather tight space; mighty figures crowd around *the* table; if they were to stand up there would not be enough for them. This illustrates for *the* first time one of *the* principles of *the* classic composition: *the* super proportions of *the* figures in relation to space. *The* correct perspective of *the* setting is still maintained; *the* apparent continuation of *the* refractory required *a* clearly comprehensible and unambiguous space construction. This is achieved by *the* use of apparently simple but expert demarcations of coffered ceiling, tapestry – hung walls and background windows. Within this space than there actually is. This space creating force which pervades their movements is one of secret causes of *the* monumental effect of *the* picture. We shall see how far Leanardo himself developed this principle of "Super dimensions" in his subsequent compositions, the St. Anne and Battle of Anghiari. Through Leonardo, it became from then on, *a* formal principle of *the* classic High Renaissance style; Raphael makes use of it; as well as Michelangelo, who in his Sistine ceiling develops *the* conscious imprisonment of colossal forms in *a* tight space ad extremism. (from Ludwig H. *Heydenreich: Leanardo da Vinci*).

9

Determiners

"Like everything metaphysical, the harmony between thought and reality is found in the grammar of the language."

—Ludwig Wittgenstein

Introduction

Determiners are little words that modify the nouns that occur after them. They have the same function as that of adjectives, i.e. to modify nouns but they are different from them in that they belong to *a close set* whereas adjectives belong to an open class. To become a fluent reader or writer of English, it is necessary to learn the correct use of determiners. Look at the following sentence:

'Hey! There's **an egg** on your chin.'

The use of *an* before *egg* leads to a ludicrous remark because what the speaker wants to say is that there is some substance of an egg on the listener's chin. Therefore, the correct sentence would be:

'Hey! There's egg on your chin.'

In this lesson, we shall discuss what a determiner is, classes of determiners and uses of determiners. It is assumed that by studying the lesson, the readers would be proficient in the correct use of determiners.

What is a Determiner

Read the following passage and pay attention to the bold words:

The inspector of **the** workshop was so hated by **the** prisoners that he often had recourse to Claude Gueux to enforce **his** authority; and when **a** tumult was on **the** point of breaking out, **a few** words from Claude had more effect than **the** inspector was glad to avail himself of **this** influence, he was jealous **all the** same, and hated **the** superior prisoner with **an** envious and implacable feeling—**an** example of might over right, **all the** more fearful as it was secretly nourished. But Claude cared so much for Albin that he thought little about **the** inspector. (From Claude Gueux, King of Thieves by Victor Hugo in 5 French Masters)

The bold words in the above passage (**the**, **his**, **a few**, **this**, **an**, **a**, **all**) are called **determiners**. They are called determiners because they limit the meanings of nouns by restricting the reference and signal the occurrence of nouns. The determiners are given below.

A, an, the, my, our, your, his, her, their, this, these, that, those, some, any, no, enough, each, every, either, neither, which, what, whose, whatever, whichever

Thus, we see that determiners are words that determine the reference of a noun or a noun group. They signal that a noun will follow. It is a sort of noun modifier used before a noun to specify the reference of a noun including quantity rather than attributes. This reference could be specific or unspecific/general.

(i) **Most people** in this world are corrupt. (general reference)
(ii) Most of the people in this village are honest. (specific reference)

Table 9.1 provides the types of determiners.

TABLE 9.1 Types of determiners

Articles	*Possessives adjectives*	*Demonstratives*	*Interrogatives*	*Quantifiers/ Distributives*
a, an, the	Including possessive nouns (my, our, your, his, her, its, their) John's, my mother's	this, these, that, those	which, what, whose, whatever, whichever	some, any, no, enough, each, every, either, neither Quantifiers answer the question how many how much

Thus determiners limit the reference of a noun and thereby restrict the meaning of a noun.

EXERCISE 9.1

Identify determiners in the following passage and point out the class to which each determiner belongs.

Example: **What a** beautiful person she is!
Ans.: Determiners: **What** (Interrogative), **a** (article)

She came to know what heavy housework meant and the odious of the kitchen. She washed the dishes, using her dainty fingers and rosy nails on greasy pots and pans. She washed the soiled linen, the shirts and the dishcloths, which she dried upon a line; she took the slops down to the street every morning and carried up the water, stopping for breath at every landing. And dressed like a woman of the people, she went to the fruit seller, the grocer, the butcher, a basket on her arm, bargaining, meeting with impertinence, defending her miserable money, sou by sou.

(From The Necklace by Guy de Mau passant in 5 French Masters)

Classification of Determiners

Determiners and nouns are fellow travellers. Nouns are of two types: count and uncount

The types of nouns affect the use of determiners. Some determiners go with count nouns whereas others keep company with uncountable nouns. For example, a, an, any, each, every are used with singular count nouns: every boy, an orange, an elephant, any book, each student. Further, plural count nouns occur with several, many, all, some, etc: several doctors, some people, all people, many patients. Uncount nouns go with all, enough, much, most, etc.: enough milk, much money, all ice cream, etc.

Note further that some nouns in certain situations do not take any determiners at all.

1. Singular uncount nouns used in the general sense:
   - (i) **Honesty** is a good policy.
   - (ii) **Gold** is a precious metal.
   - (iii) **Wheat** is more nutritive than **barley**.
2. Plural count nouns when they refer to the whole class.
   - (i) **Cows** are worshipped in India.
   - (ii) **Horses** are faithful animals.
3. Singular proper nouns.
   - (i) **Jaipur** is the capital of **Rajasthan**.
   - (ii) **Ramesh** is a good painter.
   - (iii) **Amer** is famous for tourist spots.

Like nouns, determiners can be classified into three categories:

- Pre-determiners
- Central determiners
- Post-determiners

This classification of determiners is based on ordering of determiners:

I met	**all**	**my**	**many**	friends at the party.
	pre-det	cent det	post-det	

Pre-determiners (so called) occur before central determiners and are of several types as given below.

1. **Intensifiers:**
   (i) This man is **rather** a bore, isn't he?
   (ii) He made **quite** a noise when he came in.
2. **Multiplying:**
   (i) **Twice** his income
   (ii) **Double** my income
   (iii) **Ten times** my income
3. **Fractions:**
   (i) **Half** my income
   (ii) **One-fourth** my income
4. **All and both:**
   (i) **All** my income
   (ii) **Both** my friends
5. **Many** a man:
   (i) **Many** a man knows this.

The class of central determiners includes the main determiners, which are mutually exclusive. They include *articles*, *possessives* and *demonstratives*.

All *the* books
All *these* books
All *your* books

We cannot say, all your these books (because your and these are mutually exclusive).

Post-determiners are the words that occur after central determiners. They include:

1. **Cardinal and ordinal numbers**:
   (i) The **three** teachers
   (ii) The **fortieth** wedding anniversary
2. **General ordinals:**
   (i) His **next** birthday
   (ii) Our **last** meeting
   (iii) Your **previous** work
   (iv) Their **subsequent** decision
3. **Other quantifying expressions:**
   (i) His **many** friends
   (ii) Your **several** complaints

(iii) The **few** friends that I have
(iv) The **little** milk in the refrigerator

Notice unlike pre- and central determiners, post- determiners can co-occur.
My **next two** books; **several other** projects
Because of this characteristic, some grammarians treat them as adjectives rather than as determiners.

EXERCISE 9.2

Identify all the determiners in the following sentences as also indicate each type (i.e. whether it is a pre-determiner, central determiner or post-determiner) in each case.

Example: **All his** desires were fulfilled.
Ans.: all (pre-determiner), his (central determiner)

1. Both his friends will arrive today.
2. He has several friends but these two are invaluable.
3. Only those friends are trustworthy who help you in need.
4. All those people are lucky who have trustworthy friends.
5. When he was in the States, he made several new friends forgetting all his previous friends.
6. If you don't have any reliable friends in this world, your life is miserable.
7. My brother, who died last year, had no friends at all.
8. He always felt jealous whenever he saw me surrounded by a number of friends.
9. My many friends helped me with my homework.
10. Come and take lessons from me as to how you can make many friends.

Characteristics of Determiners

As said earlier, traditional grammarians did not use the term **determiners** to talk about the little words that we are dealing with in this chapter. They used terms like possessive adjectives (my, our, your, its, his, her, their); articles (a, an, the), demonstrative adjectives (this, these, that, those), distributive adjectives (each, every, either, neither); numerical adjectives (one, two, first, second, last, previous, etc.); and quantifiers (half, no, some, much, enough, little, a little, few, a few, all, any, no, many, most, a lot of, etc). We have chosen a blanket term 'determiners' to encompass all the above grammatical categories because of two reasons. First, the above categories show the same pattern of distribution. They fit into the same syntactic frame:

The yellow book.
The several yellow books.

Secondly, except numerical adjectives, the above categories belong to a closed set of determiners. They are limited in number. It is a moot point whether we should include numerical adjectives under determiners or adjectives. We leave this question open.

Determiners show a particular order or sequence in their occurrence. It would be better to sub-classify determiners as pre, central and post so that the order and co-occurrence restrictions can be specified. Pre- and central determiners (articles, possessives and demonstratives) are mutually exclusive whereas more than one post-determiner can co-occur. Look at the following example:

All	the	**first**	**five**	students
pre-det	central det	post-det	post-det	

There are co-occurrence restrictions in the use of determiners in the nouns. Some determiners occur only with count nouns, some with uncount nouns whereas others occur with both count and uncount nouns. Table 9.2 makes it clear.

TABLE 9.2 Co-occurrence restrictions on nouns

With countable nouns	*With uncountable nouns*	*With both count and uncountable nouns*
all/every car(s), most, many, some, a few, few, a number of, several, a large number of, a great number of	all (money) most, much, some, a little, no, a bit of, a great deal of, a large amount of	no/none, not any, some, any, a lot of, plenty of, lots of *Example:* (i) There wasn't any milk in the fridge. (ii) There weren't any students in the class.

In the above table, a further sub-classification is possible. We can say that **a**, **an**, **another**, **any**, **each**, **either**, **every**, **neither**, **no** are used with singular countable nouns.

(i) **Every student** in the class wore a green uniform.
(ii) He is wearing **a red tie**.

Further, *all*, *any*, *both*, *enough*, *few*, *fewer*, *many*, *more*, *most*, *no*, *other*, *several*, *some* are used with plural countable nouns.

(i) Some people always complain about their service conditions.
(ii) Several students joined the strike against the principal.

Furthermore, *all*, *any*, *enough*, *less*, *little*, *more*, *most*, *much*, *no*, *some* are used with uncountable nouns.

(i) You have to find **more evidence** to prosecute him.
(ii) I don't have **enough money** to let you study engineering.

The violation of these rules will result in ill-formed sentences:

(i) Do you want another more tea? (×)
(ii) Do you want some more tea? (✓)

Many and *much* (quantifiers) are gradable.

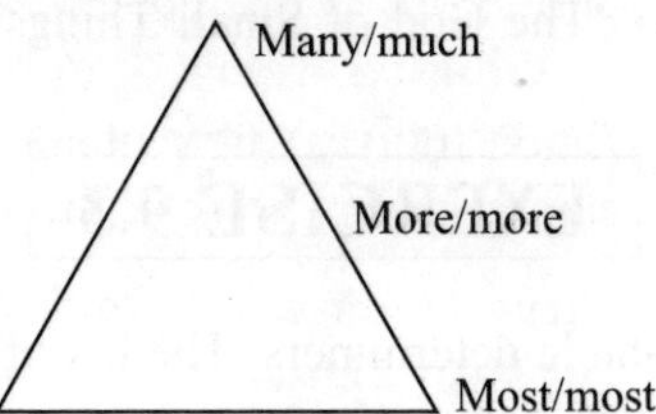

And so are **little** and **few**:

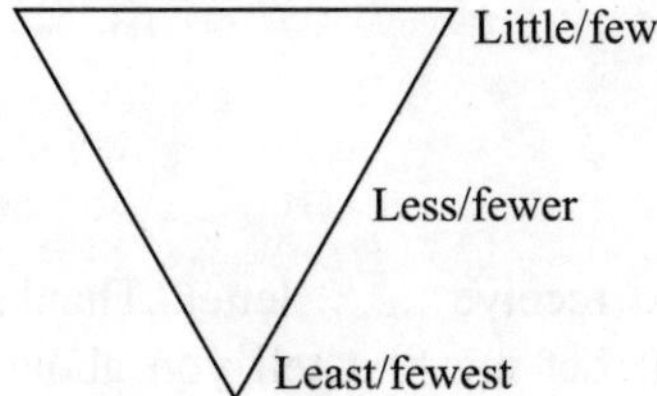

(i) There are many poor people in the village; **more** in the town; but **most** in Mumbai.
(ii) **Much information** was given to the police by the lookers; **more** by the friends of the victim; and **most** by the parents of the victim.
(iii) **Few people** are intelligent; **fewer** are stupid; and **fewest** are the stupidest.
(iv) There was **little milk** in the jug; **less** in the pot; and **least** in the fridge.

Some grammarians have categorized determiners as specific and general. Specific (known to the speaker and the listener) determiners include *articles*, *possessive adjectives* and *demonstrative adjectives*. The rest fall under the category of general determiners. All pre-determiners (all, half, both), numerical adjectives and quantifiers will come under general determiners.

There is a considerable overlap between the determiners class and the sub-class of pronouns. Many words have the same form as pronouns and determiners (see Table 9.3).

TABLE 9.3 Pronouns and determiners

Pronoun	*Determiner*
This is a very expensive car.	*This* car is very expensive.
That's an excellent book.	*That* book is excellent.

Notice determiners occur before nouns whereas pronouns are used in place of nouns. Pronouns can be substituted by nouns but not the determiners.

That's an excellent book → 'The God of Small Things' is an excellent book. (✓)

But not the following:

That book is excellent → 'The God of Small Things' book is excellent. (×)

EXERCISE 9.3

Fill in the blanks with suitable determiners. The list of determiners from which you have to choose is given below:

Your, your, all, this, his, a, his, the, some, a, our, his, the, the, his, a, any, your, this, your, my, a, a few, his, his, such, a

New York
9 April, 2012

Dear Ravi,

I was very happy to receive .... letter. Thanks for promising to take care of .... friend John. Let me first tell you about John. He is .... very famous dress designer for children. Within .... months of starting .... business, he started getting big orders. .... kind of clothes was .... hit with children that you have to book .... Johnies' shirts for .... kid three months in advance. With .... success, John became so stressed out that all of us are very worried. When he developed chest pain, John was also worried. He has been advised by .... doctor to relax and take .... break from .... business. I told him about .... wonders of India and persuaded him to spend .... time in Chennai. He is planning to stay for 15 days. So please arrange for .... place for him to stay. .... Weekend seaside cottage would be ideal.

He is arriving by Boeing 707 Indian Airlines on 5th September. .... flight lands at Chennai at 10:30 in .... morning. Please be there to receive him, for he does not know anybody in .... city. .... full name is John D. Sallivan. He is tall, fair, bland, and has .... slight limp. If there is .... confusion please call me.

Mom and Dad said hi to you and .... parents. Again thanks a lot for .... help.

Bye.

Love,

Shyam

(*Source: English for Engineers Students* 1, Vikas, 2004.)

Uses of Determiners

The classifying and specific uses of *a* and *an* and the identifying uses of *the* have been dealt with in a separate Chapter on 'The Uses of Articles'.

Possessive determiners such as *my*, *our*, *your*, *its*, *his*, *her* and there are used to show possession:

(i) It's not **her** book, it's mine.
(ii) **Your** behaviour to me is shocking.
(iii) **Their** house is excellent.

Demonstrative determiners such as *this*, *these*, *that* and *those* show nearness to or distance from the speaker. The *nearness* or *distance* can be in terms of time, space or thought.

(i) **This picture** belongs to the 16th century but I'm not sure of **that picture** over there.
(ii) **These houses** belong to the lower middle class but **those houses** over there have been constructed for the high-income group.

Some and *any* both refer to quantity or number. *Some* refers to a quantity or number, which is not precise whereas *any* refers to a number or quantity that may or may not exist. *Some* is used in affirmative sentences or in question expecting agreement or the answer 'yes':

(i) I have **some problem.**
(ii) There are **some students** waiting for you.
(iii) Would you like **some tea**? (Expecting the answer 'yes' from the listener)

Any is used in sentences that are negative in *form* or *meaning*.

(i) We haven't got **any** book on the subject.
(ii) There isn't **any** butter left in the fridge.

Words having negative meanings such as **barely**, **hardly**, **never**, **rarely**, **scarcely**, **seldom**, **deny**, **fail**, **forbid**, **refuse**, **prohibit**, **impossible**, **unlikely** take **any** with them.

It is impossible for him to do **any work**.
Any is also used in questions:
Are there **any** problems that I can solve?

Any is used in if- constructions:

If you have **any** problem, let me know.

Any is also used having the meaning 'it doesn't matter which':

To go to town you can catch **any** bus. (They all go to town.)

EXERCISE 9.4

Complete the sentences with **some** or **any**.

1. Were there .... questions difficult?
2. The paper didn't have .... difficult questions. All were easy.
3. Would you be going on holiday alone or with .... friends?
4. It is unlikely for him to do .... work by 7 o' clock.
5. If you have .... questions, please shoot them.
6. Are you going to Jaipur? Yes. You can take .... train. All go to Jaipur.
7. I have .... money that I want to invest in mutual funds. Which one would you recommend?
8. I don't have .... trustworthy friend.
9. There is seldom .... entertainment in the evenings.
10. .... students who are late will not be allowed to sit for the exam.

Much (of) and *many* (of) are used to talk about quantities and amounts. Much (of) is used with uncount nouns whereas many (of) with plural count nouns.

Many people watch too **much television**.

Much (of) and *many* (of) are used in negative sentences to talk about smaller quantities than expected and in interrogative sentences to ask about quantities or amounts.

(i) **Not many** friends help you in time of need.
(ii) He did not take **much interest** in his studies.
(iii) **How much money** do you want?
(iv) **How many people** were present at the party?

In affirmative sentences, *a lot of*, *lots of*, *plenty of* are used in informal writing or speech to talk about large quantities.

(i) He took **a lot of** interest in extra-curricular activities.
(ii) He devoted **lots of/plenty of** time in studies.
(iii) He spent **a lot of/plenty of** days staying in the Northeast.

The opposite determiners of *much* and *many* are *little* and *few*.

We use *little* to talk about a small quantity of things and *few* to take about a small number of things or people. Table 9.4 summarizes the use of **little** and **few**.

The meanings of *little* and *few* are given below:

Little = not much

Few = not many

A little = some, a small amount

A few = some, a small number

A couple of = two, a small number (informal)
Several = more than two but fewer than many

Table 9.4 Uses of little and few

	Affirmative	*Negative formal*
(a) few (used with plural countable nouns)	I have **a few** good books that I read again and again (= enough)	I have **few** good friends. (the number is low; not enough)
(b) little (used with uncount nouns)	I had **a little** money left so I went out to buy 'Vinci De Code' (= enough)	I have **little** money left (= The quantity is low; not enough)

EXERCISE 9.5

Complete the sentences with (a, the) few (of), (a / the) little (of), much, many, a lot of, plenty of, lots of.

1. Sarla had only ₹ 20 on her. The lunch cost ₹ 30. She could not buy lunch because she had .... money.
2. Sarla had only ₹ 100 on her. The dinner at Plaza restaurant cost ₹ 90. Sarla bought dinner at Plaza restaurant with .... money she had.
3. Five friends went to Jaipur. They had ₹ 200 altogether. They spent .... money they had on having ice cream.
4. He isn't romantic. He has .... girl-friends.
5. The correspondent asked him .... questions.
6. The class had very poor attendance but .... students who came enjoyed the lesson.
7. I was leaving for the States for further studies. I went to Ram for some advice but he didn't give me .... advice.
8. I had .... questions to ask from him but he didn't show .... interest.
9. .... people were present at the meeting.
10. .... critics have rated her as one of the best poets of the 21st century.
11. .... food was left uneaten.
12. He had .... drinks and then drove home safety.

Just For Fun

At painful times, when composition is impossible and reading is not enough, grammar and dictionaries are excellent for distraction.

Elizabeth Barett Browning

Both, *either* and *neither* are used for *two things*.

Suppose you go to Jaipur and want to stay in a hotel near the railway station. There are two hotels nearby.

(i) **Both hotels** are comfortable.
(ii) **Neither hotel** is costly.
(iii) Your can stay in **either hotel**. (either = one or the other, it does not matter which one)
(iv) Both of these hotels are comfortable.
(v) Neither of the hotels was comfortable.
(vi) **Neither** Ram **nor** Shyam came to college.
(vii) He is **either Indian or Nepalese**.

All, *half*, *no*, *none* determiners have interesting uses. Consider the following sentences:

(i) **All men** are mortal (All = sum total of people or things)
(ii) I have **no** money. (no = not any)
(iii) I have **no** friends. (no = not any)
(iv) **None of this money** is mine. (We cannot say none of money ×)

Compare *all* as a determiner with its pre- determiner counterpart.

(i) **All** my friends are in Jaipur.
(ii) **All** of my friends are in Jaipur.
(iii) Half these people or half of these people belong to OBC.

Compare *no* and *none* in the following sentences:

(i) We had to go by bus, as there was **no train**. (= there wasn't a train)
(ii) **None of this** property is mine.

Each and *every* have the same meaning in certain contexts. They are replaceable in these situations.

(i) There was a television in **each/every** room of the house.
(ii) **Each/every** time I see you, you look gorgeous to me. (= whenever I see you ....)

But in some uses, *each* is different from *every*. *Each* has two different meanings. First, *each* is used for things when we think of them separately, one by one:

Study each book seriously. (= study the book one by one)

The second meaning of *each* is that it is used *for a small number*:

(i) There were four persons in the room. **Each person** belonged to a different nationality.
(ii) In a card game, **each player** is given 10 cards.

Each (not every) is used for *two* things in a cricket match.

Each team has 11 players. (not every team)

Every, on the other hand, is used for things when they are viewed as a group. Here **every** is equal to **all**.

Every person must have feelings. (= all persons have feelings)

Unlike each, *every* is used for *a large number*:

I would like to dispel the sorrows of **every person** in the world. (= all the persons)

Every (not each) is used for **how often something** happens:

(i) There is a flight to Chennai **every** day.
(ii) There is a flight to London **every** week. (not each week)

EXERCISE 9.6

Fill the blanks with **each** or **every**.

1. .... student is worried about his exams.
2. Two to four players play badminton. .... player has a racket to smash the shuttlecock.
3. I practice yoga .... week.
4. The class will be divided into three sections and .... section will contain 20 students.
5. Is there a metro for Dwarka? 'Yes'. How often does it go? '........... ten minutes'.
6. Helmets are life savers. .... scooter driver should wear one.
7. I have visited .... village in Koyambatur district.

EXERCISE 9.7

Below is given a letter written by Pandit J.L. Nehru to his daughter Indira Gandhi. Fill in the blanks with suitable determiners.

Central Prison, Naini
October 26, 1930

My dear Indira,

On .... birthday you have been in .... habit of receiving presents and good wishes. Good wishes you will still have in full we assure, but what present can I send you from Naini prison? .... presents cannot be very material or solid. They can be of .... mind and .... spirit that even .... high walls of prison cannot stop. I have always thought that .... best way to find out what is right and what is not right, what should be done and what should not be done is not by giving .... sermon but by talking and discussing and out of discussion sometimes .... little bit of truth comes out. .... Letter can hardly take .... place of .... talk; at best it is .... one-sided affair. Imagine that I have made .... suggestion to you for you to think over, as if we really were having .... talk… I have written .... very long letter to you. And yet there is so much I would like to tell you. How can .... letter contain it?

With .... love and good wishes.

Your loving father,
(J.L. Nehru)

EXERCISE 9.8

Identify pre-determiners, central determiners and post-determiners in the following sentences and phrases:

1. All his colleagues.
2. A few lectures.
3. John would be the first person to come.
4. Most people are cheats.
5. Some people do not follow rules.
6. What sort of decision is this?
7. Whose house is this?
8. Which train goes to Kolkata?
9. Many a young man has arrived to attend the party.
10. What a beautiful woman she is?
11. I hate the very expression on your face.
12. He has a little knowledge of English. So we can communicate with him in English.
13. He has little knowledge of French. Therefore, we cannot communicate with him in French.
14. Half a glass of milk a day is not enough for this growing child.
15. Your speech makes no sense.
16. He lost all his wealth in gambling.
17. Most lectures do their work with perfect dedication.
18. Most of the lectures in this college have a doctorate.
19. Do you have any cold drink in the fridge?
20. The first impression is the last impression.
21. I will see you next week.
22. Such a shock.
23. All such necessary furniture.
24. Much of the food.
25. No such person.
26. Such an interesting debate.
27. My mother's hair.

28. Mother's teeth.
29. A bit of entertainment.
30. A lot of knowledge/spectators.

EXERCISE 9.9

In the following sentences, fill in the gaps with one of the following quantifiers: much, many, few, a few, little, a little, most, any, a lot of.

1. He has had .... successes this year.
2. How .... money do you want to borrow from me?
3. How .... students have not come to class?
4. She has already faced .... problems because her father died when she was very young.
5. I cannot read in this light because there are too .... insects.
6. I haven't eaten .... ice cream for the last one year and this has made .... differences to my weight.
7. I'm afraid I haven't attended my computer classes .... times and I have .... understanding of computer languages.
8. He gave me .... advice, which didn't help me to improve my life.
9. When did you last see your parents? .... days ago.
10. 'My exams are starting from tomorrow.'
    'I wish you .... luck.'

Key to Exercise 9.1

what (interrogative), the (article), the (article), the (article), her (possessive), the (article), the (article), the (article), a (article), the (article), the (article), every (indefinite), the (article), every (indefinite), a (article), the (article), the (article), the (article), the (article), a (article), her (possessive), her (possessive).

Key to Exercise 9.2

1. both (pre-determiner), his (central determiner)
2. several (determiner), these (central determiner), two (post-determiner)
3. only (pre-determiner), those (central determiner)
4. all (pre-determiner), those (central determiner)
5. several (determiner), all (pre-determiner), his (central determiner), previous (post-determiner)
6. any (determiner), this (determiner)
7. my (determiner), last (determiner), no (determiner)
8. a (determiner)
9. my (central determiner), many (post-determiner), my (determiner)
10. many (determiner)

Key to Exercise 9.3

Your, my, a, a few, his, his, such, a, your, your, all, this, his, a, his, the, some, a, our, his, the, the, his, a, any, your, this

Key to Exercise 9.4

1. any
2. any
3. some
4. any
5. any
6. any
7. some
8. any
9. any
10. any

Key to Exercise 9.5

1. little
2. a little
3. the little
4. few
5. a few
6. the few
7. much
8. a lot of, much
9. many/ a lot of (in spoken English)
10. many (Formal/ academic writing)
11. a great deal of/ much/ a large amount of (Formal)
12. a couple of, several, a few (= a small number, informal) (literally a couple of means two)

Key to Exercise 9.6

1. every
2. each
3. every
4. each
5. every
6. every
7. every

Key to Exercise 9.7

Your, the, my, the, the, the, the, a, a, a, the, a, a, a, a, all, a, my, a lot of

Key to Exercise 9.8

1.	all	=	pre-determiner
	his	=	determiner
2.	a few	=	determiner
3.	the	=	determiner
	first	=	post-determiner
4.	most	=	determiner
5.	some	=	determiners
6.	what	=	determiner
7.	whose	=	determiner
8.	which	=	determiner
9.	many	=	pre-determiner
	a	=	determiner
	the	=	determiner

10. what = pre-determiner
    a = determiner
11. the = determiner
    very = post-determiner
    your = determiner
12. a little = determiner
13. little = determiner
14. half = pre-determiner
    a = determiner
    a = determiner
    this = determiner
15. your = determiner
    no = determiner
16. all = pre-determiner
    his = determiner
17. most = determiner
    their = determiner
18. most of = pre-determiner
    the = determiner
    this = determiner
    a = determiner
19. any = determiner
    the = determiner
20. the = determiner
    first = post-determiner
    the = determiner
    last = post-determiner
21. next = determiner
22. such = pre-determiner
    a = determiner
23. all = pre-determiner
    such = determiner
24. much of = pre-determiner
    the = determiner
25. no = pre-determiner
    such = determiner
26. such = pre-determiner
    an = determiner
27. my = determiner
    mother's = post-determiner
28. mother's = determiner
29. a bit of = determiner
30. a lot of = determiner

Key to Exercise 9.9

1. many
2. much
3. many
4. a lot of
5. many
6. any, a lot of
7. few, little
8. little
9. a few
10. a lot of

10

Prepositions

Introduction

Prepositions occur before nouns or pronouns and they show relation between one noun/pronoun with another. They can be classified according to form and meaning.

Formwise, prepositions can be *simple* (in, on, at, up, with, under, behind, among, etc.); *compound* (into, onto, as to, as for, alongside, instead of, out of, etc.); *phrasal* (with reference to, in comparison with, in the direction of, at the back of, in spite of, etc.) and *participial* (considering, concerning, regarding, respecting, barring, excepting, pending, etc.).

Meaningwise, there can be prepositions of place, time, position and direction, instrument/means, agent, beneficiary/recipient/goal, accompaniment, reason/purpose and ingredient or material. Below we shall discuss prepositions functionwise.

In the discussion of prepositions of *place, direction* and *location,* notions like *point, line, surface, area* and *volume* have been used. Therefore, it would be quite in order to discuss these concepts before the discussion of prepositions.

The use of the *prepositions of place* very much depends upon the perception of the place on the part of the speaker/writer.

The place can be seen as a *point.* That means it is viewed as a place having length, width or height. Consider the following sentences:

(i) He went **to** Jaipur.
(ii) He is **at** home.
(iii) They came (away) **from** the city centre.
(iv) They stayed away **from** the city.

Another view of looking at a place is in terms of *a line.* That is, it is seen in terms of *length* but not *breadth* or *height.* Interestingly enough, the place vis-à-vis preposition *on* and its related prepositions can be viewed as *a line* or *a surface.* Consider the following sentences where the place is viewed as a line:

(i) The car swerved **off** the road and rolled back **on to** the road after a minute.
(ii) My village is situated **on** the Ganges.
(iii) He swam **across** the Ganges.
(iv) Chennai is two miles **off** the sea.
(v) The houses **along** the Marina Beach were painted white.

Now consider the following sentences in which the place is seen as *a surface.* That is, it is viewed as having *length* and *width* but not *height* or *depth,* showing the use of preposition o*n and* its related counter-parts:

(i) He put the book **on** the table.
(ii) He threw the book **on to** the table.
(iii) He fell **off** the horse.
(iv) He went **across** the fields.
(v) She looked **through** the window.

Further, the place can be seen as *an area* (i.e. an area of ground or territory enclosed by boundaries). Preposition *in* and its type are used in this case.

(i) Thousands of birds poured **into** Ghana Birds Sanctuary from Afghanistan.
(ii) He has found cheap lodgings **in** the outskirts of the town.
(iii) He went **out of** the country.
(iv) She went out **through** the park.

Furthermore, the place can be seen as a *volume*, i.e. having *length, width,* and *height* or depth. *In* type prepositions are used in this case:

(i) She ran **into** the school.
(ii) Put the food **in** the refrigerator.
(iii) He went **out off** the room.
(iv) He was **out off** the school.
(v) She went **through** the grass.

Prepositions of Time

Look at the following sentences:

(i) I reached the college **at** 10 a.m. yesterday.
(ii) I get up **at** 6 a.m. every day.
(iii) What are you doing **at** this moment?
(iv) Will he come **at** Christmas?
(v) He does his work **at** night.
(vi) What are you doing **at** the weekend?
(vii) It is not so cold **at** Dipawali time.
(viii) I will meet you **in** the evening.
(ix) I will be rich **in** two months time.
(x) He was born **in** January.

(xi) He came here **in** 1970.
(xii) It is very pleasant here **in** winter.
(xiii) The train will depart **in** five minutes/**in** four or five minutes time.
(xiv) He was born **on** a Sunday.
(xv) I saw him **on** that particular night.
(xvi) He was born **on** lst August 1940.
(xvii) I will give him a watch **on** his birthday.
(xviii) I met her **on** a Sunday afternoon.

The rules are as follows.

1. *At* is used for an exact point of time, that is, with hour, moments and the names of festivals. (see sentences i–vii)
2. *In* is used with seasons, years, parts of the day, months and period within which an action will take place. (see sentences viii–xiii)
3. *On* is used with days, dates and general points of time. (see sentences xiv–xviii)

Consider the following sentences which illustrate some other prepositions of time such as *by, for, since, from, to, during, before, after, throughout, till/until, ago* and a few more.

(i) He was at the theatre **from** 3 pm **to** 6 pm.
(ii) He works hard **from** morning **till** evening.
(iii) He came to see me **during** day.
(iv) He fell ill **during** Dussehra break.
(v) He was busy **throughout** the vacation.
(vi) Come **before** 9 p.m.
(vii) You can leave **after** 5 p.m.
(viii) I have lived here **for** the last 20 years.
(ix) We go to Kashmir **for** a month every year.
(x) He has lived here **since** 1985.
(xi) My father died 10 years **ago.**
(xii) He will perhaps come **by** 7 p.m.
(xiii) He has been ill **since** last week.
(xiv) He has been ill **for** the last week.
(xv) I haven't seen him **since** childhood.

The rules are as follows.

1. *By* is used for the latest time by which an action will be finished. (see sentence xii)
2. *For* is used for period of time. It is generally used with perfect tenses but is also found with the other tenses. (see sentences viii and ix)
3. *Since* is used with point of time and is found in perfect tenses. (see sentences x, xiii and xv)

4. *From* is used with the starting point of an action in the past or future and is generally found with *to* or *till/until.* (see sentences i and ii).
5. *During* emphasizes period of time. (see sentences iii and iv).
6. *Throughout* indicates entire period of time. (see sentence v).
7. *Before* and *after time* show particular points of time. (see sentences vi and vii).
8. *Ago* refers to a past action or event.

EXERCISE 10.1

Fill in the blanks with suitable prepositions.

1. The meeting will be over .... 5 p.m.
2. He reaches the college .... 9 p.m. sharp.
3. The college timings are .... 9 p.m. .... 4 p.m.
4. My class starts .... 10 a.m.
5. It lasts .... 10 a.m. .... 11 a.m.
6. I will be back .... 7:30 p.m.
7. The college is from 10 a.m. to 5 p.m. So, you meet me .... 5 p.m. or .... 10 a.m.
8. We go to South .... winter.
9. He was born .... 10 January 1940.
10. He passed his B.A. .... 1989.
11. He has been a social worker .... his life.
12. I have known him .... last January.
13. I have known him .... the last 2 years.
14. .... my stay in Orissa, I hardly met her.
15. Will you come home .... Dipawali?

Prepositions of Place

Look at the following sentences which illustrate *at, in, on, inside, under, above, outside,* as prepositions of place:

(i) The college is situated **at** the junction near Pepsi Factory.
(ii) There is a cultural programme **at** Suchna Kendra today.
(iii) He was present **at** the meeting/function/match.
(iv) I met him **at** the dentist's clinic.
(v) He was born **at** Patna in Bihar.
(vi) He lives **at** A –165, HKM Nagar.
(vii) My Institute is **on** the road to Perry.
(viii) The book is **on** the table.
(ix) Read the poem **on** page 46.
(x) He lives **on** the second floor of the apartment.
(xi) My suitcase is **in** the room.

(xii) Madhya Pradesh is a state **in** India.
(xiii) The kite is flying **in** the sky.
(xiv) He has acted **in** the film **Ham Apke Hain Kaun.**
(xv) I live **in/on** street No. 20, Shivaji Park.
(xvi) He is **inside** the house.
(xvii) He is waiting **outside** the house.
(xviii) There is a fan **above** my head.
(xix) He is sitting **under** the table.
(xx) He waited for half an hour **at** the corner of the street.

The rules are as follows.

1. *At* is used to indicate the exact point of places; houses, stations, small villages whereas *in* is used to show a larger area such as bigger towns, valleys, and countries. Further, *in* is used for a point in an enclosed place. (see sentences i, vi and xi, xiv). *At* is used for institution such as the post office, at school.
2. *On* is used for a point touching a surface or close to a line. (see sentences vii, x)
3. For addresses, with the house number we use *at.* (see sentences vi)
4. With the name of the street we can use *in/on* (see sentence xv) and with the word floor we use *on.* (see sentence x)
5. *Above* means higher than whereas *under* means vertically lower than.
6. *Inside* gives the idea of being surrounded by whereas *outside* is the opposite of *inside.*

EXERCISE 10.2

Fill in the blanks with suitable prepositions.

1. He was born .... Tricharapalli .... in Tamil Nadu.
2. I don' have any money .... me.
3. There are five fans .... the ceiling.
4. There are two tube lights .... the wall.
5. Who is that .... that photo?
6. How much do you have .... the bank?
7. Rajiv Gandhi was killed .... Sri Perumbudur .... Tamil Nadu.
8. I put the clothes .... the box.
9. The British Prime Minister lives .... 10 Downing Street.
10. I live ...., street No. 54, Nampally.
11. Where is he? He is .... the house.
12. Who is standing .... the house?
13. What is the cat doing .... the table?
14. He put the bell .... the table.
15. How much money do you have .... your purse?

Prepositions of Direction and Location

To, on, in are used as prepositions of destination and position. So are prepositions such as *away from, off* and *out of. To* and *at* refer to a point of destination and position respectively, *on* (*to*) *on* and *off* refer to line or surface, whereas *in* (*to*) and *out of* refer to an enclosed area or volume. Look at the following sentences:

(i) He is going **to** Jaipur tomorrow.
(ii) He threw a book **onto** the table.
(iii) He went **into** the room.
(iv) He is **at** the door.
(v) The book is **on** the table.
(vi) He is **in** the room.
(vii) He fell **off** the horse.
(viii) He came **out of** the room.
(ix) He is **out of** breath.
(x) When you are **away from** your country, you feel home sick.
(xi) Our college is **near** the Pepsi Factory.
(xii) If you sit **far off** from the blackboard, you won't be able to see the letters clearly on the blackboard.
(xiii) There is a graveyard **in front of** the college.
(xiv) There is a road **behind** the college.
(xv) He is sitting **on the top** of the table.
(xvi) There is a cat **below** the table.
(xvii) The Frigidaire is **beside** the television.
(xviii) I had to appear **before** the court yesterday.
(xix) There is a restaurant **opposite /facing** our college.
(xx) He is resting **under** the tree.
(xxi) Water is running **over** the bridge.
(xxii) He came **down** the hill.
(xxiii) He climbed **up** the hill.

The rules are as follows.

1. *Into* shows movement. (see sentence iii)
2. *At* refers to point of position. (see sentence iv)
3. *On* refers to line or surface. (see sentence v)
4. *To* shows a point of destination. (see sentence i)
5. *Onto* shows a point of movement. (see sentence ii)
6. *Off* refers to line or surface and is used for away from a line.
7. *Out of* refers to destination and is used for an enclosed area or volume.
8. *Out of* is also used for position. (see sentence ix)
9. *Opposite* or *facing* is used to refer to things that are on opposite sides of a room, road, or river. (see sentence xiv)

10. *Over* means vertically higher and *below* means lower than. *Under* also shows direct or vertical relationship.
11. *Up* and *down* are used for vertical axis. (see sentences xxii and xxiii)

EXERCISE 10.3

Fill in the blanks with suitable prepositions:

1. I shall come .... your house at 5 O' clock.
2. The train .... Delhi leaves in 5 minutes.
3. Kings used to lead their armies .... the enemy in person.
4. They ran .... the scene of the murder.
5. He died .... cholera.
6. It is not expected .... you to behave like this.
7. This table is made .... wood.
8. Curds are made .... milk.
9. Take the book .... the table.
10. She took the parcels .... the car and carried them .... the house.
11. He wants to marry a girl .... pink dress.
12. I saw a man .... an umbrella.
13. He ran into a man .... red hair.
14. For a man .... sixty, he looks quite young.
15. Our house is .... Mohan's.
16. He laughed/stared/aimed .... me.

Prepositions in Fixed Phrases

Some prepositions collocate with certain nouns. These are to be learnt by heart. Here we give a list of these collocations:

(i) at dinner
at work, play
at war, peace
at once
at present
at ease
at will, at a loss
at a profit
at home, church, sea, school
at all costs
at heart

(ii) by land, sea, air
by ship, plane, car
by letter, post, hand, telegram
by chance, by mistake
by himself
by all means
by degrees
by surprise
by the way

(iii) in fun, play
in a hurry
in public, private
in love
in need
in other words

	in debt, difficulties, danger	in a way
	in ink, pencil, paint	in all likelihood
	in place	in bed
	in tears	in trouble
	in any case	in hand
	in fact	in the long run
	in particular	in due course
	in short, brief	in general
(iv)	on fire	on purpose
	on business, holiday, vacation	on the other hand
	on duty, watch, guard	on the contrary
	on sale	on the whole
	on foot, horseback	on second thoughts
(v)	out of breath	out of doors
	out of work	out of reach
	out of sight	out of practice
	out of danger	out of date
	out of use	out of the question
	out of control	out of stock

As the above are fixed phrases, no rules can be given for them.

EXERCISE 10.4

Replace the bold expressions by suitable prepositional collocations. One sentence is done for you:

She is only 25. **Anyhow,** that is what she says.
She is only 25. **At any rate,** that is what she says.

1. Children make a lot of noise **while they are playing.**
2. I am **unable to explain** why I have failed the exam.
3. He bought his shares when prices were low and now has sold them **for more money than he paid.**
4. You must sue him in the court **whatever it may cost** you.
5. You must reply to him **immediately** if you want to marry her.
6. I am sure that you can't possibly carry all that **alone.** Let me help you.
7. Don't punish him. He broke that tumbler **accidentally.**
8. I have informed him **through the telegram** of his success in the exam.
9. Oh dear! I have left my calculator **intentionally.**
10. This letter is not for me. It got delivered here **in error.**
11. When you ask him to do something, he always does the opposite **deliberately.**
12. He walked into the principal's room **crying** and said that his classfellow had hit him.
13. If I don't get a bus, I go **walking** to the office.

14. It is strange that children behave badly when they are **having their holidays.**
15. I haven't played cricket for years. I **lack practice.**

Verbs and Adjectives Followed by Prepositions

There are some verbs which are followed by fixed prepositions. Similarly, some adjectives are followed by certain fixed prepositions. Here is a list (Table 10.1).

TABLE 10.1 List of verbs and adjectives followed by prepositions

Verbs followed by prepositions	*Adjectives followed by prepositions*
apologize for, arrive at, accustom oneself to, exclaim at, glance at, appeal to, attend to, attribute to, compare to, knock at, smile at, laugh at, condemned to, confirmed to, reduced to, responded to, surrender to, stare at, surrender to, turn to, yield to, reply to, act on, believe in, took revenge on, engaged in, drawn on, operate on, trust in, work on, beware of, assure him of, complain of, differ from, consist of, convict of, cure of, eliminate from, suffer from, think of, exchange for, begin with, interfere with, disgusted with, communicate with, search for, part with, reason with, satisfied with, wait for, quarrel with	blind to, clear at, efficient at, expert at good at, fatal to, new to, kind to, obedient to, surprised to, peculiar to, surprised to afraid of , angry with, careful of, certain of, consistent with, grateful for, identical with, ready for, ignorant of, responsible for, sorry for, thankful for, devoid of, tired of, sure of, unworthy of, fortunate in, dubious of, proficient in, different from, popular with, jealous of, honest about, dependent upon, right about, interested in, sad about, doubtful/curious about, safe from, uneasy about, reluctant about

EXERCISE 10.5

Fill in the blanks with suitable prepositions.

1. He stared .... the stranger when he saw him.
2. Last night he came to see me but when he found the door closed, he went away without knocking .... it.
3. This book does not belong .... me.
4. Has he replied .... your letter?
5. Do you object .... my walking up late in the morning?

6. You should not depend .... me for financial matters.
7. You can rely .... him completely.
8. He has been eliminated .... the chess tournament.
9. I am tired .... arguing with you.
10. He is very much afraid .... your dog.
11. Mathura is famous .... temples.
12. He is very envious .... my new car.
13. The manager is well qualified .... his position.
14. You will be responsible .... providing the drinks.
15. You are not worthy .... the post you are holding.

EXERCISE 10.6

Fill in the blanks with suitable prepositions.

1. I have the habit .... leaving my seat and waiting .... the door of the bus.
2. There is hardly any industrial area .... steel furniture .... ship building which does not use welding.
3. He built a very nice house .... Jack .... only ₹ 50,000.
4. The passengers may leave the articles .... the conductor's permission but the company will not be responsible .... these articles.
5. I will walk round .... a circle .... some time if you have no objection.
6. We arrived .... Sydney .... exactly 6 O' clock.
7. She cannot accept proposals of marriage without the consent .... the court.
8. After the ladies had withdrawn, Lord William went to his room to take his collar .... and get bedroom slippers.
9. I know most .... the things a father should know .... his daughters.
10. What ...... the writer's view are the beautiful things .... life?
11. The emphasis is .... a direct approach .... the teaching of grammar.
12. I could not carry it .... home .... short notice.
13. What did he say .... his letter?
14. He is late .... work every day.
15. He hid himself .... the enemies.
16. I have an appointment .... 5:30 p.m.
17. I do a lot .... work in the garden.
18. The Prime Minister lives .... 10, Downing, Street.
19. For information you should apply .... the secretary.
20. Sherlock Holmes lived .... Baker Street.
21. He refused to answer. .... me.

22. Which hand do you write ....?
23. It will be over .... five minutes.
24. He has been living in his new house .... last week.
25. The railway line runs .... the river and the road.
26. The dog buried the bone .... the ground.
27. He started going .... School .... the age of five.
28. He is always .... a hurry. He drives .... a tremendous speed.
29. Have you spoken .... John .... my job?
30. Remember to be .... time .... the opera.
31. Aren't you coming .... us?
    No, I'm waiting .... Ram.
32. The lawyer accused the prisoner .... murder.
33. My friend agreed .... the plan.
34. What will you do now and .... five o' clock.
35. The new bridge .... the river has now been completed .
36. The chief guest arrived .... the party shortly .... seven o' clock.
37. At zero degree centigrade water changes .... ice.
38. The dinner should be over .... ten minutes.
39. I expect him to call me .... any moment.
40. We have had no rains now .... three months.
41. The train .... Delhi leaves in two minutes.
42. This device is entirely new .... me.
43. She is very efficient .... her work.
44. This is quite different .... what I expected.
45. The young man is very keen .... cycling.
46. Come and see me .... six o' clock tomorrow evening.
47. He was born .... 1st August 1940.
48. He has gone .... the States.
49. This table is made .... wood.
50. He is responsible .... this loss.

Key to Exercise 10.1

1. at/by	2. at	3. from, to
4. at	5. from, until	6. by
7. after, before	8. in	9. on
10. in	11. throughout	12. since
13. for	14. during	15. at

Key to Exercise 10.2

1. at, in	2. on	3. on
4. on	5. in	6. in
7. at, in	8. in	9. at

10. on/in
11. inside
12. outside
13. under
14. on
15. in

Key to Exercise 10.3

1. to
2. for
3. against
4. from
5. of
6. of
7. of
8. from
9. off
10. out of, into
11. in
12. with
13. with
14. of
15. opposite
16. at

Key to Exercise 10.4

1. they are at play
2. at a loss to explain
3. at a profit
4. at all costs
5. at once
6. by yourself
7. by accident
8. by telegram
9. by chance
10. by mistake
11. on purpose
12. in tears
13. on foot
14. on holiday
15. out of practice

Key to Exercise 10.5

1. at
2. at
3. to
4. to
5. to
6. on
7. on/upon
8. from
9. of
10. of
11. for
12. of
13. for
14. for
15. of

Key to Exercise 10.6

1. of, at
2. of, in
3. for, for
4. with, for
5. in, for
6. in, at
7. of
8. off
9. of, about
10. according to, of
11. on, to
12. to, at
13. in
14. for
15. from
16. at
17. of
18. at
19. to
20. in/on
21. to
22. with
23. in
24. since
25. along
26. in
27. to, at
28. in, at
29. to, about
30. in, for
31. with, for
32. of
33. to
34. between
35. over
36. at, before
37. into
38. in
39. at
40. for
41. to
42. to
43. at
44. from
45. on
46. at
47. on
48. to
49. of
50. for

11

Tenses

Introduction

Study the following sentence:

I usually **get up** at 6 a.m.

The bold verb is in the simple present tense. Tense refers to the absolute location of an event or character in time, either the present or the past. Tense refers to the form of the verb. There is no one to one correspondence between tense and time. When we study tenses in English, we should pay attention to three things: (i) Form, (ii) Function or Use and (iii) Adverbials used.

Simple Present Tense

Form of Simple Present Tense

I/we/they/you get up.
He/she/it gets up.
Do we get up?
Does he get up?
She does not/doesn't get up.
They/you do not/don't get up.

Uses

1. Simple present tense is used for habitual action:

   (i) He plays football every day.
   (ii) They generally come late to college.

2. It is also used for universal truth:

   (i) The sun rises in the east and sets in the west.
   (ii) Two and two make four.

3. Simple present tense is also used for timetables, newspaper headlines, demonstrations, commentaries and recipes.
    (i) The train **leaves** for Delhi at 6 p.m.
    (ii) The Prime Minister **arrives** in Chennai tomorrow.
    (iii) Take this piece of thread and put it round your wrist. The thread **turns** a gold chain.
    (iv) Mohan **passes** the ball to Sohan and Sohan **scores** a goal.
    (v) I **take** a spoonful of tea-leaves and **put** it in the boiling water. I **add** sugar and milk and the tea is ready.

Adverbials Used

This tense is generally used with adverbs or adverbials such as often, sometimes, rarely, seldom, hardly, ever, never, usually, generally, always, every day, twice a week, every other day, three times a week, regularly, on Fridays, every Saturday, in the morning, in the afternoon, in the evening, etc.

(i) I go there **every day**.
(ii) He **often** comes late to college.
(iii) He practices hard **on Fridays**.
(iv) He attends French classes **twice a week.**

Tenses are generally studied in pairs. Contrast simple present tense with the present progressive or continuous. Whereas simple present tense expresses permanent activities or situations, present continuous tense expresses temporary situations.

Present Continuous

Forms in Present Continuous

Forms of present continuous are given in Table 11.1.

TABLE 11.1 Forms of present continuous

Affirmative	*Negative*	*Interrogative*
I am studying	I am not studying	Am I studying?
You are studying	You are not studying	Are you studying?
He/she is studying	He/she is not studying	Is she/he studying?
They are studying	They are not studying	Are they studying?

Uses

1. Present continuous tense is used for those actions, events that are happening at the time of speaking.

(i) It **is raining** now.
(ii) They **are making** a noise in the park.
(iii) The pudding **is burning** and I can smell it.

2. This tense is also used for those situations that are not happening now but which are of limited duration.

(i) I **am writing** a book these days. (The book is not being written at the moment of speaking, but it involves an activity which will last for a while.)
(ii) He **is attending** dance lessons nowadays. (not necessarily at the time speaking).

3. Note further that the present progressive is generally *not used* with verbs denoting mental activities such as *think, feel, suppose, consider, imagine, know, understand, want, wish, desire, remember, recall, believe, forgive, seen, appear;* verbs of senses such as *smell, hear, see, feel, look, taste, hate, like, dislike, mind* (= *care*), *respect, value;* verbs of possession such as *belong, owe, own, possess;* other verbs such as *concern, consist, contain, hold* (= *contain*), *keep* (= *continue*), *matter, signify* and *sound* (= *seem/appear*).

(i) I like bananas but bananas don't like me.
*I am liking bananas. (wrong)
(ii) I love her but she detests me.
*I am loving her but she is detesting me. (wrong)
(iii) He owns a car and she has a fat bank balance.
*He is owning a car but she is having a fat bank balance. (wrong)
(iv) How much do you owe me?
(v) This room measures 20 × 20 square feet.
(vi) I believe she will top the university.

These verbs are called **stative verbs**. When some of them are used as activity verbs, they can be used in the present progressive. But notice in such circumstances, they lose their original meaning and acquire a new meaning.

(i) I see/can see a bird in the tree. (physical act of seeing)
(ii) I am **seeing** the principal this afternoon. (Here, *see* is being used in the present progressive but notice the meaning has changed. Here *seeing* has the meaning of *meeting*.)

Adverbials Used

The adverbs or adverbial phrases used with this tense are *now, at the moment, these days, nowadays, at present, still,* etc.

These adverbials may be overt or covert. If they are not present, they can be subsumed to be there. For example:

What are you doing?

I am writing a book. (It is ambiguous between I am writing a book now or I am writing a book these days.)

The context disambiguates the sentence under consideration. Anyway, the adverbs can be understood on the basis of the context.

EXERCISE 11.1

Put the verbs in brackets into the correct present tense: continuous or simple.

1. Ajay regularly .... (attend) classes but today he .... (cut) classes because he is sick.
2. He generally .... (walk) to college but today he .... (go) by bus because he is not well.
3. We always .... (spend) our summer vacation in Rajasthan but this year we .... (go) to Kerala.
4. You .... (enjoy) working in the garden as a rule?
5. She usually .... (play) badminton for two hours but today she ..... (play) for three hours.
6. It .... (rain) now though it .... (not rain) here in June.
7. I .... (not understand) what you .... (say).
8. You .... (know) how selfish he is?
9. He .... (have) a bath at the moment, therefore he can .... (not see) you.
10. Ram .... (come) in to bowl, Shyam .... (fling) his bat, Sohan .... (fall) on the ground .... (miss) the catch and the ball .... (go) to the boundary.
11. He .... (have) a Mercedes car and a big house. He must be very rich.
12. Where is Ram? He still .... (sleep). Should I wake him up?
13. What .... he .... (do ?). He .... (play) football at the moment.
14. He usually .... (sit) in the front row but today he .... (sit) in the third row.
15. He generally .... (love) Indian classical music.
16. Who .... (knock) at the door? It's I. Oh God! Another grammarian has come.
17. What .... you .... (study) these days? I .... (take) lessons in waltz.
18. I .... (prefer) tea to coffee? What about you?
19. How often .... you .... (wash) your hair? Twice a week.
20. Hurry up! Sohan .... (wait) for you.
21. He usually .... (tease) girls outside the college.
22. He .... (watch) TV. He .... (like) to watch thrillers.

23. The Ashram Express is never late. It always .... (leave) Ahmedabad on time.
24. Sohan is very careless. He always .... (leave) his things all over the place.
25. Can you drive? I .... (learn). My friend .... (teach) me.

Present Perfect vs Simple Past

Look at the following two sentences:

I **have reached** a dead-end.
We **have had** a breakdown.

The bold verb groups are said to be in the present perfect. That is, the use of have/has + verb+ed/en. Let us discuss this tense from the point of view of our framework (form, uses and adverbials).

Form

The form of the present perfect is given in Table 11.2.

TABLE 11.2 Forms of present perfect

Affirmative	*Negative*	*Interrogative*
I have done it.	I have not done it.	Have I done it?
You have done it.	You have not done it.	Have you done it?
He/she/it has done it.	He/she/it has not done it.	Has he/she/it done it?

Notice, we use *yet* in negative and interrogatives whereas we use *already* in affirmative sentences:

Have you done the homework?
No, not **yet.**
I have **already** done the homework.
Have you tried to do the homework **yet?**

Uses

The present perfect tense has three main uses. As the name suggests, this tense is used for those actions/events that started in the past but has some kind of relationship with the present. This tense can be called **pre-present**.

1. The tense is used for those actions/events that started in the past and have continued up to the moment of speaking and may or may not continue in future.
   (i) He came to Mumbai in 1982.
   (ii) He has lived here ever since.
   (iii) During his stay here, he has earned a good name.

This use shows a linkage with the present. The sentence 'He has lived here for two years' shows that he is still here or has just left.

2. The second use of the present perfect is the *resultative* use. That is the focus is on the completion and the result of the activity. For example:

   (i) He has published six books. (You can see the books.)
   (ii) She has gone to Jaipur. (She is in Jaipur now.)
   (iii) He has painted a picture. (The picture is complete.)
   (iv) Have you done your homework? (Is it here?)
   (v) He has cleaned the blackboard. (The blackboard is clean.)

   This use is also called **evidential use**.
   She has taught in a number of Summer Institutes. (Here is the certificate as a piece of evidence.)

3. The third use of the present perfect is the *experiential* use. The participant did something at an indefinite time in the past but he still has the knowledge/experience/memory of it. It is a part of his experience. Look at the following sentences:

   (i) I have seen the Taj. (No time adverbial is given because the emphasis is not on when it was seen but on the remembrance of it.)
   (ii) I have been the student of this college. (I still remember some of the things.)
   (iii) He has been to the States. (He still remembers his experience.)

Adverbials Used

Some of the adverbials that are used with the present perfect tense are being given below:

ever, *never*, *already*, *yet*, *all my life*, *since I was a child*, *for a long time*, *recently*, *lately*, *so far*, *up till now*, *just*, *today*, *this morning*, (*week*, *month*), *still*, *all day*, *all night*, etc.

Notice *since* is used for point of time and *for* for the period of time.

(i) I haven't seen him **since** last week.
(ii) I haven't seen him **since** the war broke out.
(iii) I haven't seen him **for** the last one week.
(iv) He has just left **for** the States.
(v) He has lived here **all his** life.
(vi) He has had good fortune **lately**.

Simple Past Tense

Simple past tense refers to the occurrence of activities, events and existence of states and situations in the past. The *second* form of the verb is used in this tense and there is an overt or covert definite time expression denoting past time. Below we discuss this tense under three heads: (i) form, (ii) uses and (iii) adverbials used.

Form

As said above, the second form of the verb is used in this tense. There are two types of verbs: **regular** and **irregular**. The regular verbs are formed by the addition of *–ed* in the past and past participle form such as *walk*, *walked*, *walked*. The irregular verbs are formed by the change of vowel in the past and past participle form: *ring*, *rang*, *rung*. Some irregular verbs remain unchanged: *cut*, *cut*, *cut*. Below are given the form of the simple past tense (Table 11.3).

TABLE 11.3 Forms of the simple past tense

Affirmative	*Negative*	*Interrogative*
I rang the bell.	I did not ring the bell.	Did I ring the bell?
He rang the bell.	He did not ring the bell.	Did he ring the bell?
You rang the bell.	You did not ring the bell.	Did you ring the bell?
They rang the bell.	They did not ring the bell.	Did they ring the bell?

Look at the following question answer forms:

Did you do the homework?
Yes, I did.
No, I didn't.

Uses

1. The simple past tense is used for those actions and events that happened at a definite time in the past.
   (i) I went to the United States of America in 1976.
   (definite time shown)
   (ii) I got an East West Centre Scholarship.
   (definite time understood)
   (iii) I did M.A. and Ph.D. in Linguistics there.
   (These events occurred at a stated or understood definite time in the past.)

2. It is also used to refer to present time with verbs such as *wonder*, *want*, *hope* and *think:* This use makes the utterance more polite and tactful:
   (i) I **wanted** to speak to the principal.
   (ii) I **wondered** whether you would do me a favour.
   (iii) I **thought** I would succeed.
   (iv) I **hoped** to speak to the principal.
   (The use of the present tense in the above sentences will make them sound peremptory.)

3. It is also used in doubtful or hypothetical condition to refer to future time.

   (i) If a ghost **came** into the room, I **would** faint.
   (ii) If I **were** the P.M. of India, I **would** remove poverty.

4. It is also used in reported speech.

   (i) I said, "I'll go to Jaipur tomorrow."
   (ii) I said that I **would go** to Jaipur tomorrow/the next day.

Adverbials Used

The following time adverbs/adverbial phrases are used in this tense: *yesterday, last night, last week, last year, a moment ago, three days ago, long time ago, the day before yesterday, last Friday*.

Adverbial clauses introduced by *when, while, until, before, as soon as, after, once, the moment that*.

I *saw* a ghost in my room *yesterday*.

The ghost *said* hello to me. (The time expression is understood from the previous sentence.)

Notice, it is not acceptable to use a past time adverbial with the present perfect tense. It will be wrong to say:

*I have done the homework yesterday.

The correct version would be

I have done the homework.

I did the homework yesterday.

Difference between Simple Past and Present Perfect

It is important to note the difference between the simple past tense and the present perfect tense. As we know, in both the tenses we denote the action done in the past. The difference between the two is that whereas in the simple past, the focus is on *the time of the activity*, the focus in the present perfect is on the *current relevance* or result of the past action.

For example:

Have some breakfast.

I have just had my breakfast.

(I am not hungry.)

I had my breakfast. (can answer the question: When did you have breakfast?)

Further, it does not say anything about the current relevance.

EXERCISE 11.2

Put the verbs in brackets in the following sentences into the correct tense either simple past or present perfect:

1. I .... (go) to the States in 1976 for higher studies.
2. I .... (stay) in the States for 5 years.
3. During this period, I .... (do) extensive research on communication, culture and the English language.
4. I .... (publish) several papers on Linguistics and ELT in national and international journals.
5. I .... (teach) Grammar and Linguistics in several summer Institutes in English.
6. The United States is a marvellous country. I .... (enjoy) my stay there.
7. A: Hey, your body smells.
   B: Impossible! I .... (have) a bath with Life Buoy Gold.
8. A: Which perfume .... you .... (use)?
   B: Este Lauder. Would you like to try?
9. Farewell Address: Ladies and Gentlemen. Thank you very much for every thing. I .... (serve) this Institute for two and a half years. I .... (enjoy) every minute of my stay here. I .... (learn) many things.
10. You ever .... (see) a ghost?
    No. .... you (have)? Having said this, the man disappeared.
11. I am mortally afraid of the hostel warden. He .... (prohibit) me from sleeping during nights.
12. I .... just (see) a cockroach hurrying fast towards my food. But I can't see it now. May be it .... (fall) into my curry and I .... (eat) it.
13. You look quite thinned, Dan ? How .... you............ achieve this miraculous feat?
14. I .... (wonder) whether you .... (lend) me ₹ 2000.
15. I ……..(hope) to discuss the matter with the Principal.
16. The captain .... (declare) that nobody .... (be involved) in match fixing in 1996.
17. The hero .... (buy) all the tickets of "Kahin Payaar Na Ho Jaaye". It is an example of ticket scam.
18. A famous captain .... (confess) accepting $100000 in cricket match fixing.
19. It .... (be) a week since I .... (write) home.
20. The police .... (catch) a thief yesterday afternoon near Hope Circus.
21. They .... (not visit) us after we had quarrelled.
22. It is three months since we .... (meet).

23. Come and meet me when you .... (have) your lunch.
24. Once you .... (drink) that beer, you will never want to drink any other brand.
25. .... you (remember) to switch off the lights before going out of the room?

Present Perfect Continuous vs Present Perfect

Study the following sentence:

I **have been travelling** for the last ten hours but **haven't reached** Jaipur yet.

The bold verbal phrases are in the perfect continuous tense and in the present perfect. The form of the present perfect continuous is given below.

Form

The form of present perfect continuous is given in Table 11.4.

TABLE 11.4 Forms of present perfect continuous

Affirmative	*Negative*	*Interrogative*
I have been sleeping.	I haven't been sleeping.	Have I been sleeping?
He has been sleeping.	He hasn't been sleeping.	Has he been sleeping?
They have been sleeping.	They haven't been sleeping.	Have they been sleeping?

This tense is formed by have/has + been + verb + ing. In the negative, not or n't is placed immediately after the helping verb have/has. In interrogatives, have/has precedes the subject.

Uses

1. The present perfect continuous tense is used for the action that started in the past, continued up to the moment of speaking and are still continuing.

   (i) I have been living in Alwar for the last 20 years. (I am still living in Alwar.)

   (ii) She has been learning music since January.

2. It is used for those actions that are not taking place at the moment of speaking but to indicate that the actions have been *uninterrupted.*

   Why are you panting?
   I **have been running.** (The particular person is not running at the moment of speaking.)
   You have paint all over your clothes. What is the reason?
   I **have been painting** the door.

The above sentences show the visible effect of an event, i.e. *running* or *painting*.

3. This tense is also used to show the unfinished activity as against the completed activity in the present perfect tense.

   He **has been painting** a picture.
   (not finished yet)
   He **has painted a** picture. (The picture is complete.)

Adverbials used

The adverbials used in this tense are *for*, *since all day*, *all week*, *all morning*, etc.

Look at Table 11.5 for the use of *for* and *since*.

TABLE 11.5 Uses of since and for

point of time	since	25 February, last year, Wednesday, he was a boy.
period of time	for	three days, a long time, ten minutes, ten years.

Difference between Present Perfect and Present Perfect Continuous

The difference between the present perfect and present perfect continuous can be illustrated by the following table (Table 11.6):

TABLE 11.6 Difference between present perfect and continuous tense

Present perfect	*Present perfect continuous*	*Difference*
Indefinite time in the past: I have seen the Taj.	No parallel available	Not applicable
Linkage with the present: I have lived in Alwar for 20 years.	I have been living in Alwar for 20 years.	No difference in meaning
Current relevance: I have typed ten letters.	Why do you look tired? I *have been running*.	In the present perfect, the focus is on the completion of activity whereas in the present perfect continuous, the focus is on *the activity* itself.

The difference can be made clear by the following sentences:

(i) Who has eaten my candy? (None left)
(ii) Who has been eating my candy? (Some left)
(iii) Ram has cleaned the car. (The car is clean now, completed activity.)
(iv) Ram has been cleaning the car. (Incomplete activity. The car is not yet clean.)

EXERCISE 11.3

1. The master says to the servant, "you .... (clean) the floor. You may go now."
2. There are tears in his eyes. He .... (cut) onions.
3. It .... (rain) for the last three days and there seems to be no way of stopping it.
4. This tea .... already .... (get) cold. I can't drink it.
5. I can't reply to his letter as I .... (mislay) it.
6. What have you decided about buying this home?
   I .... still .... (think).
7. I .... (take) a decision not to buy this house.
8. The dog .... (sit) in front of the gate for the last half an hour.
9. I .... (look) at this painting for an hour but I can't understand it.
10. He is tired because he .... (work) in the garden all morning.
11. Tell me what you .... (do) since I last met you.
12. The dentist said to the young girl, "What .... you .... (do) to your teeth? They are in such a bad shape."
13. Shyam .... (paint) the house since last week.
14. What .... you .... (do) to my screwdriver? The edges are bent.
15. .... you .... (see) the Eiffel Tower?
16. The authorities .... once again .... (open) the leaning Pisa for public viewing.
17. The authorities .... (close) the public park for holding marriage receptions.
18. Though the Engineering College started only 2 years ago, it .... (earn) a name for itself.
19. He is quite an experienced teacher. He .... (teach) in several colleges.
20. I can tell you story of this novel. Still you don't believe me that I .... (read) the novel.

Simple Past Tense vs Past Continuous Tense

Look at the following sentence:

His head **was hurting,** and some blood **was showing** on his knee.

As we know that present continuous tense refers to the actions that are going on at the moment of speaking, the past continuous is used to express actions that *were going on in the past*. We shall study three things about this tense: (i) form, (ii) uses and (iii) adverbials used.

Form

This tense is formed by was/were +verb+ing. Look at the following table (Table 11.7).

TABLE 11.7 Form of past continuous tense

Affirmative	*Negative*	*Interrogative*
He was driving a car.	He was not driving a car.	Was he driving a car?
They were driving a car.	They were not driving a car.	Were they driving a car?
You were driving a car.	You were not driving a car.	Were you driving a car?
He/she was driving a car.	He/she was not driving a car.	Was he/she driving acar.

Notice we use was + verb + ing with *I/he* and *she*. We use were + verb + ing with *you/we* and *they*.

Uses

1. This tense is used for those actions that were in progress when something else happened. This tense serves as a time frame for something else to happen. For example:

   (i) He **was watching** TV when I reached home.
   (ii) She **was writing** letters when I opened the gate.
   (iii) He **was sleeping** when I rang him up.

2. This tense is also used to say that someone was in the middle of doing something at a certain time in the past.

   What were you doing at 9 o'clock last night?
   I was watching TV.
   I was quarrelling with my sister.

Notice the action of *watching* or quarrelling had started before 9 o' clock and hadn't finished.

Adverbials Used

Look at Table 11.8.

TABLE 11.8 Adverbials used in past continuous

Definite past time adverbials	*Adverbial clauses of time*
at 9 pm.	*As* he was crossing the road,
this time last year	*When* he came in, ...
all afternoon	
all last week	
all morning	*While* I was watching TV.....
all yesterday	

Relationship with the Simple Past

The past continuous serves as a time framework for a past action to happen.

He was sleeping when I arrived home.

This shows that my arrival at home occurred during his sleep. He went to sleep before my arrival and was still sleeping when I arrived.

This tense can also be used to denote two simultaneous activities in progress in the past:

While I **was watching** TV, **she was writing** letters.

EXERCISE 11.4

Fill in the blanks with either past continuous or past simple of the verbs given in brackets.

1. When I .... (enter) the class, the students .... (draw) a cartoon of the teacher on the blackboard.
2. When I .... (teach) in the class, some students ....(make) a noise.
3. When my mother .... (cook) food in the kitchen, some boys .... (play) football in the street.
4. While I .... (water) the plants, some birds .... (chirp).
5. While I .... (sip) coffee, he .... (drink) Coco cola.
6. The cook .... (prepare) food in the kitchen, when I .... (enter) the dining hall.
7. Some students .... (watch) TV in the TV room when I .... (open) the gate.
8. Shyam .... (play) table tennis, when I .... (go) up to him to give him the telephonic message received from his father.
9. When I .... (teach), Divya .... (walk) in.
10. While he .... (study), the electricity .... (break) down.
11. It .... (rain) hard when Shyam .... (reach) the station.
12. While Ram .... (play) in the park, a dog .... (bite) him.

13. As the old man .... (cross) the road, a speeding car .... (hit) him.
14. He .... (play) the guitar when I .... (go) to his house.
15. The thief .... (stab) him, when he .... (say) his prayers.
16. We .... (encounter) a tiger when we .... (cross) the jungle.
17. She .... (practise) yoga when her friend .... (call) on her.
18. What were you doing at 9 pm?
    Yesterday I .... (read) a book.
19. I .... (have) dinner when the telephone .... (ring).
20. What .... you .... (do) when I .... (knock) at the door?
21. She .... (break) down when she .... (hear) the news.
22. The gardener .... (dig) in the garden when he .... (find) a diamond necklace.
23. I .... (try) to ring you up all afternoon but your telephone .... (not work).
24. Did you see Geeta in the theatre last night? She .... (sit) in the first row.
25. They all .... (have) lunch when I .... (reach) home.

Simple Past Tense vs Past Perfect Tense

Look at the two sentences:

> The last room **had just been taken** before Sachin **reached** there. Luckily **he had entered** the main gate before the watchman **closed** it for the night.

The bold verbs are in the *past perfect* and in the simple past. The past perfect tense is formed by *had + third form of the verb* and the simple past is formed by the *second form* of the verb. We shall study the past perfect by discussing (i) form, (ii) uses and (iii) adverbials.

Form

Table 11.9 illustrates the form of this tense.

TABLE 11.9 Form of past perfect

Affirmative	*Negative*	*Interrogative*
I had reached the station.	I had not reached the station.	Had I reached the station?
He had reached the station.	He had not reached the station.	Had he reached the station?
They had reached the station.	They had not reached the station.	Had they reached the station?
We/you had reached the station.	We/you had not reached the station?	Had we/you reached the station?

The form of the past perfect is very straight forward. *Had + third form of the verb* constitutes this tense.

Uses

This tense is used for those actions or events that happened before some other actions or events:

The patient **had died** before the doctor **arrived.**

Here two actions occurred in the past.

(a) Death of the patient.
(b) Arrival of the doctor.

The death occurred before the arrival of the doctor. Therefore, we use *past perfect* for the action of dying and simple past for the arrival of the doctor, because it is the subsequent act. Other examples of the past perfect are:

(i) The train **had left** before I **reached the station.**
(ii) After the thief **had escaped,** the **police arrived.**
(iii) The **bell rang** after the students **had finished** their work.

The present perfect and the simple past become past perfect in the reported speech if the reporting verb is in the past tense:

(i) He said, "I **have done** the homework."
He said that he **had done** the homework.
(ii) He said, "I **lost** my book **yesterday."**
He said that he **had lost** his book **the previous day.**
(iii) Radha said, "I **have learnt** dancing."
Radha said that she **had learnt** dancing.

Adverbials Used

This tense generally occurs in company with the simple past tense. The subordinating conjunctions used are *when*, *until*, *before*, *after*, *as soon as*, *till*, *the moment*, *by the time*, etc.

(i) When he reached the class, the teacher **had already come.**
(ii) As soon as I **had finished** the work, I went home.
(iii) After the **patient had died,** the doctor arrived.
(iv) I **had spent** all the money before he asked me for a loan.
(v) When **I reached** home I **found** that I **had lost** my purse.
(vi) He **had not understood** till the teacher explained it to him.

Relationship with the Simple Past and Present Perfect

The past perfect denotes an action or event that happened before some other action or event in the past.

He *had lived* in Jaipur before he *moved* to Delhi.

The sentence shows that his living in Jaipur was completed before his movement to Delhi.

Sometimes it is difficult to decide which action happened before the other in the past. In such a situation, it is better to use simple past in both the clauses.

(i) The moment he reached home, the light went off.
(ii) As soon as he reached home, the light went off.

The past perfect tense shows a time earlier on in the past than the simple past tense; the present perfect shows a time earlier than the simple present tense.

(i) He had studied in Jaipur for 5 years before he went to Delhi. (Shows he was in Jaipur for 5 years before moving to Delhi.)
(ii) He has studied in Jaipur for 5 years. (Shows that he has already studied in Jaipur for 5 years and is still here.)

EXERCISE 11.5

Put the verbs in brackets into the correct tense, simple past or past perfect. (*Hint:* Figure out which action happened before the other. Use past perfect for the earlier action and simple past for the subsequent action.)

1. Rekha .... (put) the clothes in the cupboard after she .... (iron) them.
2. The players .... (start) playing after the referee .... (blow) the whistle.
3. When I .... (reach) home I .... (realize) that I .... (leave) the key in the department..
4. He .... (revise) all his lessons before the exam .... (start).
5. As soon as he .... (recover) form illness, he .... (start) going to college.
6. Last night I .... (go) to see him.
7. We .... (go) inside as soon as it .... (begin) to rain.
8. After his friend .... (cheat) him, he .... (lose) faith in all humanity.
9. I .... (wait) for him until he .... (come).
10. Last year when she .... (have) money she .... (buy) a colour TV.
11. His chin .... (begin) to bleed as soon as he .... (cut) himself.
12. I .... (be) not able to understand the lesson until he .... (explain) it to me.
13. I .... (expect) that he .... (will) pass.
14. The teacher .... (want) to know why I .... (not do) the homework.

15. He .... (make) a will before he .... (die).
16. The teacher .... (be) in the class for 15 minutes when I .... (reach) the college.
17. The principal .... (not allow) him to attend classes until he .... (apologise).
18. He .... (tell) me that he never .... (meet) you.
19. She .... (burst) into tears the moment she .... (come) to know that she .... (fail) in the exam.
20. He .... (exclaim) with joy that they .... (win) a match.
21. He .... (be) happy to learn that he .... (pass) the RPET.
22. After he .... (pass) the RPET, he .... (admit) to JECRC, Jaipur.
23. When she .... (perform) the show, she .... (sit) down.
24. When she .... (enter) the room, she .... (realize) that there .... (be) a burglary.
25. He .... (refuse) till he .... (see) all the show.

Six Ways of Expressing Future

There is no future tense in English. As said earlier, tense refers to the form of the verb. As there is no corresponding form of the verb for the future tense, there is no future tense in English. There are six ways of expressing futurity in English. Read the following paragraph:

The caretaker gave Rahul a nice room. The room was cosy and well ventilated. The linen was neat and clean. Lying in the comfortable bed Rahul said to himself, "I'll reach Jaipur at 10 am tomorrow. I'll be attending the counselling session at MREC. I am going to take the first available bus to Jaipur tomorrow morning. The bus leaves at 6 am. I hope I'll reach Jaipur bus station by 9 am."

Enveloped in these thoughts, Rahul did not know when he went to sleep. He woke up; hearing chirping of the birds in the morning. The sun light had already entered the room through window-panes. He got up perplexedly and looked up his watch. To his dismay, it was already 6:30 am.

Look at the following sentences from the passage.

I'll reach Jaipur at 10 am tomorrow; *I am going to take* the first available bus to Jaipur tomorrow morning, and the bus *leaves* at 6 am.

The above three sentences illustrate three out of six ways of expressing future in English. Below we discuss all the six ways one by one.

Use of Will/Shall

Will/shall + the first form of the verb is used to denote what we think will happen in future. The difference between *will* and *shall* is fast disappearing in future. The contracted 'll form is generally used in speech.

The adverbials used are future time adverbials such as *tomorrow*, *day after tomorrow*, *next week*, *next month*, *on coming Friday*, *in 2016*, *etc*. Study the following sentences:

(i) I shall go to Jaipur tomorrow.
(ii) I'll meet my friend Mohan there.
(iii) Together we shall go to see the Vice-chancellor.

Notice the future time adverbials may be stated as in sentence (i) above or it may be understood as in sentences (ii) and (iii).

Use of Will/Shall + be + verb + ing

This form is used to express three things

1. When we are in the middle of doing something in the future:

   Can I come and see you tomorrow at 8 pm? Please don't come at that time. Why? **I'll be having** dinner then.

2. It is used to denote a part of the plan or arrangement especially when you want something to be done:

   Will you be passing the post office? Why?
   Could you buy me some stamps?

3. It is used to express a happening which occurs as a matter of course or routine:

   Will you give this letter to Mohan?
   No problem.
   I'll be meeting him in the office anyway.
   Compare:
   I will meet him in the office. (shows the speaker's volition)
   I'll be meeting him in the office. (matter of fact/course/routine. That means the speaker works there.)

Use of is/am/are + Going to + First Form of the Verb

This construction is used to express three things in future:

1. It expresses future intention:

   (i) I am going to buy a car next year. (I intend to buy a car….)
   (ii) He is going to marry a rich girl. (He intends to marry a rich girl.)
   (iii) She is going to visit the States next year. (That is her intention.).

2. It is used to express something that is sure to happen in future. There is a sufficient present cause to show the expected future result.

   (i) There are dark clouds in the sky. It is going to rain.
   (ii) It is already 8.30. He has to reach office by 9 a.m.
   (iii) It takes about 45 minutes by bus. He is going to be late.

3. This construction is also used for what the speaker has decided to do.

   (i) Your room is dirty. I'm going to clean it.
   (ii) Your shoes are torn. I am going to get them mended.

   In this use, there is very little difference between the present continuous and going to form. But for making plans in future, the use of present continuous is more natural.

Use of Present Continuous

The present continuous tense with future time adverbials (tomorrow, next week, day after tomorrow, etc.) is used to denote future arrangements or plans.

(i) I'm leaving for Jaipur tomorrow. (My visit to Jaipur is planned. I have already bought a ticket.)
(ii) We **are starting** the construction of the college building next week. (Every thing for the construction work has been arranged. Cement, mortar, concrete, etc. have already been bought.)
(iii) He is **joining** his duties tomorrow. (He has already been appointed.)

Use of Simple Present Tense

This tense is used to denote fixed plans, railway time tables, aeroplane schedules, programmes for public transport, cinema, etc.

(i) The train **leaves** Alwar at 7.00 pm and reaches Delhi at 10.00 pm.
(ii) The Prime Minister **arrives** in Agra tomorrow. (A newspaper headline. The visit has been fixed.)
(iii) The programme **starts** at 11.00 am tomorrow.
(iv) The film **starts** at 8.15 am this morning.

Use of Be + about to + First Form of the Verb

We use this construction for immediate future. The future time adverbial used should also indicate immediate future.

(i) The train is about to leave in two minutes.
(ii) It is already 9.59 am. The exam is about to start.
(iii) The sky is overcast with clouds. It is about to rain.

EXERCISE 11.6

Put the verbs in brackets into is/am/are + going to + first form of the verb or will/shall + first form of the verb.

1. Have you decided on the subject you are going to choose. Oh, yes, I .... (go in for) Science-Biology.

2. What do you think you are doing? I .... (take) the car back. Be careful. If you are not careful, it .... (fall) into the nearby ditch.
3. Why have you brought this book here? I .... (read) it. Hide it, if the chairman sees it, he .... (fire) you from service.
4. What are doing for the weakend? I .... (start) the construction of my house. The bank has sanctioned the loan. The raw material has arrived.
5. I .... (start) a computer centre. I don't know how many students .... (join) it.
6. She .... (have) a baby next month.
7. I think he .... (pass) the exam.
8. He has won a lottery. What is he going to do with it? He .... (buy) a car.
9. There is a volleyball match between Ist year and 2nd year students the evening. .... you .... (go) to watch it?
10. This food looks bad. I .... (not eat) it.

EXERCISE 11.7

Put the verbs in brackets into will/shall + first form of the verb or into will/shall + be + first form of the verb + –ing according to the context.

1. There is a possibility of power strike tomorrow. Everybody .... (look) for candles tomorrow.
2. Ajay has got a job in the Engineering College of Alwar. He .... (leave) for .... Alwar tomorrow.
3. Please do me a favour. Forward my name to 13 Malviya Nagar Jaipur. I .... (to stay) there for a week.
4. It .... (be) very late by the time I get home and my parents .... (wonder) about my getting late.
5. Don't come at 8 pm. I .... (teach) in the PMT class. Ok, I .... (come) later.
6. He says he .... (meet) me at the railway station but I'm sure he .... (forget) to come.
7. Don't drink coffee without milk. The milk vendor .... (come) any moment.
8. Ram usually walks home. But tomorrow he .... (come) by bus as he has to take his mother to hospital.
9. The air hostess said, "Fasten your seat belts please. We .... (take) off in a few minutes."
10. I don't know what I .... (do) next year. I hope you still .... (work) in the same college.

EXERCISE 11.8

Put the verbs in brackets in correct tense form:

1. Bose (be) the first Indian scientist to work with Madam Curie. He (have) a good command of three languages.
2. They (go) to New York? How many hours (do) it take?
3. A man who I (see) three times already that afternoon (follow) me.
4. He (work) for the Crowe Brothers for 22 years and never once (be) late.
5. Throughout his years at St. Stephen's College Delhi, he (smoke) and (play) poker and (score) the lowest marks in the college.
6. But I still (not see) why more people (not think) freely.
7. I (get) into the club when a stylish woman (come) up to me.
8. I (not be) able to give Joan all she (be) used to.
9. You (know) what symphony means?
10. My wife (not wear) stockings very often when we were on holiday.
11. When John entered the room, the thief already (escape).
12. I am sorry to hear you (leave) so soon. I (not know) the facts, all I know is that Peter (ring) up.
13. Mason (follow) him to the car. Tom drove. The men (be) silent.
14. He (lose) his books. He (look) for them all afternoon but has not found them.
15. She (go) shopping tomorrow. You (go) too?
16. Why you (type) so fast? You (make) a lot of mistakes.
17. If you (heat) butter, it (melt).
18. I just (open) the letter when the wind (blow) it out of my hand.
19. I (not see) him for three years. I wonder where he (be).
20. As soon as everyday (go) to bed, the mice (come) out of their holes.
21. She (cook) dinner when the door bell rang.
22. They (not visit) us after we had quarrelled.
23. They just (arrive) from New York.
24. Mr. Jones usually (sell) only newspapers.
25. You (know) that boy who (sit) in the last seat?
26. The house opposite the college (be pulled) down. That is why we (use) the back entrance at present.
27. Hello, Jack! I (not see) you for ages Where you (be)?
28. I (not know) you (be) left handed.
29. I (see) my bank manager tomorrow. I'm going to ask him but I expect he (refuse).
30. I (work) for Videocon for six months. I left because the men always (go) on strike.
31. My aunt (walk) in the park when I met him.
32. I was washing my hands when the telephone (ring).

33. They (live) here since January.
34. You ever (read) "War & Peace"?
35. Whenever I (go) to see him, he was not there.
36. He lost his new knife shortly after he (buy) it.
37. The patient (die) already by the time the doctor arrived.
38. When I .... (cross) the road, a truck hit me. I .... (fall) on the road but the truck driver fled. The passersby (come) to help me. They .... (surprise) to notice that there was not even a scratch on my body. I .... (thank) God for saving me.
39. He (come) to see me every day last week.
40. We usually (have) breakfast at seven o'clock.
41. You (see) the house on the corner? That is where I was born.
42. I (knock) on the door ten times now without any answer.
43. When I was young, my father always (give) me some money on Saturdays.
44. In the past, men frequently (fight) duels. Now-a-days they seldom (do).
45. Buses usually (run) along this street, but today they (not run) because it is under repair.
46. Sita still (do) her homework. Her sister, who always (work) quicker, (play) already in the garden.
47. What you (do) at this moment? If you (not do) anything, please help me.
48. We nearly always (spend) our holidays at the seaside, but this year we are going to Dehradun.
49. I'm sorry you can't see her she (sleep) still. She usually (wake) much earlier.
50. You (smell) gas? I (think) the new stove is leaking.
51. Look at Ram! He (drink) up his medicine, but I can see that he (hate) it.
52. Do you (remember) the name of that boy who (walk) on the other side of the street?
53. The chairman (study) your proposal and regrets he cannot accept it.
54. Ram (write) letters all morning, but Shaym (not start) to write any as yet.
55. The company (build) the building over a year but it still isn't finished.
56. Radha (go) to the dentist off and on for three months.
57. Shaym (try) to get in touch with you for several hours now.
58. Yesterday afternoon the police (catch) a thief at the Hope Circus.
59. It is nearly four years ago that we (get) married.
60. Ram (get back) very late last night.
61. As soon as he had opened the door, his dog (rush) out to greet him.
62. When you last (see) your father?
63. She broke down when she (hear) the news.
64. I (wash) my hands when the telephone (ring).

65. The patient (die) before the doctor arrived.
66. When Ram (get) home, night already (fall).
67. What your wife (do) at the moment?
She (take) bath.
She (bath) every day?
Yes, she (do).
68. Gopal (throw) the ball to Ganesh, but he (lose) it, Suresh, then, (give) the ball to Mahesh, Mahesh (go) past two men, he (shoot) hard and (score) a goal.
69. Ganesh (not go) to the theatre last night because he (see) the play before.

Key to Exercise 11.1

1. attends, is cutting
2. walks, is going
3. spend, are going
4. do you enjoy
5. plays, is playing
6. is raining, does not rain
7. do not understand, are saying
8. do you know
9. is having, not see
10. comes, flings, falls, misses, goes
11. has
12. is still sleeping
13. is he doing, is playing
14. sits, is sitting
15. loves
16. is knocking
17. are you studying, am taking
18. prefer
19. do you wash
20. is waiting
21. teases
22. is watching, likes
23. leaves
24. is leaving
25. am learning, is teaching

Key to Exercise 11.2

1. went
2. stayed
3. did
4. have published
5. have taught
6. enjoyed
7. have had
8. do you use
9. have served, have enjoyed, have learnt
10. have you ever seen
11. has prohibited
12. just saw, has fallen, have eaten
13. have you achieved
14. wondered, would lend
15. hoped
16. declared, was involved
17. has bought

18. has confessed
19. has been, wrote
20. caught
21. did not visit
22. met
23. have had
24. have drunk
25. did you remember

Key to Exercise 11.3

1. have cleaned
2. has been cutting
3. has been raining
4. has already got
5. have mislaid
6. have still been thinking
7. have taken
8. has been sitting
9. have been looking
10. has been working
11. have been doing
12. have you been doing
13. has been painting
14. have you done
15. have you seen
16. have once again opened
17. have closed
18. has earned
19. has taught
20. have read

Key to Exercise 11.4

1. entered, were drawing
2. was teaching, were making a noise.
3. was cooking, were playing
4. was watering, were chirping
5. was sipping, was drinking
6. was preparing, entered
7. were watching, opened
8. was playing, went
9. was teaching, walked
10. was studying, broke down
11. was raining, reached
12. was playing, bit
13. was crossing, hit
14. was playing, went
15. stabbed, was saying
16. encountered, were crossing
17. was practising, called
18. was reading
19. was having, rang
20. were you doing, knocked
21. broke down, heard
22. was digging, found
23. was trying, was not working
24. was sitting
25. were all having, reached

Key to Exercise 11.5

1. put, had ironed
2. started, had blown
3. reached, realized, had left
4. had revised, started
5. had recovered, started
6. went
7. went, began
8. had cheated, lost
9. had waited, came
10. had, bought
11. began, had cut
12. was, had explained

13. had expected, would
14. wanted, had not done
15. had made, died
16. had been, reached
17. did not allow, had apologized
18. told, had met
19. burst, came, had failed
20. exclaimed, had won
21. was, had passed
22. had passed, was admitted
23. had performed, sat down
24. entered, realized, had been
25. refused, had seen

Key to Exercise 11.6

1. am going to go in for
2. am going to take, will fall
3. am going to read, will fire
4. am going to start
5. am going to start, will join
6. is going to have
7. will pass
8. is going to buy
9. are you going to
10. am not going to eat

Key to Exercise 11.7

1. will be looking
2. will be leaving
3. will be staying
4. will be, will be wondering
5. will be teaching, will come
6. will meet, will forget
7. will be coming
8. will be coming
9. shall be taking
10. will be doing, will be working

Key to Exercise 11.8

1. was, had
2. are they going, does
3. had seen, followed
4. has worked, has never once been
5. smoked, played, scored
6. do not see, do not think
7. was getting, came
8. have not been, has been used to
9. do you know
10. did not wear
11. had already escaped
12. are leaving, do not know, rang
13. followed, were
14. has lost, was looking
15. is going, will you go
16. are you typing, are making
17. heat, melts/ will melt
18. was just opening, blew
19. have not seen, is
20. had gone, came
21. was cooking
22. did not visit
23. have just arrived
24. sells
25. do you know, is sitting
26. has been pulled down, are using
27. have not seen, were/have you been
28. did not know, were/are
29. am seeing, will refuse
30. have worked, are always going
31. was walking
32. rang
33. have been living

34. have you ever read
35. went
36. had bought
37. had died
38. was crossing, fell, came, were surprised, thanked
39. came
40. have
41. do you see
42. have knocked
43. gave
44. fought, do
45. run, are not running
46. is still doing, works, is already playing
47. what are you doing, are not doing
48. spend
49. is still sleeping, wakes
50. do you smell, think
51. is drinking, hates
52. do you remember, is walking
53. has studied
54. has been writing, has not started
55. has been building
56. has been going
57. has been trying
58. caught
59. got
60. got back
61. rushed
62. did you last see
63. heard
64. was washing, rang
65. had died
66. got, had already fallen
67. is your wife doing, is taking bath, does she bathe, does
68. throws, loses, gives, goes, shoots, scores
69. did not go, had seen

12

Modal Auxiliaries

Introduction

Auxiliary verbs are helping verbs that are used with main verbs to indicate *person*, *tense*, *voice* and *aspect*. The auxiliary verbs have been bold in the following sentences.

(i) I **am** helping my mother in the kitchen.
(ii) He **didn't** come yesterday.
(iii) I **have** passed the examination.

There are three types of helping verbs in the English language as shown in Figure 12.1.

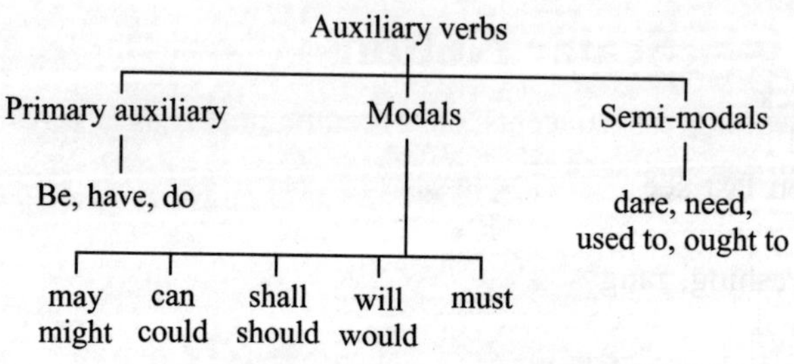

FIGURE 12.1 Auxiliary verbs

Characteristics of Modals

Modal auxiliaries have certain characteristics which differentiate them from other helping verbs.

1. A modal verb is always the first element in a verb phrase. It has no ending with –s, –ing, or –ed. It is followed by a base infinitive:

   (i) Jaipur **will be** windy tonight.
   (ii) You **should obey** your parents.

2. A modal verb usually does not have a tense.

   (i) He **may come** tomorrow (refers to future time).
   (ii) He **might come** tomorrow (refers to future time).
   (iii) He **may have come** by now (refers to past time).
   (iv) He **might have come** by now (refers to past time).

3. A modal verb can go with progressive or perfective aspect or with passive voice.

   (i) They **may be building** a house.
   (ii) They **may have built** a house.
   (iii) The house **may have been completed** by now.

4. Modal verbs are used to denote concepts such as necessity, possibility, probability, obligation, advice, permission, certainty, ability, etc.
5. *Dare*, *need*, and *used to* have been listed under the semi-modals because sometimes it is possible to use them as main verbs.

   (i) He **daren't** go. (as a modal)
   (ii) **Dare** you challenge me? (as a modal)
   (iii) He doesn't **dare** to challenge him. (as a verb)
   (iv) He **needn't** come. (as a modal)
   (v) **Does** he **need** to come? (as a verb)
   (vi) He **usedn't** to attend classes regularly. (as a modal)
   (vii) He **didn't use to** attend classes regularly. (as a verb)

Modality is a Scalar Notion

Modal auxiliaries express concepts on a continuum. It is always helpful to think in terms of various scales:

1. Scale of politeness

   (i) Could you help me? (more polite)
   (ii) Would you help me.
   (iii) Can you help me.(?)
   (iv) Will you help me?

2. Scale of formality

   (i) May I come in? (formal)
   (ii) Can I go out? (informal)

3. Scale of possibility

   (i) He may come tomorrow.
   (ii) He might come tomorrow. (less possible)

It is also possible to think in terms of theoretical and factual possibility.

(i) Electricity can kill people. (theoretical possibility)
(ii) There are dark clouds in the sky. It may rain soon. (factual possibility)

Concepts are Atomic

It is useful to think in terms of concepts as atomic. For example, obligation can be broken into sub-concepts such as giving advice or making recommendation or talking about responsibility or duty. Making recommendation can depend upon outside authority or can be self-motivated.

(i) You look terribly sick. You should/ought to see a doctor (giving advice or making a recommendation).
(ii) The manual says that the cooler **should** be disconnected from the mains before the cooler is filled with water. (Do not use **ought to** here because the recommendation is based on outside authority.)
(iii) I **should** reserve my ticket in advance if I were you. (Do not use **ought to** if the recommendation is self-motivated.)
(iv) You **should/ought to** obey you parents. (duty/responsibility)
(v) He **should/ought to** have taken my permission before he took my book. (past obligation)
(vi) If you are not well, you **should/ought to /had better** ask Radha to go instead. (use **had better and first form of the verb** in spoken English for advice. Do not use **had better ...** construction in referring to past time or general recommendation.)
(vii) **I'm supposed to** be here at 10:00 a.m. (refers to less strong obligation)
(viii) Eating sweets is **supposed** to be bad for teeth. (What many people think is true. Do not use **should** in this case.)

For willingness in the past, we shall have to make a distinction between *repeated willingness* and *willingness* on a particular occasion.

(i) Whenever I went to Delhi, Ram **would give** me a lift. (repeated)
(ii) I was late, so Ram gave me a lift to town. (particular occasion)

A difference is made in the use of one modal over the other along the axis of formality versus *informality*. For example:

(i) We **would** lend him money when he wasn't employed.
(ii) We **used to** lend him money when he wasn't employed. (repeated action in the past with the implication that **used to** is more common in informal English.)
(iii) Can I borrow your book? Of course you can. (asking permission – informal)

(iv) May I borrow your book? Of course. (asking permission – formal)
(v) Might I borrow your book? (asking permission, it is both formal and tentative.)

Necessity can be because of an outside authority or a speaker can decide something to be necessary. The former warrants the use of *have* (*got*) *to* and the latter warrants the use of *must*.

(i) I **have (got)** to see the principal. (He has called me to his office.)
(ii) I must see the principal. (I want to discuss something with him.)
(iii) He has got a Mercedes and a big bungalow. He **must** be rich. (For logical conclusion, use **must**, not **have (got) to**)
(iv) You want to borrow money from me. **You've** got to be joking. (Here the use of **have (got) to** instead of **must** suggests that it is an **informal** use.)
(v) That can't be right. That couldn't be right. (For negative conclusion, **cannot** or **could not** is used. We cannot use **mustn't** or **haven't got to**.)

Lack of necessity can be further viewed as general necessity or necessity not to do something. For general necessity, don't *need to* is used whereas to give permission not to do something, we can use either *needn't* or *don't need to*.

(i) You **don't need** to be over 18 to drive a car. (general necessity)
(ii) You **needn't** to be over 18 to drive a car. (not possible)
(iii) You **don't need/needn't** sweep the floor, I'll do it later. (to give permission not to do something)

Further, we shall have to make a distinction between having *general permission* to do something and having permission for a particular past action. For the former, *could* or was *allowed to* is used but for the latter, only *was/were allowed to* is used.

(i) Women **weren't allowed** to vote (couldn't vote) in the 19th century. (general permission)
(ii) I **wasn't allowed to** travel to Bombay alone. (here *couldn't* is not possible)

To make an *offer*, would (you) like, not *will you like* is used. In accepting the offer, one can say either *would like* or *should like* but not *will like:*

(i) What would you like to drink? (offer)
(ii) I would like to have an orange juice.
(iii) I should like to have an orange juice. (formal).

Compare the difference of meaning in the following sentences:

(i) What will you have to eat/drink? (not what would you ...?)
(ii) What would you like to eat/drink? (not what will you like ...?)

The use of *not* in modals needs special attention.

(i) He can't be successful. (It is not possible (that he is successful).)
(ii) He may not be successful. (It is possible (that he is not successful).)
(iii) You don't have to go now. (It is not compulsory (for you to go now).)
(iv) You must not go now. (It is compulsory (for you not to go now).)

Mood, Modals and Modality

Traditional grammarians talk about different kinds of moods. Mood is a formal or grammatical category. They refer to the following moods:

1. Declarative mood: makes a statement.

   (i) She is a doctor.
   (ii) I request you to open the door.
   (iii) I am amazed that you fared so badly in the exam.

2. Interrogative mood: asks a question.

   (i) Is she a doctor?
   (ii) Who is a doctor?
   (iii) Will you join me for lunch?

3. Imperative mood: makes a request or an order.

   (i) Bring me a glass of water.
   (ii) Please come with me to see a movie tonight.

4. Exclamative mood: expresses a strong emotion.

   (i) What a grand building!
   (ii) How fantastic your performance is!

5. Subjunctive: expresses a wish.

   (i) If I were the Prime Minister of India!
   (ii) May you prosper!

Notice sentence 1(ii) above is in declarative mood, but it makes a request. Similarly 2(iii) is an interrogative but expresses a request. A sentence like he is the principal of the college, said with a rising intonation is a question though it is in a declarative mood. This shows that there is no one to one correspondence between mood and semantic labels like statements, questions, requests, etc.

Mood refers to the way a sentence is structured whereas statements, questions, requests, wish, etc. refer to the meaning of sentences. For these semantic categories, the term **modality** should be used. Other concepts expressed through modality are ability, permission, probability, necessity, request, etc. These meanings are expressed either through mood or modals. Consider the following sentences:

(i) She is a doctor.
Mood: declarative
Modality: statement

(ii) I request you to open the door.
Mood: declarative
Modality: request

(iii) If only I were the P.M. of India.
Mood: subjunctive
Modality: wish

Notice the expression of modality is the most important function of modals.

Table 12.1 discusses the meanings of modal verbs.

TABLE 12.1 Meanings of modal verbs

Modals	*Meaning*	*Examples*
must/have	necessity	(i) You *must* reserve your ticket in advance to go to Bombay. (The speaker feels the necessity.) (ii) I *have to* buy the ticket before I get on the bus. (That's the rule.) (iii) I *must* attend *classes* regularly. (I am getting behind in my studies.) (iv) I *have to attend* classes regularly. (The teacher has told me to do so.) (v) Compare: I'm *to go* on a diet. (order by a person or authority) (vi) Compare: You *are obliged to/required to* enter into an agreement. (expresses necessity) (vii) *Must* has no perfective or a continuous form, no past time, no infinitive or – ing form. We use *have to* instead of *must*. I had to go to Mumbai last week. We've had to make some changes in the syllabus. You'll have to pay the fine.
must	logical necessity	(i) He has a BMW and a big house. He *must* be rich. (ii) He has come walking 20 miles. He *must* be tired. (iii) He has secured 90% marks in the exam. He *must* be hard working.
needn't/ don't have to/haven't *got to*	no necessity	(i) You *needn't* always make a complaint. (ii) You *do not* always *have to* make a complaint. (iii) The figures *do not have to/ don't need to* match.

(*Contd.*)

TABLE 12.1 Meanings of modal verbs (*Contd.*)

Modals	*Meaning*	*Examples*
mustn't	necessity not to do something	(i) You *mustn't* use calculators in the examination hall. (You are prohibited ...) (ii) I *mustn't* run. I've got a weak heart. (not allowed). (iii) You *mustn't* forget your admit card. (= Don't forget your admit card. You must remember your admit card.)
Should/ ought to/ had better	obligation/ advice	(i) They *should /ought to* build more hospitals. (That is the right thing to do.) (ii) You should travel in a group. (It is a good idea too.) (iii) Visitors *should* come one hour before the commencement of the show. (*should* is more polite and less emphatic alternative to *must.*) (iv) You are sick. You'd better see a doctor. (*had better* is stronger than *should/ought to.*) (v) We *had better* not waste time. (vi) Too much butter and sugar are *supposed to be* bad for you. (It is the normal thing to do or because it has been ordered or arranged.)
should/ ought to	probability	(i) They *should have/ought to have* reached the station by now. (ii) The train *should be* on time. (= if all goes well.) (iii) We're *likely to* know the result soon. (iv) We'll *probably* know the result soon.
Can/could may/might	permission	(i) You *can* use my bike if you like (giving permission). (ii) Any girl over 18 years *may/can* marry a boy over 21 years. (permitted by law, *may* is formal.) (iii) Can I use your phone? Of course, you can. (asking permission) (iv) May we come in? Of course. (asking permission) (v) I can stay up as late as I like. My parents don't mind. (talking about permission. Compare I'm allowed to stay up as late as I like.) (vi) Compare: May we go early? (What's the rule?)
will/ must/ can't	certainty	Comment: These verbs are used to say that something is certainly true or untrue. (i) Who's at the door? It'll be the postman. (ii) Who *can/will* be at the door? (iii) He walked twenty miles. He *must be* tried. (logically true) (iv) That can't be Ram. (can't is the opposite of *must.*)

(*Contd.*)

TABLE 12.1 Meanings of modal verbs (*Contd.*)

Modals	*Meaning*	*Examples*
		(v) The face looks familiar. I *must* have seen him before (past certainty) (vi) You've got exams soon. You *must* work hard. (order) (vii) Ram isn't at home. He *must* be working. (logical necessity)
may/might can/could	possibility	(i) That old furniture *may/might* be valuable. (something is possibly true.) (ii) You *may/might* get stuck up in the traffic if you do not go early. (uncertain prediction or intention; no difference of meaning between *may* and *might*, except *may* is a little stronger.) (iii) I can't repair his transistor. I *might* as *well* throw it away. (that's the best thing to do under the circumstances.) (iv) You can/could go on the bus (possible future actions; *can* is stronger than *could*). (v) Can/could you give me a lift (request, *could* is more tentative.) (vi) Can I give you a lift? (offer) (vii) Ram *could have* forgotten to post the letter. (for something that is possibly true, (for uncertain prediction, we use *could*, *may* and *might* but not *can.*)) (viii) You can make wine from apples. (something generally possible) (ix) We can feel lonely in the village. (Here *can* has the meaning of *sometimes*). (x) You can't/couldn't have seen Ram this morning. He is in Tamil Nadu. (impossibility) (xi) This answer can't be right. It must be wrong. (xii) This answer may/might not be right. It may/might be wrong. (xiii) He may/might/could have missed the train. (possibly true in the past)
can/could/ be able to	ability	(i) Ram can play western music. (present ability) (ii) Ram could speak French when he was a boy. (past ability) (iii) We can keep a dog in this house. (an opportunity) (iv) One day people *will be able* to go on a package tour of the solar system. (future ability or opportunity) (v) He could have phoned but decided to wait.

(*Contd.*)

TABLE 12.1 Meanings of modal verbs (*Contd.*)

Modals	*Meaning*	*Examples*
will/would	unreal situations	(i) We're going to throw a party Oh, that'*ll be nice.* (prediction about the future) (ii) We're thinking of throwing a party. Oh, that *would be nice.* (prediction about an unreal situation) (iii) Will /would you pass me the salt? (request, *would* more tentative than *will*) (iv) I wouldn't agree with that. (The use of *would* avoids impoliteness especially when disagreeing with someone.) (v) I would like to have a drink. (*would like* less direct than I *want to have a drink*) (vi) Would you rather stay or go? (preference) (vii) I'd rather not take any risks. (viii) I'd sooner walk than hover around for a bus. (ix) I would/should like to thank you for all you've done.
will/would/ used to	habits	(i) Every day Ram will come home and ring up Shyam. (ii) In those days people would make arrangement for dried vegetables. (iii) I *used to sit* on the bank of the river when I was a child. (*Used to* also shows past habit but it is used in informal English.)
will/would can/could may/might	request/ request for permission	(i) Will you come with me for the picnic? (ii) Can you pass me the salt please? (iii) Can I eat some chocolate? (iv) May I be going? (v) Would you do me a favour, please? (vi) Could you lend me ₹ 2000, please? (vii) Could I go out with Manish, please? (viii) Might I come in, sir?
shall/will	prediction	(i) I shall leave for Jaipur tomorrow. (ii) There will be a dust-storm tomorrow. (iii) The weather will be fine on Monday.
will/would	willingness	(i) I will lend you ₹ 5000. (ii) I would use that for you. (shows tentativeness) (iii) I would have used that for you. (= I was willing to do that for you.)
shall/should	volition of the listener	(i) Shall I wait for you? (Do you want me to wait for you?) (ii) Shall/should (AmE) the cabdriver wait for you?

(*Contd.*)

TABLE 12.1 Meanings of modal verbs (*Contd.*)

Modals	*Meaning*	*Examples*
shall/will/ would	insistence	(i) He shall be punished. (ii) He will go. (the subject insists on going) (iii) He shall go. (I (the speaker) insist on his going.) (iv) He would act the fool. (persistence)
May	benediction/ malediction	(i) May you live long! (ii) May you rot! (iii) May you fail in the exam!
can/could/ would	empty use	(i) I can see a bird in the tree. (with verbs of sensation) (ii) I would like to say a few words. (would has no meaning) (iii) I could hear some music when I passed through the hall. (with verbs of sensation)

EXERCISE 12.1

Paraphrase the following sentences by using modals.

Example: He *is able to* speak English.
Ans.: He *can* speak English.

1. You are advised to send the soup back.
2. It is my duty to visit my parents more often.
3. I'm sorry we didn't take a taxi when it rained.
4. If you are not well, it would be sensible to ask Ram to go instead.
5. He has travelled five times abroad during this year. We can logically conclude that he is rich.
6. We hear people say that eating salty and fatty food is not good for heart.
7. I am willing to give you another opportunity to improve your grade.
8. We thought people were willing to buy the new detergent.
9. Every day Ram is in the habit of listening to spiritual music.
10. She was in the habit of leaving all taps on whenever she went out.
11. He was in the habit of playing in the garden.
12. He was in the habit of playing hockey for India, wasn't he?
13. When Ram gets a job, it is possible for me to get my money back.
14. It is possible for temperature to soar to 45°C sometime in June.
15. Are you likely to visit Thailand again this summer?
16. There isn't a possibility of any milk being left in the fridge.
17. It is possible that it won't happen for another ten years.
18. It is possible for the P.M. to call an election in August.
19. I'll write the date of my wedding anniversary in my diary, otherwise it is possible for me to forget it.

20. He thought it was possible for his sister to be playing with the ball.
21. Don't wait for me. It is possible for me to be a few minutes late.
22. Sita is able to read well though she is only five.
23. He was able to contest the election on the support of the voters of his constituency.
24. I am not able to decide where I should go for my holidays.
25. To get a confirmed ticket to Mumbai, it is necessary for you to book in advance.
26. To be eligible to sit for the annual examination, it is the rule that every student has 75 per cent attendance.
27. The hall is packed. It is logical to conclude that there are 2000 people in the hall.
28. The car broke down, so it became necessary for us to get a taxi.
29. It is not necessary for her to come with us if she does not want to.
30. Am I permitted to have another cup of tea?
31. You are allowed to have another ice cream.
32. You are not allowed to have another chocolate.
33. In 1940, women were not allowed to vote.
34. We were not allowed to see the pictures during the exam days.
35. I suggest that you should use my car.
36. Do you want me to call a taxi for you?
37. I request you to pass me salt.
38. I offer you a glass of orange juice.
39. I request you to lend me ₹ 2000.
40. You are prohibited to smoke in here.
41. You are not permitted to bring your own food in this cafeteria.
42. Do you allow me to go out with Ram?
43. I request you to do me a favour.

Key to Exercise 12.1

1. You should/ought to send the soup back.
2. I should visit my parents more often.
3. We should/ought to have taken a taxi when it rained.
4. You'd better ask Ram to go instead.
5. He must be rich.
6. Eating salty and fatty food is supposed to be bad for heart.
7. I'll give you another opportunity to improve your grade.
8. We thought that people would buy the new detergent.
9. Every day Ram will listen to spiritual music.
10. She would leave all taps on whenever she went out.
11. He used to play in the garden.
12. He used to play hockey for India, didn't he?

13. When Ram gets a job, I may get my money back.
14. Temperature can sometimes soar to 45°C in June.
15. Might you visit Thailand again this summer ?
16. There can't/couldn't be any milk left in the fridge.
17. It may not/might not happen for another ten years.
18. The P.M. may conceivably call an election in August.
19. I'll write the date of my wedding anniversary in my diary, otherwise I may/might/could forget it.
20. He thought his sister might be playing with the ball.
21. Don't wait for me. I might be a few minutes late.
22. Sita can read well though she is only five.
23. He could contest the election on the support of the voters of his constituency.
24. I cannot decide where I should go for my holidays.
25. To get a confirmed ticket to Mumbai, you must book in advance.
26. To be eligible to sit for the annual examination, every student has got to have 75 per cent attendance.
27. There must be 2000 people in the hall.
28. The car broke down, so we had to hire a taxi.
29. She needn't come with us.
30. Can I have another cup of tea?
31. You can have another ice cream.
32. You can't have another chocolate.
33. In 1940, women couldn't vote.
34. We could not see the pictures during the exam days.
35. You can use my car.
36. Shall/should I call a taxi for you?
37. Could you pass me the salt, please?
38. Would you like to have a glass of orange juice?
39. Would/could you lend me ₹ 2000, please?
40. You mustn't smoke in here.
41. You may not bring your own food in this cafeteria.
42. Can I go out with Ram?
43. Could you do me a favour?

13

Passive Voice

Introduction

Read the following message which appeared on a poster.

WORLD'S MESSIEST ROOM AWARD

As a unique and priceless example of complete chaos, the room has been declared National Hysteric Sight. No part of this area may be rearranged, reorganized or removed so that future generations may enjoy this breath taking natural wonder.

In the above message, the following sentences are in the passive voice.

(i) The room has been declared National Hysteric Sight.
(ii) No part of this area may be rearranged, reorganized and removed.

Changing an active construction into a passive construction involves three processes. They are discussed below.

ia Ram killed a snake. (Active Voice)
ib A snake was killed by Ram. (Passive Voice)

Look at the changes (Figure 13.1) that take place when we convert (ia) into (ib).

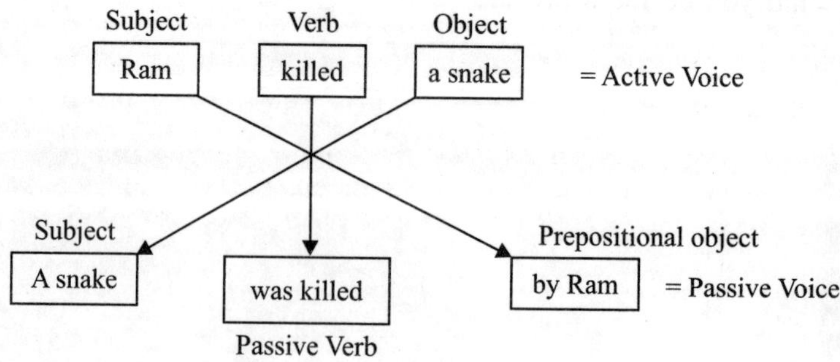

FIGURE 13.1 Active and passive voice.

There are four changes.

1. The object becomes the subject.
2. The subject becomes by + object.
3. The verb changes into be + third form of the verb.
4. The tense of the construction does not change. That is, if the active sentence is in simple present tense, the passive construction also remains in simple present tense (see Figure 13.2).

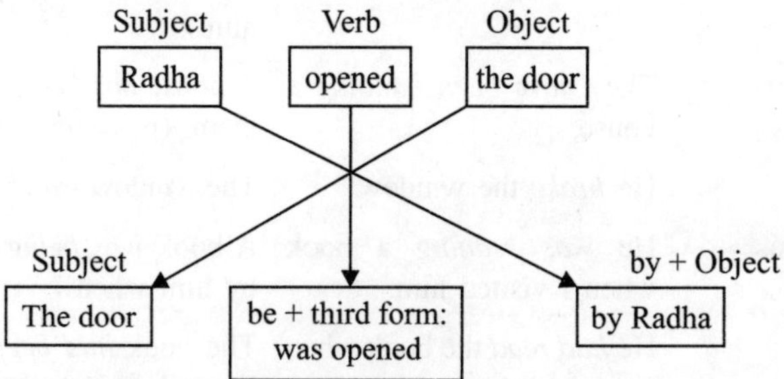

FIGURE 13.2 Active and passive voice.

Notice that the syntactical pattern of the sentence does not change. That is, if an active sentence is a statement, the passive sentence also remains a statement. If an active sentence is a question, the passive sentence also remains a question, so on and so forth.

Note further that only transitive verbs can have passive constructions. There are three types of verbs in English.

1. Intransitive verbs: weep, run, sleep, laugh, jump, and many more.
2. Transitive verbs: play, read, eat, give, and many more.
3. Linking verbs: seem, remain, resemble, become, and many more.

Intransitive and linking verbs cannot be passivized.

He became a king.
A king was become by him. (not possible)
She is **jumping**. (intransitive) (passive not possible)

Passive Verbs in Different Tenses

As said above, be + third form of the verb is the hallmark of a passive verb. Let us look at different configurations of the passive verb in different tenses (see Table 13.1).

TABLE 13.1 Passive verbs

Tense	*Active construction*	*Passive construction*
Simple present	He *eats* a banana every day.	A banana *is eaten* by him every day.
Present continuous	He *is eating* a banana now.	A banana *is being eaten* by him now.
Present perfect	He *has eaten* a banana.	A banana *has been eaten* by him.
Present perfect continuous	They *have been building* a house.	A house *has been being built* by them. (possible but rarely used)
Simple past	He *broke* the window.	The window *was broken* by him.
Past continuous	He *was reading* a book when I visited him.	A book *was being read* by him when I visited him.
Past perfect	He *had read* the book when I reached there.	The book *had been read* by him when I reached there.
Past perfect continuous	He *had been playing* football when I reached the playground.	Football *had been being played* by him when I reached the playground. (possible but rarely used)
Will + first form of the verb	He *will complete* his Ph.D dissertation next year.	His Ph.D. dissertation *will be completed* by him next year.
Will + be + verb + ing form	He *will be visiting* us tomorrow.	We *will be being visited* by him tomorrow. (possible but rarely used)
Will + have + third form of the verb	He *will have passed* the exam by June next year.	The exam *will have been passed* by him by June next year. (possible but rarely used)
Modal verbs + first form of the verb	You *must do* it.	It *must be done* by you.
To-infinitive	I would like him *to take me out* for dinner.	I would like *to be taken out* for dinner by him.

Note also that where the agent is unknown or understood by context, it is left out in the passive construction.

(i) Somebody has broken the window.

ia. The window has been broken. (agent is unknown)

(ii) People speak English all over the world.

iia. English is spoken all over the world. (agent is understood)

In addition to be + *third form of the verb*, sometimes *get* + *third form of the verb*, *become* + *third form of the verb* are also used.

(i) They **got married** last week.
(ii) She is **getting** dressed.
(iii) The auditorium **become filled** with people.
(iv) The water **becomes frozen** into ice.

In addition to the by + agent form, some other prepositions are also found in some fixed expressions.

(i) I know him.

ia. He is known to me.

(ii) This box contains five books.

iia. Five books are contained in this box.

(iii) A stone hurt him.

iiia. He was hurt with a stone.

(iv) Your behaviour astonished me.

iva. I am astonished at your behaviour.

Double Object Verbs

There are some verbs such as *show*, *tell*, *give*, *write*, *bring*, *buy*, *offer*, *pray*, *promise*, and *send* which take two objects: indirect object (denoted generally by a person) and direct object (denoted generally by a thing). If a sentence has two objects, there can be two passives of such a sentence.

1. I gave Mary a book.

ia. Mary was given a book by me.
ib. A book was given to Mary by me.

Compare double object verbs with the verbs that are followed by object and objective complement:

2. They appointed him chairman.

iia. He was appointed chairman.
iib. Chairman was appointed of him. (not possible)

In such cases, only one passive construction is possible.

EXERCISE 13.1

Change the following sentences into the passive.

1. Shahajahan built the Taj Mahal.
2. He told the child a story.
3. They called him stupid.
4. They elected him secretary of the club.
5. They explained the matter to him.
6. I gave my daughter a wrist watch on her birthday.
7. He offered her a new job.
8. In America, people are wearing broad ties these days.
9. He eats twenty bananas every day for his breakfast.
10. The cat is chasing the mouse.
11. He has written a good book on Auyurveda.
12. When I reached home, he was watching TV.
13. He had played football for two hours when I reached there.
14. They must have been building a house.
15. He will regret his decision of quitting the job.
16. The new management has called him for the interview.
17. People say that he is naughty (Begin with it is said...)
18. Carelessness causes many serious accidents.
19. They have decided to open a new branch of the bank next year. (It has been decided...)
20. He believes that he will pass in the first division.
21. Someone lent me two books on Shakespeare.
22. I don't like people looking at me.
23. I would like you to do this work.
24. People generally agree he is a bore. (It is generally agreed...)
25. Everybody knows that Armstrong landed on the moon.

Passive of Questions and Commands

In the previous section, we discussed how to convert statements into passives. In this section, we shall discuss the rules of conversion of imperatives and interrogative sentences into passive.

A question asks information whereas an imperative gives commands, orders and makes requests. Look at the following imperative sentences and their passive counterparts:

(i) Bring me a glass of water.

  ia. Let a glass of water be brought to me.

  ib. You are requested to bring me a glass of water.

(ii) Don't make a noise.

iia. Let no noise be made.
iib. You are ordered not to make a noise.

(iii) Please help me.

iiia. Let me be helped by you.
iiib. You are requested to help me.

Note the following points about the pattern:

(i) Use *let* in the beginning for imperative constructions.
(ii) Object is used in the objective case form after *let*.
(iii) The verb becomes *be* + *third form*.
(iv) By + agent is generally not used.
(v) Note that *let construction* is generally not used. The alternative construction *you are requested to*, you are *ordered to* ... is more common.

There are two types of questions in English:

(i) Yes-no questions: Are you married?
(ii) Wh-questions: Where do you live?

In question-formation in English, inversion of the verbs is a must.

You are married
inversion: Are you married?

This syntactical pattern remains unchanged in passive constructions also. Look at the following sentences (Figures 13.3 and 13.4).

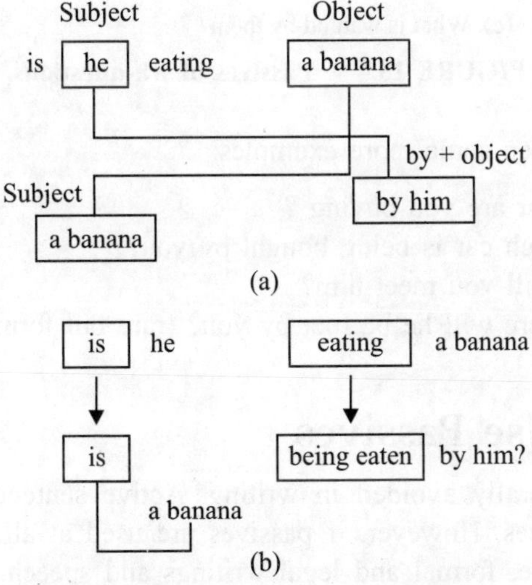

FIGURE 13.3 Passives of yes-no questions.

wh-questions

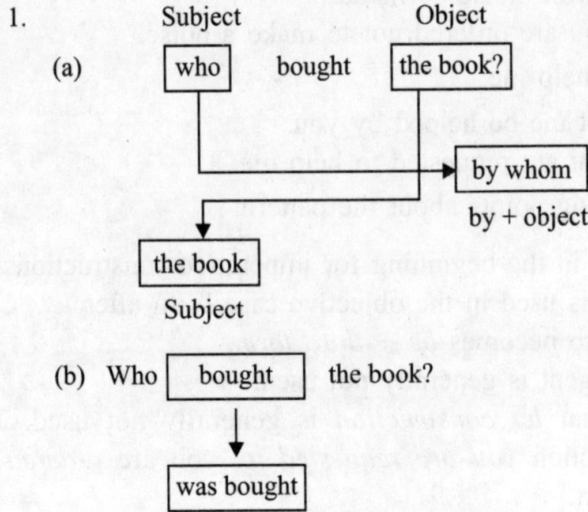

(c) By whom was the book bought?

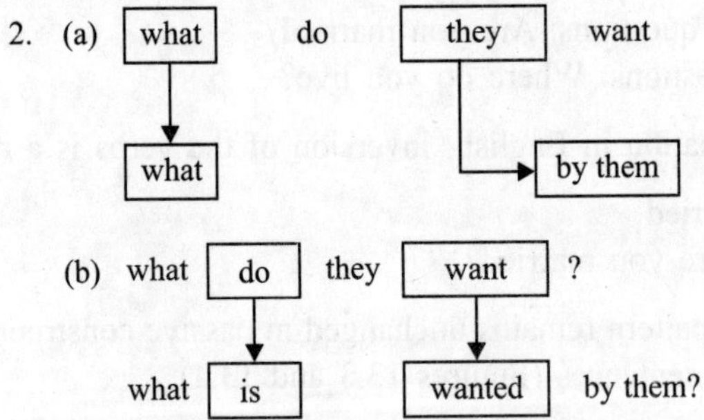

(c) What is wanted by them?

FIGURE 13.4 Passives of wh-questions.

Below are given some more examples.

(i) Which car are you buying ?
  ia. Which car is being bought by you?

(ii) Where will you meet him?
  iia. Where will he be met by you? (rare but formally possible)

Where to Use Passives

Passives are generally avoided in writing. Active sentences are preferable to passive sentences. However, if passives are used at all, they are used in scientific, objective, formal and legal writings and speech. The passives are generally used when the agent is unknown or self-evident or when the process /action denoted by the verb is more important than the active subject. Study the following sentences:

(i) My book has been stolen. (agent is unknown)
(ii) The duty on colour TVs has been reduced by ₹ 1000. (by the finance minister is self-evident)
(iii) Sedimentation and decantation processes are applied for separation of soluble salts from an impure sample. (process is more important than the agent.)
(iv) Nearly 40 people were injured in a bus accident near Jaipur yesterday. (Newspaper headlines)

EXERCISE 13.2

Change the following sentences into passive:

1. What do you eat for breakfast?
2. What does he serve for breakfast?
3. Who will cook the food?
4. Who will punish him?
5. Which book are you buying?
6. When will you join your new job?
7. Why did you treat him so shabbily?
8. How can you do it?
9. How many persons did the police arrest?
10. How much income tax did you pay?
11. Send him this letter.
12. Lend me ₹ 2000, please.
13. Don't pluck these flowers.
14. Don't cut the trees.
15. Switch on the light.
16. Don't touch me.
17. Don't comb your hair in the class.
18. Polish my shoes, please.
19. Don't disturb me.
20. Don't grow tomatoes in this field.

EXERCISE 13.3

Change the following into the passive voice:

1. Nearly forty years ago engineers realized that they needed a new engine.
2. Rontgen showed that the impact of cathode rays produced X-rays.
3. The police ought to put him in prison.
4. You must iron this dress for tonight.
5. You will have to amuse him with fiddles and bed-time stories.
6. They discovered a new pill to stimulate the appetite.

7. It fascinated me.
8. A Duke of the 15th century had killed his wife in this room.
9. Fear of death oppresses some old people.
10. The judge advised me to settle the matter out of court.
11. Rajiv chose the words with care.
12. You don't need to wind an automatic watch.
13. If in the 16th century they could make history by building monuments, in the 20th century they can make it by selling and reselling them.
14. They returned my keys to me.
15. They were handing round apple and orange juice.
16. They have pulled down the sky scrapper.
17. Fog held up the trains.
18. They performed his symphony for the first time.
19. Have they carried out his instructions?
20. We have to pick the fruit very early in the morning.
21. The water of the Moti Jheel flooded Bharatpur.
22. Have you stamped the letter?
23. You should read the introduction carefully.
24. They will alter the notice.
25. The nurse is looking after the invalid.
26. Please, sit down.
27. You can rely upon that man.
28. Our friend is making special preparations.
29. A special messenger brought the letter.
30. What do you call the baby?
31. They are sending all their children to public schools.
32. The book I bought yesterday has won the first prize in the exhibition.
33. Though foreigners praised Rabindranath's Gitanjali, Indian critics ignored it in the beginning.
34. They did everything possible to save the child's life.
35. The State Government founded this college 30 years ago.
36. They first washed the cars and then polished them.
37. Did they give you enough sugar?
38. People heard the Pope's message all over the world.
39. No one has climbed this mountain before.
40. You must look into this matter.
41. They presented Kanta a new doll for her birthday.
42. They will give you some new instructions before you leave.
43. Someone built this bridge last year.
44. They have proved all his calculations wrong.
45. He is eating a banana.
46. Who broke the window?
47. Somebody has stolen my purse.
48. People speak English all over the world.

49. Don't make a noise.
50. Poor John! A bus has run him down.
51. Has any other company ever refused you a Life Insurance Policy?
52. What are you eating ?
53. Close the door, please.
54. You cannot expect children to understand these problems.
55. I don't like him to cheat me.

Key to Exercise 13.1

1. The Taj Mahal was built by Shahajahan.
2. The child was told a story by him.
3. He was called stupid (by them).
4. He was elected Secretary of the club.
5. The matter was explained to him.
6. My daughter was given a wrist watch on her birthday.

   or

   A wrist watch was given to my daughter on her birthday.
7. She was offered a new job.
8. In America, broad ties are worn these days.
9. Twenty bananas are eaten by him for breakfast.
10. The mouse is being chased by the cat.
11. A good book on Ayurveda has been written by him.
12. TV was being watched by him when I reached home.
13. Football had been played for two hours by him when I reached there.
14. A house must have been being built by them.
15. His decision of quitting the job will be regretted by him.
16. He has been called for an interview.
17. It is said that he is naughty.
18. Many serious accidents are caused by carelessness.
19. It has been decided to open a new branch of the bank next year.
20. That he will pass in the first division is believed by him.
21. I was lent two books on Shakespeare.
22. I don't like being looked at.
23. I would like the work to be done by you.
24. It is generally agreed that he is a bore.
25. That Armstrong landed on the moon is well known.

Key to Exercise 13.2

1. What is eaten by you for breakfast?
2. What is served for breakfast?
3. By whom will the food be cooked?
4. By whom will he be punished?

5. Which book is being bought by you?
6. When will your new job be joined by you. (funny but possible)
7. Why was he treated so shabbily?
8. How can it be done?
9. How many persons were asked by the police?
10. How much income tax was paid by you?
11. Let this letter be sent.
12. You are requested to lend ₹ 2000.
13. Let these flowers not be picked./Let no flowers be picked.
14. You are forbidden to cut these trees.
15. You are asked to switch on the light.
16. You are forbidden to touch me.
17. You are asked not to comb your hair in the class.
18. You are requested to polish my shoes.
19. You are asked not to disturb me.
20. You are forbidden to grow tomatoes in this field.

Key to Exercise 13.3

1. That they need a new engine was realized by engineers nearly forty years ago.
2. That the impact of cathode rays produced X-rays was shown by Rontgen.
3. He ought to be put in prison by them.
4. This dress must be ironed tonight by you.
5. He will have to be amused with riddles and bed time stories by you.
6. A new pill was discovered by them to stimulate the appetite.
7. I was fascinated at it.
8. His wife had been killed by the Duke of the 15th century in this room.
9. Some old people are oppressed with fear of death.
10. I was advised by the judge to settle the matter out of court.
11. Words were chosen with care by Rajeev.
12. An automatic watch doesn't need to be wound.
13. History could be made by them in the 16th century by building monuments, it can be made in the 20th century by selling and reselling them.
14. I was returned my keys by them. / The keys were returned to me by them.
15. Orange and apple juice was being handed round by them.
16. The sky scrapper has been pulled down by them.
17. The trains were held up with fog.
18. His symphony was performed by them for the first time.
19. Have his instructions been carried out?
20. The fruit is to be picked very early in the morning.
21. Bharatpur was flooded by the water of Moti Jheel.

22. Has the letter been stamped?
23. The instructions should be altered by them.
24. The notice will be altered by them.
25. The invalid is being looked after by the nurse.
26. You are requested to sit down.
27. That man can be relied upon.
28. Special preparations are being made by our friend.
29. The letter has been brought by a special messenger.
30. What is the baby called?
31. All their children are being sent to public schools by them.
32. First prize has been given in the exhibition to the book I bought yesterday.
33. Though Rabindranath's Gitanjali was praised by foreigners, it was ignored in the beginning by Indians critics.
34. Every thing possible was done to save the child's life.
35. This college was formed 30 years ago by the State Government.
36. The cars were first washed and then polished by them.
37. Were you given enough sugar by them?
38. Pope's message was heard all over the world.
39. This mountain has not been climbed before.
40. This matter must be looked into.
41. A new doll was presented to Kanta for her birthday.

    or

    Kanta was presented a new doll for her birthday.
42. Some new instructions will be given to you before you leave.

    or

    You will be given some new instructions by them before you leave.
43. This bridge was built last year.
44. All his calculations have been proved wrong.
45. A banana is being eaten by him.
46. By whom was the window broken?
47. My purse has been stolen.
48. English is spoken all over the world.
49. Let no noise be made.
50. John has been run down.
51. Have you ever been refused a life insurance policy?

    or

    Has Life Insurance Policy been refused to you?
52. What is being eaten by you?
53. You are requested to close the door.
54. Children cannot be expected to understand these problems.
55. I don't like to be cheated by him.

14

Letter Writing

Introduction

There was a time when lovers used to send their love letters through pigeons. The letters written by several great men like Abraham Lincoln, Mahatma Gandhi and Jawaharlal Nehru are read with great interest even today by people. The Times of India news (July 10, 2004) is that James Joyce's highly erotic love letter written to Barnacle (a wild-eyed whore) in December 1909 was sold in London in an auction for $ 446000. From Naini Prison, Pt. Jawaharlal Nehru wrote letters to Indira Gandhi, which were later on published in the form of a book entitled "Discovery of India".

Lately, under the influence of e-communication, the habit of writing letters is on the decline. People generally exchange messages through telephone or send fax messages or e-mail. Even then, it is necessary for every learner of English to know how to write personal and business letters. Letter writing involves conventions of writing in addition to the content part of letter writing. Below we discuss the art of letter writing in great detail.

Types of Letters

Table 14.1 summarizes the types of letters.

TABLE 14.1 Types of letters

Personal letters	*Business letters*
Invitations	Letters of enquiry
Condolences	Letters of quotations
Congratulations	Letters of placing orders
	Letters of inviting tenders
	Sales letters
	Claim letters

(*Contd.*)

TABLE 14.1 Types of letters (*Contd.*)

Personal letters	*Business letters*
	Adjustment letters
	Credit and collection letters
	Letters of application
	Letters of invitation
	Letters of sympathy

Before we present examples of each type of letter, it would be in order to discuss the structure and layout of letters on the one hand and the principles of letter writing, on the other.

Structure and Layout of Letter

The structure of personal letters differs from that of business letters. Personal letters refer to letters written to friends and relatives. These are *newsy* and *chatty* and *conversational* in style. It can be about any subject – one's home, family, school or any experience one has had. It is simple, sincere and friendly in tone.

The aim of a business letter, on the other hand, is to "transact some particular business". It is written *to get something done.* It is formal, and not casual or informal in tone. But the letter should not be cold but friendly in tone. Business letters are written to people whom we do not know or if we know we have *business relationship*, and not any personal relationship with them.

In order to discuss the parts of a personal letter, we shall start by presenting an example of a personal letter. This has been written by Prakash to Mahesh from Las Vegas (Exhibit 14.1):

EXHIBIT 14.1 A sample letter

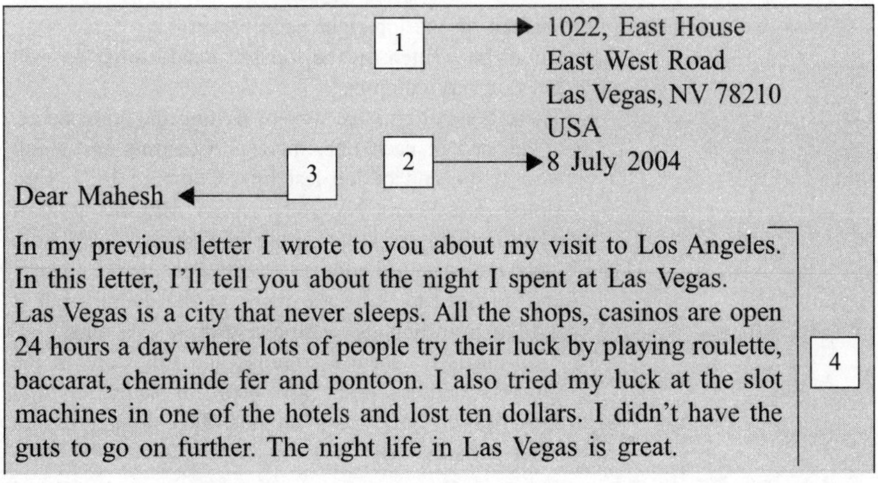
1 → 1022, East House
East West Road
Las Vegas, NV 78210
USA
2 → 8 July 2004

Dear Mahesh ← 3

In my previous letter I wrote to you about my visit to Los Angeles. In this letter, I'll tell you about the night I spent at Las Vegas.
Las Vegas is a city that never sleeps. All the shops, casinos are open 24 hours a day where lots of people try their luck by playing roulette, baccarat, cheminde fer and pontoon. I also tried my luck at the slot machines in one of the hotels and lost ten dollars. I didn't have the guts to go on further. The night life in Las Vegas is great. 4

There're lots of floor shows by American beauties. What a pity! A visitor isn't allowed to shoot.
There are lots of restaurants selling all kinds of grub. You name any kind of food and it's here.
Las Vegas has grown at an incredible rate. The population of this city was 45000 in 1950 that has gone to 5 lac in 2004. Every day 5000 to 8000 people visit this place and get lost in the gambling dens here. The sins of night life are washed away by their prayers in about 500 churches and 50 synagogues. My description of Las Vegas reads like a book of facts. More about my personal experience in the next letter. 4

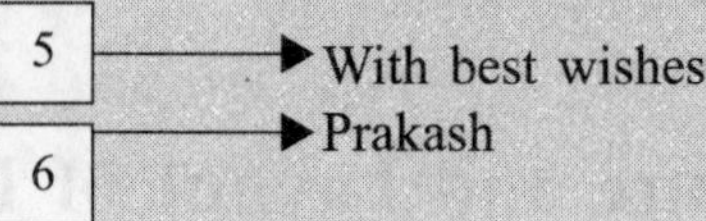

A personal letter has the following six parts:

1. The address of the sender
2. The date
3. The salutation or greeting
4. The body of the letter
5. The subscription or complimentary close
6. The signature

Notice these parts are shown in the specimen letter by arrows and numbers in boxes. We shall discuss these parts one by one (Table 14.2).

TABLE 14.2 Parts of personal letter

Part of personal letter	*Discussion*
Address of the sender	• Written on the top right hand corner • Could be written on the top left hand corner as well but not very common • There is an alternative way of writing the address, i.e. at the end of each line, there is a comma and a full stop at the end of the last line. Compare 1022, East House, Las Vegas, NV 78210, USA. But this style of writing addresses is going out of fashion • Need not write full address if written inside the country and no need to write the name of the country but if written from outside, complete address is a must • The rule is if you use commas and full stops in the sender's address, then use them in salutation and subscription, but if you do not, then do not use in other parts as well

(*Contd.*)

TABLE 14.2 Parts of personal letter (*Contd.*)

Part of personal letter	*Discussion*
Date	• Written generally below the sender's address. • Many ways of writing the date: July 8th, 2012 8 July 2012 8th July 2012 8th Sept., 2011 8/7/2012 8/7/'12 8-7-2012 8.7.2012 7.8.2012 ***Note:*** The last four but one forms are *ambiguous* because in the States, for example, they would mean 7 August 2012
Salutation	• To a friend, address him by name: Dear Mahesh *Don't write* Dear Friend Mahesh • Don't write the address of your friend at all • Address him by the name you use while speaking to him: Dear Mittu (not Dear Mrityanand) • To father, mother, brother and dear friends: My dear father My dear mother My dear sister My dear Reeta • The *punctuation* after salutation is in agreement with the sender's address. If you use *comma* there, use *comma here* also, otherwise no punctuation mark.
Body of the letter	• Simple and pleasant to read • It's *newsy*, full of details which appeal to the reader • Write to him as you would speak to him
Ending	• Different ways of ending the letter • Most common to close a letter to a friend: Yours sincerely Ever sincerely yours • Some people close their personal letters as: Your sincere friend Yours ever Yours affectionately Your loving son • In BE (British English) • To family members and close friends: Love Love from Lots of love

(*Contd.*)

TABLE 14.2 Parts of personal letter (*Contd.*)

Part of personal letter	*Discussion*
	• To friends and acquaintances: Best wishes All the best Take care • *Punctuation*, if you use *comma* after the greeting, use *comma* here too, otherwise *don't*.
Signature	• To a friend and close relatives • *No full signature*, only first name. For example Not: Shyam Sunder Sharma *but* Shyam Similarly, *Bala* *Not* Balasubamaniyam

EXERCISE 14.1

1. Write a letter to your friend telling him about the film that you saw last night.
2. Krishana has come for the first time to live in the college hostel. He is feeling very homesick. He is also being ragged by the senior students. Write a letter to his mother as Krishana would write to his mother about his experiences.
3. Write a letter to your father telling him about your experiences of the first day in the college.
4. Your uncle has sent you a personal computer on your birthday. Write a letter to him thanking him to send you such a lovely and useful gift.
5. A pen friend of yours from the USA has asked you a number of questions about India, especially about the Taj Mahal, classical dance and music. Write a reply to him/her telling him/her about the rich heritage of this country.
6. Below are given two paragraphs of a personal letter. The first paragraph is informal in tone whereas the second paragraph is quite formal. Rewrite the second paragraph in such away that it matches the style of the first paragraph.

    - This is just a quick note to tell you how much I enjoyed my week-end at your place. You took every care to make it really great.
    - On this occasion I think it is my bounden duty to express my sincere gratitude to your mother who left no stone unturned in making my stay unforgettable and to provide me with all the amenities of life.

7. Here is a personal letter which is defective in form. Rewrite the letter after correcting the errors of the form.

Satnama

8 -7 -2012

From
Manish Agarwal,
2 Kshipra path,
Mansarover,
Jaipur, 20.
To,
Madhu Jain,
C/o
Jagdish Jain,
C-88 Karmchari Colony,
Alwar 301001
Dear friend,
I am well here and hope you are well there. In particular, I passed my Senior Secondary Exam in the first. I will take admission at MNIT, Jaipur.
What are your plans?
I saw your roll numbers in the list of successful candidates perhaps you will try for admission at Bhilwara Engineering College.
Thanking you,

I remain,
Yours sincere friend
Manish Agarwal

8. Your pen friend from Canada wrote you the following letter. She has asked a number of questions about India, specially about the places that are worth seeing and she also wants to know why they are famous. Write a reply to the following letter.

2500 University Drive
N.W. Calgary
Alberta
Canada T2 N 1N4
July 8, 2012

Dear Madhu
I got your address from the World Penpals Club. From the description there I gather that like me you too are fond of travelling. Hence I am writing this letter to you.
My name is Tess. I am twenty years old and have black hair and blue eyes. I have a younger sister, who is 18 years old. We both go to college and are doing our courses in world history.
I understand there are plenty of palaces and castles in India. I also gather there are lots of places of pilgrimages.

I am very eager to have a small description of some of these places, especially six or seven places that you would like to recommend me to see during my visit for two weeks in India. In fact, I am planning to visit India next year with my friends. Please send me some picture post cards of these places too.
Please reply to my letter soon. With best wishes.

Yours sincerely
Tess

9. The following phrases and sentences have been taken from two different letters. One is a letter from Mahesh, who writes to his friend Manish sending condolences on his father's death. The other has been written by Mahesh to his mother telling her about his exam result. Write the two letters after selecting and arranging the parts that belong to each other.

    (i) I'm sorry to hear of the untimely death of your father.
    (ii) You'll be delighted to know I've passed the BE-II third semester examination with highest marks in the class.
    (iii) Tell Shikha also to be bright like me
    (iv) Dear mom
    (v) Please accept my heart-felt condolences
    (vi) Dear Manish
    (vii) Lots of love
    (viii) He was such a wonderful man!
    (ix) She spends all her time watching TV
    (x) Mom, now you must buy me the passion motor bike that you promised
    (xi) I remember how much pain he took to make me feel at home when I spent the week-end with you last year.
    (xii) May his soul rest in peace!
    (xiii) I'm coming home next week to see you all.
    (xiv) May God grant you strength to bear this irreparable loss!

10. Write a letter to your friend congratulating him on passing the IAS examination.
11. Write a letter to your friend who is in another town inviting him to spend the Diwali holidays with you and your family.
12. Write a letter to your brother describing your visit to Neemarana Fort Palace Hotel.

Structure of Business Letters

As said earlier, business letters are written to transact some business. In order to understand the structure of a business letter, it would be in order to start a few specimen business letters. These specimen letters (Exhibits 14.2–14.9) are *authentic* and have been received from various countries such as the UK, the USA, Canada, Saudi Arabia, Cairo, British Council, Indian Universities and Corporate world. The name of the recipient of the letter has been changed to maintain the secrecy of the recipient. You would notice that there are minor differences among these business letters. These differences have been pointed out briefly after each exhibit by way of comments. We comment on the *departures* from usual *conventions* of letter writing.

EXHIBIT 14.2 Reply to a job letter

Institute of Public Administration
P.O. Box 205
Regadh, Saudi Arabia

Bablo Tpadmix
Tel. 61600
Telex: 21160 S.J
7546
date: 9 May 1981

Dr. Anil Gupta
Assistant Professor of English
Plot No. 54, Teej Ki Road
Scheme-1 Extension
Alwar 301001, Rajasthan, India

Dear Dr. Gupta

Thank you for your letter expressing an interest in joining the English Language Programme of the Institute of Public Administration.

After giving your application a full consideration, we are sorry to tell you that, at the time being, we do not have any vacancies which meet the qualifications you have. However we took the liberty of keeping your application in our files for future consideration.

Sincerely Yours,
Director
English Language Programme

Comments:

1. The inside address has no punctuation marks.
2. The salutation has no comma(,) or colon(:).
3. The ending is *Sincerely Yours* instead of 'Yours sincerely' Further, notice capital 'Y'.
4. The use of [,] after *sincerely yours* is *not* required.

EXHIBIT 14.3 A letter from the British Council

British High Commission
British Council Division

Del/607/50 TT

17 Kasturba Gandhi Marg
New Delhi – 110 001
Telephone 3711401
3710111, 3710555
Telex 65460
Fax 3710717

12 December 1997

Dr. Anil Gupta
A-165, H.K.M. Nagar
Alwar 301001
Rajasthan

Dear Dr. Gupta

We are in receipt of your letter dated 8 December 1997 and wish you too a Happy New Year. This is to inform you that we have your request on our BEC file. Should an opportunity arise to induct new teachers for the BEC teacher training programme we will get in touch with you.

With best wishes
Yours sincerely
Parul Sena
(For) Dr Rajni Badlani
English Studies Officer

Comments

1. This letter is a model business letter which conforms to the latest conventions of business letter writing.
2. *Look at the signature. As a junior officer signs the letter, the form shown here is used..*

EXHIBIT 14.4 A letter from LSI

Telephone : 27231 (by request) Telegram: Care Deccolinst Pune

Linguistic Society of India

C/o Deccan College Postgraduate and Research Institute, Pune 411006 (India)

Dr. Anil Gupta
Shakti Nagar
Vijay Mandir Road
Alwar 301001

RS/304
20. VI 86

Dear Dr. Gupta,

Thank you for your letter regarding your paper on assertion transformations in Hindi. I am very sorry to hear that your father has died; my heart-felt condolences.

Please take your time over revising the paper. We have now finalized the 1986 and 1987 volumes anyway, and they are full; so your paper will appear in 1988. But that will, I hope, not be a problem for you. You see, our press takes a year to print anything we give it; we are planning to submit vols. 47 (1986) and 48 (1987) to two different presses so that printing goes on concurrently. We expect both volumes to appear around July 1987.

Lack of resources prevents us from making our volumes as big as we would like; hence that fact that vols. 47 and 48 are already full, in the sense that we cannot make them any bigger. Most of the contributors to these volumes submitted their work considerably earlier than you did, and have thus been waiting for a long time. We can shorten the waiting period only if we get more money, and that does not seem very likely!

With best wishes (for everything),

Yours sincerely:

Probal Dasgupta
Editor, IL

P.S. : I won't be editor for much longer in future; when writing to me, please mention just my department and college, not the Society, i.e. use the address 'Dasgupta' Linguistics, Deccan College, Pune 411008.

Comments

1. Notice the date 20. VI. 86, which is *not followed* these days.
2. No punctuation after *inside address.*
3. *Comma* after salutation has been used.
4. But the use of colon (:) after ending is quite *unconventional.*
5. P.S. The postscript gives the information left out in the body of the letter. Quite useful.

EXHIBIT 14.5 A letter from UH

University of Hawaii at Manoa

An Equal Opportunity Employer
Department of Linguistics
Moore Hall 569. 1890 East-West Road
Honolulu, Hawaii 96822.

November 14, 1980

Professor Shivnath Singh
Joint Director of College Education
Government of Rajasthan
Gandhi Nagar
Jaipur-4 Rajasthan
India

Dear Professor Singh,

I am writing to you about Anil Gupta, who is my dissertation advisee. I understand that he may lose his job in India unless he returns to his post immediately. Although I have no way of knowing how compelling are the reasons for not extending his leave, it would be a great pity if he cannot complete his Ph. D work now that so many years have been invested and now that he is so near to completing it.

Mr. Gupta has now completed our program save for defending his dissertation. His dissertation will concern Hindi relative clauses, and he has placed an entire draft in my hands. I have now read this in detail.

Mr. Gupta's thesis seems to me to have genuine merit, since he has uncovered many new facts and has proposed novel theoretical interpretations. It is a work of very considerable scholarship. Yet, at the same time, it is not a polished, finished product. I have recommended to Mr. Gupta a number of revisions, and I expect to recommend additional ones. I view this as an entirely ordinary procedure, and it is something I have gone through with all my previous dissertation advisees.

This process of criticism and revision is not something that can be very well carried out at long distance, by mail. At least, this has been my experience. I am afraid that if Mr. Gupta must now return to his post in India, the completion of his dissertation may be protracted by many years.

I therefore ask your indulgence in extending Mr. Gupta's leave until June, 1981, by which time I expect his dissertation to be in final form and to have been successfully defended.

Thank you for your
consideration,

Gregory Lee
Assistant Prof. of Linguistics

Comments

1. No punctuation after *inside address* and the date.
2. American convention of letter writing.
3. Notice the use of comma, after greeting.
4. Notice the ending, quite novel indeed.
5. *Thank you for your consideration*, and then the *signature* with *job description.*

EXHIBIT 14.6 A letter from AH Cairo

The American University in Cairo

June 21, 1981

Dr. Anil Gupta
Assistant Professor of English,
Plot No. 54,
Teej Ki Road,
Scheme-1 Extension, Alwar 301001,
Rajasthan,
India.

Dear Dr. Gupta,

Thank you for your application for a faculty position in the E.L.I.

Unfortunately despite your excellent qualifications, we do not foresee being able to make you an appropriate offer in the near future. However, we would like to keep your papers on file for future consideration. If interested, please fill out the enclosed application form and return it to us at your convenience.

Thank you for your interest in our University, and best wishes.

Sincerely,

Dr. Yehia El- Ezabi
Director
English Language Institute

Encl.
cc: Dean of the Faculties
Ms. P. Blakemore, N.Y.O.

English Language Institute P.O. Box 2511 – Cairo Egypt.

Comments

1. Follows the British tradition of letter writing in *date*, *inside address*, and *salutation.*
2. But the ending with *Sincerely* is American usage. Age of *mixing.*

EXHIBIT 14.7 A letter from ASRC Hyderabad

E-Mail : babu@asrchyd.ernet.in
Fax : 91-040-7017114

Telegram : AMCENTRE
Telephone 7018608, 7018609, 7017658 (D)
Res. 3741963

American Studies Research Centre
Hyderabad 500 007 India

Prof. B. Ramesh Babu
Fund Raising CO-ordinator

8 July 1998

Dr. Anil Gupta
A –165
Hasan Khan Mewati Nagar
Alwar - 301001
Rajasthan

Dear Dr. Gupta:

Thank you very much indeed for your valuable contribution to the *Save ASRC Fund.* Here is the official receipt which entitles you to the Tax exemption under

80G. Your name will be listed in the next newsletter as one of the contributors to the *Save ASRC Fund.*

With warm regards,

Sincerely,

B. Ramesh Babu

Encl. Receipt

Comments

1. The inside address has no punctuation marks.
2. Notice colon (:) occurs after the salutation. Quite common in AE.
3. Letter ends with *sincerely* followed by a *comma.*
4. Enclosure occurs after signature as per convention.

EXHIBIT 14.8 A letter from UoE

University of Edinburgh
Department if Linguistics

Adam Ferguson Building, George square, Edinburgh EH 8 9 LL
Telephone 031-667-1001
SPC/SM.
Mr. Anil Gupta
Lecture in English
Govt. College,
Karauli – 322241
Dist. Swaimadhopur Rajasthan
India.

5th January, 1973

Dr. Mr. Gupta,

I received your letter of 15th December asking me to provide a testimonial in connection with your application for a post in the Hyderabad Centre. Unfortunately you letter did not fall into my hands until after the date of submission of your application. Therefore I have not done anything about it since I suppose it will be too late.

I am sorry that the possession of a Diploma does not seem to be of much use to you from the educational point of view. This is something which is causing us some considerable disquiet and we are considering the possibility of a one year degree in Applied Linguistics. I am afraid that this will not be able to benefit you if it is introduced, but your successors might get something out of it.

With best wishes for the New Year

Yours sincerely,

Professor Pit Corder

Head of Department S.P. Corder Extension 6515 & 6318

Comments

1. Notice punctuation after *salutation, inside address* and the ending.
2. The date comes at the right hand side.
3. Initials of the sender and the recipient come after the inside address. Generally, they come after the signature.

EXHIBIT 14.9 A letter from UoC

The
University
of Calgary

Faculty of Social Sciences
Department of Linguistics

2500 University Drive N.W. Calgary, Alberta, Canada T2N 1N4
Telephone (403) 286-5469

April 9, 1981

Dr. Anil Gupta
Assistant Professor of English
Plot No. 54
Teej Ki Road
Scheme-1 Extension, Alwar 301001
Rajasthan, India

Dear Sir:

Thank you for your letter of March 28th. Unfortunately, we do not have any openings that would be suitable to your background at this time.

We will, however, keep your letter and curriculum vitae on file.

Thank you for your interest in our programme.

Yours sincerely,

E.D. Cook
Head

/ko

Comments

1. No punctuation marks after *inside address and date*.
2. Notice *colon* (:) after greeting. This convention is becoming popular.
3. The initials at the end simply lists the *typist's initials* (/ko) because it is clear who dictated the letter.

After presenting nine specimen business letters from different countries and organizations, let us present a *model/business* letter which conforms to the latest conventions of business letter writing.

EXHIBIT 14.10 Model business letter

[1] **Latest Computer Company**
25, Chaura Rasta Jaipur – 302001
Tel: 0141-2395507, 2395508 Fax. 0141- 2395509
E-mail: lcc01@rediffmail.com

8 July 2012 [2]

Your Ref: WF/21/6/04 [3]
Our Ref: MKT/29/7/04 [4]
Sunrise Computers
Hope Circus, Alwar – 3011901

Attention: Mr. Atul Sinha [5]

Dear Sir [6]

[7] Sub: Our order for P III computers

Your letter containing a statement of Pentium III computers with you was received today.

We do not think the Pentium III with the configuration given by you will meet the requirements of our customers. Could you please, therefore, send us details of P-IV computers with the latest configurations within a week ?

We are enclosing a full statement of the configurations that we need in P-IV computers. We should be happy to hear from you soon. [8]

[9] Yours faithfully
For Latest Computer Company

[10] (M. Sinha)
Managing Director

MS: SM [11]

Encl: 1 [12]

cc: Sales Supervisor, Hardware Section [13]

Parts of Business Letters

The parts of a business letter are as follows:

1. Sender's address/heading
2. Date
3. Reference
4. Inside address
5. Attention
6. Salutation
7. Subject (what the letter is about)

8. Body
9. Complimentary close
10. Signature
11. Identification marks
12. Enclosures
13. Carbon copies given to other persons

A standard business letter contains the above thirteen parts. We shall discuss briefly each part one by one.

Sender's Address

There are three ways of writing addresses in business letters:

1. Heading as given below.

Infotech Private Ltd.	
House of Computer Experts	
Telephone: 0144246351	21 Hope Circus
Cable: Infotech	Alwar 301001
Fax: 0144246352	
E-mail : info@rediffmail.com	

An example of letterhead

(i) On a letterhead, the name and address are printed on the top middle of the page.
(ii) Other information is shown in margin.
(iii) 1/5 of space of the paper is used for the letterhead.
(iv) There can be variations in the style of a letterhead.

2. The second way of writing the sender's address is the same as in the personal letter:

Infotech Private Ltd.
21 Hope Circus
Alwar – 301001
14 July 2004

Sunrise Computer Ltd.
Bus stand
Behror

3. The third way of writing the sender's address is that both the sender's address and the inside address occur on the left hand side. *From* may be used for the sender's address and *To* is used for the recipient's address. But these two addresses can also occur without *from* and *to*, i.e. only with 2 spaces below each other. This style is found in government official letters but now it is getting out of use.

14 July 2012

From
Infotech Private Ltd.
21 Hope Circus
Alwar
To
Sunrise Computer Ltd.
Bus stand
Behror

Date

Date is printed on the upper right hand corner just 2 spaces below the last line of the letter head. The way of writing date is

14 July 2012
or
July 14, 2012

The first way of writing the date is logical.

References

There are different conventions for writing references.

1. In the letterhead itself
   Telegram: Oils

   Tel. 0141-2385312

   Ropar Oil Mills
   Chauki Dani
   Jaipur 302015

   Your Reference:
   Our Reference:
2. Two spaces above the inside address as shown in the model business letter in this book.
3. Some writers prefer to begin the business letter by the reference No. of the firm from which they received the letter.

Thank you for your letter No. 523 dated 12 June 2012.

Inside Address

1. Written on the left margin two or three lines below the line of the date (which is on the right). Here are some examples:

   (i) Infotech Private Ltd.
   24 Hope Circus
   Alwar – 301001
   (Addressed to the Company)

(ii) The Superintendent of Police
Alwar District
Alwar
(Addressed to the officer)

(iii) Mr. R.P. Chadda
Manager
Infotech Private Ltd.
24 Hope Circus
Alwar 301001
(Addressed to the officer by name)

Attention

1. Two spaces below the inside address and two spaces above the *salutation.*
2. The purpose is to attract the attention of a particular officer in an organization to attend to the letter.
   Examples:
   Attention : The Purchase Officer
   Attention: Mr. K.S. Subramanian

Salutation

Table 14.3 discusses the different forms of salutation.

TABLE 14.3 Different forms of salutation

Form of salutation	*Where used*	*Dialect of English*
Dear Sirs	a firm a company a board	British English
Dear Madams	a club a society an association a post box a newspaper box number	
Gentlemen or To whom it may concern:	a firm a company a board a club a society an association a post box a newspaper box number	 American English

(*Contd.*)

TABLE 14.3 Different forms of salutation (*Contd.*)

Form of salutation	*Where used*	*Dialect of English*
Dear Sir Dear Madam	officer by designation	BE and AE
Dear Mr. Gupta* Mrs. Miss Ms Dr.	a person known to you; use title and surname	BE and AE
My dear Shri Gupta My dear Shri Nath My dear Kusum Sharma	used with the person whom we know but *it is less formal*	Indian English
Dear Investor Dear Member Dear Reader Dear Subscriber	a general term of address	Circular letters, Sales letters

*John Seely (1998:18) suggests that some writers find Dear Dr. Gupta *too formal* and Dear John too informal. Therefore, some writers use the intermediate form:

Dear Ramesh Gupta

Some find it rather artificial.

Use of Punctuation

After the salutation, there are three conventions of punctuation:

1. Comma (,)
   Dear Sir,
2. Colon (:) especially in AE
   Dear Sir:
3. No punctuation
   Dear Sir

Subject

There are two conventions:

1. Between *attention* and *salutation*
   Attention: SM Sharma
   Subject: Admission to BE I
   Dear Sirs,
2. After salutation to BEI
   Dear Sirs,
   Subject: Admission to BEI

The word *Subject* can be left out. We can write the main topic boldly.

Dear Sirs,
ADMISSION To BEI

Body

The body of a letter may contain several paragraphs:

1. The first paragraph introduces the subject matter or states the *purpose* in writing.
2. One or more paragraphs. Facts of the case should be developed logically and clearly. If more than one paragraph, each paragraph should state a separate aspect of the subject matter and there should be links between paragraphs.
3. The final paragraph should state what you would like to see happen.
4. According to Sharma and Mohan (2003:45), if the body of a letter ends with 'Hoping to hear from you soon', we should add 'I am,' as shown below:
   Hoping to hear from you soon,

   I am,
   Yours faithfully,

   (SM Sharma)

Complimentary close

1. Typed two spaces below the last line of the letter.
2. It is a polite way of leave taking.
3. The close must agree with the salutation as shown in Table 14.4.

TABLE 14.4 Different forms of complimentary close

Salutation	*Complimentary close*	*Kind of English*
Sir Dear Sir	Yours faithfully, Yours Truly	BE AE
Dear Sir, Dear Madam, Dear Sirs, Dear Madams,	Yours faithfully, Yours Truly	BE AE
To whom it may concern:	Sincerely	AE
Dear Dr. Gupta	Yours sincerely, Sincerely Yours,	BE AE
Dear Investor,	Yours sincerely, Regards,	BE IE

Signature

1. Placed below the complimentary close.
2. The name of the writer is typed four spaces below the closing line, providing enough space for the signature.
3. The signature is put above the typed name in brackets and below the typed name appears the job description.

Yours faithfully,
(S.M. Sharma)
Sales Manager

4. If there is a firm or organization, the convention for signature is to put *on behalf of* or *per pro* (a Latin) phrase which is legally binding on the company.

Yours faithfully
on behalf of or per pro
Gupta and Company
Moti Das
Managing Director

5. The word *for* also is used for signing in place of an officer. This kind of putting down of signature is not legally binding on the company:

Yours sincerely
Parul Sen
(For) Dr. Rajni Badlani
English Studies Officer

Identification Marks

1. Placed in the left margin to identify the typist of the letter.
2. Placed two spaces below the signature.
3. Usually the initials of the officer who dictated the letter are put first.

SMS/LS
SMS/LS
/KO

The last two initials show the initials of the typist, the name of the officer is self evident.

Enclosure

1. Typed two spaces below the identification marks.
2. The shortened form *Encl* is typed against which the number of enclosures is shown: Encl 3
3. If the attachments are important, they may be specified:

Encls: 1. Photocopy of 10th Marks sheet
2. Photocopy of 12th Marks sheet

Copies

If copies of the letter are sent to anyone else, that is shown after the list of enclosures.

CC. Director, Finance Section
Or
Copy to
(i) Director
(ii) Chairman

Characteristics of a Good Business Letter

Remember the five *Cs* in a good business letter:

1. Courteous
2. Considerate
3. Concise
4. Clear
5. Complete

When we write a business letter we have to

1. Remember the purpose of the letter
2. Use a suitable style

Below we shall show how these five principles of courtesy, consideration, conciseness, clarity and completeness work in a business letter.

Study the following four letters.

1.

Dear respected Sir,

Your esteemed letter was received in this office yesterday and we perused the contents thereof. We are extremely delighted to apprise you of the fact that we stock the products desired by you and we shall act expeditiously the moment we receive your esteemed order because we value our customers as gods.

We feel honoured to enclose the required papers for your perusal and necessary action.

Yours faithfully,

2.

Dear Sir,

Thank you very much for your letter of 5 July 2012. We are enclosing the required papers as desired by you.

Yours faithfully,

3.

Dear Sir,

Thank you very much for your letter asking us to send you the pricelist of our products. We are enclosing the catalogue and the pricelist of the items that we produce.

We shall be able to supply the goods within a period of 15 days from the date of the receipt of the order. However, we are not obliged to guarantee the damage caused to the products in transit.

While ordering care should be taken to give us at least 15 days time to send you goods in time.

Yours faithfully,

4.

Dear Sir,

Thank you very much for your letter asking us to send you the pricelist of our products.

We are enclosing the catalogue and the pricelist of the items that we produce.

We shall be able to supply the goods within a period of 15 days as desired by you.

Currently we are offering 10 per cent discount on our entire range of products. We hope that you will order the goods at an early date to take advantage of our discount offer.

I once again thank you for showing interest in our company and look forward to hearing from you soon.

Yours faithfully,

Notice letter (1) is extremely courteous but quite verbose and lacks clarity. Expressions such as *respected sir*, *esteemed letter*, *customers ... as god*, *feel honoured*, *etc.* make us feel uncomfortable.

Letter (2) is extremely short and therefore lacks clarity.

Letter (3) is brief and precise, but the last paragraph where he says 'we are not obliged to guarantee' 'care should be taken' are *curt* and put the reader off.

Letter (4) is quite balanced; it is clear, precise, complete, courteous and considerate. Therefore it is suggested that in business correspondence, you should be:

1. Polite but not timid
2. Direct but not rude
3. Concise but not abrupt
4. Firm but not inflexible

In business correspondence your language should be **simple, direct, courteous.**

In business correspondence avoid:

1. Curtness
2. Verbosity
3. Jargon
4. Irrelevant details

Style and punctuation should be as suggested below:

1. Block style is in fashion. Use it.
2. No punctuation at sender's address, date, inside address, salutation and complimentary close.

EXERCISE 14.2

1. The following letter containing a request for payment is not courteous. Rewrite the following letter in such a way that it becomes more polite:

Dear Sir

You have owed us ₹ 2000 since May, which means you haven't paid us for three months.

We wrote to you and surprisingly you didn't bother answering us, yet you've been a customer for years. Anyway, this cannot go on like this, so if you don't tell us why you haven't paid or sent the money you owe us in 7 days, we'll sue you. After all we've got bills from our own suppliers and besides we explained our rules for giving credit, i.e. payment on final dates, some time ago.

Yours sincerely

(S.M. Sharma)

2. The use of words given in Table 14.4 makes your writing pompous, officious and long-winded.

Table 14.5 contains simpler alternatives in a jumbled form.

Match the words given in Table 14.5 with their counterparts in Table 14.6.

TABLE 14.5

1. accede	2. accustomed to
3. acquaint yourself	4. address
5. aforesaid	6. apprise
7. as a consequence of	8. attribute (verb)

(*Contd.*)

TABLE 14.5 (*Contd.*)

9. cease	10. cognizant of
11. commence	12. concerning
13. consequently	14. construe
15. corroboration	16. deem
17. defer	18. despite the fact that
19. disburse	20. due to the fact that
21. dwelling, domicile	22. envisage
23. equitable	24. eventuate
25. expedite	26. expiration
27. for the duration of	28. for the purpose of
29. henceforth	30. heretofore
31. hitherto	32. if this is not the case
33. in accordance with	34. in as much as
35. in conjunction with	36. in lieu of
37. in receipt of	38. interim (noun)
39. in the event of	40. in view of the fact that
41. nevertheless	42. nonetheless
43. notwithstanding	44. peruse
45. provenance	46. thereafter
47. truncate	48. whereby
49. whilst	50. with reference to

TABLE 14.6

1. about, concerning	2. while
3. by which, because of which	4. slice, portion, share, chunk
5. then, afterwards	6. source, origin
7. read, study	8. even if, despite, still, yet, but
9. even so, however, yet	10. even so, however, yet
11. as, because	12. if, when
13. meantime	14. get, have, receive
15. instead of	16. with
17. because, in that	18. in line with
19. in not	20. until now
21. until now	22. from now on
23. to	24. during, while
25. end	26. agree, grant, allow
27. used to	28. find out, read
29. tackle, deal with, consider	30. above mentioned
31. inform, tell	32. because
33. earmark	34. stop, end
35. aware of, know about	36. start, begin

(*Contd.*)

TABLE 14.6 (*Contd.*)

37. about	38. so
39. interpret	40. evidence, proof, support
41. treat as, consider	42. put off, postpone
43. although, despite	44. pay
45. as, because	46. home, property
47. expect, imagine	48. fair
49. result, occur, happen	50. hasten, speed up

EXERCISE 14.3

The following excerpts taken from business letters are wordy, indirect and imprecise or discourteous. Rewrite them so as to make them free from these faults.

1. A position where my experience aids in organizational excellence and the opportunities provided leads to avenue for continued professional and personal growth. I like to work in group where there is a cooperation and regular give and take of knowledge. I work towards my employer's prosperity and especially to develop my experience of instilling loyalty and enthusiasm in the people for whom I am responsible.
2. Objective: To go forward and achieve all the destinations keeping intensive eyes on my labour and faith in God.
3. Objective: Utilizing my knowledge, ideas and experience for performing and producing results in order to achieve prime goals of the organization. To explore opportunities and contribute in overall growth of the organization.
4. Objective: Seeking a challenging position and for adding a new component of knowledge and betterment of my professional qualifications.
5. Sub: Application for the post of lecturer in Electrical Engg. Deptt.

   Respected Sir,

   With due respect I would like to make a humble request that I consider myself eligible for the above post.

   With that reason, I am applying with the hope that you will consider me to work for your esteemed concern.
6. Objective: Seeking a position to utilize my skills and abilities in the Electronics and Telecom Sector which offers professional growth being resourceful, innovative and flexible.
7. To have a challenging position in the production and maintenance field combined with an opportunity to learn and enhance self-skill.
8. Having known about your college I am appending my Bio-Data for your perusal and kind consideration. If granted opportunity I am confident to

come up to your expectations and I would try my level best to prove an asset to your institution through serving with fullest devotion and dedication.

9. I am Master of Computer Applications (MCA) from IMS Ghaziabad and M.Tech. in Communication Engineering from VIT, Vellore (TN) with 3 year hands of Experience in Java Technology.
10. To put in the best of me and use present skills and to take up greater challenges especially in the field of Information Technology. Also to update present skill sets in order to scale greater heights. To use intellectual abilities towards mere result – oriented personality.
11. The cheque that was received from Reliance Infotech was received on 20 July.
12. The standard of traffic management on the NH8, NH12 and NH13 is of lower standard than on the major roads in Jaipur.
13. We attach herewith a financial statement.
14. A new bank account is in the process of being set up for you.
15. I must point out that I am legally obliged to charge rates on the property's current value.
16. I would like to take this opportunity to apologize for the delay in replying to your complaint.
17. It is only fair for me to point out at this point that the committee showed great concern about your case at its last meeting.
18. It should be appreciated that there is always an element of underreporting of accident, particularly if no one is injured. It should also be noted that our accident figures exclude occurrences where the system for explosion relief operated effectively.

EXERCISE 14.4

Make changes to the following letter so that it sounds more formal:

Thanks for sending us ₹ 1000 the other week, but don't forget you still owe us ₹ 2000 which we want you to pay before the end of September. If you're having problems finding the money, why don't you give us a ring? We could arrange a different way for you to pay us.

EXERCISE 14.5

In the following sentences, the *italicized* words are not very appropriate for formal correspondence. Choose a more suitable alternative from the list:

Inform, overdue, request, promptly, sufficient, elapsed, confidential, acceptable, competitive, settle

1. Thank you for forwarding the documents so *quickly.*
2. We feel that enough time has passed for you to *pay.*

3. I am writing *to ask for* open account facilities.
4. We remind you that this information is highly *secret.*
5. Your quarterly settlement is three weeks *late.*
6. We are pleased to tell you that the credit facilities you asked for are *fine.*
7. Our prices are very *low.*

EXERCISE 14.6

Change the following sentences into a more acceptable form for business letters.

1. I can't come to the reception because I'll be on holiday next month. I regret that ....
2. It's such a shame that your brother is dead. I'm really sorry. I was ....
3. So you've been elected chairman of the company! Well done! I would like ....
4. Mr. Sharma wants to drop in and see you next week about a contract, OK? Mr. Sharma would ....
5. I can't see you next Sunday for our appointment after all. I am sorry to tell ....
6. Can you come to our Sales Conference on 18 March? We would like ....
7. Thanks for helping me when I was in Delhi last week. I would ....
8. It'll be good to see you on Saturday. I look ....

EXERCISE 14.7

Read the following letter requesting payment and choose the best words from the options in brackets.

Data Scooters Ltd.
20 Hope Circus
Alwar 301001

Our Ref: DS 350
The Managing Director
Meena Scooters
Alwar Road
Rajgarh
Account No. 32305
20 July 2012
Dear Mr. Meena

We wrote to you on 20 June concerning the above (account, bill) for ₹ 12000 which has now been outstanding (for, since, about) three months. When we agreed to offer you credit facilities we pointed out that it was essential to (pay up, clear, handle) accounts (in, at, on) the exact date, particularly as we generally do not (allow, give, offer) credit terms.

As you realize, delayed payments can create problems for us (by, to, with) our own suppliers. Therefore, we would appreciate it if you could either let us know why the (account, credit payment) has not been cleared, or let us have a remittance (within, for, during) the next ten days. We hope this receives your immediate attention.

Yours sincerely

(S.M. Sharma)
Accountant

EXERCISE 14.8

Your college wants to buy Pentium – IV computers manufactured by WIPRO. As principal of the college, write a letter to Softdeal Computers, 20 Daryaganj, Delhi who have been using these computers to ask whether they are satisfied with the working of these computers.

EXERCISE 14.9

Imagine that you are accountant of Parley-G, RIICO Industrial Area, Neemarana. The Goyal Kirana Merchant, Bus Stand Behror have not yet made the payment of ₹ 12000 due to your company for the last three months. Write a letter to Kirana Merchant asking them to clear your accounts within a week failing which you will be forced to take a legal action.

EXERCISE 14.10

Write a letter of complaint to Richolook Garments, Tehsil Road, Alwar. You bought a pair of trousers from them, but after the very first wash the trousers have developed ball like figures all over. You want a refund of the money.

EXERCISE 14.11

Imagine that you are the proprietor of Richolook Garments, Tehsil Road, Alwar. Write a reply to the customer who has made a complaint about the defective piece of trousers.

You don't want to lose a customer, so make your letter frank and polite, in order to retain his goodwill.

EXERCISE 14.12

You are the librarian of your college. Write a letter to the Manager, Macmillan India Ltd. Imli Ka Phatak, Jyoti Nagar, Jaipur asking for a catalogue of books on engineering subjects. Also make an enquiry as to how much discount they offer to colleges on the catalogue price of the books.

EXERCISE 14.13

As Secretary of your class, write a letter to the General Manager, Parley-G, RIICO Industrial Area, Neemrana, requesting him to allow your class to visit the factory. Also give the date and time of the visit, the number of students in the group and telling him what you would particularly like to see.

EXERCISE 14.14

Write a letter to the Naveen Magazine Agency, Road No. 2, Alwar as librarian of your college asking them to send *India Today*, *Frontline* and *Outlook* on a regular basis. Also ask them to send their sales person to collect the year's subscription from the college accountant.

EXERCISE 14.15

Imagine that you are starting a detergent company. Design a letterhead for the company. On this letterhead write a letter to a commission agent in Jaipur appointing him sole distributor of your product for Rajasthan State.

EXERCISE 14.16

You ordered a watch as a birthday present for a close friend of yours. As you wanted it to be a surprise, you asked the shopkeeper not to mention your name. When your friend received the gift packet, he found the price tag on the watch along with a bill in your name. This was a matter of great embarrassment for you and your friend. Write a letter to the shopkeeper complaining about his carelessness.

EXERCISE 14.17

Put yourself in the place of the shopkeeper of the previous exercise and write a letter to the customer apologizing for the error.

Memos

A memorandum (a Latin word, plural: memoranda) is a short piece of writing generally used by the officers of an organization for communicating among themselves. Therefore, it is also called **interoffice memorandum**.

1. The purpose is to record or convey information, decisions or to make short requests.
2. Also used in some organizations for short reports to enable another officer to take decisions.
3. A very useful device for smooth flow of information and for maintaining social relationship.
4. Written in easy to understand, objective and matter of fact language.
5. A memo establishes acceptability within the organization and fixes responsibility of a wrong or faulty decision.

Structure of a Memo

The following items find a place in a memo:

1. Designation of the receiver
2. Designation of the sender
3. Reference
4. Date
5. Subject
6. In printed form, the name of the organization is written on the top
7. If copies of a memo are sent to other officers, its indication is given at the bottom.

Examples of Memos

A few examples of memos are given in Exhibits 14.11–14.12.

S.M. Sharma is the Managing Director of Jain Systems, Road No. 2, Alwar and Lata is his Secretary.

EXHIBIT 14.11 Example of memorandum

Memorandum

To: Lata

From: SM
Date: 20 July 2012
Please place an order with Data Infosys for the items I've indicated on the catalogue attached. Remind him in the accompanying letter that the terms we agreed on were payment by banker's draft and delivery within 2 weeks.
Thanks.

EXHIBIT 14.12 Example of memorandum

Suman Garments Ltd.
Church Road Alwar

To: All Staff
From: Personnel Officer
Date: 20 July 2004
Subject: Staff Discounts
We intend to introduce a staff discount scheme on 20 July for everyone working for the company. The discount will be fifteen percent off the retail price of any items in the store.
When purchases are made, staff keep receipt of anything they have bought until after exit security checks have been made. It would also be advisable for staff to keep receipts for three months after purchase to prove when & where the item was bought.
If you have any questions, see your manager or supervisor who will be able to help you.

Faxes

A fax is a short form of *facsimile.* It is a technological way of sending a message from one person to another. Since the fax is new, there are fewer conventions to write it. The following points are, however, important:

1. The company or organization to which the fax is addressed.
2. The person for whom the fax is intended.
3. Their fax No.
4. The number of pages (purpose to check whether all the material has been received).
5. The sender's name.
6. The sender's company or organization.
7. Their fax number as also their phone number in case there has been a problem in sending or receiving the fax.
8. The date.
9. The fax is quick, cheaper than a telephone call; can use words as well as pictures and the recipient need not be there to receive it.
10. There are three types of faxes:
    (i) Informal and handwritten
    (ii) Based on the letter
    (iii) Based on the memo

The *first type* of fax is similar to the second type except that it is hand-written. Therefore, we shall not give any example for the first one. The examples for the remaining are given below (Exhibit 14.13).

EXHIBIT 14.13 Example of fax

Suman Garments
Church Road, Alwar
Tel: 0144-2731946
Fax: 0144-2731947

Fax Cover Sheet[1]
Date 20 July 2012 To Fax No.:01494246352
To: Rajeev Goyal From: Lata Sahni
Number of pages including this cover sheet: 1

Dear Rajeev,
It was good to hear from you again. The enclosed catalogue gives you details of the latest additions to our range. It you require any further information, please do not hesitate to contact me.
Best regards,
Lata Sahni

This fax may contain confidential information[2]. If you are not the intended recipient[3], advise the sender[4] and destroy this document. If you do not receive all pages or if any pages are illegible, please phone 0144-2731946 immediately.

1. Cover sheet: The first page of a fax showing who it is *from*, who it is *to*, etc.
2. Information that others should not know.
3. The person who should receive the Fax.
4. Tell the person who sent it.

Suman Travels Agents
AND
Tour Planners

Church Road
Alwar 301001
Phone: 0144-2731946
Phone: 0144-**By Fax**
Fax: 0144-2731947

To:	Rajeev Goyal
Company:	Gupta Bus Company
Fax No.:	01494-246352
From:	Lata Sahni
No. of Pages:	1
Date:	20 July 2004
Subject:	Requirement of 5 Deluxe Buses

This month we have 250 tourists willing to travel to Tamil Nadu.
Therefore, we need five deluxe buses on next Monday. The buses will be travelling through Tamil Nadu for a month.
How much will you charge from us for this tour arrangement. Let us know immediately. We shall pay 50% of the total cost as advance plus the required gas. The remainder shall be paid on completion of the tour.

We look forward to hearing from you.

E-mail

Electronic mail or e-mail is increasingly used instead of letters or faxes. The chief advantages are:

1. It is quick.
2. It is cheap.
3. Replying to messages is easy.
4. Messages can be copied to others and re-routed.
5. The receiver can incorporate an e-mail message into a computer program (e.g. a word processed text).
6. One can attach computer files to an e-mail message (e.g. a graphics file)

Figure 14.1 from "Business Vocabulary in Use (p.114)" illustrates the layout of email:

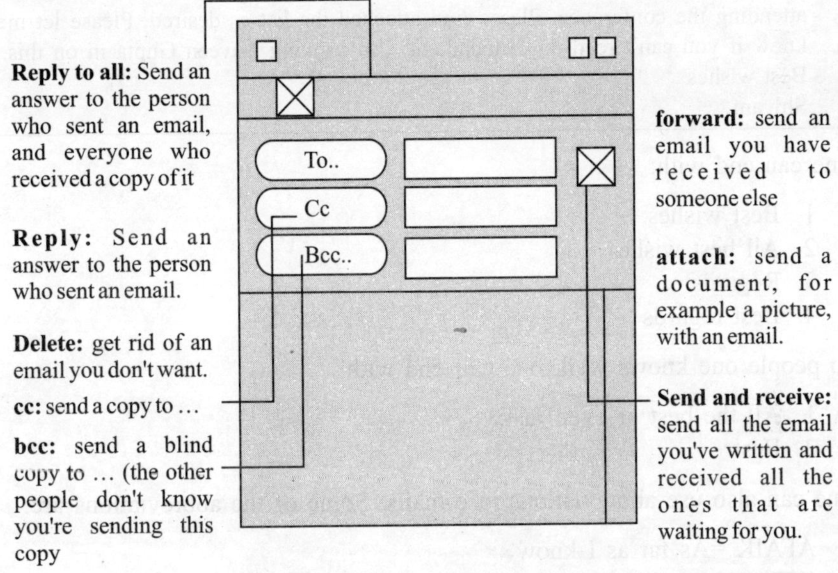

FIGURE 14.1 Layout of e-mail.

Email is an electronic mail. You can send an email to someone, or email them. They will reply to your email or email you back.

Exhibit 14.14 given an example of an e-mail.

EXHIBIT 14.14 Example of an e-mail

E-mail expressions

Previous	Next	Reply	Forward	Delete

Date: 20 July 2012

To	guptasag01@rediffmail.com
From	sharma01@yahoo.com
CC	guptasag02@yahoo.com
BCC	

Sagar,
Thanks for your e-mail asking to send you the list of persons who will be attending the conference. Please find attached the list as desired. Please let me know if you can't read this attachment. I'm copying Naveen Gupta in on this.
Best wishes
Shivam

One can end with:

1. Best wishes
2. All best wishes
3. Regards
4. Best regards

To people one knows well, one can end with:

1. All the best or even just:
2. Best

One can also use abbreviations in e-mails. Some of the abbreviations are:

AFAIK =As far as I know
HTH= Hope this helps

Telegram

Telegram is a miniature version of a memo. Function words are left out. It is a quick way of sending a message. An example is given in Exhibit 14.15.

EXHIBIT 14.15 Example of a telegram

Rajeev Goyal
C/o Goyal Garments
Bus stand, Behror – 301701
List of seminarists sent today by courier.
Amit Sharma
Not to be telegraphed
Amit Sharma
A-16 HKM Nagar
Alwar - 301001

Notices, Agenda and Minutes

An organization consists of several bodies and committees who look after the different aspects of funding of the organization. There are a general body, finance committee, purchase committee, Board of Directors, etc. Each committee has an executive committee comprising chairman, secretary, treasurer, etc. The secretary of committee issues a notice for a meeting to be held indicating day, date, time, place and agenda of the meeting to all the members who have a right to attend the meeting.

Agenda means the main business to be transacted at the meeting. This can form a part of the notice or can be appended separately with the notice.

During the meeting, the Secretary records the *minutes* (*main points of discussion and the decision taken*) which form the basis for further action and decisions. Minutes form an important part of the record of the organization. Sometimes, a member of the committee may not agree with the decisions taken at the meeting; in such a case, he may write *a note of dissent* which will be appended to the minutes and will form a part of the record of the organization.

Below we shall present examples of *notice*, *agenda* and *minutes* (Exhibits 14.16–14.18).

EXHIBIT 14.16 Example of notice

St. Thomas Arts & Science College Triveni Marg Behror-301701
20 July 2012
Notice
Notice is hereby given that the second meeting of the Staff Council will be held in the staff-room at 3.30 pm on Tuesday, 27 July 2012.
The agenda is attached.
To: All the staff members
SM Sharma
Secretary

EXHIBIT 14.17 Example of agenda

St. Thomas Arts & Science College
Triveni Marg Behror-301701

20 July 2004

Agenda for the Second Meeting of the Staff Council to be held at 3.30 pm on Tuesday, 27 July 2012 in the staff-room.

2.01 Confirmation of the minutes of the last meeting
2.02 Ratification of the proposed syllabus for BA II
2.03 Issue of prospectus
2.04 Problem of Indiscipline in the college
2.05 Teacher Training Programmes
2.06 Any other matter with the permission of the chairman

SM Sharma
Secretary

EXHIBIT 14.18 Example of minutes

St. Thomas Arts and Science College
Triveni Marg Berhor-301701

Minutes of the Second Meeting of the Staff Council held in the staff room of the college at 3.30 pm on Tuesday, 27 July 2012.

Present :	Avinash Gaur	Principal & Chairman
	Akhilesh Gupta	
	R.L. Singh	
	S.K. Sharma	
	Abhinav Gupta	
	Lata Sharma	
	Neha Khandelwal	
Absent:	Shikha Gupta	
	Brij Bhusan	
In attendance:	S.M. Sharma	Secretary

No. of minutes	*Subject of minutes*	*Details of minutes*
2.01	Confirmation of the minutes of the last meeting	The minutes of the meeting held on 10 April, 2012 were approved by the council and signed by the Principal.
2.02	Ratification of the proposed syllabus for BA II	The changes suggested by the Syllabus Committee were discussed threadbare and the changes approved.
2.03	Issue of prospectus	A committee consisting of S.K. Sharma, R.L. Singh and Abhinav Gupta was appointed to draft the prospectus and present it in the next meeting.
2.04	Problem of indiscipline in the college	The problem of indiscipline was discussed in detail. The causes were analyzed and it was resolved that strict action be taken against the offenders.

2.05	Teacher training programmes	It was suggested that a trained teacher is an asset for any institution. The principal should persuade the management to send at least two teachers every year for training on full salary. The Principal promised to discuss the matter with the management and report the outcome in the next meeting.

The meeting ended with a vote of thanks to the Chair.

Avinash Gaur
Principal
27 July 2012

S.M. Sharma
Secretary

EXERCISE 14.18

1. Imagine that you have just come back from an International Conference held at Hyderabed from 4 to 9 August 2011. You were deputed there by your college. Write a *memo* to your Head of the Department reporting to him the important matters discussed at the Conference. Also, point out their usefulness for teaching.
2. As the Principal of a college, write a memo to all Heads of the Departments of technology asking them to send the teaching plans of their departments within a week of the receipt of the memo.
3. As Principal of a college, you are worried about the amount of time lecturers are spending gossiping in the corridors, outside the main gate and in the canteen. Write a memo to all the lecturers asking them to be in their labs when they do not have classes.
4. The meeting of the Proctorial Board was held to consider the case of indiscipline of S.C. Gupta, a student of BE III. All the members of the Board were present. It was unanimously decided to expell the said student from the college. Write a notice to all members of the Board to attend the meeting. Also attach an agenda. Then write minutes of the meeting.
5. Send a fax message from International Engineering College Bidasar, to Sohan Sharma, who has applied for the job of a lecturer in Electronics in your college. Ask him to attend an interview within a week of the receipt of the fax message.
6. Send an e-mail to Infotech Computer Suppliers, Nai Sarak, Delhi to expedite the order of computers that you placed a week before from your college (imagine the name of the college) and ask them to send the consignment immediately.

Social Letters

There are other types of letters that we are called upon to write in our social life. These letters are governed by social etiquette and laid-down stringent social conventions. Among these letters are invitation, condolence and congratulation letters. Below we shall discuss two of them.

Invitations

There are two kinds of letters of invitations: formal and informal. Formal invitations are written in third person. There is also a tradition of writing RSVP (a French expression for please reply to the given telephone number or address) on the left hand bottom margin.

Here is a wedding invitation (Exhibit 14.19).

EXHIBIT 14.19 Example of invitation

Mrs. and Mr. S.M. Sharma
request the pleasure of the company of
Mr. and Mrs. R.K. Sharma
at the marriage of their son
PRATEEK
to
PRIYA
on Friday, the twenty third of July at 7 o' clock at Hotel Shubham Road No. 2, Alwar.

1. This is a formal wedding invitation.
2. Mark the use of the third person instead of *we.*
3. There is no signature or date at the end.
4. The name of invitee is handwritten.

Here is another example (Exhibit 14.20):

EXHIBIT 14.20 Example of invitation

Mrs. and Mr. B.K. Mathur
request the pleasure of the company of
Mr. R.K. Rangarao
on the occasion of the first birthday of their daughter
Namrata
at 7:00 p.m.
on Friday, July 20.

Dhyaan Niwas
Road No. 2 Alwar,
R.S.V.P.
0144-2731946

1. Courtesy demands that replies should be sent if RSVP is given.
2. The reply is also written in a formal style.

An example of letter of acceptance of the invitation letter is given in Exhibit 14.21.

EXHIBIT 14.21 Letter of acceptance

> Mr. R.K. Rangarao thanks Mr. and Mrs. B.K. Mathur for their kind invitation, which he accepts with pleasure.
>
> 210 HKM Nagar
> Alwar,
> 17 July, 2012

An example of letter of regret of the invitation letter is given in Exhibit 14.22.

EXHIBIT 14.22 Letter of regret

> Mr. Rangarao thanks Mrs. and Mr. B.K. Mathur for their kind invitation, but regrets that, owing to a prior engagement, he is unable to accept it.
> 210 HKM Nagar
> Alwar,
> 17 July, 2012

The invitation letter can also be written in the form of a letter also. Here is a specimen (see Exhibits 14.23–14.25).

EXHIBIT 14.23 Invitation in the form of letter

> Dhyoam Niwas
> Road No. 2, Alwar
> 17 July 2012
> Dear Mr. R.K. Rangarao
> I shall be extremely delighted if you could attend a party on the occasion of the first birthday of our daughter Namrata at 7.00 pm. on Friday July20, 2012 at our residence. If your son has come home for the holidays, please bring him along too.
>
> Yours sincerely
>
> Dr. B.K. Mathur

EXHIBIT 14.24 Acceptance

> 0210 HKM Nagar
> Alwar,
> 17 July, 2012
> Dear Mrs. and Mr. B.K. Mathur
> I thank you very much for your invitation to a party on the occasion of the birthday of your daughter Namrata.
> I shall be pleased to attend the party on Friday, July 20, 2012 at 7.00 pm.
> I am looking forward to meeting you and other friends at the party.
>
> Yours sincerely
>
> R.K. Rangarao

EXHIBIT 14.25 Letter of regret

210 HKM Nagar
Alwar
17 July, 2012
Dear Mrs. and Mr. B.K. Mathur

Thank you very much for your invitation to the party at your residence on Friday, July 20.

I am sorry to say that I cannot come to the party because of a prior engagement. Thanks so much for asking me. I know what a wonderful evening I am going to miss.

Yours sincerely

R.K. Rangarao

An example of letter of condolence is given in Exhibit 14.26.

EXHIBIT 14.26 Letter of condolence

Dear Mr Sharma
I am shocked to learn that your father expired yesterday. I know that he was ill, but had no idea that we would lose him so suddenly.
I express my heartfelt sympathy to you and pray to God to give you strength to bear this irreparable loss.
If there is anything I can do to lighten your burden, please do let me know.
With kind regards,

Yours sincerely

S.K. Gupta

An example of letter of congratulations is given in Exhibit 14.27.

Exhibit 14.27 Letter of congratulations

My dear Yogesh
I am delighted to know that you have gotten the highest marks (90%) in Computer Science in BE-III Semester Examination 2012. Please accept my heartiest congratulations.
You deserved this grade because you put in such hard work.
I wish you many more successes in future.

Yours sincerely
Manish

An example of letter of hotel reservation is given below.

201 HKM Nagar
Alwar-301001
20 July 2012

Manager
Taj Hotel
Dayal Bagh
Agra (U.P.)
Dear Sir,
Subject: Hotel Reservation

I, along with my family (wife and two sons aged 10 and 8), am coming to Agra on 27 July 2012 for three days.

Please book a double occupancy room for us starting 27 July for a period of three days. A draft for ₹ 3000 is enclosed as an advance.

Please confirm the booking by return post.

Yours faithfully,

S.M. Sharma

EXERCISE 14.19

1. Write a letter of sympathy to a friend of yours who has lost his mother.
2. An old classmate of yours has passed the RAS examination and is ranked first. Write a letter congratulating him on his brilliant success in the examination.
3. Your sister's marriage is going to take place after 15 days. Draft a formal and informal letter of invitation.
4. You have received a wedding invitation from a friend of yours. His sister's marriage is to take place after 15 days. Draft a letter of acceptance and a letter of refusal.
5. You are going to Shimla with your family for holidaying. Write a letter to the Manager, Hotel Grand, Mall Road, Shimla requesting him to book a room for you for 3 days.

Letter of Application

Most important among business letters is a letter of application which is usually written in reply to an advertisement. A highly qualified person offers his services to a firm or organization. Getting a job, of course, depends upon one's qualifications, experience and eligibility requirements but getting called for an interview will depend upon your cover (AE) or covering (BE) letter and the resume (AE) or CV or bio-data (BE). If your CV and cover letters are well organized, precise, to the point and attractive, then that will definitely get you a call for an interview which might result in your getting a job.

Curriculum Vitae (CV)

The Shorter Oxford Dictionary defines CV as:

"A brief account of one's life and career, especially as required in an application for employment."

A traditional CV includes the following basic information.

1. Full name
2. Address and telephone number
3. Age, date and place of birth
4. Nationality
5. Marital status
6. Number of children
7. Dates and places of primary, secondary and tertiary education
8. Educational qualifications (public examinations, grades and degrees achieved)
9. Employment record including name of the company, position held and the period
10. More detailed information about present position and salary
11. Interests
12. Name of persons who will provide references for character and work

An example of CV is given in Exhibit 14.28.

EXHIBIT 14.28 An Example of CV

Name:		Rati Mohan Sharma
Address:		A-165, HKM Nagar, Alwar-301001
Telephone:		0144-2731317
Born:		1 August 1950, Kanwat, Sikar, Rajasthan
Age:		54
Nationality:		Indian
Marital status:		Married
Children:		2
Educational Qualifications	1955–1961	Govt. Primary School, Kanwat
	1961–1966	Govt. High School, Kanwat
	1966–1969	Govt. Polytechnic, Sikar Physics (A), Maths (A), Chemistry (B), Electronics (A)
Employment:	1969–1974	Graduate trainee with Data Infosys Alwar
	1974–2000	Rainbow Mobile Phones Assistant Area Sales Manger,

	2000–2004	(Current position) Sales Manager, Hutch India Ltd. Jaipur. Current Salary ₹ 25000 per month
Interest:		Swimming, reading, playing golf, Member of Rotary Club Alwar
References:		Mr. Ravi Kant, MLA, 102 Moti Dunagri, Alwar (Telephone:0141-2395507)

The above is adapted from Seeley (2002). The above CV is a bald recital of facts. It does not say anything about the selling points of the candidates. This work will have to be done by the cover letter. Therefore, it is wise to make your CV a 'selling document' which gives a list of the applicant's virtues along with supporting details.

A successful CV is a product of careful thought and planning. An employer looks for an applicant who has the right experience, skills and personal qualities for the job. A person who is called for an interview is the one who not only has the above traits but also presents them in an attractive way. The applicant should prepare rough notes on the following:

1. Experience includes:
   (i) education
   (ii) professional training
   (iii) periods of employment including part time jobs and 'proper' jobs
   (iv) Other jobs like a foreign job or a foreign travel
   (v) Any voluntary work.

2. Skills include:
   (i) the skills which a person already has
   (ii) the skills on which the applicant has made improvement
   (iii) the skills that he/she has learnt
   (iv) In the enumeration of your skills, mention all the sub-skills and variety of skills such as:
   (v) Organizing events
   (vi) Making presentations
   (vii) Editing
   (viii) Chairing meeting
   (ix) Negotiating
   (x) Supervising
   (xi) Giving advice
   (xii) Counselling
   (xiii) Monitoring

   and a host of other skills, too detailed to be listed here.

3. Personal qualities are too numerous to be mentioned. Some of them could be as given here.
   Choose some of these qualities; also support them with incidents of your life.

accurate	competent
adaptable	cooperative
astute	courteous
can work under pressure	decisive
careful	dedicated
committed	energetic
extrovert	orderly
flexible	organized
friendly	positive
get on well with people	practical
good communicator	receptive
good sense of humour	relaxed
good time keeper	reliable
hardworking	self-confident
imaginative	self-motivated
independent worker	sensitive
lively	thorough
logical	thoughtful
loyal	vigilant
methodical	work well with others
meticulous	

After making rough notes on experience, skills and personal qualities, one can order one's CV in two ways:

1. Chronologically
2. Functionally

In chronological CV, the applicant presents his education and work experience as they happened or in the reverse order (i.e. starting with the latest and then the descending order). The advantages of the chronological order are that this order shows continuity and emphasizes the key periods of employment. The disadvantages are that it does not highlight skills and also shows inexperience and periods of unemployment.

A *functional CV*, on the other hand, is organized by skills and qualities. The advantages are that it highlights skills and conceals periods of inexperience and unemployment. The disadvantages of this approach are that it does not focus on important periods of employment and continuity and reliability of employment. Below we present *chronological CV* (Exhibit 14.29) and *functional CV* (Exhibit 14.30).

EXHIBIT 14.29 Example of chronological CV

Suraj M. Sharma
'The Saikripa'
A-165,
HKM Nagar,
Alwar-301001
Tel: 0144-2730317
e-mail:sharma@yahoo.com

Experience

2000–present
Lecturer in English at Mary Convent College of Engineering and Technology, Teaching English Literature, Humanities to BE II Students; organizing debates, quizzes for BE I students; conducting personality development programmes for both BE I and II year students.

1996–2000
Head of English Department at Govt. Arts College Alwar. Responsible for preparing the syllabus and teaching load of lecturers; teaching Poetics and TS Eliot to MA Final students. Responsible for organizing programmes for the Literary Association.

1994–2000
Teacher of English language at Govt. College, Behror. Responsible for teaching General English classes of BA –I and BA –II students.

Qualifications and Training

Postgraduate Diploma in Teaching English from CIEFL, Hyderabad.
Postgraduate Diploma in Applied Linguistics, Edinburgh University. 'A' level in French and German.

Interests:

Foreign travel
Parachute jumping
Rock-climbing
Voluntary social work on AIDS awareness programme among truck drivers.

Referees

Dr. A.C. Garg
Professor of English
P.G. Arts College
Alwar

Dr. S.K. Sharma
MLA Alwar
102, Shantikunj
Alwar

EXHIBIT 14.30 Example of functional CV

Pawan J. Kumar
Alwar Nagar-301001
Tel/Fax: (0144) 2731946

Profile

Enthusiastic, responsible, postgraduate with a Ph.D. in Linguistics and good knowledge of French and German. Able to work independently, using initiative as a part of a team. With excellent skills in oratory, communication and teaching effectively.

Training

Has recently completed the Post-graduate Diploma in teaching English from IGNOU, New Delhi.

Skills gained

- Pre-preparation of lectures
- Delivering lectures by using power point
- Interactive method of teaching
- Organizing literary meets
- Inviting experts in the field of literature

Experience

- Two years experience of teaching English language and literature to undergraduate students at Chirawa College, Chirawa
- Five years experience of teaching English Literature at Govt. College, Kota
- Currently teaching Communication Techniques to BE I at St. Mary Convent School of Technology, Neemrana

Education

Research Degree: Ph.D in Linguistics from University of Hawaii
Degree: M.A. (English Literature) from University of Rajasthan
B.Ed. from M.D. University, Rohtak
B.A. from University of Rajasthan with English, Sanskrit and Hindi

Interests

Music: playing the guitar
Cinema and theatre going
Foreign books
Listening to light and classical music

Referees

Dr. G.K. Biswas
Professor and Head
Department of English
University of Rajasthan
Jaipur

Dr. C.K. Nair
Principal
St. Mary Convent
School of Technology
Neemrana

The document or CV should be well presented, suitably word-processed, printed on a high quality paper using a good laser printer to print and the layout and typefaces be chosen with extreme care.

A word of caution is necessary. A CV should be adjusted to suit a particular post for which one is applying. It should be updated from time to time.

Cover Letter

The CV should be accompanied by a cover letter.

This letter has a number of purposes:

1. It emphasizes the applicant's selling points.
2. It enables the applicant to list his personal qualities that do not appear in the CV.
3. It shows the prospective employer that the applicant can write a letter.

The cover letter should include:

1. The details of why you are applying for the jobs and where you saw the advertisement, etc.
2. In two or three paragraphs, emphasize your personal qualities and the skills that make you suitable for the job. You can also emphasize periods of employment and experience that are relevant.
3. In conclusion, leave the reader with a positive image and show your willingness to provide any further information that the reader may want.

It is the layout, printing and typefaces and the selling points of the covering letter, which will attract the prospective employer to call you for an interview. So, a covering letter is like a neat packaging of your material. The more attractive it is, the better it is.

An example of a covering letter is given in Exhibit 14.31.

EXHIBIT 14.31 Example of a cover letter

S.C. Gupta
C –129, HKM, Nagar Alwar-301001
Tel/Fax (0144) 2731-946
The Registrar
Sobhasaria Engineering College
Gokulpura
Sikar (Rajasthan)
Dear Sir
Professor/Assistant Professor of English language

I wish to apply for the above post, advertised in the Rajasthan Patrika. Currently I am working at St. Mary Convent School of Technology Neemrana. I am teaching Communication Techniques, Making Presentations and Personality Development Programmes to BE I students. I have a wide range of responsibilities in addition to teaching. I am looking after the admission work; correspondence to the University of Rajasthan and problems of indiscipline among the students. I am doing all this work with great enthusiasm and commitment. The management, the principal and the students are quite happy with my work.

I have been here for more than two years but there is no longer the scope to use all my knowledge and experience. I am seeking a position that offers me greater responsibility and challenge especially in the field of English Language Teaching. For example, I want to set up an ultra-modern language lab, which can train the students of technology in effective communication techniques of English. I think your college may provide me this opportunity. I would welcome the opportunity to discuss the letter and my resume. The telephone number given is that of my son-in-law. He will be pleased to pass on the message to me.

I look forward to hearing from you.

Yours sincerely

S.C. Gupta

Before we end our discussion on CV, it would be worthwhile to give adapted examples of CV, from the Advanced Learner's Dictionary both in British and American style. The American style is becoming more popular. The first example in British style (Exhibit 14.32) is a covering letter, followed by CV (Exhibits 14.32 and 14.33).

EXHIBIT 14.32 Example of a covering letter for CV in British style

C-129
HKM Nagar,
Alwar-301001
20 July, 2004
The Registrar
Apex Institute of Technology
Jaipur
Dear Sir

I am writing to apply for the position of lecturer in Electronics and Communication. Engineering advertised in Dainik Bhaskar of 15 July 2012. Please find enclosed a copy of my CV.

I have a degree in Electronics and Communication Engineering from Balaji College of Technology Jaipur. Since graduation last summer I have been working for Rainbow, Raja Park, Jaipur on a contract basis. I have particularly become interested in mobile technology and now wish to develop my career in that direction. I would welcome the chance to work as part of a small, dynamic team where I could make a significant contribution while developing my skills yet further. I would like to show the small research work that I have done. I look forward to hearing from you.

Yours sincerely

(S.C. Gupta)

EXHIBIT 14.33 CV in British style

Name	S.C. Gupta
Address	C–129, HKM, Nagar Alwar-301001
Telephone	0144-2731946
Nationality	Indian
Date of birth	11 April 1982
Marital status	Single
Education/Qualifications	
1999–2003	Balaji College of Technology, BE in Electronics and Communication Engineering (First class)
1997–1999	Senior Secondary Exam from Martin Senior Secondary School, Jaipur Physics (Distinction), Maths (Distinction), Chemistry (Distinction)
Employment to date	
2003–Present	Rainbow Jaipur, Network Engineer
Skills	Computer expertise in DSA, Visual Basic and C++
Interests	Tennis, swimming, classical music

Exhibit 14.34 Example of resume in American style

S.C. Gupta	Married
C –129	No children
HKM Nagar	
Alwar-301001	
Tel: 0144 2731946	
e-mail: guptascol@rediffmail.com	
Objective	To obtain a position of lecturer in Electronics and Communication Engineering in a highly reputed college of technology
Education	
1999–2003	BE in Electronics & Communication, Engineering from Balaji College of Technology Jaipur (First class)
1997–1998	Senior Secondary Exam from Martin Senior Secondary School, Jaipur, Physics (Distinction), Maths (Distinction), Chemistry (Distinction)
Experience	
2003–Present	Rainbows, Jaipur Network Engineer
Language	Fluent French and Russian
Personal	Interests include tennis, swimming and classical music
Reference	Dr. S.K. Munjal, Chair, Department of Electronics and Communication, Engg., IIT Delhi

EXERCISE 14.20

Answer the following advertisements

1. Merchandising: Kitex, the largest garment manufacturers in the state of Kerala, seeks the following elegant, diligent and ingenious candidates for its ongoing expansion project of 200 crores.
   Manager—Merchandising
   Senior Merchandisers
   The minimum qualification is Degree/Diploma in Fashion Technology/Textile Technology with relevant experience in garment industry/buying house.
   Interested persons will apply with detailed bio-data to:
   Kitex Garments Ltd.
   3rd floor Shenoy,
   Chambers, Shanmughan, Road,
   Cochin-31.
2. Power Links
   Transmission Limited
   (A joint venture of Tata Power and Power Grid)
   Powerlinks invites application for the position:

   Project Engineers

   Requirements: Degree in Electrical/Mechanical/Civil Engineering with 8–10 years experience in Construction and Maintenance of 440 KV/220 KV Transmission Lines and Project Management in respective areas.
   CV may be forwarded within 7 days to:
   Head, HRD and Administration, Powerlinks Transmission Limited, 4th Floor, Kanchenjunga Building,18 Barakhamba Road, New Delhi-110001.
   Fax: 011-55306377
   e-mail: pkumar@powerlinkstransmission.com
3. Shapoorji Pallonji and Co. Ltd.
   Require for their Interior Division in Mumbai/Bangalore/Delhi

   Project Managers

   5/8 years experience B.E. Civil/B.Arch

   Quality Surveyors

   3/5 years experience
   Project Engineers/Supervisors
   2/3 years experience

Commercial Assistants

Fresh/1–2 years experience, graduate.
Apply to: **Shapoorji Pallonji and Co. Ltd**
New India Centre, 10th Floor, 17, Cooperage Road,
Mumbai – 400 001. Fax No.: 2281 9363
Email: spcmghrd@rediffmail.com

4. Hindustan Petroleum Corporation Limited

Corrigendum

Recruitment of Officer Trainees

This has reference to our Advertisement in Hindustan Times dated 22/06/2004 inviting applications for the position of Officer Trainees.

The total number of vacancies notified have been revised to 270 (SC-42, ST-20, OBC-73 and Locomotor Disability-2).

The Eligibility Criteria with regard to Qualifications in addition to the same stated in the earlier advertisement is as follows: Those candidates who possess the Degree in Engineering (B.E./B.Tech) in the disciplines of *Chemical* and *Instrumentation* or appeared in the Final Year Examination and are awaiting results can also apply. However, they be interviewed only on production of evidence of having passed their final examination with the stipulated percentage of 60% for General/OBC (Pass class for SC/STs) as notified in our advertisement.

The Discipline Code for Chemical Engineering is *05* and Instrumentation Engineering is *06*. The other terms and conditions of recruitment remain unchanged.

The last date for receipt of applications in the prescribed format as per our Advertisement is extended for 15 days from the date of release of the Corrigendum.

5. Dairy Technologist

Metro Dairy Limited is a joint sector company with an annual turnover of ₹ 145 crores. The Company's project was totally funded by the World Bank under the Operation Flood Programme.

For its fully automated plant located near Kolkata, the company wishes to recruit:

Executive

Graduate in Dairy Technology with M. Tech in Dairy Chemistry/Dairy Microbiology, preferably with 2–3 years of experience in Quality Assurance in a large milk processing plant. Ability to work in shifts is a must. Age: around 28 years.

Please apply within 10 days, superscribing the position on the envelope to:
Managing Director
Metro Dairy Limited
21 Gopal Mukherjee Road,
Kolkata-700002.

6. Urgently Required for Libya

   A reputed company requires the following personnel for their project in Libya:

   (i) For fully computerized automatic Mosaic Tile Plant (ESSANI Make), capacity 4500 sq.m./day.

   Computer Programmer 1/Computer Engineer 1

   (ii) For Manual Mosaic Tile Plant (LONEINETT), capacity 3600 sq.m./day

   Supervisor/Foreman 2

   (having knowledge of Mosaic Tile manufacturing)

   (iii) For stone quarry

   Blasters (having valid license) 2 Rock Drillers 4

   Contact Tel. No. 9871237088 or apply to:
   Box HTD-46712 Hindustan Times, New Delhi-110001.

15

Precis Writing

Introduction

Précis writing is a very important activity. It is a frequently asked question in all home and competitive examinations. It is also a very useful activity for business executives, newspaper reporters and research scholars. It is not possible to read all the latest dissertations for a Ph.D. dissertation abstracts. Précis is an exercise in comprehension, concentration and condensation.

In this chapter, we shall discuss what précis is, and what tips are useful for précis writing. We shall also present two model pieces of précis. The model pieces of précis will be followed by exercises.

What is a Précis

A precis is not

1. Simply a summary of a passage.
2. Simply an abstract of a passage.
3. An outline of a passage.
4. A mere selection of a few important sentences from a passage.
5. A collection of unconnected facts and statements.

A précis is a **restatement of reconstruction in a shortened form** (could be anywhere between one-third to one-fifth of the original passage) of the **main ideas** of the **original passage** usually in one **paragraph** which reads as a well-connected piece.

Features of a Good Précis

A good précis:

1. is marked by clarity, brevity and precision.

2. is not just lifting of the sentences from the original. It should be written in the précis writer's own words.
3. demands a lot of practice and effort.
4. is written in reported speech.
5. of a speech or dialogue is written in third person and in reported speech.
6. must have a title.
7. must have a logical order and be well-knit and well connected.
8. must have coherence; must use linking devices such as *so*, *therefore*, *and because*, *further*, etc.
9. must follow the order of ideas of the original.
10. must not contain any details not found in the original.

Steps to Write a Precis

We list the steps given bellow that should be followed in attempting a précis of a passage with the help of an algorithm (Figure 15.1).

Notice in steps 6 and 9 of the visual representation, we talk of leaving out of unimportant ideas and condensation respectively. This refers to two kinds of *reduction* in writing a précis.

1. Conceptual reduction
2. Linguistic reduction

Below we shall tell you how to achieve the two kinds of reduction.

Conceptual Reduction

If we study the structure of a paragraph, we notice that each paragraph contains a topic sentence and a number of major support and minor support sentences. The purpose of a major support sentence is to develop the idea contained in the topic sentence and the purpose of a minor support sentence is to develop the idea contained in the major support sentence. While attempting précis of a paragraph, we should go sentence by sentence noting down *the main idea* expressed by each sentence. In most cases, it is possible to leave out minor support sentences or we can refer to the idea expressed therein by one or two words.

Let us take an example:

(i) White's is a good drug store.
(ii) It is very modern and clean inside.
(iii) It has air conditioning and the most up-to-date refrigeration equipment.

In the above short paragraph, sentence (i) is a topic sentence because the passage is about White's drug store and its goodness. Sentence (ii) is a *major support* sentence because it tells us why White's is good drug store. sentence (iii) is a minor support sentence because it tells us why it is modern and most up-to-date (see Figure 15.2).

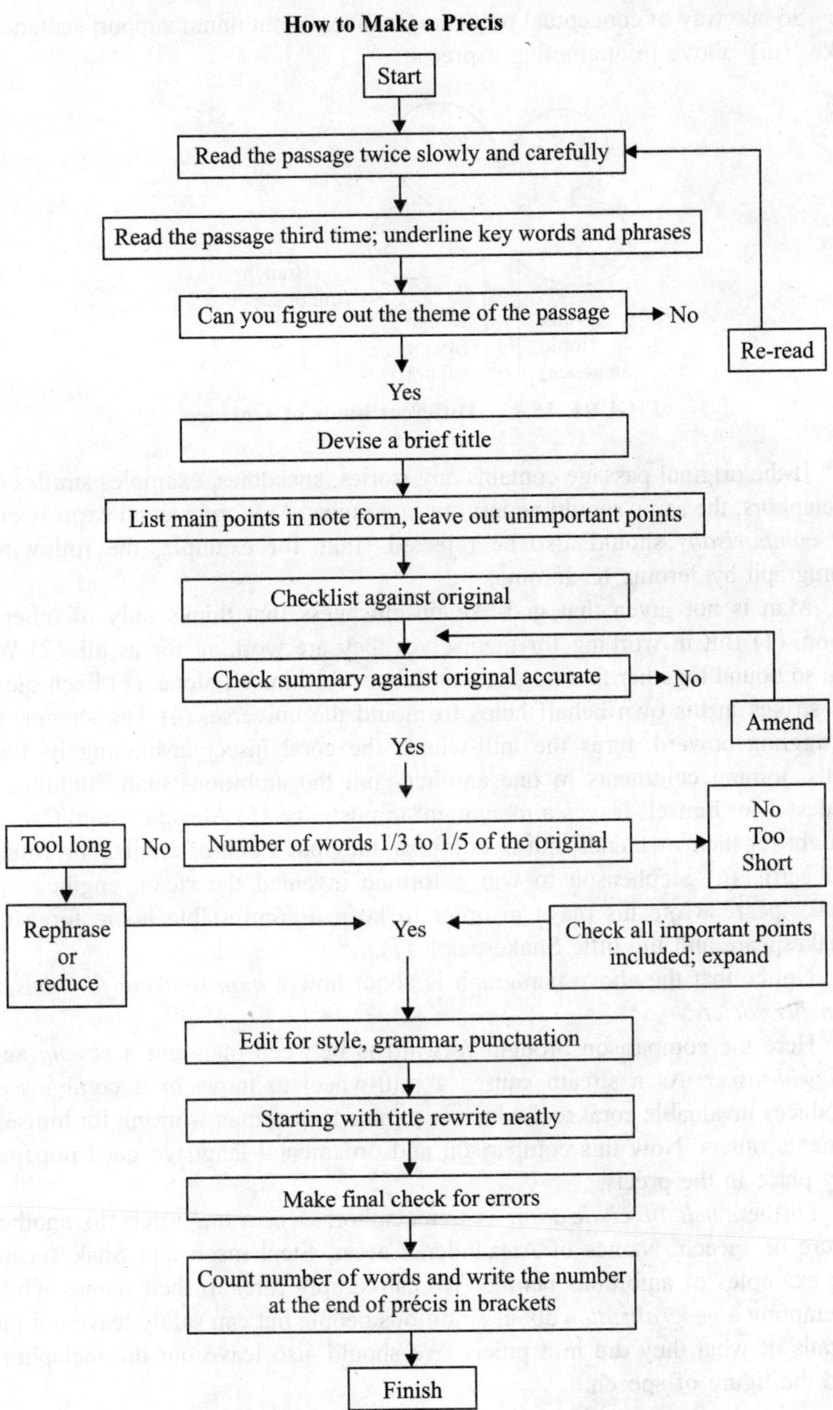

FIGURE 15.1 Steps in writing a precis.

So one way of conceptual reduction is to leave out minor support sentences like '(iii)' above in attempting a précis.

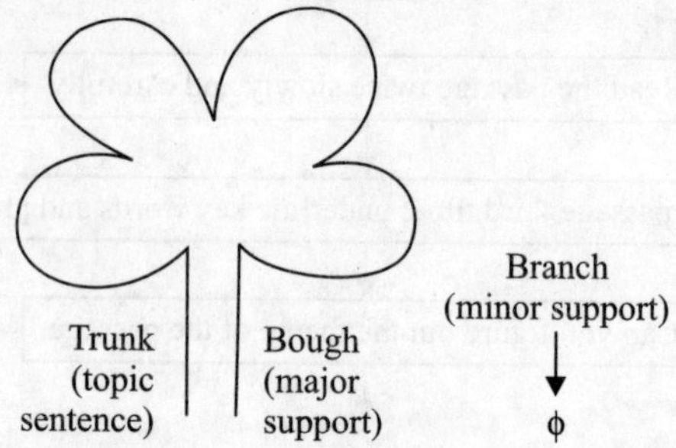

FIGURE 15.2 Different kinds of sentences

If the original passage contains any stories, anecdotes, examples similes or metaphors, the same should be left out in a précis. Any ornamental expressions or *comparisons* should also be rejected. Take for example, the following paragraph by Jerome K. Jerome:

Man is not given that god-like unselfishness that thinks only of other's good. (1) But in working for themselves they are working for us all. (2) We are so bound together that no man can labour for himself alone. (3) Each blow he strikes in his own behalf helps to mould the universe. (4) The stream, in struggling onward, turns the mill-wheel; the coral insect fashioning its tiny cells, joining continents to one another; and the ambitious man, building a pedestal for himself leaves a monument to posterity. (5) Alexander and Caesar fought for their own ends, but in doing so, they put a belt of civilization round the earth. (6) Stephenson to win a fortune invented the steam engine; and Shakespeare wrote his plays in order to keep a comfortable home for Mrs. Shakespeare and the little Shakespeare (7).

Notice that the above paragraph is about how a *man working for himself benefits society.*

Here the comparison brought forward is between man and a *stream* and a *coral-insect.* As a stream causes a mill-wheel to move or a coral insect produces invaluable coral reef which is so nice to see, man working for himself benefits others. Now this comparison and ornamental language need not find any place in the précis.

Further, *belt of civilization* is a metaphor; *a pedestal* refers to another figure of speech. Names of Alexander, Caesar, Stephenson and Shakespeare are examples of ambitious people. We can simply refer to their names while attempting a *generalization* about ambitious people but can safely leave out the details of what they did in a précis. We should also leave out the metaphors and the figure of speech.

Now look at the précis of the above paragraph:

> Man is not selfless like God. Often the ambitions men working for themselves benefit society. Ambitious men like Alexander, Caesar, Stephenson and Shakespeare while working for themselves enriched society.

Notice in the above précis, we have left out all ornamental language, examples and figures of speech. We have simply retained the names of four great personalities while generalizing the ambitious people.

Other simple examples could be

Indira Gandhi was brave like a lioness.
(simile)
or
Indira Gandhi was the lioness of India.
(metaphor)

The above two sentences can be compressed as;

Indira Gandhi was very brave.

Another way of compression at the level of ideas is attempting *selection*, *rejection* and *generalization*. Let us clear this point by taking an example. Once again we are reproducing a paragraph from Jerome K. Jerome:

> Contended, unambitious people are all very well in their way. They form a neat, useful background for great portraits to be painted against; and they make a respectable, if not particularly intelligent audience for the active spirits of the age to play before. I have not a word to say against contended people so long as they keep quiet. But do not, for goodness sake, let them go strutting about, as they are so fond of doing, crying out that they are the true models for the whole species. Why they are the deadheads, the drones in the great hive, the street crowds that lounge about, gaping at those who are working. And let them not imagine either—as they are also fond of doing—that they are very wise and philosophical, and that it is a very artful thing to be contended. It may be true that 'a contended mind is happy anywhere' but so is a Jerusalem pony and the consequence is that both are put anywhere and are treated anyhow.

In the above paragraph, the following phrases:

the contended people
the deadheads
the drones in the great hive
the street crowds that lounge about
the Jerusalem pony

could be compressed by using a *generalizing* phrase, the *unambitious people.*

Linguistic Reduction

There are many devices to achieve compression at the linguistic level.

1. Use one word substitutions for phrase or sentences. Examples are given in Table 15.1.

TABLE 15.1 Linguistic reduction

Phrases or clauses	*One word substitute*
The Secretary's proposal was accepted with full agreement *among all the members.*	The Secretary's proposal was accepted *unanimously.*
The member often made remarks *that had no bearing on the subject under discussion.*	The member often made *irrelevant* remarks.
Do not put off *till tomorrow what you can do today.*	Do not *postpone* matters.
You cannot trust him *because he is a person who believes easily whatever he is told.*	He is a *credulous* person.
My efforts *did not meet with success.*	My efforts were *futile.*
There was no means by which the enemy could attack the fortress.	The fortress was unassailable.

2. Change the structure of the sentence to make it short. This can be done by changing *complex sentences* into *simple ones* (Table 15.2).

TABLE 15.2 Linguistic reduction

Complex sentences	*Simple sentences*
He confessed *that he was guilty of the crime.*	He confessed his guilt.
Ram hoped *that he would succeed.*	Ram hoped to *succeed.*
The S.P. ordered *that the trouble makers should be arrested.*	The S.P. ordered the *arrest of the trouble makers.*
Ram is unable to think of any advice *that he can offer Sita.*	Ram has no advice to *offer Sita.*
There is little hope *that Ram will recover.*	There is little hope *of his recovery.*

3. Circumlocutory phrases or sentences are replaced by simple ones. Repetitions and enumerations are removed. Bombastic language is replaced by simple one. High flown and verbose language is also replaced by simple and direct language. Illustrations and examples are done away with (see Table 15.3).

TABLE 15.3 Linguistic reduction

Circumlocutions repetitions, verbosity, etc.	*Simple, direct, concise language*
It *is not outside the bounds of possibility* that *a man who is an expert in the study of Languages* can write the grammar of a language *that he does not know.*	*It is possible* that a linguist can write the grammar of an *unknown* language.
Despite the fact that *he was by no means well*, the man, *who was very old*, *went out with the intention of bringing back* the cows and sheep.	In spite of being unwell and very old, the man went out to bring back the cows and sheep.
This is a *mechanically propelled road vehicle.*	This is a car/scooter.
Aunts, uncles, grand parents and cousins are useful when they give *money, books, bicycles, and similar items as presents.*	Relatives are useful when they give expensive gifts.
The stamp is the *only one of this design ever printed.* It is *absolutely unique.*	The stamp is *absolutely unique.*
We went to the zoo and spent an enjoyable day looking at the various creatures in the zoological garden; *tigers, panthers, hippopotami, lions, crocodiles, snakes, parrots, eagles, and all kinds of birds.*	We went to the zoo and enjoyed the day by looking at different *animals* and *birds.*
After a considerable period of cerebral activity the teacher replied in the negative to an inquiry by a member of the faculty in the same institution, where the teacher works as to whether the meteorological conditions would be favourable for taking the students out. (example of verbosity)	After much thought the teacher said 'no' to a query by a colleague whether the climate was favourable to take the students out.

Examples of Précis Writing

Passage 1

There is an enemy beneath our feet—an enemy the more deadly for his complete impartiality. He recognizes no national boundaries, no political parties. Everyone in the world is threatened by him. The enemy is the earth itself. When an earthquake strikes, the world trembles. The power of a quake is greater than anything man himself can produce. But today scientists are directing a great deal of their effort into finding some way of combating earthquakes, and it is possible that at some time in the near future mankind will have discovered a means of protecting itself.

An earthquake strikes without warning. When it does, its power is immense. If it strikes a modern city, the damage it causes is as great as if it has struck a primitive village. Gas mains burst, explosions are caused and fires are started. Underground railways are wrecked.

Whole buildings collapse, bridges fall, dams burst. Gaping crevices appear in busy streets. If the quake strikes at sea, huge tidal waves sweep inland. If it strikes in mountain regions, avalanches roar down into the valley. Consider the terrifying statistics from the post. 1755: Lisbon, capital Portugal—the city destroyed entirely and 450 killed. 1970: Peru: 50,000 killed.

In 1968, an earthquake struck Alaska. As this is a relatively unpopulated part, only a few people were killed. But it is likely that this was one of the most powerful quakes ever to have hit the world.

Geologists estimate that during the tremors, the whole of the state moved over 80 feet farther west into Pacific Ocean. Imagine the power of something that can move an entire subcontinent! This is the problem that faces the scientists. They are dealing with forces so immense that man cannot hope to resist them. All that can be done is to try to pinpoint just where the earthquake will strike and work from there. At least some precautionary measures can then be taken to save lives and some of the property.

(330 words)

Based on the above paragraphs, we arrive at the following main points for the four paragraphs:

1. Earthquake – the deadly enemy of mankind
2. Damage caused by an earthquake in general
3. Damage caused by an earthquake in particular
4. What can scientists do?

The above four main points can be developed into the following outline:

1. Earthquake – the deadly enemy of mankind
   - (i) Earthquake strikes all without a distinction of national boundary or political affiliation.
   - (ii) The power of a quake is greater than that of a man-made weapon of destruction.
   - (iii) Scientists trying to find out means to combat earthquakes; they will find some way to protect themselves from earthquakes.
2. Damage caused by an earthquake in general
   - (i) Strikes without warning.
   - (ii) Modern city when struck reduced to a primitive village.
3. Damage caused by an earthquake in particular
   - (i) Quake strikes plains, seas and mountains causing all round destruction.

(ii) In 1755, Lisbon destroyed, 450 killed.
(iii) 1n 1970, Peru struck, 50,000 killed.

4. What can scientists do?
   (i) In 1968, Alaska hit, subcontinent moved 80 feet into the pacific ocean.
   (ii) Scientists cannot resist the powerful earthquake.
   (iii) They can predict the place of origin of the quake so that precaution can be taken to save man and property.

Based on the above outline, we can make the following rough draft:

Rough Draft

Earthquake – The Great Destroyer

Earthquake is the deadly enemy of mankind. Earthquake strikes all without a distinction of nationality or political affiliation. The power of a quake is greater than that of any man-made weapon of destruction. An earthquake strikes mankind without a warning. A modern city when struck is reduced to a rubble. A quake strikes plains, seas and mountains causing all round destruction. Alaska in 1968 moving it 80 feet into Pacific Ocean. Scientists are trying to find out means to combat earthquakes and they are able to predict at least where the earthquake will hit so that precaution can be taken to save man and property from destruction.

(122 words)

As the number of words in the rough draft are more than required, say, (110), we shall have to reduce it further without reducing the ideas. The final draft would look as follows:

Final Draft

Earthquake – The Great Destroyer

Earthquake is the mankind's deadly enemy. Earthquake strikes all without a distinction of nationality or political affiliation. The earthquake's power is greater than that of any man-made weapon of destruction. An earthquake strikes mankind without a warning. A modern city when struck is reduced to a rubble. A quake strikes plains, seas and mountains causing all round destruction. The quake struck Lisbon in 1755 killing 450; Peru in 1970 killing 50,000; Alaska in 1968 moving it 80 feet into Pacific Ocean. Scientists are trying to find out means to combat earthquakes to predict the origin of the quake so that precaution can be taken to save man and property from destruction.

(113 words)

Passage 2

Fascism rejected democracy based on the rule of majority. It denied that numbers alone can govern by means of periodical consultation. The receptivity of the masses is very limited, their intelligence is small. The principle of equality is replaced by the principle of one man leadership or the Nietzheana doctrine of the superman. The pattern of democracy is that of a pyramid balanced on its apex. The principle is supposed to apply to all branches of life. In industry, for example, the employer was the leader of the factory and the workers his followers. It is for this reason the communists hated fascists. They thought the equation of the employer to the leader and workers to the followers in the German Labour Code was nothing but a smoke screen to hide the totalitarian designs of the capitalists. For them, fascism was the last desperate attempt of capitalism to save itself, it was not so much capitalism in decay as capitalism fighting for life. Fascism adopted a clever posture. It dissolved all working class organizations. It also limited the initiative of the employers. It accepted capitalism and yet stressed its subordination to the ideal of welfare state. Hitler declared that it was the duty of the state to see that "capital remains the servant of the nation". Both tried to advance their own idea of corporate state. Based on Hegel's concept of three classes – the agricultural, the industrial and the universal or governing, Mussolini argued that these classes were not antagonistic in the Marxian sense but complementary. Each call was accepted by the state as having the right to pursue its own welfare. Labour must do its job, the employers theirs. The third element– party must govern both. Both workers and capitalists are subservient to it. It was hoped that such a state would abolish class conflict and create a most satisfactory harmony.

(313 words)

The following are the main points of the passage:

1. Fascism rejected democracy.
2. Subscribed to pyramidal structure of democracy.
3. Communists hated fascism.
4. Clever posture of fascism.
5. Subscribed to Hegel's three class theory.

Now these points can be developed into an outline.

1. Fascism rejected democracy.
   - (i) Numbers cannot govern by periodical consultation.
   - (ii) Masses are not intelligent enough.
   - (iii) Equality pyramidal structure of democracy.
2. Subscribed to pyramidcal structure of democracy.
   - (i) Democracy– a pyramid balanced on its apex
   - (ii) In industry, employer = leader, workers = followers

3. Communists hated fascists.
   (i) Views about employer and workers show totalitarian designs of capitalism
   (ii) Fascism—an attempt to save capitalism.
4. Clever picture of fascism.
   (i) Working class organization dissolved.
   (ii) Initiative of employer limited.
   (iii) Subordination of capitalism to welfare state.
   (iv) Supports idea of corporate state like capitalism.
5. Subscribed to Hegel's three class theory.
   (i) Complementary role for agricultural, industrial and governing classes.
   (ii) Each class attends to their jobs.
   (iii) Workers and capital subservient to Government.
   (iv) Such corporate state will have harmonious relationship among three classes.

Rough Draft

Characteristics of Fascism

Fascism rejected democracy. Democracy is based on majority and periodic consultation cannot rule. The electorate is not intelligent enough. The principle of equality is replaced by the superman in fascism. Fascism subscribes to the pyramidal structure of democracy and regards employers as leaders and workers as followers in industry. Communists hated fascism because they did not subscribe to the fascists' view of employer (leader), workers (followers) and regarded it as having totalitarian designs of capitalism. They thought that fascism is an attempt to save capitalism. Fascism very cleverly dissolved working class organizations; limited the employer's initiative, subordinated capitalism to a welfare state and upheld the concept of corporate state. Fascism subscribed to the complementary role of Hegel's three class (agriculturists, industrial workers and governing class) theory. It upheld that workers and capitalists were subservient to Government. This idea of corporate state led to harmonious relationship among the classes.

(142 words)

As we see that rough draft is a little lengthy, it should be compressed to 111 words as against the present 142 words. Below we attempt the final draft.

Final Draft

Characteristics of Fascism

Fascism maintains that democracy is not viable because majority of the electorate is less intelligent. In fascism, equality is replaced by Nietzscheism. Fascism subscribes to pyramidal structure of democracy in which employers are leaders and workers followers. Communists rejected this view of democracy. They thought this view will impose totalitarian designs and perpetuation of capitalism on people. Fascism very cleverly dissolved working class organizations; limited the employer's initiative, subordinated capitalism to a welfare state and upheld the concept of corporate state. Fascism subscribed to the complementary role of Hegel's (farmers, workers and rulers) theory. It upheld that workers and capitalists are subservient to Government. This idea of corporate state led to harmonious relationship among the classes.

(116 words)

Passages for Practice

Passage 1

For diabetics in India, therapy is witnessing a revolution with the introduction of many new classes of diabetes medication. But none of the new drugs have been so significant as the unique breed of products called 'designer' insulins, or insulin analogues, that have entered the market recently. "In the last few years, there has been a paradigm shift in the way diabetes is treated," says Shashank Joshi, consultant endocrinologist at Lilavati Hospital in Mumbai.

While the paradigm shift has taken place at every level of managing diabetes, the impact on patients' lives has been the most notable with these insulin analogues. Being a new segment, the analogues market is still a very small one. According to estimates from market research agency ORG-IMS, the market is estimated at over ₹ 2.3 crore, but is growing very rapidly at 75%. Insulin analogues are a class of products that are designed to more closely mimic the body's own physiological insulin regulation of blood glucose levels than conventional insulin. "Insulin analogues represent a useful advance for those patients aiming for tight control, and will probably replace conventional insulin," writes Simon Heller, reader in medicine, Sheffield, UK in the *Diabetes Digest.*

Though there are many advantages to insulin therapy, it has traditionally been relegated to the last option with both doctors and patients preferring oral drugs.

"Patients have many apprehensions concerning insulin therapy," says Dr Kris Iyer, a US-based expert on diabetes.

Passage 2

We don't know for certain if the fruit that Shabari offered Ram was a produce cultivated through organic farming methods. But NDA at the Centre is seriously debating the pros prior to formally launching the proposed National Project on Organic Farming with an outlay of ₹ 99.58 crore during the Tenth plan. The government may christen organic farming 'Vedic Krishi'.

At the recently held three-day National Conference on Organic Farming for Sustainable Production under the aegis of the Horticultural Society of India, the ICAR and the Central Institute for Sub-tropical Horticulture, the subject of finding a "suitable" nomenclature in Indianese for organic ranked high on the agenda.

That the phrase, the only other serious contender appears to have been the phrase "Jaivik Krishi", had found tacit acceptance a la the Swadeshi thinking of the ruling coalition was apparent when Mr. Sompal, the chairman of the Farmers' Commission, asserted, 'Although there are a number of other systems prevailing in the world which are also non-chemical use systems, in my view the system that suits our conditions best is Vedic Krishi. This is a concept that evolved thousands of years back and is a way of life for Indian farmers. This involves different traditional practices followed even by ancient civilizations and can be an integrated form of organic farming system."

Ironically, finance minister Jaswant Singh may have exhorted Indian agriculturists to ring in the Second Greeen Revolution, replace with bio-tech, state-of-the-art farming methods and land use systems including contract farming, but Farmers' Commission, set up virtually as a parallel outfit to the agriculture minister (Mr. Sompal, as Chairman, ranks on par with a Cabinet minister for his term), is having none of that, it appears.

Referring to the first Green Revolution of the late 60s, he emphasized that high input uses in that case had "reached a plateau and is now sustained with diminishing return or dividends. The nutrient efficiency and factor productivity is on the decline." The second-generation problems of the Green Revolution need to be corrected by adopting alternate technology in farming, a technology which should be "eco-friendly, farmer-friendly and low-cost" but also "preserve traditional bio-diversity and knowledge."

Passage 3

The last day of Governor Madan Lal Khurana's controversial programme for the poor ended amid high drama at Raj Bhawan here on Thursday when thousands seeking aid thronged Khurana's doorstep and took the administration, the police and the Governor himself by surprise.

Police efforts to disperse a 6,000-odd crowd jamming traffic in Civil Lines area ended up in a mini-stampede. Policemen, dressed in riot gears and complete with helmets and shields, had to stay guard at Raj Bhawan most of the day. Khurana later admitted that there were arrangements for 1,000 people with reinforcements for another 500 and but no more.

The ire of the crowd—the larger number that was forced out of the place—marred Khurana's programme. Interestingly, those who failed to enter Raj Bhawan knocked the doors of the Opposition leader BD Kalla seeking help. A section of the crowd proceeded to stage a dharna outside Kalla's residence. Kalla tried to pacify them—even hosting them to snacks and water—but when nothing worked out, he called up the Governor's office, asking to send "ration" for the poor.

A visibly upset Governor described the incident as "unfortunate". But there was much more to it than met the eye. "Otherwise how do you explain needy people going over to the Opposition leader to seek relief when they know very well that my house is open for such people," Khurana told media persons. He said the protests at Kalla's residence appeared motivated. "Even I have spent some time in politics. I know all about it," he added, though he denied reports of lathicharge.

Kalla, in turn, described the Governor's remarks as unfortunate. "I tried and helped him out by pacifying the irate people and what I got in return was allegations," he said. Contrary to Khurana's statement, Kalla said lathicharge had taken place and that hundreds of people had come to his place to escape police wrath. "Most of the people who came to my place were physically challenged and widows and were looking for pension," he said, denying charges that congress workers caused the disruption.

Around ₹ 4 lakh was distributed to the needy people at Raj Bhawan on Thursday. ₹ 1 lakh was contributed by the Governor's Relief Fund while the remaining sum was donated by Asaram Bapu.

Passage 4

India's bitterness at the United States over recent slights – including the manner in which Washington has coddled Pakistan – boiled over on Thursday with the country's outgoing envoy warning that continuing hyphenation between the two countries casts a shadow on Indo-US relations.

Ambassador Lalit Mansing, who leaves Washington next month at the end of his three-year term here, started a gathering of South Asian scholars and analysts at George Washington University with some blunt words, including suggestion that the Bush administration was displaying double standards in the war on terrorism.

"This war cannot be won completely and durably if short-term political calculations come into play and there is ambiguity about allies as well adversaries," Mansingh said in remarks that clearly alluded to the cozy ties between US and the military regime in Pakistan that is widely recognized as having fostered and rationalized terrorism.

"In the global war against terrorism, there cannot be two touchstones for judging acts of pre-meditated violence against innocent human beings."

The Indian envoy also publicly invoked charges of nuclear proliferation against Pakistan which the Bush administration has been trying to sweep under the carpet by implying it is the work of a few individuals, ostensibly for Islamabad's support in capturing the Al-Qaida big fish as a political payoff.

"The nexus between terrorism and WMD is frightening. What was only a theoretical construct a few months ago, is a palpable reality today, as the cover is blown off one of the most bizarre proliferation scandals emanating from Pakistan," Mansingh said.

The ambassador's blunt address at the Eliot School of International Affairs in what is probably his swansong before Washington's strategic community barely masked the disappointment at three years of excellent progress in Indo-US ties being wrecked by three weeks of disaster.

Ever since US secretary of state Colin Powell's visit to the region last month ending with his granting of Major non-Nato Ally status to Pakistan, a degree of mistrust and recrimination appears to have crept into Indo-US ties.

Mansingh indicated it was not the granting of the MNNA status but the manner in which Powel did it that had left a bad taste.

Passage 5

In a world that swears by progress, here's a town where people have forced politicians to promise that whoever wins will not disturb anything in the name of development.

If you think that's weird, folks in Patapatnam-literally Old Town – in Andhra's Srikakulam district couldn't careless. "Spare us the wide roads, efficient sewerage and all that. We're doing fine," say residents.

They call themselves traditional. "People from neighbouring constituencies are often taken aback by our backwardness. What they don't realize is that we're proud to be the way we are. They call us primitive. Why must you be progressive?" asks Lakshma Reddy. "We have a deep bond with our ancestors and we cherish this."

Houses here are built of brick and mortar, but a touch of urban sophistication isn't to be seen anywhere. Roads are narrow. Residents say government babus came here for a road widening project but were sent back. "We did not want to disturb properties of our forefathers," says Reddy.

Only when local MLA Kalamata Mohan Rao (TDP) mediate did they allow the team to broaden a couple of thorogh-fares and top them with concrete. Here, nobody creates a fuss about civic amenities or drainage.

"Rama Naidu and Krishna Rao are the elders in our community. They told us to block government efforts to build drains and roads. These would destroy the natural beauty of our town," a resident explained.

"Is there a stench here? No. The air is clean and people don't fall ill like in big cities. They have drains, sewage systems, neat roads. There shouldn't be any health problem," Rao says.

They also brought Janmabhoomi and Neeru-Meeru to Patapatnam. But residents just wanted a girls' school and a degree college for women. Candidates promised both before last elections. But, once the polls were over the promises were forgotten.

This election, the TDP's Mohan Rao is facing Gorle Haribabu of the Congress. But whoever wants to win here must give an undertaking. Whatever they do, they must not disturb the town in the name of development. The one who convinces the residents that their old institutions and traditional ways won't be tinkered with will win Patapatnam.

Passage 6

It happens all the time on the streets, on public staircases, railway stations, promenades and buses. Women being pinched, pawed and brushed against, women at the receiving end of lewd and unprintable remarks. But police records show that only about 60 cases of eve-teasing are registered annually in this city which has population of 12 million.

Everyone knows that this is an absurd figure. Mumbai, which has always prided itself on being a city where women are safe, is waking up to the realization that increasingly this is not so. The ludicrously low figure belies the seriousness and frequency of the crime, underlined by two recent eve-teasing incidents, one on a waterfront and the other in a local train. In the first case, one of the offenders lost his life when a concerned and cornered husband pulled the trigger.

In the second case, the lecturer who dared to intervene on behalf of the harried girls in a local train was roughed up by the bullies, who, much to every Mumbaikar's shock, turned out to be medical students.

The low number of cases registered is a reflection of the victim's reluctance to follow up on the matter. Joint police commissioner (law and order) Ahmed Javed, who exhorts women to register even the smallest offence, may well say, "One should remember that not registering a compliant is equivalent to indirectly encouraging the perpetrators." But women have a different take on the issue. Help even from the person in uniform is not necessarily guaranteed, and registering a police complaint can turn into a humiliating experience given the insensitivity with which a complaint of this sort is treated.

Devi Pacher, former member of the Mahila Dakshta Samiti and now a member of Nirbhaya, an organization that works in the field of crimes against women and children, recalls an incident where a policeman registering a complaint told the victim, "He only touched you, but didn't do anything more." However, policemen say that despite such disheartening responses, victims should pursue cases. "They can send across a letter or a fax to a senior official like me," says Javed.

In one heartening instance, an enterprising activist went the extra mile to bring eve-teasers to book. Film-maker –activist Madhushree Datta slugged it out for ten years to get justice after two policemen beat her up because she declined their propositions. The constables lost their jobs, but Datta says, "Ironically enough, I would never advise a victim of eve-teasing to lodge a police complaint." Her statement hints at the emotional toll the decade-long battle took.

Eve-teasing is considered a minor crime and a non-cognizable offence. It is a bailable offence under Section 354 of the Indian Penal Code, allowing offenders to be let off easily.

Passage 7

Despite an increase in the number of women contesting in the polls, many of them have not been able to prove their mettle at the hustings.

The first general elections in 1952 saw not a single woman returning to the Lower House with only two women contestants in the fray – a Jan Sangh nominee and an independent – and both lost security deposits.

In the 1957 polls, not a single woman candidate was in the fray.

It was only in 1996 polls that the largest number of women – two each from Congress and BJP – entered the Lok Sabha from Rajasthan. Later, a woman candidate won in the bypoll from Banswara.

However, it is from Rajasthan only that a woman candidate, former Maharani of Jaipur, Gayatri Devi, got her name entered in the Guinness Book of World Records by bagging 77.8 percent of the votes polled in 1962.

Gayatri Devi also scored a hat-trick by winning three Lok Sabha polls. Even the present chief minister of the state, Vasundhara Raje Scindia has won five successive parliamentary polls from Jhalawar since 1989.

Former Pradesh Congress committee chief Girija Vyas also won three Lok Sabha elections in 1991, 1996, and 1999, losing 1998 polls. Nirmala Kumari of Congress won Chittorgarh seat twice for her party in 1980 and 1984.

The former royals have also played a major role in opening the doors of political arena for the fairer sex with Gayatri Devi contesting on a Swatantra Party ticket in 1962 polls when total six woman contestants were in the fray.

Another royal, Maharani Krishna Kumari form Jodhpur, joined the election fray in 1971 as an independent with Gayatri Devi. Both won at the hustings.

Congress succeeded in sending its first women candidate to the Lower House in 1980 when Nirmala Kumari won Chittorgarh seat while four other women nominees from different seats lost.

The 1991 polls saw number of women contestants rising to 14, of which three returned successful. Besides Raje, BJP nominee, former Maharani of Alwar, Mahendra Kumari, succeeded while Congress candidate, Girija Vyas, too made her entry into LS from Udaipur.

Passage 8

Their crowns may have passed on, but the Bangalore beauties who once walked the international ramps and held titles, have moved on to greener pastures. Here's what some of them are doing now:

Veena Sanjani, Miss India 1970, is busy working and doing a bit of theatre. "I'm marketing manager for a company in Bangalore. I will soon visit Delhi to act in *Tughlaq* where I play the role of queen mother. I also do TV serials and ad films."

Rekha Hande, Miss India in 1983, still does modelling. "I'm also involved in the beauty business and compere shows." Rekha has also acted in Kannada and Hindi serials.

Sandhya Chibb, Miss India Universe in 1996, is enjoying being a full time mother in the US. Between taking her two daughters aged five and three to ballet, swimming and school, she manages to do some modelling too.

Rani Jeyraj, Miss India World in 1996, was so passionate about direction that she went to the London International Films School to study the subject. "I now work in a production company where I am assistant – director. I am trying my hand in directing ad films and should be able to do some on my own soon."

Sara Corner is now married and settled abroad. She has also completed a course in tourism which she always wanted to do. Nafisa Joseph has her hands full with TV show productions and corporate shows. Celina Jaitely and Lara Dutta are busy with films. Jaitely is also campaigning for the Congress. Other Bangaloreans have found their feet in other walks of life.

Passage 9

Ace photographer Raghu Rai is excited as he awaits the release of his second book *The Enigmatic Indira Gandhi.*

Perhaps the only Indian lensman who had unlimited access to Mrs. Gandhi, Rai dug out a huge chunk of negatives of his earlier work on the woman he had done during his first book, *A Life in the Day of Indira Gandhi in 1974.* Sixty percent of these pictures were unused. These include candid moments with her close friends and even one of her sons, Sanjay Gandhi, holding a party worker by his neck, symbolizing the power she had, explains Rai.

The 62-year-old Padma Bhushan awardee states that Indira as a subject has never been as politically potent as in 2004. "She represents an umbrella of power under which no one was allowed to grow, thriving sycophancy and legacy of staying in power. These factors are the hallmark of politics today."

What about her daughter-in-law Sonia being touted as the other Indira? "Indira rose to become a dignified leader. The Congress has installed Sonia where Indira left, but she has to work hard to justify her position," says Rai. Indira-Sonia similarities fascinate him. Sonia not only dresses like her, she even talks and walks like her in the rallies! How does he feel the generation X of the Gandhi family in the poll fray? "I feel Varun Gandhi is a good orator and more focused. Rahul and Priyanka are sweet children, but they should not bask in the glory of the family for too long."

After more than 40 years in the business, Rai looks disinterested in the 2004 Lok Sabha campaign.

Passage 10

Scholars of Indian origin won two prized appointments in the United States this week, attesting to their growing influence in academia.

Management scholar Yash Gupta has been named Dean of the University of Southern California's Marshall School of Business. An alumnus of Punjab University, who later studied management sciences in England, Gupta has been Dean of the University of Washington's business school for the last five years.

Gupta was the first person of Indian origin to head a US business school, and was followed by Dipak Jain, who was named Dean of the Kellogg School of Business in May 2001. Several top business schools have a significant contingent of Indian teachers, sometimes more than 10% of the faculty.

Meanwhile, the influential Asia Society is slated to name Indian arts scholar and performer Vishakha Desai as its new president.

The Ahmedabad–born Desai is an alumnus of Bombay University. She will be the first woman and the first Asian–American to head the organization founded by John Rockefeller in 1956.

Desai is married to China scholar Robert Oxfam, who was the society's president from 1981 to 1992. She succeeds Nicholas Platt, a former ambassador to Pakistan, who followed Oxfam as president.

Desai reportedly won the high-profile job over candidates who included an American ambassador and a university president. Meanwhile, Marshall School of Business, which is counted among the top 25 B-schools in the US, also announced that it had chosen Gupta after "an extensive search for the very best individual to lead the school in the 21st century".

16

Reading Comprehension

Introduction

The Kothari Commission for Higher Education characterized English as a **library language**. This label highlights the role of acquisition of reading skills in English. However, the role of English since then has changed and English has now become a global language. In this changed scenario, it is not enough to master only reading skills but one has to acquire listening, speaking and writing skills in English as well. However, the acquisition of reading skills, to my mind, is by far the most important in the study of the English language. Most of the books, journals and magazines on science, technology, medicine, law, social sciences and humanities are in English. Therefore, to acquire the latest and up-to-date material in all these disciplines, one has to read books and journals written in English and make notes. Hence the importance of reading comprehension.

Comprehending a passage requires syntactic, semantic and pragmatic strategies. The knowledge of sentence structure, interrelationships between ideas, knowledge of vocabulary, linguistic means showing interconnections between sentences, background knowledge, knowledge of cohesion and coherence and interpretation of ideas are some of the prerequisites to understand a passage.

Reading is more than recognizing and understanding isolated words. It requires one to think, feel and imagine. It involves visual and auditory perception, discrimination, association of auditory and visual patterns and a capacity for detailed analysis of the structure of individual words. It is not a process of rapid recognition of words one after another, but a process of fusing the meanings of the single words into connected sequence. It is an activity which involves the interpretation of ideas symbolized by written or printed language.

Reading always means reading with comprehension. The degree of comprehension depends upon the subject-matter, the reader's linguistic competence and the purpose of reading. Fry classifies reading into three main categories:

1. Study reading requires a speed of reading between 200 and 250 words per minute with 80 percent to 90 percent comprehension. The material to be read is difficult. This is also called **intensive reading**.
2. Average reading involves the reading of newspapers, magazines, novels and other easier texts. The desired comprehension is 70 percent and the speed of reading is about 250–300 wpm. This is also called **extensive reading**.
3. Skimming and scanning come under the fastest form of reading with 800 wpm and with 50 percent comprehension.

Comprehension involves four different levels

1. Reading the lines: This involves the literal meaning of the material read. It includes the precise meaning of familiar words and guessing the meaning of unfamiliar words from the contextual clues.

2. Reading between the lines: In this kind of reading, besides the literal meaning of the text, the reader tries to get the author's intent or purpose. The reader tries to interpret on the basis of the various literary devices employed by the writer.

3. Reading beyond the lines: This involves making a critical evaluation of text. This entails numerous factors such as deriving implications, speculating about consequence, drawing generalizations not stated by the author and arranging ideas into patterns. By careful analysis and synthesis, the reader gains new insights or higher level of understanding.

4. Reading with involvement: In this process, the reader attains the highest level of comprehension. He not only gets ideas but ideas get him. He identifies himself with characters; he sympathizes with them; he becomes aware of the moral problems involved. For example, Mahatma Gandhi was deeply influenced by Ruskin's 'Unto The Last'.

Davis (1972) distinguishes between three approaches to the analysis of comprehension in reading—a broad subjective analysis called 'arm-chair' analysis, subjective analysis based on specific studies and multi-variety analysis.

Both Bloom and Barrett give a list of behaviours in reading comprehension. The more complex behaviours seem to include the singular ones through a system of hierarchy. Bloom lists remembering, reasoning, problem solving, concept formation and creative thinking; Barrett lists as main heading: literal comprehension, re-organization, inferential comprehension, evaluation and appreciation. These aspects of comprehension have already been discussed under levels of comprehension.

Types of Reading Comprehension

There are different kinds of reading comprehension: study reading, average reading, skimming and scanning, intensive and extensive reading. Below we discuss skimming and scanning.

Skimming

Skimming involves getting a quick general, superficial overall idea of a text ignoring all details. The main purpose of skimming is to look for main ideas generally found in the topic sentences of a text.

We adopt the strategy of skimming when we look through a book in a bookstore before deciding whether to buy it or not. We also skim when we read a newspaper. We quickly go through the headlines before deciding to read the details. The reading speed in skimming is quite high; 500–600 wpm and the comprehension in skimming is quite low but not lower than 50 percemt.

Strategies for Skimming

One way to skim through a text is to concentrate on the main ideas ignoring the details. Study the following paragraph below. Many words have been left out. Read the paragraph quickly without pausing and then answer the questions that follow:

> Engineering .... productive and purposeful use of .... sciences .... also called Technology. Chemist studies elements .... scientist. When he applies ..... knowledge ..... produce synthetic products .... Technologist. .... Technology .... purposeful use .... knowledge of materials .... sources of energy. Therefore it .... essential .... life (34 words).

Tick the correct alternative:

(i) Science is an essential part of modern life.
(ii) A technologist is greater than a scientist.
(iii) The paragraph is mainly about what technology is.

If your answer is '(iii)', you are right. Notice how even without whole paragraph, you are able to guess the main idea of the paragraph just by reading 50 percent of the text.

Now take a look at the whole paragraph.

> Engineering involves the productive and purposeful use of the sciences. It is also called Technology. A chemist studies the elements in Nature; he is a scientist. When he applies his scientific knowledge to produce synthetic products and medicines, he becomes a Technologist. Thus technology is the purposeful use of the knowledge of materials and sources of energy. Therefore, it is an essential part of modern life. (66 words)

The above paragraph illustrates that in skimming, we read fast and concentrate only on the main ideas and ignore details.

EXERCISE 16.1

When we read a newspaper in the morning sipping a cup of tea lazily, we skim through the newspaper headlines. When the newspaper headlines are not intelligible, we quickly read the report given thereunder. The process of skimming is very useful and widely used in reading a newspaper.

Below you will find a few news headlines and their reports. The order of the reports has been changed. Skim through the reports and match them with their headlines. Time the exercise; the quicker you do, the better skimmer you are.

(A) '4000 years' history gone in 48 hrs
(B) People in 'cages', tigers roam free
(C) Genetic code can tame SARS
(D) The million dollar home
(E) New tourism circuits to be developed
(F) Basra pearls for the rich and famous
(G) Egypt opens up its market to Indian wheat
(H) Right to privacy is not absolute, rules SC
(I) Sanjan Shards may give insight into Parsi history

1. **New Delhi, April 14 (TOI):** While the constitution provides every citizen with the right to privacy, the Supreme Court has ruled that the freedom is, by no means, absolute.
2. **Mumbai, April 14 (TOI):** An important find at Sanjan—one of the first Parsi settlements in India – is expected to provide fresh insights into the Zoroastrians' flight from Iran to India, about 1400 years ago. The find at Sanjan's Varoli riverside dig includes six whole skeletons and a few partial ones, coins, pieces of pottery, glass and beads.
3. **New Delhi, April 14 (TOI):** Egypt on Friday agreed to import wheat from India, opening up its seven million-tonne a year market to Indian exporters. The breakthrough came after Egyptian quarantine authority approved Indian wheat quality for imports.
4. **Jaipur, April 14 (TOI):** The port city of Basara which has fallen to the coalition forces has age-old trade links with Rajasthan. The Pink City, which is also a gems city, has been getting its stocks of the world famous Basara pearls from the Persian Gulf.
5. **Vancouver/Hong Kong, April 14 (TOI):** Scientists in Canada have broken the genetic code of the virus suspected of causing SARS, the first step towards developing a test for doctors to diagnose victims of the killer flu or, in future, a possible vaccine.

6. **Bagdad, April 14 (TOI):** The Nature Museum of Iraq recorded a history of civilizations that flourished in Mesopotamia more than 7000 years ago. But it took only 48 hours for it to be destroyed. At least 170000 artifacts were carried away by looters.
7. **New Delhi, April 14 (TOI):** No more open jeep-thrills in tiger reserves. Following the recent attack by a tiger on tourists in Bandavgarh reserve in Madhya Pradesh, Project Tiger has asked all 27 tiger reserves to fit all open tourist vehicles with iron grills and sliding windows.
8. **New Delhi, April 14 (TOI):** Liz Hurley has splashed out a princely $ 2.75 million on her new luxury home, of eight bedrooms and 72 acres of grounds in the Cotswold's.
9. **Jaipur, April 14 (TOI):** The government is developing tourism circuits in the state, while old circuits are being strengthened and new are being developed. The tourism department has proposed to develop Jaipur Shekhawati-Bikaner-Jodhpur-Jaisalmer circuit.

Now check your answers with the answers given at the end of the chapter.

Comments on News Headlines

The headlines a and b make us go to the reports as the headlines themselves are not self-explanatory. Headline b is very interesting and until we quickly read the report given in 7, the main idea dose not become clear. Headlines c, g, h are self-explanatory and require only a quick survey of the reports.

However, to understand the significance of headlines d, e, f, and i, the reader will have to read the reports given under each of them quickly.

EXERCISE 16.2

We use the strategy of skimming while selecting books at a book-shop. We take a look at the title, index and blurb to see whether to buy the book or not. Below are given some titles with their blurbs. Skim through them quickly and match the title with the blurbs.

(A) Looking from Within
(B) An Anthology of Commonwealth Poetry
(C) From Paragraph to Essay
(D) Professional Communication Skills
(E) A Short History of English Poetry

1. The book is specially designed to train engineering students to have that critical edge over others in the competitive world of global industries and organizations. It is created specifically to suit engineering and other professional students to learn the basics of what they would be expected to do as they advance in their careers.

2. Three chief categories of seekers have been kept in view in selecting passages for this compilation: Those who wish to obtain a greater life mastery and self-mastery; those who, while pursuing the common goals of life, also aim at something beyond the ordinary life and seek to grow towards a higher or spiritual state of being; those for whom spiritual growth is the primary purpose and pre-occupation of life ...
   All of the many approaches for the attainment of mastery and inner growth involve the cultivation of certain attitudes which … are related to inner or psychological states from which we look at and react to everything in life; both within us and outside us. This book deals with such basic attitudes in the light of Sri Aurobindo's yoga.
3. This is intended for advanced students who need training in writing clear and well organized essays in English.
   A variety of paragraph styles are presented and analyzed in the form of model passages, with accompanying written exercises. At regular stages the techniques and paragraph styles are developed into essay form and the final chapter combines all the techniques and styles introduced throughout the book.
4. The compilation of 181 selections confirms the multiple faces of Commonwealth poetry from India, Australia, New Zealand, Canada, the West Indies, Africa, Singapore, Malaysia, Sri Lanka, Pakistan and Bangladesh. As a source and reference work for students and teachers of the subject, it is invaluable.
5. This revised edition of a highly successful text makes available to the undergraduate students of literature the main approaches to English poetry listed chronologically with short bio-sketches of major poets. It presents in a concise manner the developments that have been responsible for the literary aspect of each period and cites examples of various kinds of poetry that have been in vogue at different times in history. The distinctions of each age will help the students understand the significance of each poet's oeuvre and the sensibilities that have been portrayed by the poets in their poems.

Now do this exercise. As you have skimmed through the blurbs, say which book each one of the following should read. Write their titles in the space provided.

1. A person who wants to improve his inner self and spiritual life

   ....
2. A student who wants to learn how to write essays

   ....
3. A student of literature who wants to have the knowledge of the history of poetry

   ....

4. Suraj is doing research in Commonwealth poetry
   ....
5. An engineering student who wants to learn basics of Communication Skills
   ....

   (Check your answers with the answers given at the end of chapter)

EXERCISE 16.3

Whenever we come across the description of a new product in a newspaper or a magazine, we quickly read the description to see what the product is and whether we would like to buy it or we can afford it. Below are given some descriptions of the new products launched. The headings do not match the descriptions. Quickly read the descriptions and write the name of the product with which the description matches in the space provided.

A. Dress up in Style

Weikfield adds another feather to its crown by launching Glucovin-D in India. Glucovin-D comes in an attractive reusable plastic glass with lid. Normally sweet product packets when opened attract all kinds of insects, but with the introduction of this new reusable plastic glass with lid that is not the case to be. This gives children a quick source of food; an energy drink that is convenient to make while playing indoors or outdoors.

B. The Energy Powerhouse

No more sweating inside the shoes for Indian feet during this summer. With the arrival of these long sweaty days, Superhouse Leathers, the manufacturers of Allen Copper brand of shoes and leather accessories, has now come up with a new range of sandals for the Indians Men. Ultra light sole, which is there for greater flexibility, also makes the sandals light in weight and the extra grooves for the extra grip provides the anti, skid features. These sandals are available in the range of ₹ 899 to ₹ 1099.

C. Carving Styles, Touch Wood!

IBM India Ltd. has announced the availability of a completely redesigned range of notebook, computers with industry leading performance and new standards for battery life, portability ergonomics and the most secure wireless access. The new notebooks are the top of line ThinkPad T-40, the ultra portable ThinkPad x 31 and new models of the ThinkPad Ruo. It is IBM's competitively priced line of ThinkPad notebooks, which now offers up to 10.3 hours of battery life.

D. Smart ThinkPad's

In the developing furniture market, one of the players is Esthetix. The specialty of Esthetix is the availability of historical and traditional furniture, which gives the eyes catching variation to the consumer: Esthetix has over 500 different ranges of furniture designs. In these designs the traditionally designed furniture has its own speciality. Esthetix also offers the diverse range of furniture for house, farm houses, offices, factories, corporation and government, etc.

A ....

B ....

C ....

D ....

(Now check your answers with those given at the end of the chapter.)

Scanning

Scanning is a reading process involving location of specific information, say, a word or a number, a name or an idea. Janice Abbott defines scanning very lucidly in the book Meet the Press:

Scanning is a reading skill we use when we want to find the answer to a specific question. We use it when we look up a word in a dictionary, when we consult an encylopaedia or the index of a reference book, when we look up a telephone number or the time of the next train to Liverpool. We also use it when reading a newspaper-to find out the football results, the name of the newly elected President, the time of a television programme or the temperature in Madrid. In all these cases we are not concerned with understanding the whole article or text but only with locating one item information.

The question arises as to how to scan. If we are looking for the name of a person or town, we should look for a capital letter. If we want to find out date or time, the best thing is to look rapidly for numbers. If we are looking for ideas, we should look for words that are likely to occur to convey those ideas. Once we have located the key words, the best thing for us is to read the information contained therein most slowly and carefully. It is desirable that we should not read extra material once the answer to the specific question is found out.

EXERCISE 16.4

Below are given two types of matrimonial advertisements. In the first part, parents are looking for suitable boys for their daughters. In the second part are given 14 advertisements of boys. Scan these advertisements quickly and match the boys' advertisements with those of the girls'. In some cases, there may be more than one choice. Note the time of your starting and finishing the advertisements. (If you are good at scanning, you should not take more than 5 minutes to complete the task.) Write the advertisement number in the brackets.

Part I

1. Affluent Punjabi Khatri business family of high status residing in posh South Delhi locality seeks alliance for slim, fair, beautiful and caring daughter, 24/165, DU and NIFT graduate owns independent business of garment exports. Father established industrialist.
   Looking for business professional or industrialist Khatri family of high status only. Please respond with complete details and a photo of the boy to Box No.230212. The Times of India, New Delhi-2. [ ]
2. Proposals invited from qualified professionals working in USA/Australia for smart beautiful 1976/5'6"/52 kg, Convent educated, well qualified, Gujarati Vaishnav girl. E-mail: sribelajisri@rediffmail.com.. or write to Box No. BAN 305899 R Times of India, Bangalore-560001. [ ]
3. Wanted a Rajasthani based Doctor/Engineer match for 36 yr/5'4" MD Doctor girl/senior demonstrator medical college, Jaipur. Caste no bar, divorcees please excuse. Box 937, Rajasthan Patrika, Jaipur. [ ]
4. Suitable match for Sindhi Girl MA., 38/5' Govt. job. Send biodata, horoscope Box No. 954, Rajasthan Patrika, Jaipur. [ ]
5. Beautiful slim 28/160 MA English, MBA Punjabi Brahmin girl from status family. Send BHP 1049 Rajasthan Patrika, Jaipur. [ ]
6. Beautiful, intelligent, slim girl, 32/5'3". RJA result awaited. Preferred upper caste. Contact 0141-2591605, 1, Sachivalya colony, Barkat Nagar, Jaipur. [ ]
7. Suitable match for Agarwal Garg manglik girl, Convent educated. Dec. 72, born in business family, fair, slim 155/45, attractive, sharp features. PG, Professionally qualified, interior designer. Decent marriage. Send BHP or call 0-987053335.

Part II

1. Alliance invited for handsome 31/5'6" boy working as Manager in Pharma Company. Caste no bar. Royal marriage, Udaipur, call 2428084 or 9829042531.
2. Alliance invited for 45/179 smart presentable Brahmin bachelor, private tutor, fluent in English, owns MIG flat, earns five figures per month. Caste, creed, language, etc. not restrictive at all. Write to Box No. 967, Rajasthan Patrika, Jaipur.
3. Rajasthan based Hindu Bengali boy divorcee 36/175/10,000. Teacher, M.A. B.Ed. Ph.D. BH. No dowry. Apply only virgin girl; Pensionable , service, caste, province no bar. Box no. 10124. Rajasthan Patrika, Jaipur.
4. Suitable Bengali/non-Bengali graduate, preferable govt. service, match for smart postgraduate 32/5'6"/65kg, 17000, private sector, father is doctor, own house, only son, caste no bar, early marriage. Send details for early progress. Simple marriage, no dowry. Box. No. 17044, Rajasthan Patrika, Alwar (Raj.).

5. Goyal BE, MBA, 30/162/16000 pm income, handsome boy looking for a beautiful, educated girl of reputed family. Write to Box No. 002, with photograph Kohinoor Publicity, Chhawani, Kota (Raj.).
6. Medio match (preference P.G. doing/selected) for Bansal handsome 25/175 doing PG 2nd year DVL (skin) Cosmetic surgery /hair transplantation, Jodhpur. Only brother, final MBBS. Contact Bikaner 0151-2233084, Box No. 14149, Rajasthan Patrika, Bikaner.
7. Goyal BE 26/5'7"/56/14500 pm, lecturer in Govt. Polytechnical college looking for beautiful educated family. Contact 0151-22334506. Send biodata to Box No. 12288, Rajasthan Patrika, Kota.
8. Qualified cultured match for US-based handsome Agarwal boy, 29/170/, State Attorney at Orlando Florida. Boy visiting India during December. Send BHP to Bikaner 2003@yahoo.com or contact 0141-2523336.
9. Suitable match for Agarwal (Kansal) boy BE (Electrical), 5'7", January 1980, Lecturer in Engineering College, Jaipur, salary 10500/-, preferred professionally qualified B.E. C.A., decent marriage desired. Contact 0141-2334706.
10. Bhardwaj College lecturer 32/5'8". M.Sc. NET, Ph.D. 15500/- seeks professionally qualified, MBA preferred. Write to Box 935, Rajasthan Patrika, Jaipur.
11. For Smart Arora Khatri boy MBA 25/5'5" high status family, own factory, looking for beautiful slim, educated girl. Send biodata and horoscope. Writer to Box No. Luc 505825C, Times of India, Lucknow-226001.
12. Professional, beautiful, slim girl for Bisa Agarwal, fair, MCA, DNIIT SW professional USA 31/176/65 boy currently visiting India. Write to Box No. DEL 230264C, Times of India, New Delhi-110002 or contact Tel. No. 011-255552587.
13. Suitable match for Sindhi businessman, 40 year divorcee with no encumbrances. No dowry. Early marriage. Govt. service preferred. Write to Box 936, Rajasthan Patrika, Jaipur.
14. Wanted professionally qualified employed, slim beautiful girl for smart MBA well settled, 32/173. Saryuparnin Sadliya non-manglik boy. Father prof. Send BHP. Write to Box No. All 5311767 K, Times of India, Allahabad.

(Match the answers with those given at the end of the chapter.)

EXERCISE 16.5

We use the strategy of scanning in consulting a word in a dictionary or finding a telephone number in a telephone directory or the arrival or departure of a particular train in the Railway Time Table. Below is given an exercise on finding the meaning of particular words in a dictionary.

1. He *is licking his boots*.
   Find out the meaning of the *italicized* phrase.
2. Give the meaning of *nymphomaniac*.
3. What is the past tense of 'tread'
   trod or treaded or trodden?
4. Are the words 'pale' and 'pail' pronounced alike?
   Yes/No
5. What is the complete name of 'SARS'?
6. 'Felled' is the past tense form of 'fall' or 'fell'.
7. What is the full name of the word 'flu'?
8. He is a *slowcoach*.
   What is the meaning of *italicized* word?
9. What is 'dip-net' used for?
10. What is the full form of DNA?

EXERCISE 16.6

The world had been in the grip of SARS for the last four or five months. It is a contagious disease. Scan the extract given in India Today, May 2003 and then answer the questions. Write T if it is true, F if it is false and NI if there is no information about it in the extract.

1. What is SARS?
   (i) Serve Acute Respiratory Syndrome [ ]
   (ii) It is a kind of 'flu'
2. Is there a cure for SARS?
   (i) It is too new. So there is no proven medicine for it [ ]
   (ii) It is treated with ribavirin and steroids [ ]
3. How does it spread?
   (i) Through droplets released by the patient while coughing [ ]
   (ii) Infected objects could spread the infection [ ]
4. What are its symptoms?
   (i) Fever less than 100 degrees [ ]
   (ii) Difficulty in breathing [ ]
   (iii) Virus lasts 5 hours outside body [ ]
5. How is it tested?
   (i) DNA based test called PCR [ ]
   (ii) Elisa test is also being developed [ ]
6. Which mark to use?
   (i) Three layer mark costing ₹ 3 [ ]
   (ii) Eu 871 costing ₹ 80 [ ]
   (iii) N-95 costing ₹ 300 [ ]

7. How can it be avoided?
   (i) Screening at point of entry and quarantine of infected of patients [ ]
   (ii) Washing hands frequently [ ]
   (iii) No Spiting or urinating in public place [ ]
8. Is there a scope for the virus to spread?
   (i) Patients are discharged once the cough and fever subside [ ]
   (ii) Quarantine of SARS victims is difficult to implement [ ]

Extract on SARS

SARS defined: Severe Acute Respiratory Syndrome. A viral disease caused by a deadly new member of the common cold family. Surfaced in China six months ago. Has killed over 260 people and infected 4400 people globally.

Spread of SARS: Through droplets released while coughing, in close contact with patient.

Infected objects like doorknobs could spread infection. But much is still unknown.

In Hong Kong, savage, faeces and cockroaches were suspected transmitters.

Symptoms: Similar to flu. Fever of more than 100 degrees, dry cough, bodyache. SARS can develop into pneumonia and cause difficulty in breathing. Symptoms appear up to 10 days later, virus lasts just four hours outside body.

Tests conducted: No full proof method. Most common is a DNA based test called PCR. A cell-based on fluorescence test shows best results 10 days later. An antibody based test called ELISA is also being developed.

Cure: It's too new. It has a mortality rate of 5 percent. SARS is treated with an antiviral called *ribavirin* plus steroids.

Masks: The Ministry of Health has recommended three types: a three-layer mask costs ₹ 3 and is to be given to employees at airports, an Eu 871 costs ₹ 80 and is a must for paramedical staff and an N-95, recommended by WHO for doctors and medical staff, costs ₹ 300.

Control: Screening for SARS at points on entry like airports. Quarantine for infected patients.

Maintaining strict personal hygiene, such as washing hands frequently.

Keeping neighbourhoods clean, with no spitting or urinating in public places.

India at Risk? SARS loves crowds. Cough droplets from a SARS victim could spread to many others in a bus or on a train.

SARS could be mistaken for the flu. Symptoms may not show till 10 days after infection. So screening at airports could fail. SARS is still evolving.

Patients may not show all the clinically defined symptoms. A negative test results does not rule out SARS. Patients given the clear signal may not be free of SARS. There is no way of being sure.

Patients prefer private doctors. About 75 percent of Indians visit private doctors who have only just been briefed about SARS. All four SARS patients initially went to private doctors. The Real worry so far, India has had only four SARS cases, with no deaths. But as quarantine of SARS positive patients is voluntary, it is difficult to implement. Patients are discharged once the cough and fever subside; so there is scope for the virus to spread.

More About Comprehension and Reading

The word 'comprehension' is derived from the Latin word *comprehendere*, which means 'to grasp', 'to comprehend', as John Donne, the famous English poet has said, 'is to know thing as well as that thing can be known.'

Reading is an interactive activity. It involves the interaction among the printed page, the reader and the message. The comprehension of a text involves the *knowledge of language system* and the knowledge of the world on the part of the reader.

The knowledge of the language system consists of:

(i) The matching of sounds with the alphabet
(ii) The meaning of words
(iii) The meaning of sentences
(iv) The interrelationship between sentences
(v) The use of cohesive devices and the meaning generated by them; the topic sentence generating the main idea and the supporting sentences contributing to the main idea.

The knowledge of the world involves:

(i) The knowledge of the subject being read
(ii) The expectation or understanding of what the author may have to say
(iii) The relevant past knowledge or earlier experience of a reader
(iv) The relevant background knowledge
(v) Analysis of information in the light of one's experiences and emotions
(vi) Relating the text to broader social issues and exploring larger social implications
(vii) The relationship between the reader and text
(viii) The attitude and tone of the text.

What Does Reading Comprehension Involve?

This involves the processing of information contained in the text through various sub-skills. Theses sub-skills involve:

(i) Comprehension at word, sentence and paragraph level
(ii) Predictability or guessing
(iii) Inferencing: simple or complex
(iv) Sifting of information
(v) Problem solving
(vi) Processing
(vii) Comprehension of tone, attitude, opinion
(viii) Transferring of information, i.e. visual to verbal or vice versa
(ix) Selecting information
(x) Identifying topic-shift, cause-effect, point of view

Below are given time-tested strategies to attempt comprehension passages.

Strategies for Attempting a Comprehension Passage

The strategies for comprehensing a passage are given in Figure 16.1.

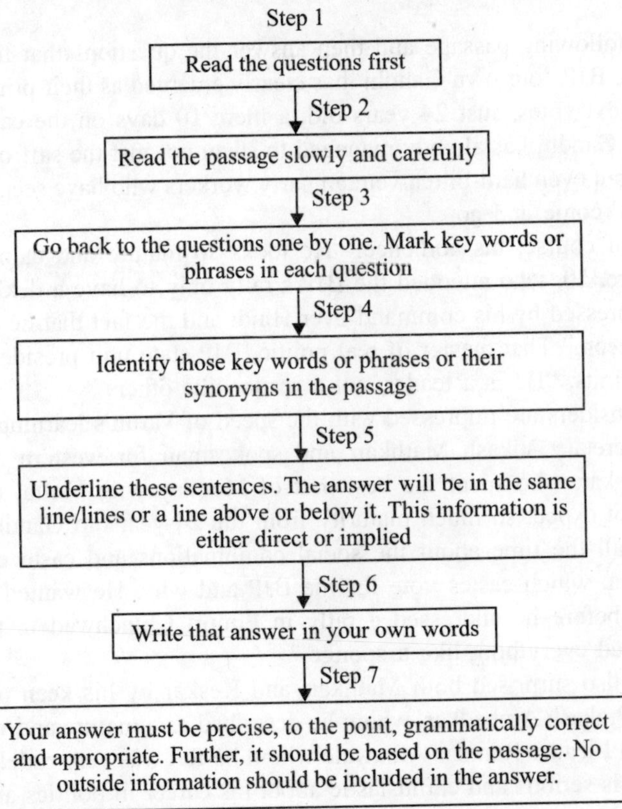

FIGURE 16.1 Strategies for comprehension.

This seven-step strategy will work wonderfully well for factual and information seeking questions where the answers are contained in the passage. This strategy may also work for answering those questions that require inferencing, e.g. logical reasoning. But this strategy will not work for answering those questions that require the interaction between textual information and knowledge of the world.

For answering true-false type questions, *the elimination technique* should be used. First, eliminate the obvious wrong answers by matching the facts given in questions with the facts given in the passage. This will give you the correct answer.

Multiple-choice questions can also be answered by *elimination technique* except in those cases where the distractors have been very cleverly framed.

Evaluative or critical analysis type questions will require the analytical ability on the part of the reader to answer the questions because here he will have to compare his previous knowledge or experiences with the ones given in the passage and then arrive at the correct answer.

Below, we shall illustrate the above strategies by giving practice passages.

Passage 1

Read the following passage and then answer the questions that follow:

For the BJP, 'our own Gandhi' has clearly emerged as their prime pitchman for Gen Next votes. Just 24 years old, a mere 10 days on the campaign trail and Varun Gandhi has already managed to sway not just the saffron combine's top brass, but even hard-bitten veteran party workers who have seen all manners of 'leaders' come and go.

And, of course, his audience. "He looks so mature and calm," enthuses Neha Khare, 20, who attended the BJP's rally only to have a dekko at Varun. "I was impressed by his command over Hindi and the fact that he did not read out his speech." That master of real politic, BJP state unit president Gopinath Munde, admits, "He is a leader, not a reader like others."

Party insiders are impressed with the speed of Varun's learning curve. BJP general secretary Vikash Mathkari and spokesman for western Maharashtra Ujjwal Keskar, who spent the best part of Monday with Varun, confess that they did not expect so much maturity from the 24-year old Gandhi. "He was asking us all the time about the social combinations and caste equations in Maharashtra, which castes vote for the BJP and why. He wanted some local references before he addressed a rally in Pimpri Chinchwad in the evening and absorbed everything like a sponge."

Varun also surprised both Mathkari and Keskar by his keen observations about MP Prakash Ambedkar, whom he described as a mature and well-studied man and RPI leader Ramdas Athawale whom he felt was very rude! "We could see that he is serious and enthusiastic about his career in politics and wants to learn as much as he can during his campaign tour," Keskar adds.

A sentiment echoed by the BJP's saffron partner Shiv Sena—His description of the down-to-earth BJP candidate from Pune, Pradeep Rawat as *seeda saadha apna Pradeep dada* is a testimony to his powers of quick observation and assessment, says Sena corporator and media manager Prashant Badhe.

No wonder the BJP is rolling out the red carpet—106 public rallies for Varun and a special helicopter for his use! Mathkari said, "Usually heirs of dynastic families are arrogant and brash, but Varun has no airs, he is transparent, level headed and showed that he has his feet firmly anchored to the ground. May be it has something to do with his being a poet." No fads while eating and no complaints about the heat. There is another aspect of this 'Swadeshi' and 'saccha Gandhi' as the BJP projects him, which appealed to the audience.

Questions

1. 'Our own Gandhi' refers to
   (i) Mahatma Gandhi (ii) Varun Gandhi
   (iii) Rahul Gandhi (iv) Priyanka Gandhi
2. Varun Gandhi has impressed
   (i) Leaders as well as workers (ii) Only leaders
   (iii) Only workers (iv) Only audience
3. Varun gives his speeches
   (i) In Marathi (ii) In Gujarati
   (iii) In Hindi (iv) In English
4. Which expression shows that Varun is a fast learner?
   (i) Absorbed everything like a sponge
   (ii) Asked questions about social combinations and caste equations
   (iii) Which castes voted for BJP
   (iv) The speed of his learning curve
5. Varun is a keen observer because
   (i) His remark about Ambedkar is correct
   (ii) His remark about Athawale is correct
   (iii) His remarks about both Ambedkar and Athwale are correct
   (iv) He takes politics seriously and enthusiastically
6. Pradeep Rawat is a candidate who belongs to
   (i) BJP (ii) Shiv Sena
   (iii) Vishav Hindu Parishad (iv) Congress
7. Another quality of Varun which attracted the people is
   (i) He belongs to the Gandhi dynasty
   (ii) He has airs of belonging to a high family
   (iii) He is a poet
   (iv) He is transparent, clam and practical

Let us now examine the answers. As suggested, we should read the questions first. As the questions are multiple choice questions, the statement before each set of choices should be read. These statements will give us a rough idea that this passage is about Varun Gandhi and his performance at election rallies. This also outlines some of his qualities as a speaker and leader.

Then we shall read the passage slowly and carefully. Having done that, we shall go back to questions one by one.

1. We shall match 'our own Gandhi' in the question with the phrase 'our own Gandhi' in the text and underline it. Then we shall go down the phrase and discover that the word, Varun, occurs 25 words after in the text. We shall eliminate the three remaining choices (i), (iii) and (ii) as incorrect choices and choose (ii) Varun Gandhi as the correct answer.
2. In question No. 2, the word 'impressed' occurs. We shall look for this word in the text or its synonym. We find the word sway and underline it. The answer then is quite obvious, i.e. (i) because he impresses both leaders and workers. Others are automatically eliminated.
3. Answer to question No. 3 is not directly given in the passage. It is, in fact, to be inferred. This inference is based on the following lines: "I was impressed by his command over Hindi and the fact that he did not read out his speech." By combining his command over Hindi and not reading out his speech, we can infer that he gave speeches in Hindi.
4. 'Fast learner' matches with learning curve but this meaning is to be eliminated. The correct answer in this case is (i) and this meaning is to be inferred based on our knowledge of the world that a sponge absorbs everything fast. Similarly, Varun learns everything quickly. Other choices are to be eliminated.
5. By the process of elimination, (iv) is incorrect. (i) and (ii) are partially correct, and therefore (iii) is the only correct choice.
6. Choices (iii) and (iv) are eliminated as they do not occur in the passage. As BJP candidate from Pune and Pradeep Rawat are in opposition to each other, (i) is the only correct choice.
7. The elimination of (i) and (iii) is quite difficult because all these qualities are found in Varun. Choice (ii) is incorrect, hence eliminable. But what makes (iv) as the correct choice is because it is his transparency, calmness and practicality that impresses people most. Therefore, the correct answer is (iv), and (i) and (iii) are eliminated.

Passage 2

Read the following passage and then answer the questions that follow:

Electric Current and Its Effects

Electricity plays a very important role in providing us with comforts and necessities of human life. Electrical energy is the cheapest form of energy which can be converted into other forms of energy easily.

For our present purpose it is sufficient to look upon electric current as something that flows. Just as water will flow along a pipe, so electricity will pass along a suitable path. Unlike the current of water, however, the electric current does not require a hollow pipe for its transmission; it is sufficient to provide it with a solid path of appropriate material.

Electricity is present in all matters whether solids, liquids or gases. All matter consists of an enormous number of minute particles called *atoms*. An atom resembles a miniature solar system. There is, in the atom, a central nucleus of positive charge, around which tiny, negatively charged particles, called electrons, revolve in fixed orbits in much the same way as the planets rotate round the sun. The negative charge of all orbital electrons just balances the positive charge of the nucleus. Hence under ordinary conditions, the atom is electrically neutral.

The nucleus of the atom is made up of two fundamental particles called the proton and the neutron. The proton is relatively heavy (1840 times heavier than an electron) and has a positive charge, while the neutron has about the same mass as the proton, but has no charge at all.

The electron orbits in shells about the nucleus each having a definite number of electrons.

The number and arrangement of these electrons and protons in the atom determine the physical properties of the substance. Different combinations of electrons and protons make different substance.

A neutral atom is ionized by giving it a surplus of electrons or by causing a deficit of electrons in it. An ion is an atom that has become electrically unbalanced. An atom that has lost an electron is a positive ion while an atom that has gained an electron is a negative ion. The process of making an atom gain or lose an electron is called 'ionization'.

In certain materials, such as copper, the electrons in the outermost of the atom are loosely attached to their nucleus and move from one atom to another.

These electrons are called free electrons. When an electrical field (pressure) is applied to copper, these free electrons move in a definite (particular) direction. This movement of free electrons in a particular direction constitutes the flow of electricity. The flow of electricity is called the 'electric current'. When electric current flows through a material, the stream of electrons constituting the current will flow from the negative terminal to the positive terminal.

Materials which readily let pass an electric current through them are called conductors. Conductors contain a large amount of free electrons. There are very few electrons in some other materials. Such materials resist the flow of current through them. Consequently, it is difficult to set up a circuit in them. They are called 'insulators'. By and large, all metals are conductors while non-metals are insulators. But carbon, although a non-metal, is a moderately good conductor.

An electric circuit is one which connects a receiver of electrical energy, say, a lamp, to the source of supply of electrical energy (say, a cell) by a pair of wires. In order that an electric current may flow in a circuit, the circuit must be complete and must consist of electrical conductors.

With regard to such a circuit, three factors are important – (1) the electric current which is the rate of flow of electricity through the circuit; (2) the electrical resistance, which is the opposition offered by the electric circuit to the flow of electricity through it; and (3) electromotive force which is the driving force necessary to cause current to flow against resistance. The electrical energy required to overcome this opposition is converted into heat. The resistance of any conductor depends upon – (1) its length, (2) the cross-sectional area, (3) the material of which it is made and (4) its temperature.

The flow of electricity through a circuit cannot be seen or handled. There are three main effects by which the presence of current may be recognized: the heating effect, the magnetic effect and chemical effect. All are of great importance in the practical applications of electricity.

Questions

1. Point out the importance of electricity.
2. What is an electric current?
3. Discuss the resemblance of solar system in an atom.
4. What are the two parts of an atom?
5. What is an ion and what is ionization?
6. How does the current flow?
7. What are conductors and insulators?
8. What is an electric circuit?
9. Point out the important factors for a circuit.
10. What does the resistance of a conductor depend on?
11. How do we know that an electric current is present in an object?

Let us examine the answers. All the 11 questions in this passage contain direct information easily recoverable from the passage by underlining the key words or phrases. This was bound to happen as the passage is a factual one and is on a scientific topic.

1. The key phrase 'importance of electricity' is matchable with the first line of the passage. The answer is in the first sentence itself. The answer is: Electricity is very important in our lives because it provides comforts and necessities of life.
2. The key phrase is 'electric current' and the same phrase occurs in the text. The answer is electric current is something that flows in a solid path of appropriate material.
3. The phrase is 'solar system' and it is there in the text. As in solar system, the sun is in the centre and the planets move around it, similarly, in an atom there is a central nucleus of positive charge around which negatively charged electrons move in fixed orbits.
4. The two parts of an atom are proton and neutron. The answer is arrived at from the key phrase.

5. Again the concept of 'key word' or 'phrase' gets the correct answer. An ion is an atom that has either surplus or deficit of electrons. Further, the process of making an atom gain or lose an electron is called 'ionization'.
6. The answer based on key phrase 'flow of current' in that the current flows from the negative terminal to the positive terminal.
7. The key words here are *conductors* and *insulators*. The location of these words in the passage gives us the correct answer. Conductors are those materials that allow a free passage of electric current. On the other hand, insulators resist the flow of current through them. Usually metals are conductors and non-metals are insulators with the exception of carbon.
8. The key phrase is 'electric circuit'. It is found in the text and the answer starts right there. An electric circuit is one which connects a receiver of electric energy with the supplier of electric energy with a pair of wires.
9. Three factors are important: (a) the electric current, (b) the electric resistance and (c) the electromotive force which cause current to flow through the resistance.
10. The resistance of any conductor depends upon (a) its length, (b) the cross-sectional area, (c) the material of which it is made, and (d) its temperature.
11. The presence of an electric current is recognized by heating effect, the magnetic effect and the chemical effect.

Notice all the answers are based on direct information recoverable form the text. No inference is required.

Passages for Practice

Passage 1

Read the following passages and then answers the questions that follow:

No hocus pocus. No swirling smoke. No guru sitting cross-length on a tiger skin, swathed in yard of white muslin, bombarding you with indecipherable mumbo jumbo. Just plain and simple Sunita Menon, a tarot card reader of repute. Not that this dusky beauty can be called plain by any stretch of the imagination. Downplaying her exotic looks, this erstwhile airhostess, who could easily be walking the ramps of Paris, is quite content foretelling the future for her vast clientele.

Sunita, with her tarot cards and the assistance of palmistry, numerology, gemology and astrology—she calls them tools, tells those seeking answers to the right or most accurate path to take. Whether it's a question pertaining to whether the love of your life is really the love of your life, or whether you should be starting a business venture in a particular month, her spread of cards seem to have all the answers.

Thirty-nine-year-old Sunita Menon's name tops the phone book of many a celebrity. Karan Johar, Manish Malhotra and Ekta Kapoor being just a few.

Her list of corporate clients is rather impressive as well, but ask her to name a few and she is the soul of discretion. Obviously, a fair amount of her clients maintain a façade of scepticism about the entire business of tarot cards, for the benefit of the world.

"That's true. There have been occasions when I have sat across someone at a party and heard him deride what I do, only to have him sit across my table the next day, asking for a reading. Their explanation is that they can't let the world know that they believe in what I do," she smiles. Such cynicism she is well used to. "Most people mock what I do. There's an immense amount of disbelief that I come across. But I am detached from all that. I have taken a path and that's that," she explains, sitting in her Spartan room in suburban Mumbai.

Right from when she was in school, Sunita was always aware that she was a 'different' child. "I was always rather quiet. The other children would come to me for help as I was supposed to be the wise and gutsy one. I'd always stick my neck out, be the arbitrator and thus always be in trouble! I was often called complicated," she smiles. That was the time when she also got the reputation of having a black tongue. "I'd get a feeling, a very strong one, and I'd say it aloud. And what I spoke about would actually happen. So then I was even told not to voice my opinions," she adds. Needless to add, her 'feelings' were rather disturbing—no one really wants to know that person X's aunt is going to pass away some time soon. She learnt to keep quiet about it. And with time, this Chennai-educated girl, at the age of 18, became an airhostess. "I wanted the freedom of packing my bags and just going away. Freedom, even now, is very important for me," she states. At the age of 21, she met the person she calls her guru, who helped her to cut through the maze of 'feelings' which had been plaguing her since long, and channelise them in a fruitful manner.

"I came back, convinced that this is what I am going to do. Many people, including my family members, were shocked with my decision. But I was convinced. I started small, but with time and word of mouth, many people started coming to me. It was around 1996 that the first of my 'celebrity clients' started trickling in," she reminisces.

Considering the fact that her readings are the mainstay for many, she is always on call, literally. And that is rather draining for her. "I see the lonely side of normal people and famous personalities. What do I do with all that knowledge? It is disturbing. Many times, people come to me with problems, which are essentially psychological in nature. Just a little bit of love, affection and attention can solve that. That's when I involve the families," she says, adding, "I don't want people to make me and my readings a habit. They need to understand that I can only offer them guidelines to enhance their life. I cannot prevent anything from happening, only they can control that. I don't want that kind of dependence." Perhaps that's one of the reasons she has increased her fee from ₹ 300 to ₹ 1000 for a 45-minute session.

Sunita is also very vehement about the fact that her tarot card readings and psychic abilities cannot undo what the future holds. "If something bad is destined for you, it will happen. However, there's no harm in to be prepared. If I tell you that it's raining outside, you can at least protect yourself with an umbrella. But the rain will still be there," she maintains.

And so it will. It ultimately is a matter of faith. And Sunita Menon leaves the choice to you.

I. Choose the Correct Alternative

1. Sunita, a tarot card reader, uses the following as tools for predicting future of her clients:
   (a) Tarot cards, palmistry, numerology, gemology and astrology.
   (b) Palmistry, numerology, gemology and astrology
   (c) Numerology, gemology and astrology
   (d) Gemology and astrology
2. Sunita was .... years old when she became an airhostess.
   (a) 18 (b) 21
   (c) 39 (d) 35
3. Sunita is a black beauty. This means she belongs to:
   (a) Tamil Nadu (b) Kerala
   (c) Karnataka (d) Maharashtra
4. 'Such cynicism she is well used to.' What cynicism does the writer refer to?
   (a) Most people deride her work
   (b) There is a lot of disbelief in what she does
   (c) Most people mock at what she does
   (d) Disbelief, mockery and derision of her work of foretelling
5. At school, she was considered to be wise and gusty. She also had the reputation for making ....
   (a) Accurate predictions
   (b) Accurate but unpleasant predictions
   (c) Pleasant predictions
   (d) Accurate but pleasant predictions
6. Why has she increased her consultation fee from ₹ 300 to ₹ 1000?
   (a) Because she does not want people to make her readings a habit
   (b) Because some people suffer from psychological problems and come to her just to chat
   (c) Because she also offers them guidelines to improve their lives
   (d) Because she wants only the genuine people to come to her who would like to know about their futures

7. Consulting a tarot card reader is a matter of ....
   (a) Faith (b) Superstition
   (c) Helplessness (d) Insecurity

II. Match the words given in column A with their meanings in column B

A	*B*
(a) Undecipherable	1. Dark skinned
(b) Mumbo jumbo	2. The meaning of which cannot be discovered
(c) Dusky	3. Mysterious talk
(d) Exotic	4. A famous person
(e) Numerology	5. The state of seeing no good in anything
(f) Celebrity	6. Strange and unusual
(g) Façade	7. Simple, severe
(h) Scepticism	8. Study of the magic meaning of numbers
(i) Cynicism	9. A doubting state of mind
(j) Spartan	10. A false appearance
	11. A jumbo jet
	12. Lover of sports

Key to Passage 1

I.	1. (a)	2. (a)	3. (a)	(4) d
	5. (b)	6. (a)	7. (a)	
II.	(a) 2	(b) 3	(c) 1	(d) 6
	(e) 8	(f) 4	(g) 10	(h) 9
	(i) 5	(j) 7		

Passage 2

Read the following passage and then answer the questions that follow:

I own a flat and certain securities which have been given to me by my father. Recently I have come across a report that if a married lady dies without making a will, then her husband has no right on the property and other assets given to her by her parents. I would like to know details about this. Further, I wish to make a will stating that my husband who is a nominee in the property I own can reside in the property but after his demise, the property should revert to my brother. For this I would like to make the relevant changes in the nomination. Is the above feasible and how should I make a will incorporating the above?

Section 14 of the Hindu Succession Act provides that any property possessed by a female Hindu, whether acquired before or after the commencement of the Hindu Succession Act, 1956, will be her absolute ownership property and not as limited owner. Property includes both moveable and immoveable whether it is acquired by inheritance or devise or in partition or in lieu of maintenance or by gift from any person before or at or after her marriage. It also includes the property acquired by her own skill or exertion or by purchase or by prescription or in any other manner. Even if she has acquired any property as stridhan. Therefore, any property acquired by you from anywhere mentioned hereinabove will be treated as your own property and you have all right to dispose it in the manner you deem fit and proper. You can give it to your husband or brother as you wish.

Questions

1. Where do you think this passage has been taken from?
2. What has been given to the lady by her father?
3. What should happen to the property owned by the lady after her husband's death?
4. What change does she want to make in the will?
5. What does Section 14 of the Hindu Succession Act provide?
6. What does property include vis-à-vis the Hindu Succession Act of 1956?
7. What does property include vis-à-vis the Hindu Succession Act of 3, 1956?

Passage 3

Read the following passage and answer the questions that follow:

Post-modern art collages
"I, Me, Myself"
Conducted by Saba Hasan
On Saturday, 20 March, 2012 at 11.30 a.m.
For ages: 5 to 9 years
For 20 participants
"I have nothing to hide, or do I?"
Conducted by Sabha Hasan
On Saturday, 20 March, 2012 at 11.30 a.m.
For ages: 10–15 years
For 20 participants

These two workshops for children where they will be taught to make colleges. Collages have become a standard art technique since the time of Cubists but have again acquired a fresh lease of life with computer-generated and mixed–media art.

Children need to bring a few materials with them for the two workshops. For "I, Me, Myself, this can include their photographs, shoelaces, buttons … anything around their own selves.

For the "I Have Nothing To Hide. Or Do I?" Workshop children can bring all kinds of things they consider to be representative of their identities. In addition to these, they need to bring a poem or an article written in a language which is not their mother tongue.

Film-making Workshop

Conducted by *Bhasker Mukherjee*
On Saturday, 27 March, 2012, at 10:30 a.m.

For ages 10–15 years

For 20 participants only

As children are these days surrounded by multimedia TV, computers and cinema, it is important for them to understand the various elements which make up a movie.

The aim of the workshop is to create an awareness of the various elements which make up a film, i.e. story, location, camera, movements, editing, titling, voice and music dubbing.

The workshop will last for three hours and will use a Digital-8 camera. The participants will shoot, edit and add sound and titles. The completed film will be of approximately 10 minutes duration. A copy of the CD will be available to each participant a week later.

Registration starts on 8 March for all the workshops on a first-come-first-served basis and is limited to 20 participants. The registration fee is ₹ 100 per participant.

These workshops are only open to children, library members and children of family library members.

Questions

1. Where is this excerpt from?
2. What is the first workshop on?
3. Who will be conducting the workshop?
4. What materials are the children of first workshop expected to bring?
5. What materials are the children of second workshop expected to bring?
6. How many participants can participate in each workshop?
7. What could be the age of children for each workshop?
8. When is the first workshop opening and when will the second workshop start?
9. What is the aim of the third workshop?
10. Give details about the third workshop.
11. Point out the eligibility requirements of the third workshop.
12. What will be the outcome of the third workshop?
13. What could be the reason for restricting each workshop only for 20 children?
14. Why do they start each workshop on Saturday?
15. The first two workshops start at 11:30 a.m., whereas the third one starts at 10:30 a.m. Why?
16. What could be the reason for organizing the first workshop for the children between 5–9 years, whereas the second and third ones for children of 10–15 years of age?

Passage 4

Read the following passage and then answer the questions that follow:

There's this quote that sums up the essential theories of my life. 'Happiness is doing what is right, not what feels good.' I read this somewhere and safely preserved a cutout. In my own life, like so many others, I've been through phases that make you look at life in a new light. As a child I was adopted. Even though I was extremely young when all of this happened, I've followed every single moment of my adoption.

My biological parents are today my *mausa* and *mausi.* The problem started when my legal parents forbade me from meeting my biological parents. I was getting too much influenced by them. My adoptive father is a man of strong principles. Certain norms that dictated my life have helped me be the person I am today. He is a role model for me in every sense.

It wasn't until I got a little older that problems began to arise. My biological father began to regret the decision he had made. But, he didn't want to accept the consequences of the decision he had made. Sadly, it was too late. He could not deal with his own pain, and in turn, he caused other people pain. At that point, the importance of decisions became clear to me. It's important to not make decisions that you can't suffer the consequences of. Everybody has to stand by the decisions he/she makes. That's life.

It all boils down to that same quote. Happiness is doing what is right, not what feels good. Through my own experiences and through those around me, I've constantly learnt this. I've found that everybody has serious problems in their families. Familial issues are complex by their very nature and it is important to accept them as such.

When I turned 17, the problem got worse. It took the shape of a legal issue and it was blown out of proportion. My biological father wanted me back. He wanted to set the clock back. Obviously, it was something that he just could not get. A year later, the conflict became more and more meaningless. I was an adult by then. The question of owning responsibility didn't arise because I was my own person. In retrospect, this childhood episode has taught me so much about life and the choices one makes.

When I got out into the real world, I was brimming with energy. I was 20 and the world was my playground. I also made some terrible mistakes then. Now, I look back to realize that your mind can completely mislead you. I got corrupted because of my own desires. Then I wanted to fall in love. I thought that alone would fulfill my dreams. The reality, as I know it today, is that no other human being can make you happy. Today, I regret having done what felt good.

I went into a relationship that felt good. I must admit we had a rocking time while it lasted. When it ended, it had its customary bitterness. But now when I look at matrimony, I realize that there's nothing I need from marriage. Mentally, morally, physically, emotionally, financially, I am independent. If there's some one you meet who shares your vision, then it's the right step to take. Now when it happens, it will be because it's right. And not just because it feels good.

Questions

1. What is the writer's philosophy of life?
2. Why are her biological parents her *mausa* and *mausi*?
3. Who is the role model for the writer and why?
4. What was the problem of the biological father?
5. How are family matters different from other matters?
6. Which childhood event taught her so much about life?
7. What was her experience of falling in love?
8. What kind of a partener would she like to marry?

Passage 5

Read the following passage and then answer the questions that follow:

Very recently, our government, through the Ministry of Environment and Forests, tried (and failed) to barter ₹ 90,000 crore worth of forest lands for votes. Full-page newspaper ads were released announcing that 'encroachments' on forest lands up to December 31, 1993 would be 'regularized'. Mercifully, the Supreme Court stayed the order, thus preventing sure death for wildlife havens including the Sanjay Gandhi National Park, Melghat, Kudremukh, Nagarhole, Bandhipur, Indravati, Tiger Reserve and Gahirmatha.

Had the court not stepped in, the politicians would have reaped a short-term goldmine of votes, but the nation would have had to confront virtual anarchy in forested India. Apart from a death sentence on our wildlife, this would have exacerbated the already serious water crisis facing millions of Indians, as the foresters in questions are critical sources of the subcontinent's purest, most reliable water supplies.

I am beyond anger. Beyond frustration. Beyond despair. I abandoned such luxuries ages ago. Instead, with and almost religious trust in the fact that 'nature will find a way to repair itself'. I now work with children to prevent, delay or otherwise ensure that our precious rivers, forests and wildlife are not converted to cash, or votes. At this point, with the elections upon us, I'd like to ask the people of *India:* Why are we so collectively bovine when, before our very eyes, lawmakers become lawbreakers?

India has some of the finest environmental laws, but because we do not insist on their implementation, some people feel free to poison our rivers, lakes and wells. Others hack our forests and wipe out corals and mangroves, which are our marine breeding grounds. What is worse, the ones doing damage claim that your silence and mine is tantamount to the endorsement of their destructive agenda.

When asked why we do what we do, most of us reply, "For our children". If this is true, can we continue to be so nonchalant about their survival, allowing both health and happiness to be squandered in exchange for ephemeral gains? Eternal vigilance is the price we must pay for wanting natural India protected. The secret is not to get angry—get involved instead!

Here are some steps you can take.

- Join or support NGOs such as the Bombay Natural History Society (BNHS).
- Write to newspapers, and to all potential MPs and MLAs. Ask what they have done to protect our forests, wildlife and the environment.
- Start or join a citizen group to clean up your neighbourhood.
- Don't vote for candidates who do not respect our wildlife and environment.

I. State whether the following statements are true or false:

1. The Ministry of Environment and Forests succumbed to the pressure of encroachers to regularize the encroachments.
2. The Supreme Court concurred with the decision of the Government.
3. The forest lands were worth of 100000 crores.
4. Forest lands provide protection and shelter to the wildlife.
5. Some of the national parks in the country are Sanjay Gandhi National Park, Melghat, Bandipur and Gahirmatha.
6. The politicians took the decision of regularizing the encroachment on forest land to get votes.
7. Forest lands have reservoir of purest and reliable water.
8. The writer is very much angry and frustrated.
9. Lawmakers are lawbreakers in our country.
10. Children can help in saving environment.
11. The environment laws in the country are the worst.
12. The implementation of laws is first rate.
13. Most people keep quiet about environmental damage.
14. This gives encouragement for damaging the environment.
15. We can save environment by being ever watchful.
16. Citizens Groups have been set up to clean up our neighbourhood.

II. Match the words given in A with their meanings in B.

A	B
(i) Encroachment	1. The possibility for developing
(ii) Merciful	2. Used something wastefully
(iii) Goldmine	3. Indifferent
(iv) Exacerbated	4. Equal to
(v) Abandoned	5. Slow moving
(vi) Bovine	6. Gave up
(vii) Tantamount	7. Made worse
(viii) Nonchalant	8. A successful activity
(ix) Squandered	9. Kind
(x) Potential	10. Occupying land which does not belongs to a person
	11. Related to cattle
	12. Willing

Key to Passage 5

I. 1. True 2. False 3. False 4. True
5. False 6. True 7. True 8. False
9. True 10. True 11. False 12. False
13. True 14. True 15. True 16. True

II. (i) 10 (ii) 9 (iii) 8 (iv) 7
(v) 6 (vi) 5 (vii) 4 (viii) 3
(ix) 2 (x) 1

Passage 6

Read the following passage and then answer the questions that follow:

Kind people have attached a variety of honorifics to my name. I don't think I am worthy of any of these. I like my work. I believe that if one is in a profession, one should practice professionalism. I have set certain values and principles for myself as regards to any work. I like to follow these. I believe in living a disciplined life.

I am not superstitious. A lot of my friends and well-wishers have gifted me rings with various stones at different points in time. I wear these as a mark of respect for their feelings. In fact, people ask me why I'm wearing two rings in a certain finger—it's simple, one of them was given to my son, and he was not too keen to wear it, so I thought I would.

I don't believe in preaching people. Who am I to tell someone how to live their life? I don't know whether I am right anyway. I'm just experimenting with a variety of solutions, hoping they will work for me. I believe the biggest *dharma* is to work with total dedication. An artist should never be satisfied with anything he does. There's always scope for improvement, always a better way to complete the job, always a higher degree of perfection to reach.

Am I spiritual? Well, I believe there is a Force that is controlling all that goes on in the world. You can call it by any name. I pray every day in the temple in my house and also read the *Ramayana* and the *Bhagvad Geeta*. This is done in my private time—when I am with myself, enjoying my solitude.

When things go wrong, I try and deal with them as best as I can. Adverse circumstances—or whatever we perceive to be adverse—are a part of the life process. I try and follow what my father used to say: *Manna ka ho to achcha, na ho to aur bhi achcha*. (If your desires are fulfilled, it is good; if not, it is better.). I have been able to be a good son.

Question

1. What is the secret of the writer's success?
2. How can we say that the writer is not superstitious?
3. What is one's biggest duty?
4. What should be the aim of an artist?
5. Why can't we preach others?
6. Is the writer spiritual? Give proof.
7. What does the writer do when things go wrong?

8. Write a paragraph giving five qualities of the writer.
9. What should we do when confronted with adversity?

Passage 7

Read the following quotations and then answer the questions that follow:

It is assumed that the woman must wait, motionless, until she is wooed. That is how the spider waits for the fly.

—Bernard Shaw

Courage is fear that has said its prayers.

—Dorothy Bernard

The meeting of two personalities is like the contact of two chemical substances: if there is any reaction, both are transformed.

—Carl Jung

Leadership and learning are indispensable to each other.

—John F. Andrews

Love is not measured by how you feel but how you make the other person feel.

—Julie Andrews

Failure always made me try harder next time.

—Michael Jordan

Getting what you go after is success, but liking it while you are getting it is happiness.

—Bertha Damon

A real man does not need to romance a different girl every night. A real man romances the same girl for the rest of her life.

—Ana Alas

Egotism is the anesthetic that dulls the pain of stupidity.

—Frank Leahy

I am you and you are love and that is what makes the world go around.

—Clive Barker

Questions

1. What is Bernard Shaw's attitude towards women?
2. Define courage in your own words.
3. We often talk of chemistry of love. What happens when there is a chemistry of meeting?
4. Is a leader omniscient? What is the relationship between learning and leadership?
5. Define love in your own words.
6. What is the effect of failure on the writer?
7. What is the relationship between success and happiness?
8. How can one make one's married life romantic?
9. What kind of people talk about themselves?
10. What is the importance of love in life?

Passage 8

Read the following passage and then answer the questions that follow:

The paradox of our time in history is that we have taller buildings but shorter tempers, wider freeways, but narrower viewpoints. We spend more, but have less, we buy more, but enjoy less. We have bigger houses and smaller families, more conveniences, but less time. We have more degrees, but less sense, more knowledge, but less judgment, more experts, yet more problems, more medicine, but less wellness.

We drink too much, smoke too much, spend too recklessly, laugh too little, drive too fast, get too angry, stay up too late, get up too tired, read too little, watch TV too much, and pray too seldom. We have multiplied our possessions, but reduced our values. We talk too much, love too seldom, and hate too often.

We've learned how to make a living, but not a life, we've added years to life, not life to years. We've been all the way to the moon and back, but have trouble crossing the street to meet a new neighbour. We conquered outer space but not inner space. We've done larger things, but not better things.

We've cleaned up the air, but polluted the soul. We've conquered the atom, but not our prejudice. We write more, but learn less. We plan more, but accomplish less. We've leaned to rush, but not to wait. We build more computers to hold more information, to produce more copies than ever, but we communicate less and less.

These are the times of fast foods and slow digestion, big men and small character, steep profits and shallow relationships. These are the days of two incomes but more divorce, fancier houses but broken homes. These are days of quick trips, disposable diapers, throwaway morality, one night stands, overweight bodies, and pills that do everything from cheer, to quiet, to kill. It is a time when there is much in the showroom window and nothing in the stockroom; a time when technology can bring this letter to you, and a time when you can choose either to share this insight, or to just hit delete.

Remember, spend some time with your loved ones, because they are not going to be around forever. Remember, say a kind word to someone who looks up to you in awe, because that little person soon will grow up and leave your side. Remember, to give a warm hug to the one next to you, because that is the only treasure you can give with your heart and it doesn't cost a cent.

Remember, to say, 'I love you' to your partner and your loved ones, but most of all mean it. A kiss and an embrace will mend hurt when it comes from deep inside of you. Remember to hold hands and cherish the moment for somebody that person will not be there again. Give time to love, give time to speak, and give time to share the precious thoughts in your mind.

How to Stay Young

1. Throw out nonessential numbers. This includes age, weight and height. Let the doctor worry about them. That is why you pay him/her.
2. Keep only cheerful friends. The grouches pull you down.

3. Keep learning. Learn more about the computer, crafts, gardening, whatever. Never let the brain idle. 'An idle mind is the devil's workshop.' And the devil's name is Alzheimer's.
4. Enjoy the simple things.
5. Laugh often, long and loud. Laugh and you gasp for breath.
6. The tears happen. Endure, grieve, and move on. The only person who is with us our entire life, is ourselves. Be ALIVE while you are alive.
7. Surround yourself with what you love, whether it's family, pets, keepsakes, music, plants, hobbies, whatever. Your home is your refuge.
8. Cherish your health: If it is good, preserve it. If it is unstable, improve it. If it is beyond what you can improve, get help.
9. Don't take guilt trips. Take a trip to the mall, to the next country, to a foreign country, but NOT to where the guilt is.
10. Tell the people you love that you love them, at every opportunity.

And Always Remember

Life is not measured by the number of breaths we take, by the moments that take our breath away.

Questions

1. Give proof for the fact that we are living in a world of contractions.
2. What advice does the writer give to the readers?
3. The writer lists 10 ways to stay young. Summarize them.
4. What does the writer ask us to always remember?
5. Why do you think that steps suggested by the writer will work?
6. On the basis of the reading of the passage, what formula to be happy can you suggest?

Passage 9

Read the following passage and then answer the questions that follow:

Since it is election session in both India and United States, some thoughts about the nature of campaigning in the two countries. Indian elections are noisy, colourful, energetic and vibrant. American elections, in comparison, are generally more sanitized and are largely made for television spectacle.

India also lacks, mercifully, two major features of the US exercise. The American campaign is long winded lasting almost a year—and they are expensive, costing more than a billion dollars by the time the polls close. By contrast, we are done in a month or so for a relative pittance given our scale.

The two systems are different in one other respect. Indians canvass with graffiti, posters, banners, buntings, hoardings and those awful cut-outs. Americans are more low-key in public, and use TV ads to beam message copiously.

American citizens also don't hesitate to express their political preferences through the medium of bumper stickers on their cars. Considering that the automobile boom is underway in India, it is surprising that Indians haven't got stuck into the bumper sticker craze. It may be coming.

As the election season warms up here, Americans are already beginning to say their two cents—or two dollars—worth of political wisdom. Those of Republican persuasion have bumper stickers that warn that "That road to hell is paved with Democrats."

Democrats tweet back with "Re-elect Bush: I'm tired of waiting for the Apocalypse".

A democrat friend swears she can identify party affiliation simply by the vehicle a person is driving.

She herself drives a small-sized Toyota Echo sporting a bumper sticker that reads "What's worse? Screwing an intern or screwing a country."

She says other small car drivers, typically Democrats, honk their appreciation when they read it. But big vehicles, usually gas guzzling sports utility vehicles (SUVs), try and intimidate her.

Bill Clinton attracted a fair bit of bumper sticker sarcasm during his term. "Clinton doesn't inhale, he SUCKS," read a popular one during the tail-end of his term (pun distended).

Hillary Clinton too has her share of detractors. Even the prospect of her running for president brought out the baiters. "I don't trust President Clinton (or her husband)", read one. Two others were "impeach Clinton, and her husband", and, "Presidents should be planned and wanted. ABORT CLINTON!"

But Bush is proving to be a match for the Clintons. Among the ones in vogue "Regime change starts at home", and 'Haven't we had enough Bush-it?"

Of course, there are those who don't care a flying fig for politicians. "Forget the Flag. Burn a Politician", reads one sticker. Another says: "Democrat/ Republican: Same Stink, Different Pile." My favourite is "I love my country. It's the government I'm afraid of."

The internet Age also brought with it new dotcom—or dot come– stickers such as "WWW.sex@myplace.com.now". The most popular ones remain comments about others driving.

The hottest one says "A hundred thousand sperms and you were the fastest???"

Beep Beep.

Questions

I. 1. List two major differences between Indian and American campaigning for elections.

2. Which country used bumper stickers for campaigning. Give some examples of the catchy stickers.
3. How can one identify the party affiliation by the vehicle a person is driving?
4. What kind of stickers did Hillary Clinton have to face?
5. Quote the stickers that show that people hate politicians.
6. Which is the hottest comment about others' driving?
7. What has the Internet age brought with it?

II. Match the words given in column A with their meanings in column B.

A	*B*
(i) Vibrant	1. Last destruction
(ii) Sanitized	2. Plentifully
(iii) Spectacle	3. Unauthorized drawing or writing on a surface in a public place
(iv) Campaign	4. Solicit votes
(v) Long-winded	5. A very small amount of money
(vi) Pittance	6. Lengthy
(vii) Canvass	7. An organized course of action
(viii) Graffiti	8. A visually striking performance
(ix) Copiously	9. Hygienic
(x) Apocalypse	10. Full of energy and enthusiasm
	11. A pair of glasses
	12. Curtain

Key to Passage 9

II. (i) 10 (ii) 9 (iii) 8 (iv) 7
(v) 6 (vi) 5 (vii) 4 (viii) 3
(ix) 2 (x) 1

Key to Exercise 16.1

A: 6 B: 7
C: 5 D: 8
E: 9 F: 4
G: 3 H: 1
I: 2

Key to Exercise 16.2

1. Looking from within
2. From Paragraph to Essay
3. A Short History of English Poetry
4. An Anthology of Commonwealth Poetry
5. Professional Communicate Skills

Key to Exercise 16.3

A The Energy Powerhouse
B Dress up in style
C Smart Think pads
D Carving styles, touchwood

Key to Exercise 16.4

1. 11
2. 8
3. 5/6
4. 13
5. 10
6. 14
7. 12

Key to Exercise 16.5

1. Be excessively obsequious towards someone
2. A woman with uncontrollable sexual desire
3. Trod
4. Yes
5. Severe Acute Respiratory Syndrome
6. Fell
7. Influenza
8. A person who acts slowly
9. A long handled net for catching small fish
10. Deoxyribonucleic acid

Key to Exercise 16.6

1. (i) T	(ii) NI	
2. (i) T	(ii) T	
3. (i) T	(ii) T	
4. (i) F	(ii) T	(iii) F
5. (i) T	(ii) T	
6. (i) T	(ii) T	(iii) T
7. (i) T	(ii) T	(iii) T
8. (i) T	(ii) T	

17

Report Writing

Introduction

The word 'report' can be used in a narrow or wide sense. Its etymological meaning to carry back (re = back + *portare* (Latin) = to carry) implies the carrying of information to someone who was not present on the scene. In its broad sense, then, a report would include letters, memorandums and news items. In its narrow sense, a report is a formal account of a personal experience or incident, analysis of a problem; collection of data of a project, investigation and analysis of data, conclusions and recommendations.

A report is a formal account of a particular subject from a person or group of persons to a person or organization (who have asked for it) written for a specific purpose, which includes a description of procedures followed for collection and analysis of data, their significance, the conclusions drawn from them and recommendations, if required. [Definition adapted from *Business Correspondence and Report Writing* by Sharma and Mohan, Tata McGraw-Hill, 2003, p. 128.]

Reports in modern age of information technology have become very important. Business executives, engineers and scientists have to write a number of reports and go through a number of reports received to disseminate knowledge about their work, organization and knowledge about other's work, projects and organizations. It is the quickest way to keep oneself up to date. In organizations, important decisions are taken on the basis of reports presented. Hence, it is important to know the fundamentals of report writing.

A report is written in a *conventional form.* The data are objectively examined and presented.

Characteristics of a Good Report

A good report has the following characteristics:

1. A report is a formal account; hence avoid informal expressions (colloquialisms, contractions and interjections) in a report.
2. A report is *functional.* It gives information and suggestions to those who can take decision on the matter. Hence, avoid all *digressions* of personal letters or essays in a report.
3. A report should be arranged in such a way that a reader can pick out quickly the facts he/she needs.
4. Presentation can be done by ordering of points; section, headings and by reference numbering (1, 1.1, 1.2, 1.3, 1.1.1, etc.) and by emphasizing the important findings by appropriate phrasing.
5. A good report should be brief and precise. It should give its findings without ambiguity.
6. A good report should not go beyond the *terms of reference.* Terms of reference include the instructions received form the appointing authority for the commission which is going to investigate a particular problem and then submit its report. Terms of reference determine the scope and limitations of a report.
7. *Objective* of the report be clearly formulated *vis-à-vis* the terms of reference of the report.
8. The presentation should be logical.

Structure and Layout of a Report

If we start with the **main body** of the report, then what comes before it is called the **front matter** and what comes after it is called the **backmatter** (Figure 17.1). Below we discuss the different parts that go under these heads.

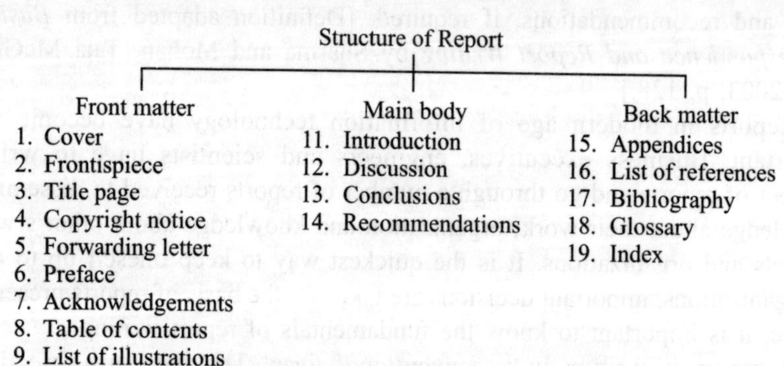

FIGURE 17.1 Structure of a report.

Notice all the above nineteen elements are not obligatory for all kinds of reports. Only *title page*, *introduction* and *discussion* are obligatory. Further, these nineteen elements do not indicate the sequence in which one finds them in all kinds of reports. They only suggest that maximally in a report these nineteen elements can appear. Below we present a brief description of each of the above nineteen elements.

Front Matter

Cover

A cover has a utilitarian value; protecting the manuscript form damage. It may contain (i) the title of the report, (ii) its number, (iii) the date and (iv) the classification (secret, top secret, etc.). A sample cover is given below (Exhibit 17.1).

EXHIBIT 17.1 Sample cover

Secret | Report No. 2354

Viability of NSS in Colleges 5 July 2004

Frontispiece

1. Found generally in bound reports
2. A kind of window display
3. The purpose is to arouse the curiosity of the reader
4. Includes photographs, maps and artistic drawings

Title page

1. First right-hand page of the report
2. Includes what has been suggested in the cover
3. Subtitle
4. Name of the author
5. Name of the authority to whom the report is submitted
6. Contract, project or job number
7. Approvals, if any
8. Distribution list

A sample of title page is given in Exhibit 17.2.

EXHIBIT 17.2 Title page

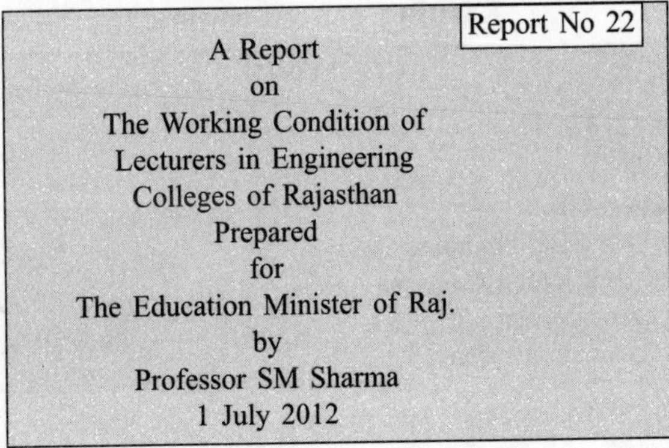

Report No 22

A Report
on
The Working Condition of
Lecturers in Engineering
Colleges of Rajasthan
Prepared
for
The Education Minister of Raj.
by
Professor SM Sharma
1 July 2012

Copyright notice

For the published report, copyright notice is given on the inside of the title page as:

@2012 SM Sharma

Forwarding letter

1. Two types of forwarding letter: covering and introductory
2. A covering forwarding letter is enclosed with the report stating that the report is submitted and a word of appreciation for those who helped.
3. Very close to preface and introduction; a word of appreciation for the assistance received; limitations of the report along with the suggestion for further work.
4. The difference between the *preface* and the *forwarding letter* is that the former is written by the author, the latter by an authority or expert in the field.

Preface

1. Introduction of the report to the reader
2. Contains all the information usually found in the introductory type of the forwarding letter.

Acknowledgements

1. Appreciation for those persons and organizations who helped in the preparation of the report.
2. Mention of permission taken from the publishers to copy copyright material.

Table of contents

1. For more than a report of 10 pages, a table of contents is a must.
2. Helps the reader to locate topics and sub-topics.

Below is given a table of contents for reference (Exhibit 17.3):

EXHIBIT 17.3 Contents

CONTENTS

List of illustrations

1. Its layout is just like the tables of contents.
2. If there are more than 12 tables and figures, a list of illustrations is given after the table of contents.
3. The list includes the page number etc.

Abstract and summary

1. An abstract is shorter than a summary.
2. The purpose of these is to enable a busy reader to gather important information without reading the whole report.
3. An abstract tells us in a condensed form what the report is about.
4. A summary presents the report in a nutshell.
5. Short reports do not carry either an abstract or a summary.

Main Body

Introduction

The introduction is a very important part of the report. It should include:

1. What the report is about?
2. What is the previous work on the subject?
3. What new work is being done in the report?
4. Scope of study including limitations
5. Method of data collection
6. Terms of reference
7. Organization of the material
8. Presentation should be clear and unambiguous.

Discussion or description

1. Includes the main body of the report
2. Presentation of data in an organized form
3. Significance and analysis of data
4. Discussion of results
5. Procedure followed
6. Explanation of the methodology used
7. Some report writers use backward order, i.e. result first and then a statement how they arrived at the results.

Conclusions

1. They include the logical inferences drawn on the basis of the analysis of data or the findings of the investigation made.
2. All conclusions must follow logically from the previous facts discussed in the report. They should be presented in a descending order of importance.

Recommendations

The purpose of recommendations is to suggest a future course of action. Some officials are interested only in this part of the report and take a decision to the effect whether to implement or not to implement them.

Recommendations should be given only when asked for.

Back Matter

Appendices

The material which is necessary to support the main body of the report but too detailed or which can interrupt the attention of the reader is included in the appendix. Questionnaires, statistical data, detailed calculations, sample documents, etc. are included in the appendix.

List of references

While preparing a report, the writer of the report consults a number of published or unpublished works. Mention should be made thereof at the end of the report in alphabetical order.

Bibliography

Generally, only a list of references is given in a report, and not the bibliography. A bibliography includes the complete list of books available on the subject under discussion and is generally included in the research proposal submitted to the University. There are set of conventions to list bibliography. Here are some entries:

1. Seely, John. 1998. *The Oxford Guide to Writing and Speaking*. Third Impression. Delhi: OUP.
2. Mohanraj, Jaya Shree and S. Mohanraj. 2001. English Online. Hyderabad: Orient Longman Limited.
3. Mahaputra, Vijay P. 1973. "Malto Object Classifiers". Indian Linguistics, Volume 34, Number 3, June: The Linguistic Society of India.
4. Singh, S.P. 1976. "Mind Your English", p. 7. The H.T. dated 8 January, New Delhi.

Glossary

A glossary refers to a list of technical words used in the report. It should be given at the end with explanations if the reader of the report is not an expert.

Index

The index is a quick guide to locate the material in the report. It should be listed alphabetically only in big reports.

Having discussed the structure and lay-out of the report, it would be worthwhile to discuss the steps to prepare a report.

How to Write a Report

There are several stages in writing a report:

1. The *purpose and scope* of the report should be defined. The report writer is given a set of instructions (terms of reference) which spell out what is required of him.
2. The tone of the report is set by the *audience/readers* for whom one is writing the report. The report should arouse the right kind of response in the reader. Moreover, the style should be in keeping with the relationship of the writer with the reader. The target audience could be superior officers, customers and general public, colleagues, subordinate employees shareholders and other organizations in similar activities.
3. After setting the objective and the audience, one should go ahead with the *collection of data*. There are several methods and sources for collecting data. We should choose the one that is relevant for the purpose. Some of the methods of collecting data are *personal observation*, *telephone interview*, *personal interview* and *administration of questionnaires*. Among the sources of collecting data are internal *records*, *library* and *internet*.
4. After one has found the relevant material from some source, the report writer should *evaluate* its authenticity and usefulness before taking notes from it.

5. Once the report writer decides that he/she has got the suitable material for writing the report, he/she should make notes topicwise, subjectwise on 3" × 5" cards. It is easy to shuffle the cards around for writing on a topic or subtopic.
6. The next step is to organize the material in a proper form. The best way to organize the material is to make an outline, which provides the starting point as well as the destination. Sharma and Mohan (2003) rightly observe:

   "As a mechanical structure, an outline is an arrangement of words, phrases or sentences which indicate the nature and sequence of topics and subtopics to be discussed in your report. The elements that constitute it are numbered and sub numbered according to their remark and relationship with one another. An outline thus shows which topics are more important, which are of equal status and which are subordinate." (p. 159)
7. Once the material is ready, then comes the question of style. A good report should contain three virtues of style and they are *precision, conciseness* and *plainness.* Precision lies in specific word against general, concrete words instead of abstract words. The use of short and familiar words contributes to the plainness in style. Clichés, jargon and foreign expressions be used only if necessary. Simple and compound sentences should be preferred over complex sentences.
8. To present data in an integrated and condensed manner, the illustrations should be used. The types of illustrations used in a report are table, graphs (reline graphs, semi-log graphs, bar graphs, pie graphs, pictorial graphs, scatter graphs, circular graphs, square graphs), charts (organization charts, flow charts, block charts), maps, photographs, drawings, circuit diagrams, sectional views and exploded views of things. The kind of information and the objective determine the type of illustrations to be used in a report.
9. Make a *rough draft* from the outline prepared.
10. Recall the layout and structure of the report. In that layout, the *cover* comes first and the *index* in the last. But while writing a report, this order should be changed. Sharma and Mohan (2003) suggest the following order: discussion, conclusions, recommendations (if any), appendices, introduction, preface, summary, abstract, glossary and index. The other parts of the report do not require any kind of rough work.
11. Go through the rough draft twice before attempting the final draft. First check the structure of the report and then the language and style. If all these things are all right, go ahead and produce the final version.

Types of Report

Reports may be oral or written. Oral reports involve face-to-face communication about something seen or observed. An oral report is ephemeral. An oral report is convenient for the reporter but is very time-consuming for the receiver. A written report is more accurate and permanent. It can be referred to again and again. It is generally formal in nature.

Some written reports could also be *informal.* An education officer visiting several primary schools in his district can write an informal report to an education officer of another district in the form of a memorandum or letter giving him information (2–3 lines or may be longer) about the working of the primary schools.

Formal reports can be of two types: *informational* and *interpretative.*

An *informational report* contains only the data collected or facts observed. It does not contain any recommendations or conclusions.

An *interpretative report*, on the other hand, contains facts as also an analysis of these facts or data and conclusions. It may also have recommendations.

There are some reports that are presented in a prescribed pro forma. These reports include annual confidential reports of the employees, inspection reports of the equipment, inventory reports of the equipment available. These reports are categories of *routine reports.*

Below we summarize all kinds of reports in the following tree diagram Figure 17.2.

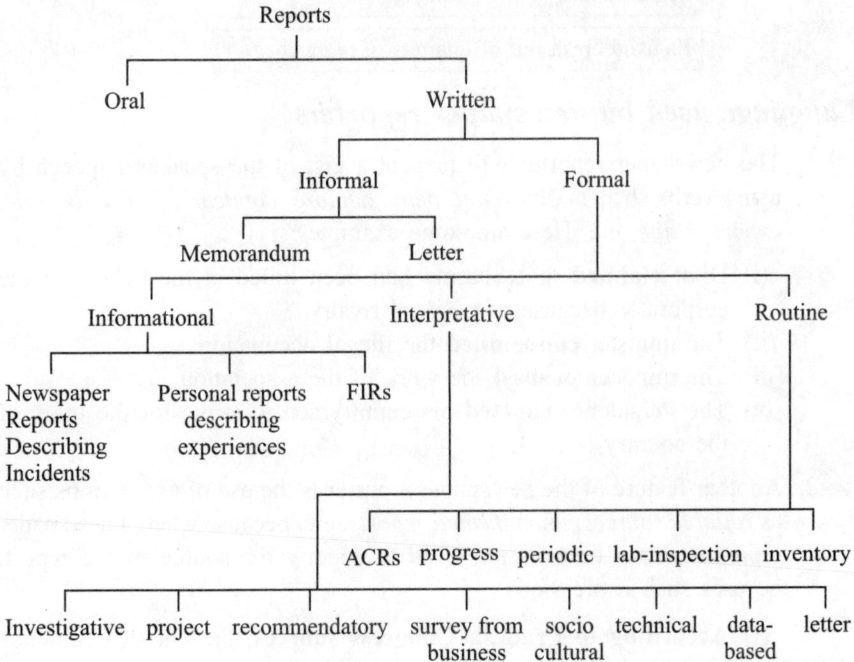

FIGURE 17.2 Types of reports.

Now, we shall discuss the above reports in great detail. We shall start with informational reports.

Newspaper Reports

Newspaper reporters report about all kinds of things: politics, accidents, new discoveries, raids by income tax department, sports, trends in shares, bullion and commodities. See Exhibit 17.4.

EXHIBIT 17.4 Newspaper headlines

Here are some newspaper headlines
Another murder accused nabbed from Kolkata
Congress hits a roadblock on highway to RS
CBI raids 74 places, books 30 officials
Water-borne diseases on the rise
Multi-murder case solved, says police
Tiwari asked to drop corrupt ministers
90 die in Iran road inferno
Sensex gains 48 pts on buying
England crash out of quarters once again

Language used by newspaper reporters

1. The newspaper reporter will present a gist of the speaker's speech by using verbs such as *call upon, deny, deplore, condemn, praise, decline, exhort, claim,* etc. Here are some examples:
   (i) Dixit **claimed** that Sharma had been killed at the behest of the corporator because of political rivalry.
   (ii) The minister **condemned** the illegal occupation ... .
   (iii) The minister **praised** the work of the association ... .
   (iv) The President **exhorted** his countrymen to strive for the unity of the country ... .
2. Another feature of the newspaper reporter is the use of expressions such as *reliable sources, unconfirmed reports,* etc. because when a newspaper reporter cannot or does not want to specify the source of the report, he uses such expressions.
   (i) **According to Pradesh Congress sources**, present PCC chief is likely to be replaced by a younger leader.
   (ii) He **is reported to be seeing** a beautiful blonde for more than a year.
   (iii) The unidentified woman **is said to have** several young children.

(iv) **It is learnt** from reliable sources that the liberal party will not contest the Lok Sabha election from the Kanpur constituency.

3. The reporter can quote the exact words of the speaker involved in the report:
   (i) "Ninety bodies have been recovered but the death toll could rise further," a Red Crescent official in Tehran **told** the student news agency ISNA.
   (ii) "Mohit has a long criminal history", he **said**.
   (iii) "Cash, valuables and securities worth ₹ 28.72 lakh have been seized...," he **said**.

Below we give some authentic examples of newspaper reports (Exhibits 17.5–17.7).

EXHIBIT 17.5 Newspaper report

Dacoity Timetable: This Time Mumbai-Howrah

Patna : In the sixth case of train robbery in less that a month in Bihar, gunmen stabbed a passenger in the early hours of Friday and looted cash and valuables worth more than ₹ 1.50 lakh from an AC coach of the Mumbai-Howrah Mail.

Seven robbers entered the AC-3 tier coach of the Howrah-bound train at Bhabhua road station on the Mughalsarai-Sasaram section of the East Central Railway and went on a looting spree, SP (railways) Vinay Kumar said. They stabbed a passenger and beat up a few others when their attempts to rob were resisted, he said. The gunmen fled after pulling the chain a few kilometers away from Bhabhua station.

Concerned over the spate of dacoities, railway minister Laloo Prasad Yadav ordered suspension of seven RPF personnel and a coach attendant of the Mumbai-Howrah Mail.

Claiming that the dreaded Gupta gang was involved in the dacoity, the minister said steps have been taken to apprehend the culprits. The railways would bear the expenses of the treatment of those injured in the dacoity.

EXHIBIT 17.6 Newspaper report

90 Die In Iran Road Inferno

Tehran: At least 90 people died in southeastern Iran when a fuel truck lost control and crashed a police post, with the explosion engulfing other trucks, cars and buses, the Iranian Red Crescent said on Friday.

"Ninety bodies have been recovered, but the death toll could rise further," a Red Crescent official in Tehran, the provincial capital of Sistan-Baluchestan province, told the student news agency ISNA.

He said 114 injured had also been evacuated from the scene of the accident, which occurred at a police post near Nosrat Abad, some 110 km west of Tehran late Thursday.

The flames engulfed six buses and five other trucks, two of which were carrying tar, causing a massive inferno, state television reported. It also quoted the Red Crescent as saying that up to 200 people may have been killed. Tehran's governor, Heydar Ali Nuraye, said it was impossible to immediately give an accurate toll as a number of bodies and blackened human remains had yet to be recovered.

According to the television, the tanker caught fire immediately after crashing.

EXHIBIT 17.7 Newspaper report

England Crash Out of Quarters Once Again

Lisbon: England's dreams of glory ended in heartbreak on Thursday after more than two hours of gut-wrenching drama culminated in a penalty shoot-out defeat to Portugal.

After finishing 90 minutes of regulation time and 30 minutes of extra time tied at 2–2, the two sides were finally divided by the heroics of Portugal's goalkeeper Ricardo.

After saving England's seventh penalty from Darius Vassell, the Sporting Lisbon keeper stepped up to the spot and slotted the ball post David James.

It was even harsher on England because they thought they had won the match in the last minute of normal time.

Sol Campbell believed he had scored—after Michael Owen's header came back off the bar—but his header was ruled out because John Terry was judged to have infringed Ricardo.

England had begun the shoot-out in the worst possible fashion when captain David Beckham skied the first penalty over the bar and stared ruefully at the penalty spot.

But England received a lifeline when Rui Costa missed Portugal's third in similar fashion.

It was an agonizing blow for England who could and should have won the match in regulation time.

Having led from the third minute thanks to the predatory instincts of Owen, Eriksson's side got to within seven minutes of victory before Postiga's headed equalizer.

Portugal also thought they had the match won when Costa went round Phil Neville and hammered in a stunning strike from just inside the area five minutes into the second period of extra-time.

But with just five minutes left, Frank Lampard latched on to a John Terry knockdown form a Beckham corner to give England another chance.

EXERCISE 17.1

Using the outlines given below, write short newspaper reports.

(i) Ranchi: Hours before train robbery in Bihar – 10 armed men – looted passenger – Ranchi-bound Patliputra Express – at Bokaro – in Jharkhand – Thrusday – dacoits thrashed 40 passengers – before looting – got down –Jhalda – sneak into West Bengal – Third robbery in this area – 8 persons arrested –earlier robberies of –Vananchal Express –Hatia Bardman Express.

(ii) New Dehi: CBI nationwide operation –Friday – raided 74 places – registered 389 cases against 50 people – 30 government servants among them. CBI director US Mishra said – 7 government servants – from UTI, BSNL, Income Tax, Customs, Central Excise, Cement

Corporation – booked for disproportionate assets- cash valuables-of ₹ 28.72 lakh seized – movable – immovable properties – ₹ 7.43 crore identified – raids at 13 places in Delhi – 24 in Mumbai, 7 in Nashik – 3 in Patna, 2 in Hyderabad and 12 in Visakhapatnam.

(iii) New Delhi: Delhi police arrested – Thursday – another accused – in double murder case – in Vasant Enclave – in Kolkata – name Bappi Duppa – main accused Bharat Bhandari – Dutta – killed – retired lieutenant general Seth and wife Roop in flat – morning – Sunday- Dutta hiding –relative's place – Kolkata – arrested Thursday – 4.40 a.m. – Deputy Commissioner Police (southwest) – Dependra Pathak said – Dutta – brought on Friday to Delhi – According to Dutta – robbery planned – by Bharat – he asked Dutta for assistance – he never told Dutta – he would kill couple while doing robbery.

FIRs

First information reports have a legal status.

These reports later on can become bases of suits in courts of law. They should be accurate giving all the details and as far as possible in a chronological order. They are formal in style.

Shyam Sunder leaves his motorbike outside the college. He has come to the college to make enquires about his son's admission to BE I. After half an hour when he comes back to the spot where he had left his motorbike, he found it missing. He lodges an FIR with the SHO Shahjahanpur. This is the report he writes (Exhibit 17.8):

EXHIBIT 17.8 An example of FIR

Main Bazar
8 July, 2012

Neemrana
The Station House Officer
Shahjahanpur
Subject: Theft of a motorbike
Dear Sir,
I, Shyam Sunder Sharma, son of Ghanshyam Sharma, resident of Main Bazar Neemrana aged 35 years went to St. Maragaret Engineering College, Neemrana to make enquires about the admission of my son Ram Sundar who has passed +2 exam this year to BEI.

I reached the college gate at 10.00 a.m. on 8 July, 2012 and left my Hero Honda Motorbike Model 2012, Registration No. RA02 C549, Engine No. N 2354967, chassis No. S 3524321 bought on 10 January 2012 from Tractor Station Aerodrome Road, Alwar, for ₹ 70000 with insurance form New India Assurance Company, Alwar outside the college gate.

I went to meet the admission officer and after one hour, i.e. at 11.00 a.m. when came back to the spot where I had left my bike I found that the bike was not there. I made enquiries form the guard standing at the gate, who said he did not know anything.

As I have not been able to trace the bike for the last 5 hours, I am lodging this FIR in your office.

I request you to find out who has stolen my bike and have it restored to me and get the thief penalized.

The copy of the bill, copies of registration papers and copy of the insurance papers are enclosed herewith.

Thanking you,

Yours sincerely
Shyam Sundar Sharma

A report in the form of a personal letter

Shyam Sunder writes about the theft of the bike to his friend, Ganesh.

Neemrana
8 July, 2012

Dear Ganesh,

Do you recall the Hero Honda Bike that I bought with you from Tractor Station, Alwar sometime in January this year? Somebody has stolen it from the Engineering College gate.

I have lodged an FIR at Shahjahanpur police station. Tell your dad to call the SHO and ask him to arrest the thief and get my bike restored.

With love and regard to your dad.

With love
Shyam

Notice the informal tone of the personal letter.

EXERCISE 17.2

1. You went to Haridwar on holidays last week. During your absence, your house was burglarized. When you came back, you discovered that all your valuables had gone. Lodge an FIR with the SHO of your locality.
2. Write a report in the form of a letter to your friend describing how you missed a train to Delhi and then managed to reach Delhi by travelling on different trains in order to appear for an important interview.
3. Write a report in the form of a letter to your friend telling him how your train met with an accident but you were lucky to survive.

Laboratory Report

A lab report is a kind of routine report. A laboratory report is characterized by the three principles of accuracy, brevity and clarity.

A lab report differs from a newspaper report and a letter report in the arrangement of the information and in the general tone. Here the information is arranged under a number of headings. The usual headings are:

1. Aim/purpose/objective
2. Apparatus
3. Theory (principle)
4. Procedure
5. Observation
6. Calculation
7. Result
8. Sources of error
9. Precautions

EXERCISE 17.3

1. Rewrite the following observed information in the form of a college laboratory report:
   I prepared copper sulphate from copper oxide in the lab. I put about 1cc of surphuric acid solution in the beaker. I placed the beaker on a gauze on a tripod and heated it over a Bunsen burner until it nearly boiled. I stopped heating and added copper oxide, a spatula measure at a time, until no more reaction, i.e. until on further heating for about a minute after addition a quantity of black solid was still present. I filtered the hot suspension through a fluted filter paper into a crystallizing dish, acidifying the solution with one or two drops of sulphuric acid and allowed it to cool. When cooled, I saw blue crystals of copper sulphate. I decanted the surplus liquid, removed the crystals with a spatula and dried them by pressing on bolting paper.
2. Write a laboratory report on determination of sodium carbonate and sodium bicarbonate by titrating against hydrochloric acid using phenolphthalein and methyl orange indicator.
3. Write a laboratory report on determination of sodium carbonate and sodium hydroxide by titrating against hydrochloric acid using phenolphthalein and methyl orange as indicator.

Inspection reports

There are two types of *inspection reports:*

1. A piece of equipment is inspected to see whether it is functioning properly or requires repairs or replacement.
2. To check a product whether it satisfies the quality control specifications in a particular factory. A specimen pro forma for an inspection report is given below in Exhibit 17.9.

EXHIBIT 17.9 Inspection report on tape-recorders

Number	Make:
Date	Model:
	Type :
	Serial No:
Checked by	

Note: please put a tick (✓) against the relevant item:

(a) Visual inspection — Case: broken/scrached/normal; Head : worn out/ sticky/dusty/normal
(b) Mechanical movement — Stopped/obstructed/run/intermittent/noisy/smooth
(c) Amplifier — Play back: dead/poor/distorted/humming/normal
(d) Recording
- (i) Direct: nil/poor/distorted/normal
- (ii) Microphone: dead/noisy/poor/normal
- (iii) Other source recording: dead/noisy/poor/normal

(e) Frequency response: high frequency missing/low frequency missing/ speaker booming/jarring/normal
(f) General remarks: Signature

Inventory Reports

At the end of each year, it is customary in every organization to take stock of equipment, furniture, stationery, etc. There is a prescribed form for this purpose which is filled in by the person who checks the stock. Here is a specimen report on office supplies (Exhibit 17.10).

EXHIBIT 17.10 Report on office supplies

S.No.	Item	Stock on hand on 31 March 2012
1.	Computer paper	10 reams
2.	Floppy cases	10 (each containing 5 floppies)
3.	File covers	250
4.	Envelopes	
	large	1500
	small	500
5.	Pencils	
	black	5 doz
	blue	3 doz
6.	Ball point pens	
	blue	100
	red	50
	black	100

(Contd.)

S.No.	Item	Stock on hand on 31 March 2012
7.	Clips	6 packets
8.	Pins	4 packets
9.	Punching machine	12
10.	Stapler	1 doz
11.	Stapler pins	12 packets
12.	Registers	20
13.	Notebooks	100
14.	Erasers	100
15.	Fevi stick	12 pieces
16.	Gum bottles	5
17.	Carbon paper	3 boxes

Place .... Checked by ....

Date ....

Signature

Annual Confidential Reports (ACRs)

In almost all organizations, an evaluation of the employee's performance and conduct is done annually. This kind of evaluation is necessary to grant promotion or increment or transfer to the other department to the employee. For this purpose, there is a prescribed pro forma in which there is a list of physical, mental and emotional qualities that are necessary for maintaining the efficiency of an employee. Along with the qualities is given the rating on a five-point scale (outstanding, very good, good, average and below average). The reporting officer simply ticks the appropriate column. The danger in this kind of assessment is that it is highly subjective and some of the reporting officers simply tick the rating of the quality as a matter of routine. Therefore, the form should be such that calls for the decision making on the part of the reporting officer and the reporting officer should use his own words to show the performance of the employee and the comment should be supported by evidence if need be.

Below is given such a form that could serve the purpose for ACRs (Exhibit 17.11).

EXHIBIT 17.11 A sample ACR

GOVT. ENGINEERING COLLEGE BARMER

Annual Confidential Report 2011–2012

1. Name of the employee:
2. Designation :
3. Date of birth:
4. Date of joining the present employment:

5. Length of service under the reporting officer:
6. Nature of work on which employed:
7. Physical personality:
   (i) Appearance
   (ii) Smartness
   (iii) Tidiness
8. Punctuality of time:
9. Character:
   (i) Candidness
   (ii) Intellectual honesty
   (iii) Moral standard
10. Knowledge of the subject:
11. Communication skills:
12. Did he finish the course in time:
13. Attitude towards students:
14. Annual results:
15. What other work he attended to in addition to teaching:
16. His behaviour to
   (i) superiors
   (ii) equals
   (iii) subordinates
   (iv) students
17. Publications during the year:
18. Conferences attended:
19. How does he conduct himself in difficult circumstances:
20. Overall rating:
21. Is he recommended for increment/promotion:
22. General remarks:

Date ....
Place ....

Signature and Designation
of the Reporting officer

The suggested ACR is in no way an ideal one. It is just a sample ACR. Better ACRs can be dervised by the organization. Further, there will be some difference between the ACR of one organization and another.

Progress Report

The progress report is related to the project report, on the one hand and the periodic report on the other. The progress report indicates the progress achieved in the completion of a certain task. The UGC or the research supervisor is always eager to know the progress of research of an individual at a particular time. Parents are very keen to know the progress of their ward at school/ college. A progress report could contain the following information.

1. Name of the work or Project: Teaching Windows 2008 to old employees in the college
2. Nature of the work or project: Practical training
3. Extent of the work to be completed: 1 month
4. The extent to which the work has been completed: MS Office
5. Amount of work left: Powerpoint, Excel and Internet
6. Estimated date of final completion of work: 15 days
7. Reasons for delays, if any: Frequent power-cuts
8. Any other relevant information: Employees are getting less practical training.
9. Signature and designation of reporting officer: S.M. Sharma, Project Officer

Periodic Report

These are the reports that are submitted periodically. For some people, there is no difference between a progress report and a periodic report. A progress report becomes periodic if one is asked to submit it periodically. For others, a periodic report occurs in the form of a printed form. Below we produce it (Exhibit 17.12).

EXHIBIT 17.12 Periodic report

Department of Telecom Mathura

Phone No: 730317
Bill date: 1-8-2012
Due date: 16-8-2012
Pay by date: 21-8-2012

Address:
SM Sharma
A-165 HKM Nagar
Alwar

Previous meter reading	Current meter reading	Total MTRD calls	Debit calls	Credit calls	Free calls	Net chargeable calls
3000	3201	201	0	0	50	151

Details		
	Rent	1-7-2012
		31-7-2012
	Local	1-7-2012
	STD/ISD	31-7-2012
	calls	
	TC/OSC/	1-7-2012
	PC	31-7-2012

Misc.	0.00
Gross AMT	475.00
Service Tax	23.75
Net AMT Payable	498.75
Delayed payment Surcharge	20.00
AMT Payable after due date	518.00

Accounts Officer Ph 237310 S.H. Khatri

Report from Industry

A survey report form a business and industrial organization is given below (Exhibit 17.13). Contents and summary have been done away with and conclusion and recommendations have been combined. The data was collected through personal contact and the conclusions reached helped the organization to decide to manufacture a new brand of detergent powder aimed at lower and lower middle classes in the villages and towns of Rajasthan.

EXHIBIT 17.13 Report No. M 30

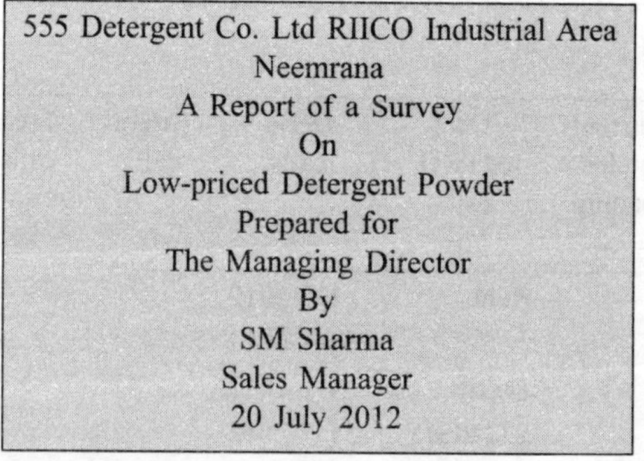

555 Detergent Co. Ltd RIICO Industrial Area
Neemrana
A Report of a Survey
On
Low-priced Detergent Powder
Prepared for
The Managing Director
By
SM Sharma
Sales Manager
20 July 2012

Introduction

Detergent cakes and powders have recently become very popular among the masses because of the rich lather and the dirt and stain fighting capacity of these products. Rin, Rin Supreme, Wheel, Nirma and other brands are very popular among the upper and upper-middle classes. Middle and lower classes find it very difficult to buy these products because of their high cost.

The company, therefore, wants to explore the possibility of entering into the production of low-priced detergent powder aimed at middle and lower classes in the villages and towns in Rajasthan.

The Managing Director, therefore, ordered a market survey with the following objectives:

1. To find out the extent of the prospect of low priced detergent powder as a washing medium
2. To identify the reasons for the popularity of brand detergent powder
3. To consider the feasibility of launching a new brand low-priced detergent powder

Sample selection

The respondents were selected from villages and towns of Rajasthan. For this purpose, two places were chosen from west Rajasthan, two from north Rajasthan, two from south Rajasthan and two from east Rajasthan. The respondents (10 from each village/town) were given a questionnaire in which they had to give answers to the above three questions (or terms of reference). The respondents were selected from middle and lower middle classes. They belonged to different occupations and age groups. A few retailers were also interviewed. The place-wise break up of the respondents is given in Table 17.1:

TABLE 17.1 Place-wise break-up of respondents

Place	*No. of Respondents*
Behror	10
Deeg	10
Bara	10
Bundi	10
Churu	10
Ratangarh	10
Balotara	10
Pokaran	10
Kishangarh	10
Nagaur	10
Total	100

Findings

Washing Media and Comparative Extent of their Acceptance

Detergent cakes

Cakes are very popular with all sections of society. The non-detergent cakes are not used any more. Detergent cakes are easy to use, lather easily and are great dirt and stain removers. But since these cakes are comparatively expensive, they are used only by upper, and upper middle class people.

Detergent powder

There are two types of detergent powder, high priced and low priced. High priced detergent powder includes *Surf Excel*, *Aerial* and *Tide*. Among low priced detergent powders, is Nirma, Wheel, 555, Doctor, Ghari, Fena, etc. But this powder is available only in 1 kg packs and only middle class people can buy it. It is beyond the reach of lower middle and lower class people.

Powder is more popular than cakes with all sections of society because it is easier to use, saves time and efforts.

Extent of acceptability of detergent powder as a washing medium

1. As said above, detergent powder is popular among all sections of society.
2. High priced detergent powder such as Surf Excel, Aerial and Tide is used by upper and upper middle class people.
3. Middle class people use *Wheel*, *Nirma*, *Ghari*, *Fena*, etc. because they are cheaper than the ones mentioned in 2.
4. Middle and lower class people are looking for a low priced detergent powder which has the quality of 2 and 3 but are quite cheap.
5. Middle and lower class people are looking for small sachets (priced ₹ 1 or ₹ 2) which they can buy on day-to-day basis.

Conclusions and Recommendations

Detergent power is popular among all sections of society.

To boost the sales of detergent powder 555 which is very popular, care should be taken to make it popular among middle and lower class people. This can be done by making sachets of ₹ 1 and ₹ 2 to be made available so that middle class and lower middle class people can buy it without compromising their bill on necessities of life, i.e. food, etc.

Letter Report

A letter report is written from an official to a higher authority informing him of an untoward situation that has developed in a district where he is serving as an administrator. The letter informs him what the situation is like, what measures the administrator has taken to set the things right and, lastly, what kind of help the government should give to improve the situation. Let us take an example.

The Collector of Jaiselmer writes a letter to the Chief Secretary, State Government of Rajasthan informing him of *drought* in the district (Exhibit 17.14).

EXHIBIT 17.14 A sample letter report

From 8 July 2012
The District Collector
Jaiselmer District
Jaiselmer
To
The Chief Secretary
State Govt. of Rajasthan
Jaipur.
Subject: Report about the drought in the district
Sir,

May I bring to your kind attention that the district of Jaiselmer has been in the grip of drought for the last 3 months. It has not rained at all during the Mansoon season. As a result of this, a famine like situation has developed in the district.

Last week I went on the spot to study the situation. I visited hundreds of villages that have been reduced to ghost villages. People have fled from the villages. The crops have been damaged completely because of lack of irrigation. Thousands of cattle have died because of lack of fodder and drinking water. The water level in the wells has gone very low. Some of the wells have dried up. There is an acute shortage of water. There are no jobs in the villages. As a result of this, thousands of villagers are running to the cities in search of better opportunities. There is also acute shortage of food in the villages.

Several NGOs have come to help the villagers. They have opened relief camps where they are providing food to the people, fodder to the cattle and drinking water to the thirsty. The government is sending tankers of water for distribution to the areas where there is scarcity of water. They are also sending fodder for the cattle and free ration to the hungry.

But the situation is so grim that it needs immediate attention by the government.

Larger supplies of food grains, fodder and drinking water will go a long way in easing the problem.

I, therefore, request you to send more help.

The detailed report of the drought will be sent to you later.

Yours faithfully
Suraj Sharma
District Collector

EXERCISE 17.4

1. Gupta Education Society wants to set up a technical college either in RIICO Industrial Area, Kotputli, or in RIICO Industrial Area, Behror. The land they are getting in Kotputli is 25 acres whereas the other one

in Behror is 10 acres. Further, there is no college near Kotputli whereas there is one college in Neemarana. The feeding institutions near Kotputli are four, i.e. Kotputli, Bansur, Nareda and Paota, whereas there are only three in Behror region. Write an investigation report advising where the society should set up the technical college and why.

2. The Computer Association of Rural Institute of Engineering and Technology, Bhopal, celebrated their annual function last week. They invited the State Minister for Technical Education to be the Chief Guest. The members of the Association presented a scintillating cultural programme on this occasion. The Chief Guest also gave away the prizes to those who made a mark in different sports events and debates and quizzes. Write a *report* describing the function.
3. Write a report on the Annual Result 2012 of the students in different branches of engineering. Here is a table giving you results of the last four years of Rural Institute of Engineering and Technology of Bhopal.

	Percentage			
Year	*CE*	*EC*	*IT*	*El and C*
2009	80	70	50	48
2010	30	60	40	45
2011	27	55	35	42
2012	25	50	32	40

What conclusions do you draw from the table?

4. Imagine that you are the District Collector. Your district has been affected by the worst floods of the season. Write a letter report to the Chief Secretary of your state giving him all the details about the flood situation in your district.
5. You are the Sales Manager in a detergent company. Your General Manager wants to launch upon a new kind of bathing soap containing *neem.* Write a survey report giving reasons whether this bathing soap will be popular among the people.
6. A student of your college has been injured while playing football. Write a trouble report of the accident which injured the student. Clearly bring out the cause of the accident, the nature and extent of injury, and the medical aid given to the student.

18

Vocabulary

Word Formation Processes

In each language, there are several word formation processes. Noted among these are prefixation and suffixation. Prefixes generally do not change the word class of the stem.

Suffixes frequently change the word class of the stems to which they are added. Below we shall discuss main prefixes and suffixes.

Prefixes

Table 18.1 provides a list of some prefixes.

TABLE 18.1 List of prefixes

Prefix	*Meaning*	*Example*
a-	on, in	ahead, asleep around, awake, await
a-(Greek prefix)	not, without	atheist, anarchist
a-, ab-(Latin prefix)	away from	abnormal, apart, abstain, absurd
ante-(Latin prefix)	before	ante-room antecedent
anti-	against	antipathy, anti-septic anti-corruption
al-	all	almighty God almost, alright
arch-	highest, worst	arch-enemy, arch-duke
auto-	self	autobiography, autograph, autonomy, autocracy, automatic, automobile

(*Contd.*)

TABLE 18.1 List of prefixes (*Contd.*)

Prefix	*Meaning*	*Example*
bene-	well	benevolent, beneficent benefactor
bi-	two	bicycle, bi-weekly, binoculars, bifocal
circum-	around	circumference, circumstances, circumcision
co-	together	co-operation, co-author co-education, co-ordination, co-existence
contra-	against	contradict, contraband
counter-	in opposition to	counteract, counter claim
de- (Latin)	down, from	descend, dethrone, decrease, decline, denationalize, decontrol, defrost
dis-	opposite of	disagree, disappear, dishearten, dishonor, dislike, disgrace, disconnect
ex-	former	ex-husband, ex-boyfriend, ex-minister
extra-	beyond, outside	extraordinary, extracurricular
fore-	before	forewarn, foresee, foresight, forerunner, foretell
il-, ir-	opposite of	illogical, illegible, irresponsible, illegal, irregular
hyper-	extremely	hypersensitive, hypertension
inter-	between, among	international, interchange, interstate
intra-	within	intra-class, intra-state
mal-	badly	maltreat, malfunction malpractice, malafide
mis-	bad, wrong opposite	misbehaviour, misfit, misrepresent, mislead, misguide
mono-	single, one	monologue, mono-syllable, monotheism, monogamy
multi-	many	multi-strayed, multi-national multi-purpose
non-	not	non-smoker, non-violence, nonsense, non-existence
omni-	all	omnipresent, omniscient
out-	beyond	outnumber, outsmart outline, outdo
over-	above, beyond too much	over-work, overthrow, overhaul, overtake

(*Contd.*)

TABLE 18.1 List of prefixes (*Contd.*)

Prefix	*Meaning*	*Example*
post-	after, behind	post-mortem, post-script, post-dated, posthumous, post-meridiem
pre- (Latin)	before	pre-university, pre-historic, preamble, precede, predict, precaution
pro-	forth, forward	pronoun, progress, promote, proceed, procedure
proto-	first, original	prototype
re-	again	refresh, renew, refund, reconsider, recall, recollect
semi-	half	semi-final, semi-circle semi-conscious
sub-	under	sub-inspector, sub-marine, sub-conscious, subordinate, sub-divide
sur-	over and above	surtax
super-	over, above more or greater than	superior, superlative, supervision, superfine, superficial
trans- (Latin)	across, beyond over	transplant, transfer, transport, translate, transmit, transit
tele-	distance	telephone, telegraph, television, telecommunication, telescope, teleprinter, telepathy,
tri-	three	tripartite, tricolour
ultra-	beyond what is reasonable	ultra-modern, ultra-violet, ultra-marine
un-	not	unreal, unable, unseen, unheard, unholy
uni-	one	union, uniform, universe, unique, unit, university
up-	high, over,	uplift, upgrade, uphill, upset, uphold, uproar, upkeep
vice-	in place of	vice-principal, vice-president
with-	against	withdraw, withhold, withstand

EXERCISE 18.1

Add Prefixes to the following words:
change, appear, logical, told, honesty, throne, bed, personal, filtration, soluble, -spect, -pret, lining, caution, suppose, position, merge, plus, charted, stand,

international, concerned, developed, helpful, calculable, limited, combustible, place (v), prove, able, -technique, meter, systematic, necessary, helpful, successful, fulfilled, -ester, -technical, -scale, productive, -employed, change, -national, dependent, action, arrange, cover, play, count, address, appear, affected, pure, ability, list (v), metals, balanced, audible, -data, well, connect, -crease.

Suffixes

Having discussed the role of prefixation in the word formation processes, we shall now discuss highly productive processes of suffixation. There are two types of suffixes as shown in Figure 18.1

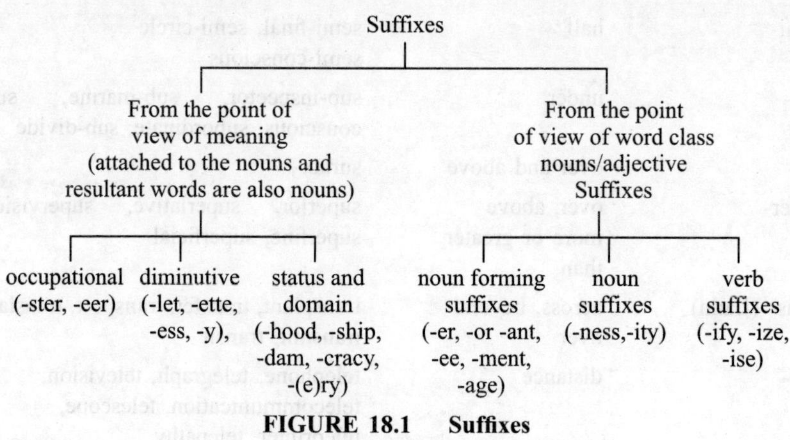

FIGURE 18.1 Suffixes

Below is given a sample list of suffixes (Table 18.2).

TABLE 18.2 Sample list of suffixes

Types of suffix	*Suffix*	*Meaning*	*Class to which added*	*Example*
occupational	-ster	person engaged in an occupation	nouns	gang + ester
diminutive	-ette	small	nouns	kitchen + ette
feminine	-ess	female	nouns	waiter + ess
status	-hood	status	nouns	boy + hood
domain	-dom	domain	nouns	king + dom
noun/adjective	-ism	attitude	nouns	ideal + ism
noun/adjective	-ese	nationality	nouns	China + ese = Chinese

(*Contd.*)

TABLE 18.2 Sample list of suffixes (*Contd.*)

Types of suffix	*Suffix*	*Meaning*	*Class to which added*	*Example*
noun	-ee	passive	verbs	employ + ee
noun	-ment	state, action	verbs	amaze + ment
noun	-ness	state quality	adjectives	happy + ness
verb	-fy	causative	adjectives	simple + fy = simplify
	-ize	causative	adjectives	popular + ize
adjective	-ful	having	nouns	use + ful
	-ly	having the...	nouns	coward + ly
other adjectives	-able	able, of, or like	gradable	read + able
	-ish	something	adjectives	young + ish
adverb	-wise	in the name of	nouns	money +wise

Below we give a detailed list of formation of words with the help of suffixes (Table 18.3).

TABLE 18.3 Formation of nouns from verbs

Verbs	*Nouns*	*Verbs*	*Nouns*
abide	abode	confide	confidence
abound	abundance	consider	consideration
accede	access	consume	consumption
act	action	contain	contents
admit	admission	contend	contention
adore	adoration	contradict	contradiction
advise	advice	convert	conversion (also convert)
agree	agreement	deal	deal, dealer
apply	application	deceive	deceit, deception
apprehend	apprehension	decide	decision
approve	approval	defend	defense
arrive	arrival	defer	deferment, deference
ascend	ascent	defy	defiance
assist	assistance	deliver	delivery, deliverance
assume	assumption	deny	denial
assure	assurance	depart	departure
attach	attachment	descend	descent
attend	attention, attendance	die	death
		diminish	diminution
avow	avowal	dine	dinner

(*Contd.*)

TABLE 18.3 Formation of nouns from verbs (*Contd.*)

Verbs	*Nouns*	*Verbs*	*Nouns*
bear	birth	discover	discovery
		dismiss	dismissal
		distinguish	distinction
behave	behaviour	disturb	disturbance
believe	belief	do	deed
belong	belongings	drive	driver
betray	betrayal	enjoy	enjoyment
bind	bond	enter	entry, entrance
bite	bite	envelop	envelope
bless	blessing	err	error
break	breach	exceed	excess
burn	burn	excel	excellence
bury	burial	exist	existence
carry	carriage	expect	expectation
certify	certificate	expel	expulsion
choose	choice	extend	extension
commit	commitment	fail	failure
compel	compulsion	float	fleet
comply	compliance	flow	flood
concede	concession	fly	flight
give	giver	receive	receipt, reception
go	goer	recover	recovery
grieve	grief	redeem	redemption
grow	growth	reduce	reduction
hate	hatred	refuse	refusal
heal	health	relieve	relief
imagine	imagination	rely	reliance
imitate	imitation	remember	remembrance
interface	interference	repeat	repetition
introduce	introduction	resolve	resolution
insure	insurance	respond	response
invite	invitation	reveal	revelation
judge	judgment	secure	security
		see	sight
know	knowledge	seize	seizure
laugh	laughter	sell	sale
learn	lore, learning	serve	service
lend	loan	shake	shock
live	life, living	sing	song
lose	loss, loser	sit	seat
maintain	maintenance	slay	slaughter

(*Contd.*)

TABLE 18.3 Formation of nouns from verbs (*Contd.*)

Verbs	*Nouns*	*Verbs*	*Nouns*
manage	management, manager	solve	solution
marry	marriage	speak	speech
mean	meaning	steal	stealth (by stealth = done *secretly*)
mix	mixture		
move	movement, motion		
obey	obedience	strike	stroke, strike
object	objection	strive	strife
occupy	occupation	succeed	success
offend	offence	sustain	sustenance
oppose	opposition	tell	tale
perform	performance	think	thought
permit	permission	trace	track
please	pleasure	try	trial
practise	practice	unite	union, unity, unison
presume	presumption	vacate	vacancy, vacation
pretend	pretence, pretension		
proceed	procedure, process	vary	variety, variance, variation
prophesy	prophecy		
protect	protection		
prove	proof	weave	web
provide	provision	wed	wedding
pursue	pursuit	weigh	weight
quote	quotation	write	writing, writ

Some examples of formation of nouns from adjectives are given in Table 18.4.

TABLE 18.4 Formation of nouns from adjectives

Adjectives	*Nouns*	*Adjectives*	*Nouns*
able	ability	noble	nobility
abundant	abundance	novel	novelty
accurate	accuracy	obedient	obedience
active	activity	one	oneness
brave	bravery	perfect	perfection
brief	brevity	pious	piety
broad	breadth	poor	poverty, poorness *quality of a material*
busy	business		
clam	calmness	popular	popularity

(*Contd.*)

TABLE 18.4 Formation of nouns from adjectives (*Contd.*)

Adjectives	*Nouns*	*Adjectives*	*Nouns*
casual	casualty, casualness	precise	precision
		private	privacy
certain	certainty	proud	pride
cheap	cheapness	prudent	prudence
cruel	cruelty	pure	purity
curious	curiosity	real	reality
deep	depth	rival	rivalry
efficient	efficiency	safe	safety
equal	equality	scarce	scarcity
excellent	excellence	secret	secrecy
false	falsehood, falsity	short	shortage, shortness
free	freedom	solitary	solitude
gallant	gallantry	splendid	splendour
gay	gaiety	strong	strength
generous	generosity	stupid	stupidity
grand	grandeur	sweet	sweetness
happy	happiness	swift	swiftness
high	height	timid	timidity
holy	holiness	true	truth
hot	heat	vacant	vacancy
human	humanity	vain	vanity
humble	humility	violent	violence
inferior	inferiority	vital	vitality
just	justice	weak	weakness
long	length	wide	width
merry	merriment	wise	wisdom
mortal	mortality	young	youth
necessary	necessity		

Some examples of formation of abstract nouns are given in Table 18.5.

TABLE 18.5 Formation of abstract nouns

Concrete nouns	*Abstract nouns*	*Concrete nouns*	*Abstract nouns*
agent	agency	hero	heroism
author	authorship	infant	infancy
baby	babyhood	king	kingship
beggar	beggary	man	manhood
bond	bondage	martyr	martyrdom
broker	brokerage	mother	motherhood

(*Contd.*)

TABLE 18.5 Formation of abstract nouns (*Contd.*)

Concrete nouns	*Abstract nouns*	*Concrete nouns*	*Abstract nouns*
child	childhood	owner	ownership
coin	coinage	patriot	patriotism
coward	cowardice	pilgrim	pilgrimage
dacoit	dacoity	priest	priesthood
enemy	enmity	robber	robbery
father	fatherhood	servant	service
friend	friendship	slave	slavery

A few examples of formation of verbs from nouns are given in Table 18.6.

TABLE 18.6 Formation of verbs from nouns

Nouns	*Verbs*	*Nouns*	*Verbs*
air	aerate (to air clothes)	danger	endanger
apology	apologize	defiance	defy
authority	authorize	dew	bedew
bath	bath, bathe	drop	drip
beauty	beautify	economy	economize
belief	believe	electricity	electrify
black	blacken	example	examplify
bliss	bless	food	feed
blood	bleed	fool	befool
body	embody	force	force, enforce
breath	breathe	fraud	defraud
brood	breed	friend	befriend
camp	encamp	fight	fight
capital	capitalize	frost	freeze
centre	centralize, concentrate	fruit	fructify
		game	gamble
character	characterize	class	classify
claim	claim, acclaim	glory	glorify
colony	colonize	gold	gild
company	accompany	grass	graze
courage	encourage	grief	grieve
critic	criticize	guile	beguile
custom	accustom	habit	habituate
harmony	harmonize	half	halve
haste	hasten	hand	hand, handle
head	behead	prison	imprison
heir	inherit	red	redden

(*Contd.*)

TABLE 18.6 Formation of verbs from nouns (*Contd.*)

Nouns	*Verbs*	*Nouns*	*Verbs*
horror	horrify	roll	enroll
idol	idolize	sale	sell
joy	enjoy	sermon	sermonize
justice	justify	shelf	shelve
knee	kneel	siege	besiege
knot	knit	slave	enslave
life	live	society	associate
light	light, lighten	spark	sparkle
mass	amass	substance	substantiate
memory	memorize, commemorate	sympathy	sympathize
		system	systematize
mind	remind	table	tabulate
monopoly	monopolize	terror	terrify, terrorize
nation	nationalize	throne	dethrone, enthrone
nature	naturalize	title	entitle
necessity	necessitate	tomb	entomb
office	officiate	utility	utilize
patron	patronize	vacancy	vacate
peace	pacify	vapour	evaporate
person	personify	vice	vitiate
	personate	victim	victimize
		vigour	invigorate
		wreath	wreathe

A few examples of formation of verbs from adjectives are given in Table 18.7.

TABLE 18.7 Formation of verbs from adjectives

Adjectives	*Verbs*	*Adjectives*	*Verbs*
able	enable	deep	deepen
abundant	abound	dense	condense
base	debase	different	differentiate
bitter	embitter	equal	equalize
bold	embolden	false	falsify
brief	abbreviate	familiar	familiarize
broad	broaden	feeble	enfeeble
calm	becalm	fertile	fertilize
certain	ascertain	fine	refine
cheap	cheapen	firm	confirm, affirm
clean	clean, cleanse	fond	fondle

(*Contd.*)

TABLE 18.7 Formation of verbs from adjectives (*Contd.*)

Adjectives	*Verbs*	*Adjectives*	*Verbs*
civil	civilize	foul	defile
clear	clear, clarify	fresh	refresh
dark	darken	general	generalize
dear	endear	glad	gladden
hale	heal	pure	purify
hard	harden	quite	quieten
high	heighten	rare	rarefy
humble	humiliate, humble (to humble oneself)	real	realize
		rich	enrich
just	justify	short	shorten
large	enlarge	sick	sicken
little	belittle	solid	consolidate
liquid	liquefy		solidify
long	lengthen, elongate	special	specialize
		stable	stabilize
low	lower	strange	estrange
mad	madden	strong	strengthen
moist	moisten	stupid	stupefy
new	renew	sure	ensure
noble	ennoble	sweet	sweeten
particular	particularize	thick	thicken
perpetual	perpetuate	timid	intimidate
poor	impoverish	vile	vilify
popular	popularize	venerable	venerate
proper	appropriate	white	whiten
public	publish, publicize	wide	widen

A few examples of formation of adjectives from nouns are given in Table 18.8.

TABLE 18.8 Formation of adjectives from nouns

Nouns	*Adjectives*	*Nouns*	*Adjectives*
accident	accidental	boy	boyish
advantage	advantageous	brass	brassy, brazen
adventure	adventurous	brother	brotherly
advice	advisable	burden	burdensome
affection	affectionate	bush	bushy
air	airy	calamity	calamitous
ancestor	ancestral	capacity	capacious

(*Contd.*)

TABLE 18.8 Formation of adjectives from nouns (*Contd.*)

Nouns	*Adjectives*	*Nouns*	*Adjectives*
angel	angelic	centre	central
angle	angular	ceremony	ceremonial,
atmosphere	atmospheric		ceremonious
authority	authoritative	character	characteristic
autumn	autumnal	cheer	cheerful
beauty	beautiful	child	childish,
black	black, blackish		childlike
blood	bloody	circle	circular
body	bodily	circumstance	circumstantial
book	bookish	class	classic, classical
climate	climatic	fire	fiery
cloud	cloudy	fish	fishy
colony	colonial	flesh	fleshy
comfort	comfortable	flower	flowery
commerce	commercial	fog	foggy
condition	conditional	fool	foolish
conscience	conscientious	force	forceful
contempt	contemptible,	fortune	fortunate
	contemptuous	friend	friendly
courage	courageous	fruit	fruitful
coward	cowardly	fury	furious
crime	criminal	ghost	ghostly
custom	customary	glory	glorious
danger	dangerous	god	godly, godlike
day	daily	gold	golden
devil	devilish	habit	habitual
dew	dewy	hair	hairy
discipline	disciplinary	hand	handy
drama	dramatic	harm	harmless, harmful
duty	dutiful	haste	hasty
earth	earthly (not an	health	healthy
	earthly being)	heart	hearty
	earthen (an earthen	heaven	heavenly
	pot)	heir	hereditary
east	eastern	hero	heroic
economy	economic,	hill	hilly
	economical	history	historic, historical
emperor, empire	imperial	home	homely
enemy	inimical	honour	honorable
envy	envious, enviable	hope	hopeless, hopeful

(*Contd.*)

TABLE 18.8 Formation of adjectives from nouns (*Contd.*)

Nouns	*Adjectives*	*Nouns*	*Adjectives*
example	exemplary	horror	horrible
expense	expensive	hour	hourly
fable	fabulous	humour	humorous
face	facial	ignorance	ignorant
faith	faithless, faithful	industry	industrial
fame	famous		industrious
fancy	fanciful	irony	ironic, ironical
fate	fateful, fatal	joke	jocular, jocose
father	fatherly	joy	joyful, joyous
fault	faulty	judge	judicious, judicial
favour	favourable	king	kingly
fear	fearful, fearless	labour	laborious
feather	feathery	law	lawful
fever	feverish	life	lifelike, lively, living
limit	limited, limitless	practice	practical
lord	lordly	pride	proud
love	lovable, loving	profit	profitable
machine	mechanical	quarrel	quarrelsome
man	manly, manful	queen	queenly
medicine	medicinal	question	questionable
memory	memorable	ruin	ruinous
merchant	mercantile	sand	sandy
mercy	merciful, merciless	school	scholastic
merit	meritorious	season	seasonable
metal	metallic		
mind	mental	service	serviceable
	miraculous	shame	shameful, shameless
mirth	mirthful		
moment	momentary	sight	sightly
	momentous	silk	silken
money	monetary	slave	slavish
month	monthly	smoke	smoky
mother	motherly	society	social
muscle	muscular	solitude	solitary
music	musical	space	spacious
mystery	mysterious		
nation	national	star	starry
nature	natural	storm	stormy
navy	naval		

(*Contd.*)

TABLE 18.8 Formation of adjectives from nouns (*Contd.*)

Nouns	*Adjectives*	*Nouns*	*Adjectives*
need	needy, needful	sun	sunny
neighbour	neighbourly	sympathy	sympathetic
nerve	nervous	system	systematic
night	nightly	table	tabular
north	northern	talk	talkative
number	numeral,	terror	terrible
	numerous,	thief	thievish
	numerical	thought	thoughtful,
office	official		thoughtless
origin	original	title	titular
ornament	ornamental	tragedy	tragic
palace	palatial	trifle	trifling, trivial
passion	passionate	trouble	troublesome
peace	peaceful	tutor	tutorial
people	popular,	type	typical
	populous	value	valuable
person	personal	verb	verbal
picture	picturesque	vice	vicious
play	playful	woman	womanly,
vigour	vigorous		womanish
virtue	virtuous	wool	woolen
voice	vocal	world	worldly
war	warlike	worthy	worthy
watch	watchful		
water	watery	wretch	wretched
week	weekly	year	yearly
will	willful, willing	youth	youthful
winter	wintry	zeal	zealous

Idiomatic Uses of Verbs

Certain verbs when followed by certain prepositions or adverbs acquire a new significance. Some examples are given here.

Back out (of): withdraw from an understanding
Back up: support one's claims
Back down: abandon claims
Bear away: win a prize
Bear with: treat forbearingly a person
Bear down: overthrow, crush opposition

Bear up: to keep up spirits, not to despair
Bear out: substantiate a charge
Blow up: *(intr.)* explode: The bridge blew up.
(Tr.): demolish by explosion: The mine blew up the bridge.
Blow out: extinguish a candle
Break with: quarrel with a person
Break into: enter a house by force
Break out: begin suddenly: Cholera has broken out. War has broken out.
Break down: fail in the middle of a speech
Break up: dissolve a meeting
Break up: disperse, disappear
Bring about: cause one's ruin
Bring forth: produce fruit or young
Bring forward: produce arguments
Bring in: introduce a new custom
Bring out: elicit facts
Bring out: publish a book
Bring round: restore to consciousness a person who has fainted
Bring under: subdue rebellion
Bring up: educate or rear a child
Call over: recite the names
Call off: divert one's attention
Call in: summon a doctor
Call up: reach a person by telephone (recollect) a matter
Call forth: evoke applause
Call for: demand an explanation
Call on a person: pay him a brief visit at his house
Carry out: execute one's orders
Carry on: manage business
Carry on with: continue
Carry though: bring safely out of difficulties
Come about: occur
Come down: descend
Come off: take place
Come out: be found out
Come round: recover from illness
Come down upon: rebuke, punish
Cry down: deprecate anyone
Cry up: extol anyone
Cut down: reduce expenditure
Cut out: surpass a rival
Cut off: isolated in the country/by snow
Cut off: disinherited without a penny

Cut off: intercept, interrupt supplies
Draw near: approach
Draw off: divert attention
Draw up: compile a code
Draw up: arrange troops
Draw up: stop at a door
Draw back: recede
Draw in: contract or shorten
Draw forth: elicit applause
Fall off (of demand): deteriorate, decrease
Fall down: collapse
Fall in: concur with another person's opinion
Fall back: retreat
Fall out: quarrel
Fall to: apply oneself to work
Fall to: begin eating a meal
Fall upon: assail an enemy
Fall through: fail, His scheme has fallen through.
Get on: advance, make progress
Get back: recover money
Get back: return to a place
Get off: escape
Get at: discover facts
Get over: surmount a difficulty
Get away: escape
Get through: pass an examination
Get out of: escape from one's clutches
Get on with: agree, live sociably with a person
Give out: emit a smell
Give out: announce a fact
Give away: present prizes
Give over: transfer charge
Give back: restore anything
Give up: surrender a point
Give up: abandon an attempt
Give in: submit, yield
Go into: examine, investigate a matter
Go back upon one's word: fail to keep it
Go thorough: examine the accounts
Go down: sink (of a ship)
Go off: explode
Go out: make public
Go out: be extinguished
Go over: change one's party or religion

Go under: sink, fail, succumb
Hold in: restrain a horse
Hold on: continue, persevere, wait a moment
Hold out: endure, last
Hold out: extend one's arm
Hold up: impede or arrest
Hold up: support anything
Hold back: restrain a person
Hold over: postpone a case
Keep up: maintain one's energy/progress
Keep on: continue
Keep under: hold in subjection
Keep to: adhere to a course, a schedule
Keep back: conceal a secret
Lay down: resign an office
Lay down: surrender one's arms
Lay out: invest money
Lay up: deposit
Leave off: discontinue
Leave out: omit a word
Let off: free a person, not punish him
Let off: discharge a gun
Let in: admit a person
Let out: liberate a prisoner
Let out: divulge a secret
Look after: take care of an orphan
Look forward to: expect with pleasure
Look into: investigate the matter
Look for: search for
Look on: regard as
Look out for: keep a watch for
Look through: glance through a book
Make out: understand one's meaning
Make out: pretend
Make up: concoct a false charge
Make up: complete an amount, a party
Make up: supply deficiency in a subject
Make it up: be reconciled
Make up one's mind: decide, resolve upon
Make over: transfer the possession of (a thing) to a person
Pick up: rally, improve
Pick out: select the best man
Put in: apply for a post
Put out: extinguish a light

Put out: disconcert a person
Put off: postpone a journey
Put on: assume haughty airs
Put down: suppress a rebellion
Put up: propose a candidate
Put up with: endure hardships
Put forth leaves and shoots: (of a plant) to grow
Run down: deprecate a person
Run after: strive after wealth
Run into: incur debt
Run through: squander away one's money
Run out of: exhaust one's stock of
Set forth: explain one's view
Set forth: start upon a journey
Set apart: reserve some money
Set aside: reject a claim
Set off: embellish a person or thing
Set off: start a firework
Set down: record in writing
Set in: begin, Winter has *set in.*
Set off or out: depart
Set on a dog: make it attack someone
Set up: erect a pillar
Set up: start business as a grocer
Spin out: prolong a story
Stand out: to be prominent
Stand out against: resist
Stand for: represent, signify; *colloq.* tolerate
Stand by: support a person
Stand up for: advocate the cause of
Take in: admit a person
Take in: deceive a person
Take in: comprehend one's meaning
Take off: remove clothes, hat, from the body
Take on: agree to do a task
Take up: occupy one's time
Take up: commence some work
Take up: accept an offer
Take over: become responsible for a duty
Take away: remove anything
Take after: resemble
Take down: write down: Take down his name and address
Throw out: reject a bill
Throw down: cause to fall

Throw up: resign an appointment
Throw off: discard, get rid off
Turn out: empty or clean out a room
Turn out: prove to be a rogue
Turn out: expel
Turn against: become hostile to
Turn up: happen
Turn up: be found, by chance
Work out: solve a problem
Work up: excite a mob

Study also the following examples:

Bear with: tolerate a man's failings
Call for: demand an explanation
Call on: visit a man at his house
Come after: succeed one's father
Come by: acquire something
Come into: enter a house
Come into: acquire a fortune
Come upon: encounter a person
Come near: approach a person
Come over: exult over an enemy or rival
Cry to: implore heaven
Do away with: abolish a rule
Fall upon: assail the enemy
Fall to: apply oneself to work
Get at: discover the facts
Get over: surmount a difficulty
Get through: accomplish a work
Go after: pursue the deer
Go against: resist, oppose the enemy
Go along with: accompany a person
Go beyond: exceed a limit
Hold to: adhere to an opinion
Jump at: eagerly accept an offer
Keep from: refrain from evil
Keep to: adhere to a promise
Laugh at: deride anyone
Lay off: discharge workers temporarily
Long for: desire rest
Look at: behold anything
Look down on: despise anything
Look for: expect anything
Look into: inspect anything

Look on: regard him as wise
Look over: examine accounts
Look up to: respect anyone
Make away with: get rid of a rival
Make off with: abscond with money
Make for: conduce to well being
Make up for: compensate for a loss
Make up to: attempt to win the favour of a person
Meet with: encounter anyone, or with an accident
Pore upon: attend closely to
Put something down to: attribute it to, They put it down to his nervousness.
See about: attend to some business
See to: give attention to one's business
See into: discern one's motives
See through: penetrate one's motives
Set upon: assail an enemy
Stand by: support a friend
Take after: resemble one's father
Think about: consider a scheme
Think of: recollect a point
Think over: consider a subject
Wait on: attend a person.

EXERCISE 18.2

Below are given some words. Make new words from the given words by adding appropriate suffixes:

1. Abundant
2. Acknowledge
3. Accurate
4. Ameliorate
5. Amplify
6. Apparent
7. Appreciate
8. Apprentice
9. Appropriate
10. Arrange
11. Assume
12. Automatic
13. Biology
14. Brilliant
15. Burglar
16. Catalyst (make a verb)
17. Category
18. Characterize
19. Classify
20. Commerce
21. Communicate
22. Consequent
23. Constitute
24. Context
25. Contribute
26. Convey
27. Corrode
28. Creative

29. Critical
30. Curious
31. Custom
32. Deprive
33. Determine
34. Direct
35. Discipline
36. Document
37. Durable
38. Efficient
39. Emit
40. Empirical
41. Equip
42. Establish
43. Estimate
44. Evaluate
45. Expect
46. Extrapolate
47. Fluctuate
48. Guide
49. Hierarchy
50. Ideology
51. Illustrate
52. Immerse
53. Impress
54. Induct
55. Infiltrate
56. Initiate
57. Inquisitive
58. Inspect
59. Insulate
60. Integrate
61. Interpret
62. Invariable
63. Invent
64. Investigate
65. Involve
66. Labour
67. Locate
68. Maintain
69. Manipulate
70. Mediate
71. Mobile
72. Moderate
73. Modern
74. Necessary
75. Neutralize
76. Novel
77. Operate
78. Orbit
79. Outline
80. Paradox
81. Persistent
82. Place
83. Precise
84. Presuppose
85. Produce
86. Provide
87. Purpose
88. Quality
89. Radiate
90. Rectify
91. Reinforce
92. Relevant
93. Reliable
94. Retard
95. Reverse
96. Revolution
97. Secure
98. Significant
99. Skill
100. Specialize
101. Specify
102. Supervise
103. Suspend
104. System
105. Transmit
106. Treat
107. Utilize
108. Valid
109. Verbal
110. Vacation

EXERCISE 18.3

Make new words by adding –al, -ed, -ful, -able, -ily, -ation, -ist, -ence, -ly, -al, -ive, -tive, -ian, -er to the following list where possible:

1. Cycle
2. Cooperate
3. Help
4. Person
5. Inform
6. Integrate
7. Intention
8. Calculate
9. Able
10. Manage
11. Technic
12. Accelerate
13. Occur
14. Misery

EXERCISE 18.4

Write out the words that end with the following suffixes:

-ive, -al, -ic, -ous, -er, –or, -ance, -ship, -ity or –ty, -ian, -ly, -en, -ize, -age, -ture, -ar –ation/tion.

EXERCISE 18.5

Give the verbal forms of the following:

1. Addition
2. Communication
3. Computation
4. Emission
5. Titration
6. Generation
7. Inspection
8. Insulation
9. Fluctuation
10. Transmission

EXERCISE 18.6

Give the noun forms of the following:

1. Audible
2. Convert
3. Direct
4. Detect
5. Operate
6. Rapid
7. Realize
8. Regulate

EXERCISE 18.7

Complete the following, choosing suitable words.

structural	perquisites	development
electrical	per………..	………..ment

metallurgical	per..........	...........ment
medical	commensurate	.............ment
..........al	com........	draftsman
...........al	provident	...........man
..........al	..............ent	
..........al	.... ent	...........man

EXERCISE 18.8

Complete the following groups:

Technocracy	technocrat	technocratic
Bureaucracy	....	....
Democracy	....	....

One Word Substitutions

Substitution is a very good way of enriching one's vocabulary. It helps one in writing summaries and abstracts. It also helps in reading comprehension.

A

Abdication: The act of renouncing the throne by a king
Aborigines: The original or natural inhabitants of a country
Accelerate: To increase the speed of
Acclimatize: To accustom oneself to a foreign climate
Adolescence: The stage between childhood and maturity
Adroitness: Skill, cleverness
Adult: One who has crossed eighteen years of age
Affidavit: A written statement made on oath before a magistrate
Agenda: List of items to be discussed at a meeting
Aggressor: One who commits the first act of attack
Agnostic: One who does not believe in the existence of God
Alien: A person who is not subject of the country in which he or she is in
Alienate: To turn a friend into an enemy
Alimony: An allowance paid by the husband to his wife after legal separation
Altercation: An argument
Alternative: Another possibility (choice)
Ambivert: One who turns thoughts both inwards and outwards
Anonymous: A communication to which no name is appended
Annihilate: To destroy completely
Ambiguous: That which has more than one interpretation

Antagonist: In a state of mutual hostility or opposition
Autobiography: Life history of a man written by himself
Arbitrator: A person who has been authorized by two parties to judge and decide the matter being neutral
Autocrat: A government by one man
Allegory: A narrative describing one subject under the guise of another
Aviary: A large cage where birds are kept
Altruist: One who engages oneself in an activity for the sake of pleasure rather than for financial gains
Alleviate: To lessen the suffering
Allegation: An emphatic charge levelled against a person or a statement against a person
Anachronism: A mistake in the chronological order
Ambassador: A diplomat of the highest rank representing his country abroad
Amnesty: General pardon for political offenders
Amnesia: Loss of memory
Anesthetic: A medicine that makes one insensible to pain
Anemia: Lack of blood
Anarchy: Absence of government; state of complete lawslessness
Anatomy: Science dealing with the structure of human body
Anniversary: The yearly recurrence of the date of past
Annual: That which happens once a year
Anthology: Collection of poems or piece of prose
Anthropology: The science of man
Antidote: A medicine that counteracts bad effect
Antonyms: Words having opposite meaning
Aquarium: Tank in which fishes are kept
Archaeology: A study of ancient buildings
Aristocracy: Government of nobles or aristocrats
Astronomy: Science of planets (sun, moon, stars)
Atheist: One who does not believe in the existence of God
Audible: Can be easily heard
Autonomy: An independent body having its own rules and regulations; a self governing community.
Arsenal: A place where weapons and ammunitions are manufactured and kept
Ambidextrous: One who can make use of both hands with equal effect
Answerable: Liable to be called upon to explain an action
Antiseptic: A medicine which prevents infection by killing germs
Antipathy: Having habitual repugnance
Aquatic: An animal which lives on water
Ascetic: One who practices strict self discipline

Astrology:	The science of prediction of human beings; fate on the basis of planets
Alloy:	A metal that is formed by mixing two types of metals together

B

Brittle:	Capable of being broken
Biennial:	That which happens in two years
Biography:	Life of a person written by others
Bachelorhood:	State of being unmarried (men)
Bigamy:	One having two wives or husbands at a time
Bankrupt:	A person unable to pay his debts
Bilingual:	Speaking two languages
Biology:	Science of living beings
Biped:	An animal with two feet
Bibliophile:	To speak irreverently of gods and sacred things
Botany:	Science of vegetable life
Bourgeois:	One who belongs to middle class
Bureaucracy:	Government by officials
Bohemian:	A man of free and easy habits
Burglar:	One who breaks into a house to steal
Bullion:	Gold and silver before coining

C

Cardiologist:	Specialist who deals with disorders of heart and circulatory system
Credulous:	A simple man who believes easily whatever is told
Cosmopolitan:	Belonging to all the world
Cannibal:	A person who eats human flesh
Catalogue:	A list of books, pictures in a systematic order
Celibacy:	State of remaining unmarried
Celibate:	One who takes a religious vow not to marry
Contagious:	A disease which spreads through contact
Centenary:	Hundredth year
Colloquialism:	Any language in speaking only
Confiscate:	To seize by authority
Compensate:	To give some one something to make good for loss, damage
Cant:	Affected manner of speech
Consummation:	Reaching the final and highest point
Caucus:	A local committee for political party organization
Capitalist:	A moneyed man having lots of investments in the private sector
Census:	Official counting of all the people of the country
Carnivorous:	Animals that eat flesh

Credible: That which can be easily believed
Continuously: Working at a stretch
Contemporary: Persons living in the same age
Congenital: Something belonging to a person from birth

D

Dead- Letter: A letter claimed by no body
Dermatologist: Specialist who deals with problems of the skin
Dictator: A person who exercises absolute power and prescribes conduct
Diplomat: The skill in managing and maintaining international relations
Despot: A tyrant ruler having absolute power, an autocrat
Desecrate: To divert a sacred person to profanity
Destitute: One who is without means of subsistence
Dessert: Item served as the final course of a meal
Duplicity: Nature of double dealing
Delinquent: A person who fails in the performance of his duty
Declamation: Act of speaking oratorically
Detergent: A chemical used for surface cleaning
Demagogue: A democratic orator or political leader or an agitator
Decisive: That which puts an end to all controversies and disputes
Dipsomania: The inability of a person to give up alcoholic drinks
Diagnose: To determine the disease by observing symptoms
Dirge: Mournful songs for the dead
Dotage: Feebleness of mind resulting from old age
Drawn: A match in which neither party wins
Durable: That which lasts for a long time
Drunkard: One who is addicted to alcoholic drinks
Drought: Want of rain
Dowry: Property which a wife brings with her to her husband in the marriage

E

Edible: That which is fit to be eaten
Egocentric: One who is excessively fixated in his own desires, needs
Extempore: Speech delivered without previous preparation
Eligible: Fit to be chosen for the post
Egoist: One who thinks of one's own interest
Egotist: One who always talks of one self
Etymology: The science that treats the origin and history of words
Emphasize: A thing or object on which stress is laid or made
Eradicate: To root out evil or diseases
Entomology: Study of insects
Ethnology: Science of human race

Epitaph: Words inscribed on a tomb in the memory of the buried
Encyclopedia: Book containing information on all subjects
Equilibrium: A state of perfect balance of mind
Effeminate: A man who is womanish in habits
Elegy: Poem of lamentations for the dead
Expedite: To quicken the work
Emancipation: To liberate from
Epic: A long narrative poem
Escapist: One who escapes from the realities of the life out of fear
Epilogue: Concluding part of literary work
Emigrant: One who leaves his country to settle in another country
Excursion: Pleasure trips by a number of persons
Ephemeral: Lasting only for a short period
Espionage: Practice of spying
Exchange: Giving and taking
Executive: A body of government which enforces law
Explicit: That which is absolutely clear
Efficacious: Medicine that produces desired effect
Empiric: One who relies on experience and observation
Expatriate: To send out of one's native country
Exonerate: To free form the burden of blame or obligation
Eulogy: A speech and writing in praise of someone.

F

Foster child: A child brought up by persons who are not his parents
Fratricide: Murder of brother
Fastidious: One who is selected in choice and taste and cannot be easily pleased
Fanatic: A man having narrow and prejudiced religious views
Feminist: One who is devoted to the welfare of women
Fire-proof: A thing that has no effect of fire
Fallible: One who is liable to be erroneous or false, one who is subject to failure
Fictitious: Unreal, not genuine, one who is not real
Flamboyant: A valuable and verbose speech, a colourful personality
Flexible: That may be easily bent
Forgery: Preparing or altering the documents fraudulently
Fortitude: Courage in adversity
Fleet: Number of ships
Fatalist: One who attributes everything to fate; one who believes that every event is pre-determined by destiny or fate

G

Genocide: Act of killing one's clan, family and community
Germicide: Medicine that kills germs
Glutton: One who eats much
Granary: A room for storing grain
Gratuity: Money paid to employees on retirement
Gullible: Capable of being easily duped
Garrulous: One who talks much
Gratis: One gets a thing without payment of charges
Grocer: One who sells fruits, vegetables, pulses
Gynecology: Study of the female ailments

H

Homicide: Murder or killing human beings
Honorary: Post without salary
Homogeneous: Containing elements of the same nature
Hospitable: Disposed to entertaining guests
Hyperbole: An exaggerated speech or writing
Humanitarian: One who generously acts for the welfare of mankind
Hermit: A person who has withdrawn to a solitary place for worshipping God
A person who lives in seclusion for peace
Honorarium: Voluntary money paid for professional services which carry no salary
Heterodox: One who is opposed to orthodoxy
Hypocrite: Pretender of that what is not
Hygienist: One who is careful about his health
Heretic: One who expresses ideas which are not in keeping with the conventional religious teaching
Heterogeneous: Containg elements of opposite nature

I

Idolatry: Worship of God or idols
Ignorant: One who knows nothing
Illegal: Contrary to law; unconstitutional
Iconoclast: A breaker of images; one who assails cherished beliefs
Illegible: Difficult to read what is written
Illicit: That which is prohibited by law
Illiterate: One who is unlettered, unschooled
Illegitimate: That which is not recognized by law
Impregnable: That which cannot be broken through by force
Immigrant: One who migrates to a country to settle there
Immortal: Permanent: undying

Immune: That which is not liable to infection
Immutable: Subject to no change and alteration
Impervious: Incapable of being influenced
Import: Goods received by one country form another
Inanimate: Having no life
Infanticide: Murder of an infant
Introvert: One whose interests are turned inwards
Imposter: One who practices fraud
Infection: Disease spreading through air and water
Infidel: Non believer of religion
Insecticide: Substance used in killing insects
Intelligible: That which can be easily understood
Incorrigible: That which cannot be reformed or corrected
Imminent: That which is likely to happen in future
Invincible: That which cannot be conquered
Inaudible: That which cannot be heard
Irritable: One who gets irritated easily
Insomnia: A disease of sleeplessness
Insurmountable: That which cannot be overcome
Invulnerable: That which cannot be wounded or hurt
Irrevocable: A decision that cannot be modified or changed
Indigenous: Produced or manufactured within the country without foreign aid or collaboration
Illusion: A deceptive appearance, belief or statement
Intimidation: The use of language or gestures which implies threat to some one
Instigation: The act of provoking and goading a man
Incurable: That which cannot be cured
Invisible: That which cannot be seen
Inseparable: That which cannot be separated
Insoluble: That which cannot be dissolved
Insatiable: One who cannot be satisfied
Infallible: One who cannot make a mistake
Inexplicable: That which cannot be explained
Inevitable: That which cannot be avoided, that which must happen
Ineligible: Not fit to be elected or selected
Indispensable: That which cannot be dispensed with
Indescribable: That which cannot be described
Indelible: That which cannot be removed
Indefatigable: That which cannot be tired out
Inaccessible: Incapable of being approached
Impracticable: That which cannot be put into practice
Imponderable: That which cannot be determined
Impenetrable: That which cannot be pierced through

Imperishable: That which cannot be perished
Imperceptible: That which cannot be perceived
Irreparable: That which cannot be repaired
Insolvent: One who is unable to pay his debts
Intimidate: One who restrains by threats
Inflammable: That which catches fire immediately
Intolerable: That which cannot be tolerated
Innumerable: That which cannot be counted
Irrefutable: That which cannot be proved false
Irrelevant: That which is not up to the point
Irrepressible: That which cannot be suppressed
Irreproachable: That which cannot be blamed
Irresistible: That which cannot be resisted
Irresolute: One not firm in purpose
Irritable: One who easily gets annoyed
Irrecoverable: That which cannot be recovered
Itinerant: Wandering from place to place
Irretrievable: That which cannot be retrieved

J

Jurist: A person well-versed in law

K

Know-how: Technical knowledge of a particular work
Kennel: A house where dogs are kept

L

Library: A place where a large number of books are kept for reading purpose
Licentious: One who is extravagant in manners and morals
Linguist: One who studies languages scientifically
Lunar: Of the moon
Legislature: That part of the government which makes law
Lexicographer: One who compiles a dictionary
Loquacious: One who talks unceasingly

M

Maiden-speech: A speech made for the first time
Manuscript: Paper written with hand
Matricide: Murder of one's mother
Mundane: Belongs to the earth. Earthly
Misanthrope: A hater of mankind
Miser: One who spends very little

Mediator: One who plays the role of bringing two opposite parties together
Martyr: One who dies for the noble cause
Mercenary: A man working for money only
Migratory: That which moves from one place to another
Mimic: One who imitates people or someone
Misogamist: One who hates marriage
Monarchy: A government headed by a king
Monogamy: System of only one marriage
Monologue: A scene in a play in which only one person speaks
Materialistic: One who is money minded
Monocracy: Rule of the crowd
Monopoly: Sole right of buying and selling
Mortuary: A place where dead bodies are kept for postmortem
Museum: A place where historical relics and curios are kept for exhibition
Missionary: One who does things with the spirit of service to others
Misogynist: A hater for womankind
Matins: Morning prayer in the church

N

Narcotic: A medicine that causes sleep
Nepotism: Showing favours of high officials to his relatives
Neurotic: One who suffers from nervous disorder
Novice: One who is new in any profession or business
Notorious: Generally known for something bad
Nihilist: A philosopher or thinker who believes that nothing is real

O

Objectionable: Open to objection
Obsolete: That which is no longer in use
Obstetrician: A specialist who takes care of babies and takes care of mother during and after pregnancy
Octogenarian: One who is eighty years old
Occasionally: From time to time
Oligarchy: A government run by a few persons alone
Octagon: An eight-sided figure
Ophthalmologist: Physician whose specialty is in disorders of vision
Optimist: One who looks at the bright side of things and life
Orthopedist: A specialist who deals with the skeletal structure of the body
Ornithology: A study of birds
Omnipotent: One who is all powerful
Omnipresent: One who is present everywhere
Omniscient: One who is of all kinds, forms and varieties

Opaque: That which cannot be seen through
Optician: One versed in optics; one who prescribes looking glasses
Omnivorous: One who eats everything

P

Polygamy: Practice of marrying more than one with at a time
Polyandry: Practice of marrying more than one husband at a time
Philanthropist: A lover of mankind
Philogynist: A lover of womankind
Philology: A study of languages
Patriot: A person who loves his country
Pacifist: One who believes in the total abolition of war
Pessimist: One who looks at the darker side of everything
Philanderer One who amuses himself by love making
Plutocracy: A government by the rich
Patricide: Murder of father
Purist: One who is particular about the purity of one's language
Pedantic: One who displays knowledge for the sake of showing
Pseudonym: An imaginary name assumed by the writer for disguise
Posthumous: A child born after the death of his father, a book published after the demise of the writer
Platitude: Commonplace remark
Plagiarism: Literary theft practiced by borrowing words and ideas from other writers and using them in one's own language
Parasol: A lady's umbrella
Panacea: A remedy for all kinds of disease
Primogeniture: Right of succession belonging to the first born
Pugnacity: Habit of quarrelling or fighting
Pioneer: One who leads others in any field or branch
Ponder: To think carefully
Popular: One who is liked or known by everybody
Pornography: A writing in which sex is dealt with too much frankness to excite the readers
Pedestrian: One who walks on foot
Phonology: A science of vocal, natural sounds
Peroration: A passage marking the close of speech
Psychiatrist: Practical psychologist
Precedent: Some previous examples from the past
Post-moterm: An examination of body made after death
Patrimony: That which is inherited from father
Primitive: That which belongs to early time

Q

Quadruped: Four footed animals
Quiz: A process to examine or test of questions

R

Rebel: One who takes up arms against the government
Remuneration: The amount of money paid to a man for his work or labour
Retrospective: An effect having reference to the past
Regicide: Murder of a king
Redtapism: Too much official formality
Reticule: A little network bag; a woman's purse
Reticent: A person of reserve nature
Ruminate: To meditate: to ponder over a question
Republic: A country where supremacy of elected candidates or representatives is acknowledged
Renounce: To give up entirely
Reminiscent: That which reminds one of something

S

Sinister: Something that is evil, threatening
Simultaneous: Things occurring at the same time
Spendthrift: One who spends his money extravagantly
Somnambulism: The habit of walking while asleep
Soliloquy: The act of speaking one's thought about when alone
Scattered: Things lying here and there
Sociable: A person who likes company
Solar: Of the sun
Sanitarium: A place for invalids
Suite: A set of rooms in a hotel
Smuggle: An illegal import of goods without payment of customs
Sanguine: Abounding in blood
Sophisticated: Extremely refined in dress, conduct and speech, fashionable and modernized
Sadist: One who takes pleasure in cruel and unnatural acts of tyranny
Sychophant: One who flatters others for personal gains and motives
Sacrilege: The act of violating the sanctity of the church
Scape-goat: One on whom the blame of other's sin can be fixed

T

Transcendental: That which is beyond ordinary or common experience, thought or belief
Transparent: Easily seen through or that through which we can see

Toper: A habitual drinker
Theist: A person who believes in the existence of God
Truant: A student who runs away from the class or school without permission
Theocracy: Government by the priests
Tensure: Ceremony of shaving the whole head
Triennial: That which happens once in three years
Twins: Two children born together of the same mother
Traitor: One who betrays his own country and gives secret to enemies

U

Unanimous: That which has been without opposition
Unintelligible: That which cannot be understood
Universal: Belonging to all parts of the world
Usurp: To seize by force and without right
Unambiguous: Order that is absolutely clear
Unnatural: Contrary to natural
Usurer: One who lends money on exorbitant rates of interest
Utilitarianism: The doctrine that actions are right because they are useful; the principle that virtue is based on utility
Unique: That which has no equal
Utopion: An imaginary social and political system

V

Venial: Able to be forgiven or pardoned, a fault that may be forgiven
Verbose: A style which is full of words
Veteran: One who has a long experience of any occupation
Verbatim: Word for word
Vegetarian: One who does not eat meat
Venue: The place of a cause of action
Venal: One guilty of accepting bribes, open to bribery
Veterinary: Science dealing with caring for the health of animals
Vibration: A continuous shaking movement or feeling
Virtual reality: Image created by a computer seen almost real

W

Wardrobe: Place where clothes are kept
Widow: A woman whose husband is dead
Widower: A man whose wife is dead
Wild: An animal that cannot be tamed
Waterproof: That which has no effect of water, able to keep out of water.

Z

Zoo: A place where animals are kept
Zoology: Science of animals

EXERCISE 18.9

In the following question, definitions of twenty words are given. Write one word against each definition.

1. One who knows many languages
2. Being unable to pay one's debts
3. Having an evil reputation
4. One who leaves his country to settle elsewhere
5. One who believes in fate
6. One who plays a game for pleasure and not professionally
7. One who has grown old or has long experience of (especially military) service or occupation
8. One who believes in the existence of God
9. One who abstains from animal food, especially meat
10. One who hates mankind
11. One who loves and works for his fellow men
12. One who lends money at exorbitant rate of interest
13. Not being able to be elected or selected under the rules
14. One who looks at the bright side of life
15. One who looks at the dark side of life
16. One who eats human flesh
17. Not being able to make a mistake
18. Knowing every thing
19. Being all powerful
20. Being present everywhere

Compounding, Blends, Reduplicatives, Clipping and Back Formation

The process of word formation through compounding is very productive in English. According to Langacker (1967), a compound word consists of two or more full morphemes; for example, teapot consists of tea + pot.

One question that arises about the compound is how it should be written, that is, as one word or two words with a hyphen (see Table 18.9)

TABLE 18.9 Different ways of writing compounds

As one word	*As two or more words*	*Written with a hyphen*
playboy	drug store	call-girl
	side sheet	bee-sting
sunrise	washing machine	air-conditioning
flashlight		story-telling
bookstore	brain washing	record-player
sidewalk	cooking apple	window-cleaner
songwriter	typing paper	birth-control
handwriting		sun-bathing
daydreamer	hydrogen bomb	factory-worker
ashtray		pot-belly
blockhead		

It is very difficult to suggest any productive rule for the writing conventions.

About the meaning of a compound word, we can say that the meaning of a compound word is the sum total of its parts in majority of cases. For example, *dancing girl* is the girl who dances. Here the meaning is derivable from its parts. But what about words like *redskin* (American Indian), *greenhorn* (an inexperienced person), *dumbbell* (a stupid person), *redcoat,* (British soldier), *turncoat* (a person who changes his party), *sourpuss* (a person who always complains) and *'paleface'* (a white person), whose meaning are not derivable from their parts.

Below we discuss derivation of compounds (Table 18.10).

TABLE 18.10 Derivation of compounds

Type of compound	*Examples*	*Derivation of first example in terms of syntactic relations*
Nouns	sunrise	The sun rises
	dancing girl	subject + verb
	sightseeing	sees sights
	taxpayer	verb + object
	songwriter	
	windows cleaner	
	blood test	
Noun	Swimming pool	Swims in the pool
	day-dreaming	(subject + verb + adverbial)
	baby-sitter	
	homework	
	searchlight	
	walking stick	
	dance-hall	

(*Contd.*)

TABLE 18.10 Derivation of compounds (*Contd.*)

Type of compound	*Examples*	*Derivation of first example in terms of syntactic relations*
Noun	wind mill toy factory bloodstain doorknob darkroom snowflake blackboard	the wind (powers) the mill subject + verb less object
Adjective	heart breaking man-eating ocean-going hard-working quick-frying	breaks heart subject + verb + object functions as adjectives
Verb	sightsee spring-clean lip-read	sees sights subject + verbs + object functions as a verb

Compounds can be classified in yet another way. This classification is based on the constituent structure (Table 18.11).

TABLE 18.11 Derivation of compounds

Types of compound		*Examples*
Compound nouns	noun + noun	bread-winner, home-maker, bagpipe, hero-worship
	noun + gerund	globe-trotting, face-saving bull-baiting, sooth-saying
	participle + noun	dancing girl, dressing room, walking stick, flying planes
	noun + adjectives	knight-errant, court-martial
	adverb + noun	post-script, after-thought, fore-sight, out-partient
	adverb + verb	outlook, input, outlet, up-start, overthrow
	verb + noun	cut throat, pick-pocket, breakfast, spendthrift passport

(*Contd.*)

TABLE 18.11 Derivation of compounds (*Contd.*)

	Types of compound	*Examples*
	adjective + noun	free thinker, stronghold, double-dealing, layman
	past participle + noun	mince-meat, charcoal skim-milk, driftwood, lock-jaw
	genitive noun + noun	draftsman, pointsman, sportsman, statesman, doomsday, child's play
	verb or noun + adverb	feedback, draw back, passer-by, go-between lock-up
Compound adjectives	nouns + adjective past participle	home side, hen-pecked, frost bitten, wonder-struck,
	adverb or adjective + participle or adjective	water-proof, knee-deep broad-based, far-fetched red hot, long suffering
	noun + present participle/adjective	heart-breaking, time saving ear-splitting, tax-paying, net-worthy
	preposition+ noun	outdoor, undergraduate, postgraduate, up-hill
	adjective+ noun	a bare foot passenger, a multi-pronged attack, a ten-rupee note, a four-year degree course
Compound verb	adverb + verb	out-vote, over-reach, under-sell, out-number, fore-see
	adjective + verb	safe-guard, white-wash, fulfil
	noun + verb	waylay, brow beat, hod-wink
Phrase compound	phrases connected by hyphens	forget-me-not, well-to-do, son-in-law, commander-in chief, good-for-nothing, examination-wise

Reduplicatives

Reduplication is a word formation process in which the sound system of the language is employed to from compounds (Table 18.12). They are generally used in informal style.

TABLE 18.12 Reduplicatives in English

Examples	*Meaning and style*	*Devices followed*
goody-goody	affectedly good informal	two identical lexical items
walkie-talkie	a two-way radio informal	initial consonants are different
criss-cross	marked by cross lines	medial vowels are different
tick-tock	imitating the sound of a clock	medial vowels are different
see-saw	suggests alternative movement	medial vowels are different
wishy-washy	suggests insincerity	medial vowels are different
tip-top	intensify the effect	medial vowels are different

Clipping

The word clipping suggests that in a word, first, middle or final syllable is clipped and the resultant shortened word is used. For example,

Phone for *telephone*
Photo for *photograph*
Flu for *influenza*

Blends

Blending is said to occur in the formation of a word when some sounds of one word are combined with some sounds of another word.

Examples:

1. brunch (br(eak fast) + (l) unch
2. motel (mo(tor) + (ho) tel)
3. smog (smo(ke) + (fo)g)
4. transistor (tran(sfer) + (re)sistor)
5. paratroop (para(chute) + troop)
6. subtopia (sub(urban) + (u)topia)
7. moped (mo(tor) + ped(al))

Back-Formation

The productive process in English is to make *nouns* from verbs. But if there is no verb in English, then in such cases verbs are formed from nouns. Such a process is called back-formation. For example, there was no verb *beg* in English but we had the word *beggar,* then the verb *beg* was formed from *beggar.* Other examples:

Verb	*Nouns*
sidle	sidling
automate	automatic
liaise	liaison
reminisce	reminiscence
baby-sit	baby-sitter
bird-watch	bird-watching
mass-produce	mass-production
hedge-hop	hedge-hopping

EXERCISE 18.10

Study the following compound words that occur in English Communication (OUP), 1977:

Withstand, word-piece, worthwhile, diesel engine, high-speed engines, marine engines, low-carbon, carbon-steel, lay-out, bio-data, cutting tool, tool-part, feed-shaft, tailstock, lead screw, heat stock, lathe bed, compound slide, cross slide, small-scale, draftsman, craftsman.

Make words on the pattern of each of the above compound words.

Compound Words Often used in Engineering Branches

Mother board
Keyboard
Seagate
Anti virus
Digital electronics
Communication engineering
Microprocessor lab
Cathode ray oscilloscope
Function generator
Digital trainer
Multimeter
Screw driver
Noseplier
Voltmeter
Ammeter
Wattmeter
Variable load
Potentiometer
Measurement lab

Descending order
Bread board
Soldering iron
Desoldering pump
Electronic tool box
Jumper wires
Thermometer
Audio oscillator
Colour coding
Photo transistor
Potassium iodide
Nitric acid
Moulding box
Conic section
Plumber block
Measuring beaker
Polarimeter
Dumbles rod
Power rider

Find the meaning of the above words in a dictionary.

List of New Words

In the 1980s and 1990s, more than 2000 high profile hot words entered in everyday parlance. Below are given some of these prominent new words for the benefit of the readers.

1. **Abortuary:** A clinic at which abortions are carried out.
   As a result of the decision we're left where 100 children a month will be killed at the *abortuary.*
2. **Abzyme:** An anti-body that has been changed to give it some properties of an enzyme.
   The new 'artificial enzymes' have been nicknamed as *abzymes.*
3. **Acid jazz:** A style of popular music in which elements of jazz blues and soul are fused with a funky beat.
   Two years ago, at the height of the acid jazz phenomena, the ICA hosted an evening of jazz meets beats.
4. **African-American:** A black American. Nobody uses the term black American, but the African-American is the preferred term now.
5. **Aids:** An acronym for Acquired Immune Deficiency Syndrome.
   Thousands of people die every year because of Aids.
6. **Anorak:** A jocular term used for a person who pursues an interest with an obsession.
   Cyberspace is no longer the preserve of techno-nerds and *anoraks.*

7. **Awesome:** Great
   You did it, Mom! You bungeed!
   You were awesome.
8. **Babe:** An attractive young woman
   You look good. John thinks you are a babe.
9. **Bad hair day:** A day on which everything seems to go wrong.
   Soon you will do less complaining even on *bad hair days.*
10. **Black metal:** A type of heavy metal music with lyrics which invoke the devil and celebrate evil.
    Black metal, a form of hard rock that features explicitly satanic lyrics, was founded by a band called Venom in the early eighties.
11. **Blue box:** A blue coloured box for the collection of recyclable items.
    Brimming blue boxes have been plunked at the end of nearly every drive.
12. **Caffeinated:** "pepped up, with added vigour".
    There is definitely something caffeinated about Nusarf Fateh Ali Khan.
13. **Challenged:** Lacking a physical or mental attribute. Words like physically challenged, mentally challenged, vertically challenged, cerebrally challenged, culinarily challenged, horizontally challenged are in use.
    Celebrity chefs … take centre stage and teach the culinarily challenged to cook.
14. **Cyber:** It is a back formation from cybernetics. It is the first element or so many words that are related to computer mediated electronic communications. Some of the important words are cyber spatial, cyberpunk, cyberart, cyberfeminist, cyberphobic, cybersuit.
15. **Download:** To transfer the contents of an electronic data file from a larger system to a smaller one.
    They now use a … heart rate monitor that download results into a lap-top computer that plots results on a graph.
16. **Dude:** a person, a guy, friend, buddy.
    He pronounced dude like a surfer.
17. **Empower:** Give power to.
    These self-empowered individuals are motivated by team work and developing boarder skills rather that just achieving conventional status.
18. **FAQ:** Acronym for frequently asked questions
    Let me give a list of FAQs for any interview.
19. **Feel-good:** Creates a feeling of well-being in people in the context of financial and material contexts. The opposite of *feel-bad.*
    Bad news for the LJP. The feel good factor was not there at all.
20. **Feminazi:** A contemptuous term for a radical ferminist.
    She is a left-wing radical, liberal feminazi who wants to save the whales.
21. **Foodie:** A person whose main interest is food.
    Foodies are discovering ingredients like red Swiss Chard.

22. **Geek:** An unfashionable, boring or socially inept person.
A geek is also a person who has an obsessional interest in a specified hobby like a *movie* geek or a computer geek.
All my friends thought I was total geek.
23. **Generation X:** Refers to young people who have no sense of direction.
24. **Get a life:** Start living a fuller life.
You should join a club and get a life.
25. **G-7:** A group of seven leading industrialized nations (Canada, France, Germany, Italy, Japan, UK, US). Unlike the UN, the GATT cannot undermine the values that the G7 champions.

Some Idioms

1. **In apple pie order:** 'In perfect order.' Bala puts his desk in apple pie order every morning.
2. **Pushing the envelope:** 'Going beyond the limits.' The new company is beginning to push the envelope in the world of technology.
3. **Laughing up your sleeve:** 'To laugh quietly.' Mahesh pretended to admire Sachin's extempore speech, but we knew that he was laughing up his sleeve at him.
4. **Ringside view:** 'An excellent view of an event'; also 'ringside seat' expression is used.
Rekha was sitting on the terrace and had a ringside view of the accident.
5. **To sail into somebody:** 'to scold someone.' He sailed into her for making such a request.
6. **Cut and dried:** 'Final and unchangeable decision.'
Mala's plans were cut and dried.
7. **A little birdie told me:** An unknown person told me.
A little birdie told me it is your birthday today.
8. **To be all ears:** 'To listen carefully.'
He was all ears when his boss talked.
9. **To be thick in the head:** 'To be stupid'
He is thick in the head.
10. **To throw a wet blanket on the discussion :** 'To discourage'
His comments threw a wet blanket on the discussion.
11. **To face the music:** 'To accept the consequences of'
Now since you have whipped up the sentiments of the students, you have to face the music.
12. **To be an old hand:** 'to be experienced.' He is an old hand at teaching.
13. **To talk nineteen to the dozen:** 'To talk fast.' It is very difficult to understand him because he talks nineteen to the dozen.
14. **To put two and two together:** 'To draw conclusion by putting facts together.'
The police have been able to put two and two together about the murder.

15. **Not to see eye to eye:** 'Not to agree'
I don't see eye to eye with the dean in this matter.
16. **To fall about:** 'to laugh uncontrollably.' We fell about when we heard her reply.
17. **Ten a penny:** 'Very cheap things.'
I bought oranges ten a penny.
18. **To make a song and dance about something:** 'To make something seem more important than it really is.'
I only asked her to move her car but she made such a song and dance about it.
19. **To hold all the aces:** 'To be in a strong position.'
In a situation like this, it is the big companies that hold all the aces.
20. **To be heads and shoulders above:** 'To be better than others.' The Secians are heads and shoulders above other teams.

Key to Exercise 18.1

exchange, disappear, illogical, untold, dishonesty, dethrone, embed, impersonal, infiltration, insoluble, inspect, interpret, underlining, precaution, presuppose, proposition, preposition, submerge, surplus, uncharted, understand, unintentional, unconcerned, undeveloped, unhelpful, incalculable, unlimited, incombustible, displace, disprove, unable, polytechnic, lactometer, unsystematic, unnecessary, unhelpful, unsuccessful, unfulfilled, polyester, non-technical, small-scale, unproductive, unemployed, interchange, international, independent, inaction, re-arrange, re-cover, replay, re-count, re-address, re-appear, unaffected, impure, inability, enlist, non-metals, unbalanced, inaudible, bio-data, unwell, disconnect, increase

Key to Exercise 18.2

1. Abundance	2. Acknowledgement
3. Accuracy	4. Amelioration
5. Amplifier	6. Apparently
7. Appreciation	8. Apprenticeship
9. Appropriateness	10. Arrangement
11. Assumption	12. Automatically
13. Biological	14. Brilliance
15. Burglary	16. Catalyze
17. Categorization	18. Characterization
19. Classification	20. Commercial
21. Communication	22. Consequential
23. Constitution	24. Contextual
25. Contribution	26. Conveyance
27. Corrosion	28. Creativity

29. Criticality
30. Curiosity
31. Customary
32. Deprivation
33. Determination
34. Direction
35. Disciplinary
36. Documentation
37. Durability
38. Efficiency
39. Emission
40. Empiricism
41. Equipment
42. Establishment
43. Estimation
44. Evaluation
45. Expectation
46. Extrapolation
47. Fluctuation
48. Guidance
49. Hierarchical
50. Ideological
51. Illustration
52. Immersion
53. Impression
54. Induction
55. Infiltration
56. Initiation
57. Inquisitiveness
58. Inspection
59. Insulation
60. Integration
61. Interpretation
62. Invariably
63. Invention
64. Investigation
65. Involvement
66. Laborious
67. Location
68. Maintenance
69. Manipulation
70. Mediation
71. Mobility
72. Moderation
73. Modernity
74. Necessarily
75. Neutralization
76. Novelty
77. Operation
78. Orbital
79. Outlining
80. Paradoxical
81. Persistence
82. Placement
83. Precision
84. Presupposition
85. Production
86. Provision
87. Purposeful
88. Qualification
89. Radiation/radiator
90. Rectifier
91. Reinforcement
92. Relevance
93. Reliability
94. Retardation
95. Reversal
96. Revolutionary
97. Security
98. Significance
99. Skillful
100. Specialization
101. Specification
102. Supervision
103. Suspension
104. Systematical
105. Transmission
106. Treatment
107. Utility
108. Validity
109. Verbally
110. Vacational

Key to Exercise 18.3

1. Cyclical
2. Cooperation
3. Helpful
4. Personal
5. Information
6. Integration
7. Intentional
8. Calculation
9. Ability
10. Manager
11. Technical
12. Acceleration
13. Occurrence
14. Miserable

Key to Exercise 18.4

Preventive, Practical, Static, Joyous, Teacher, Director, Performance, Apprenticeship, Ability/superiority, Technician, Beautifully, Lengthen/widen, Criticize/realize, Marriage, Fixture, Singular, Personification. (Alternative answers are possible)

Key to Exercise 18.5

1. Add
2. Communicate
3. Compute
4. Emit
5. Titrate
6. Generate
7. Inspect
8. Insulate
9. Fluctuate
10. Transmit

Key to Exercise 18.6

1. Audibility
2. Conversion
3. Direction
4. Detection
5. Operation
6. Rapidity
7. Realization
8. Regulation

Key to Exercise 18.7

Percentage	Improvement	
Performance	Betterment	
	Contentment	
Ethical		
Practical	Communicate	Sportsman
Biblical	Dependent	Pointsman
Orbital	Respondent	

Key to Exercise 18.8

Bureaucrat	Bureaucratic
Democrat	Democratic

Key to Exercise 18.9

1. Linguist
2. Insolvent, bankrupt
3. Notorious
4. Emigrant
5. Fatalist
6. Amateur
7. Veteran
8. Theist
9. Vegetarian
10. Misanthrope
11. Philanthropist
12. Usurer
13. Ineligible
14. Optimist
15. Pessimist
16. Cannibal
17. Infallible
18. Omniscient
19. Omnipotent
20. Omnipresent

Key to Exercise 18.10

Withdraw, time-piece, wind shield, gas engine, low-speed motors, solar engines, high profile, lay down, biochemist, measuring beaker, weight box, clamp stand, function generator, tape recorder, analog trainer, tube-light set, cathode ray oscilloscope, solder wire, large-scale, pointsman, sportsman.

Key to Exercise 18.9

1. Linguist
2. Insolvent, bankrupt
3. Notorious
4. Emigrant
5. Fatalist
6. Amateur
7. Veteran
8. Theist
9. Vegetarian
10. Misanthrope
11. Philanthropist
12. Usurer
13. Ineligible
14. Optimist
15. Pessimist
16. Cannibal
17. Infallible
18. Omniscient
19. Omnipotent
20. Omnipresent

Key to Exercise 18.10

Withdraw, time-piece, wind shield, gas engine, low-speed motors, solar engines, high profile, lay down, biochemist, measuring beaker, weight box, clamp stand, function generator, tape recorder, analog trainer, tube-light set, cathode ray oscilloscope, solder wire, large-scale, pointsman, sportsman.

Appendix 1

Types of Clauses

Different types of clauses in English with examples are discussed below.

1. Basic sentence patterns

(i) Ram is a teacher.
(ii) He is very intelligent.
(iii) He is in the room.
(iv) Ram became monitor of the class.
(v) It grew dark.
(vi) He turned traitor.
(vii) He seems to be happy.
(viii) It looks like rain.
(ix) He appears calm.
(x) He owns a big house.
(xi) They have a Mercedes car.
(xii) Birds fly in the sky.
(xiii) They killed a snake.
(xiv) I gave him a book.
(xv) They appointed him chairman.
(xvi) They reported the matter to the police.
(xvii) They put the car in the garage.
(xviii) She lay in bed.

1a. Finite clauses with finite verb phrases

(i) He *works* very hard in the college.

2. Non-finite clauses having –ing or –ed particles or an infinitive

(i) –ing clause without a subject.

- I kept tossing in bed.
- Thinking about the next day class
- Entering the room, I discovered the jewellery missing.

(ii) –ing clause with a subject.

- The sun having risen, we left for the town. (It is also called an absolute construction.)

(iii) -ed clause without a subject.

- Soaked in blood, she fainted.

(iv) -ed clause with a subject.

- The exam finished, we came out of the room to catch a bus.

(v) to- infinitive clause without a subject.

- The most important thing is to find a solution to the problem.

(vi) to- infinitive clause with a subject.

- The most important thing is for us to find a solution to the problem.

(vii) bare infinitive clause without a subject.

- All I did was collect all the coins lying on the floor.

(viii) bare infinite with a subject.

- Rather than Pradhan go, I'd like to go myself.

3. Verbless clauses: They contain no verb element and often no subject. Their subjects are the subjects of the main clauses and generally a form of verb *be* (sometimes some other verb) has been omitted. It is possible to analyze them in terms of one or more clause elements.

(i) Many V semester students failed in the exam; majority of them electronics students.
(ii) We shall start, when ready.
(iii) Whether hungry or not, he is always ready to eat.
(iv) Keen to get first division, he worked round the clock. (adjective phrase as a verbless clause)
(v) Suspicious/suspiciously, he looked at me.
(vi) Even if tasty, this food won't be good for you.

4. Cleft sentences: A sentence is divided into two parts to emphasize the most important element in it. There are two types of cleft sentences: *it-type* and *wh-type.*

(i) It was John who stole the purse.
(ii) What John stole was the purse.

5. Commands: Two types of commands
2nd person commands and
1st and 3rd person commands

(i) Open the door, please.
(ii) Behave yourself.

(iii) Let's go and see the movie. (1st person command)
(iv) Now somebody shut this door. (third person command).

6. Comment clauses: A comment clause has a threefold function as: (i) It comments on the truth of the sentence, (ii) or on the manner of saying it, (iii) or the attitude of the speaker:

(i) The governing body's suggestion, **I believe**, could lead to a multifold increase in admissions if implemented.
(ii) Notice *'I believe'* is loosely connected to the rest of the sentence and it functions as a sentence adverbial.
(iii) **What's more**, we can't go abroad now.
(iv) **Stated bluntly**, you are going to be rusticated from the college.

There are many types of comment clauses:

I see, I think, I suppose, I'm afraid, as you see, as I said, to be frank, so to say, so to speak, what's more likely, you see, you know, you bet.

7. Comparative clauses: A comparative form of an adjective or adverb is used (which constitutes *the hinge* element in the utterance), followed by *than –clause* modifying the hinge element.

(i) His comments are more interesting **than Ram's**.
(ii) She speaks French better **than her sister does.**
(iii) Ram is taller **than I am**.
Or
Ram is taller **than I**.
Or
Ram is taller **than me**.
(iv) There were **fewer than 50 persons at the meeting**.
(v) I have better things to do **than seeing a movie**.
(vi) The harder you work, the better it is.
(vii) He is the most intelligent boy in the class.

8. Exclamations: These clauses express the speaker's feelings or attitudes. They start with a predeterminer *what*, followed by an NP or with *how* followed by an adjective or an adverb.

(i) What a lovely party we had last night!
(ii) How well you are singing!
(iii) What a grand college you have!
(iv) How beautifully you sing!
(v) What a great book you write!
(vi) What a girl!
(vii) How ridiculous!
(viii) Good! Excellent! You lucky boy! What a pity! Shame! Oh God! Poor you! What an experience! Oh for a drink!
(From A Communicative Grammar of English p 132)

9. Interrogatives: Interrogative words introduce wh-questions. They are *who, whom, whose, which, what, where, how, why, whether if, how often, how long, how big, how many people.*

(i) How often do you see a movie?
(ii) How long will you stay here?
(iii) How big is your college?
(iv) How many people can it take?
(v) When are you leaving?
(vi) Where are you staying?
(vii) What's your address?
(viii) Whose children are they?
(ix) Who/whom did she marry?
(x) What/which candidate did you vote for?
(xi) Which book do you like most?
(xii) Which university did you attend: London or Edinburgh?
(xiii) What musicians do you like most?
(xiv) Which musician do you like most?
(xv) Who doesn't know Rajeev Gandhi? (rhetorical)
(xvi) Would you like tea or coffee? (alternative question)
(xvii) Ram is a doctor, isn't he? (tag question)
(xviii) Sita isn't a nurse, is she? (tag question)
(xix) Are you married? (yes-no question)
(xx) "How did you do at the interview," he asked me. (direct question)
(xxi) He asked me how I had done at the interview. (indirect question)

10. Introductory it: Introductory *it* is used to postpone the real subject. It is used in passives. In some other constructions, *it* has no real subject and it is followed by verbs like *appear*, *seem*, *happen*, *etc*. It is also used for *weather*, *time*, etc.

(i) It makes me happy to see her working hard. **To see her working hard** makes me happy. (English prefers the construction with it.)
(ii) It is suggested that new taxes should not be imposed.
(iii) It seems that it will rain.
(iv) It is interesting to read her autobiography.
(v) To talk to her was interesting.
= it was interesting to talk to her.
= she was interesting to talk to.
(vi) It's cold in here.
(vii) It's five o' clock.

11. Introductory 'there': English does not allow an *indefinite NP* to occur as a subject:

